Grammatical Relations in Change

Studies in Language Companion Series (SLCS)

The SLCS series has been established as a companion series to STUDIES IN LANGUAGE, International Journal, sponsored by the Foundation "Foundations of language".

Series Editors

Werner Abraham
Universities of Groningen, Berkeley
and Vienna

Michael Noonan
University of Wisconsin-Milwaukee
USA

Editorial Board

Joan Bybee (University of New Mexico)
Ulrike Claudi (University of Cologne)
Bernard Comrie (Max Planck Institute, Leipzig)
William Croft (University of Manchester)
Östen Dahl (University of Stockholm)
Gerrit Dimmendaal (University of Leiden)
Martin Haspelmath (Max Planck Institute, Leipzig)
Ekkehard König (Free University of Berlin)
Christian Lehmann (University of Erfurt)
Robert Longacre (University of Texas, Arlington)
Brian MacWhinney (Carnegie-Mellon University)
Marianne Mithun (University of California, Santa Barbara)
Edith Moravcsik (University of Wisconsin, Milwaukee)
Masayoshi Shibatani (Kobe University)
Russell Tomlin (University of Oregon)
John Verhaar (The Hague)

Volume 56

Grammatical Relations in Change
Edited by Jan Terje Faarlund

Grammatical Relations in Change

Edited by

Jan Terje Faarlund
University of Oslo

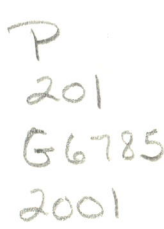

db John Benjamins Publishing Company
Amsterdam/Philadelphia

™ The paper used in this publication meets the minimum requirements of American National Standard for Information Sciences – Permanence of Paper for Printed Library Materials, ANSI Z39.48-1984.

Library of Congress Cataloging-in-Publication Data

Grammatical Relations in Change / edited by Jan Terje Faarlund.
      p.   cm. (Studies in Language Companion Series, ISSN 0165–7763 ; v. 56)
Includes bibliographical references and index.
   Six of the contributions were originally presented at a workshop held during the 14th International Conference of Historical Linguistics which was held in Vancouver, B.C., in 1999.
   Contents: How far does semantic bleaching go / Werner Abraham --"Oblique subjects," strutural and lexical case marking : some thoughts on case assignment in North Germanic and German / John Ole Askedal -- The notion of oblique subjects and its status in the history of Icelandic / Jan Terje Faarlund -- Towards personal subjects in English / Elly van Gelderen -- Focus and universal principles governing simplification of cleft structures / Alice C. Harris -- Recasting Danish subjects / Lars Heltoft -- Ergative to accusative : comparing evidence from Inuktitut / Alana Johns -- Subject and object in Old English and Latin copular deontics / D. Gary Miller -- The loss of lexical case in Swedish / Muriel Norde -- The coding of the subject-object distinction from Latin to modern French / Lene Schøsler -- Changes in Popolocan word order and clause structure / Annette Veerman-Leichsenring.
   1. Grammar, Comparative and general. 2. Historical linguistics. I. Faarlund, Jan Terje, 1943- II. Series.

P201.G6785   2001
415--dc21   2001025182
ISBN 90 272 3058 7 (Eur.) / 1 58811 034 6 (US) (Hb; alk. paper)

© 2001 – John Benjamins B.V.
No part of this book may be reproduced in any form, by print, photoprint, microfilm, or any other means, without written permission from the publisher.

John Benjamins Publishing Co. · P.O.Box 36224 · 1020 ME Amsterdam · The Netherlands
John Benjamins North America · P.O.Box 27519 · Philadelphia PA 19118-0519 · USA

Table of contents

Preface	VII
Introduction Jan Terje Faarlund	1
How far does semantic bleaching go: About grammaticalization that does not terminate in functional categories Werner Abraham	15
'Oblique subjects', structural and lexical case marking: Some thoughts on case assignment in North Germanic and German John Ole Askedal	65
The notion of oblique subject and its status in the history of Icelandic Jan Terje Faarlund	99
Towards personal subjects in English: Variation in feature interpretability Elly van Gelderen	137
Focus and universal principles governing simplification of cleft structures Alice C. Harris	159
Recasting Danish subjects: Case system, word order and subject development Lars Heltoft	171
Ergative to accusative: Comparing evidence from Inuktitut Alana Johns	205
Subject and object in Old English and Latin copular deontics D. Gary Miller	223

The loss of lexical case in Swedish   241
    Muriel Norde

The coding of the subject–object distinction from Latin to Modern French   273
    Lene Schøsler

Changes in Popolocan word order and clause structure   303
    Annette Veerman-Leichsenring

Index   323

Preface

At the XIV. International Conference of Historical Linguistics in Vancouver 1999 I organized a workshop called *Grammatical Relations and Grammatical Change*. This workshop was the beginning of the collective work resulting in this book. Of the eleven contributions in the book, six were presented at the workshop, namely those by Werner Abraham, John Ole Askedal, Jan Terje Faarlund, Lars Heltoft, Lene Schøsler, and Anette Veerman-Leichsenring. Muriel Norde submitted her paper for the workshop, but could not attend.

The workshop must be rated as a very successful one, not only in terms of the quality of the contributions, but first of all because we all felt that we did not get time to finish our discussions. We therefore agreed to meet once more, in Amsterdam in January 2000, where we would give ourselves two full days for discussion. We also agreed to try to publish the papers collectively. In order to extend the scope and the volume of the book, we decided to invite additional contributions. There were of course papers in the different sections at the Vancouver conference that also fit the topic of our workshop, and four of those were invited to join us. They were Elly van Gelderen, Alice Harris, Alana Johns, and Gary Miller. Fortunately they all agreed to participate. They joined us in Amsterdam, and contributed greatly, academically and socially. Before the Amsterdam meeting, everybody circulated revised versions of their papers among the group, so that the two days in Amsterdam could be spent efficiently discussing work that we already knew well. This book is therefore, to a larger extent than many volumes of this type, a collective work. Everybody has had an important impact on everybody else's chapter.

Amsterdam was chosen as a venue because of its pivotal location in Europe and because it is a city that nobody will want to pass up a chance to visit. We had no funding for the meeting; everybody covered it out of their own institutional (or even private) funds.

Even a small, informal meeting like ours depends on various practical and technical preparations. We are all grateful to Muriel, the local resident, for her help with these details.

The final preparation of the volume was done at the University of Oslo, with the good help of my assistants Anette Lundeby and Gro Vittersø.

Oslo, July 2000,
JTF

Introduction

Jan Terje Faarlund

Any treatment of syntactic or morphosyntactic change raises a number of methodological and metatheoretical questions related to the phenomenon of language change and to the theory of grammar. In this book, such topics are approached from different theoretical perspectives, generative grammar, valency grammar, functionalism, etc. The contributions also cover a wide range of data from many languages. What the contributions have in common, and what therefore justifies putting them together in one volume, is the topic of grammatical relations, and their role and involvement in linguistic change.

1. Grammatical relations

Grammatical relations is a rather vague or wide term. In principle it can be used about any grammatical dependency relation, in generative grammar defined as head-complement relation or specifier-head relation. In most contexts it is used about such relations within the VP, in other words about the relations between the verb and its argument phrases. This is also the meaning of the notion of grammatical relation adopted in most of the chapters in this book. In Werner Abraham's contribution, however, the term is used in a somewhat wider sense to cover also the relationship between non-lexical heads and their complements, such as modal particles, modal verbs, and the infinitival preposition.

The core relational categories, *subject* and (direct and indirect) *object*, are among the fundamental concepts of just about every grammatical theory or model. They are indispensable in descriptions of most languages. If the author of a linguistic description finds that the categories of subject and object are not useful or usable in the description of the language in question, that usually calls for special motivation and argumentation.

Grammatical relations involve various levels of linguistic description, including lexical (valency), semantic (theta-roles), morphological (case marking, verb agreement, cross-referencing), and even prosodic. But above all, grammatical relation is a syntactic notion. The syntactic description of grammatical relations involves various levels and sub-systems, such as linear precedence, configurational level, and dominance relationship, which again define the various syntactic properties of argument phrases which can be identified in a given language. There is a long tradition in the grammatical literature of describing morphological, semantic and syntactic properties of subjects and objects in various languages. There have been efforts to synthesize such descriptions into universal characterizations, the best known being Keenan (1976). It is an important subdiscipline of linguistic typology to study the distribution and correlation of different subject and object properties across languages. Some of Greenberg's (1963) universals are early examples of such correlations, e.g. Universal 41: "If in a language the verb follows both the nominal subject and the nominal object as the dominant order, the language almost always has a case system". This is but one kind of correlation. The typological distribution of the properties of subjects and objects in a wide range of languages was the topic of one of the groups working within the project *Typology of European Languages* in the 1990's. The results from this group are published in Feuillet 1998.

Generally, the notion of grammatical relations enters into grammatical descriptions and linguistic argumentation from two different perspectives. Adopting a metaphor where the abstract representation of a linguistic unit is "at the bottom", and where the overt phonological representation is "at the top", grammatical relations are *identified* in a "top-down" perspective and *defined* in a "bottom-up" perspective. In the top-down perspective, argument NPs that instantiate grammatical relations are identified in terms of their overt properties. These are either coding properties, such as position in the sentence, case marking, verb agreement, verbal valency; or behavioral properties, such as binding properties, omissibility, island properties, behavior in connection with raising, passivization, equi-deletion, etc. (Keenan 1976). In her chapter, Lene Schøsler demonstrates how especially verbal valency is an important factor in the identification of grammatical relations in a language with few coding properties.

In the bottom-up perspective, grammatical relations are defined in different ways. In the Government and Binding theory of generative grammar they are defined by their structural position, and in the minimalist program (Chomsky 1995) rather by grammatical features associated with structural positions. In Lexical Functional Grammar the relations are defined in terms of basic grammatical features, while in Relational Grammar they are considered theoretical primitives.

2. Diachronic syntax

In much recent work on syntactic change, *reanalysis* is a central concept. Harris & Campbell (1995) consider it one of three basic mechanisms of syntactic change, and define it as "a mechanism which changes the underlying structure of a syntactic pattern and which does not involve any modification of its surface manifestation" (p. 50). It should follow from this that the locus of syntactic change is the point where reanalysis takes place. According to generative grammarians, this is primarily first language acquisition. On the basis of linguistic utterances in the environment, the learner infers a grammar which is different from the grammar of the adult speakers that produced the utterances. In the context of generative grammar, reanalysis takes the form of setting parameters differently from those that underlay the input from the previous generation (Lightfoot 1991, 1999). According to Lightfoot, explaining language change requires only "(a) an account of how trigger experiences have shifted and (b) a theory of language acquisition that matches PLD [primary linguistic data] with grammars in a deterministic way" (1999: 225).

In the present volume, reanalysis is evoked as a factor in syntactic change, by authors writing within a generative framework as well as by others. Alice Harris in her contribution extends the data base of their book by examining a case of reanalysis of cleft sentences leading to monoclausal focus constructions in North East Caucasian. Anette Veerman-Leichsenring shows how NPs that are fronted because of their discourse function have been reanalyzed as subjects in the Popolocan languages of Mexico, resulting in a change from VSO to SVO as a basic order in some of these languages. Gary Miller compares the reanalysis of subjects as objects in gerundive constructions in Old English and Latin, thereby demonstrating how the same mechanism operates independently on similar constructions with similar results in different languages at different times. Elly van Gelderen examines the change from oblique to nominative in Old and Middle English, which results from a reanalysis of those NPs as subjects. In my own chapter I show how an oblique NP could be reanalyzed as a subject without changing its case in Icelandic, leading to 'oblique subjects' in that language.

It is debatable whether reanalysis can take place at any point in the life history of the speaker, or whether it is possible only in connection with first language acquisition. It is obviously true that contact situations involving adult speakers also lead to linguistic change. The internalized grammar of the adult speaker may change as a result of influence from utterances generated by a different grammar, whether in another language, another dialect, or just a different idiolect. Presumably, such influence is possible only in bilingual situations (in a wide and general sense): by adopting elements from another system (language, dialect, idiolect) grammatical rules generating that other system are mixed with the rules generating the original system. Yet such changes do not constitute a diachronic linguistic change until a future generation of speakers have adopted the mixed system as their own uniform system.

Language contact in itself does not uniquely determine or explain what the actual changes will be. The outcome of a process of change, whether triggered by language contact or not, is determined by general principles of grammar and by the cognitive and communicative properties of language (Faarlund 1990: 44–45). The cognitive aspect of language determines what is learnable, and hence what is a possible language. The possible results of a linguistic change is therefore limited by what is a possible language: a language cannot change into something which is not a possible language. Therefore Universal Grammar can be seen not only as a specification of a possible language, but also of a possible change. Another way of stating the same insight, is Lass's (1997) General Uniformity Principle: "No linguistic state of affairs (structure, inventory, process, etc.) can have been the case only in the past" (p. 28). The communicative aspects of language prevent changes from going beyond intelligibility: a language cannot change to the extent that mutual intelligibility between generations is prevented.

One crucial question in diachronic linguistics is what other constraints there are to linguistic change. The extreme hypothesis is that "anything can happen". This is a common assumption among generative syntacticians. To those scholars, the important point is that grammars are created anew by each generation. In that sense each individual speaker has his or her own grammar. Thus there can be no "rules of change" (Lightfoot 1979). To other scholars, reanalysis and other notions, such as *grammaticalization, analogy, extension* etc. are principles of change, in the sense that they specify possible linguistic changes, and thus further limit the possibilities of "what may happen" from one generation of speakers to the next (Harris & Campbell 1995).

The encoding and identification of grammatical relations may lend themselves to various possibilities of reanalysis. Certain positions in the sentence determined by pragmatic factors may be reanalyzed as the fixed position of a certain relational category, e.g. left periphery from topic to subject, or right periphery from focus to object. Such a redefinition of a positionally or structurally defined element from a discourse functional to a syntactic category is one kind of grammaticalization, as demonstrated by Lars Heltoft. Morphological marking is of course vulnerable to phonological attrition, another type of grammaticalization. Elly van Gelderen shows us its consequences for the history of subject marking in English, and Werner Abraham describes the semantic side of grammaticalization of lexical words in German, while Muriel Norde demonstrates the interplay of phonological and morphosyntactic factors in the reduction of the case system in Swedish. The move from ergative to accusative syntax in some Inuktitut (Eskimo) languages studied in Alana Johns' paper, can probably be seen as a result of grammaticalization or bleaching of a marked construction, the antipassive.

Of the eleven chapters in this book, eight deal with data from either Latin/Romance or Germanic languages. These languages have a long recorded history. The other three chapters deal with languages without an equally long history of written material. All of these base their analyses on synchronic comparative material, showing that differences between related languages or dialects can be treated as different levels along a historical development. Alice Harris compares different North East Caucasian languages, Alana Johns compares different Inuit dialects from Canada and Greenland, and Anette Veerman-Leichsenring compares different languages and dialects belonging to the Popolocan group of Otomanguean languages in Mexico. The reason why such synchronic comparison is interesting to historical linguistics is that they are based on theories about the mechanisms and principles underlying linguistic change.

3. Typology and diachrony

There is a close and interesting link between typology and diachrony. The most obvious and familiar link is embodied in the notion of "drift", which goes back to the work of Edward Sapir (1921). Drift is understood as a unidirectional series of changes whereby languages go from being more synthetic to more analytic. The changes that constitute this drift include loss of morphological case, its function being taken over by word order, and the increased use of function words. The changes described in the Lene Schøsler's chapter, as well as the contrasts presented by John Ole Askedal, are clear illustrations of the typological drift through history. Many changes involving morphology and function words cannot, however, be described simply as instances of drift in this sense, as is clearly shown by Muriel Nordes detailed study of the Swedish case system.

Despite all the theoretical and empirical work in this area, certain aspects of the nature of the link between typology and diachrony are, however, not yet completely understood. It has been suggested that word order changes tend to lead languages towards a "harmonic" stage where the order of head and complement is the same for all phrasal categories (cf. Vennemann 1975, Hawkins 1979 and others). There are, however, several serious problems about this notion of a "harmonic" state of a language. If there is such a state, it should have been attained long ago for all languages, and if it were ever disrupted in any language, we would expect it to have been "repaired" immediately. The notion also implies the possibility of a "transitional stage", which would mean that some of the world's languages are "imperfect" or "incomplete", while others have reached a stage of "perfect harmony". But since languages are learned anew by each generation on the basis of some innate capacity and the input from the environment, a transitional stage as a characterization of a language is logically impossible. In addition, some "transitional" stages seem to be lasting for a very long time. For example, a harmonic language should have the same order of head and complement in verb phrases as in noun phrases. This harmony is found in the Romance languages, which have the object after the verb (VO), and the adjective after the noun (NA) as an unmarked order, and in German and Dutch, which have basic OV and AN. English and Scandinavian, however, have VO and AN, a disharmony that has lasted for more than half a millennium.

What nevertheless seems to be an interesting connection is the historical dimension of linguistic typology. In a typological sample, living as well as dead languages may be included, and a typological class may include different historical stages of different languages, as demonstrated by Gary Miller in his study of gerundives in Latin and Old English.

4. Germanic and Romance: a case study

Since the majority of the chapters in this volume deal with Germanic or Latin/Romance, which have undergone very similar kinds of morphosyntactic changes in the course of their recorded history, I will offer a brief sketch of the changes in those languages that more or less directly concern grammatical relations.

Italic (Latin/Romance) and Germanic have basically three kinds of morphosyntactic means of marking grammatical relations: case marking, verb agreement, and position. The relative importance of these means reflect the stage on a scale from a synthetic to an analytic linguistic type. At one end of the scale are languages with case marking of all major nominal categories, agreement marking in finite verbs for all person and number categories, and relatively free word order. At the other end are languages without case marking of most nominal categories, with very reduced or no verb agreement, and with a rather fixed word order. The contemporary Romance and Germanic languages are spread out along this scale. There is also a diachronic dimension to this distribution: Latin and all the Medieval stages of Germanic are near the synthetic end, while the modern stages are spread out along the scale, with German and Icelandic still near the synthetic end, and French, English and mainland Scandinavian near the analytic end. There has thus been a typological drift through history, where the individual languages differ in terms of how far they have gone along the various parameters.

4.1 Case marking

All the ancient and Medieval stages have case marking of all major nominal categories. Subjects of finite verbs are in the nominative, and direct objects are mostly in the accusative. This system still exists in Icelandic, Faroese, German and Yiddish.

In all the languages with this type of nominal case marking, certain verbs take their complement in the dative, the genitive or the ablative (Latin only). The origin of this lexical case marking is probably semantically determined. The dative expresses the recipient role, as in double object constructions, but also in single object constructions. Being a syncretism of the Indo-European dative, instrumental, ablative and locative, the Germanic dative may also have these latter semantic functions.

The genitive was probably at one stage the case of a partitive or non-affected object, as in the Old Norse *þeir leituðu hennar* 'they searched her(GEN)'. This use of the genitive still exists in Icelandic, whereas in German there is a general tendency towards replacing the genitive with the accusative in object NPs, and in Faroese the genitive has disappeared altogether in this function.

4.2 Position in the sentence

The Germanic and Romance languages observe certain constituent order constraints, and there is a preferred or stylistically neutral order of argument NPs.

However, the languages with case marking enjoy a certain freedom of word order, depending on context and discourse functions. In addition, certain Romance languages, such as Spanish and Italian, have quite free word order although they have also lost their nominal case marking. Lene Schøsler's work shows how Old and Middle French coped with a similar situation.

In the other languages that do not have a full nominal case system, subjects and objects are tied to specific positions relative to the verb(s), and can thus be identified by their position in the sentence.

4.3 Verb agreement

With the exception of Mainland Scandinavian and Afrikaans, all the Germanic and Romance languages exhibit a certain degree of morphological marking of the verb in agreement with the subject. In languages with case marking, only nominative subjects can trigger verb agreement. If an NP in another case by certain criteria might be defined as the subject ("oblique subject") it can never trigger verb agreement, cf. the data in the chapters by Elly van Gelderen and by myself. It may also happen that a nominative subject fails to trigger agreement if it lacks typical subject properties, for example if it comes at the end of the sentence.

4.4 Subjectless sentences

The Germanic and Romance languages can be divided into two groups depending on whether they have an obligatory subject requirement or not. In Latin, Romance (except French), the Medieval stages of Germanic, and in Modern German, Yiddish, Icelandic, and Faroese, there are various sentence types that do not need an overt grammatical subject. In French and the other modern Germanic languages every finite sentence (except imperative sentences) requires a grammatical subject in its surface manifestation.

The languages that do allow subjectless sentences, however, differ as to the extent and sentence types that allow it. The following is a sketchy survey of the development within Germanic and Romance, leaving details aside, and with the proviso that this part of the grammar is particularly problematic for languages where negative data are not available.

Most Romance languages (except modern French) allow a specific subject referent to be expressed through the verbal morphology only, by a process known as *pro-drop*. With the exception of Old English and possibly Yiddish, the Germanic languages do not seem to have been typical pro-drop languages during any part of their recorded history; compare the Spanish sentence (1a), where the subject is expressed only by the verbal affix, and the Old Norse equivalent (1b), which would be incomplete without the pronoun.

(1) a. Encontr-ó   al   caballo
       found-PAST.3SG OBJ.DEF horse
    b. hann   fann   hest-in-n
       he.NOM found.PAST.3SG   horse-DEF-ACC

The old and middle stages of Germanic, as well as modern Icelandic, do, however, allow subject drop in other cases, such as with weather verbs and other verbs referring to natural processes, Icelandic: *Í gær rigndi* 'yesterday rained'. Most modern Germanic languages and French now require a grammatical subject in this type of sentences, too, cf. German: *Es regnet* 'it rains'.

Sentences without a grammatical subject, but with semantic roles assigned to other argument phrases, are somewhat misleadingly referred to as 'impersonal constructions'. For lack of a better term, we will use it here, too, and include so-called impersonal passives. In the old and middle stages, and in Modern German, cf. Icelandic and Faroese, such sentences may occur without a nominative subject, German: *Gestern wurde getrunken* 'yesterday was drunk' (i.e. 'Yesterday there was drinking going on').

As the obligatory subject requirement took effect in all the languages except those just mentioned, an oblique argument with experiencer verbs was reanalyzed as a grammatical subject. Thus the Old Norse (2a) was replaced by the modern Norwegian (2b).

(2) a. Mun þik   kal-a
       FUT you.ACC cool-INF
       'You will be cold'
    b. Du   vil   frysa
       you.NOM will freeze

For ample documentation and discussion of equivalent constructions in Old English, see Elly van Gelderen's chapter. Impersonal passives either disappeared (French, English, Yiddish), remained subjectless (German, Icelandic, Faroese), or were equipped with an expletive subject (mainland Scandinavian), cf. Norwegian: *Det vart dansa til langt på natt* 'it was danced till far on night' (i.e. 'There was dancing going on far into the night').

4.5 Passive

The main syntactic operation of passivization common to all Germanic and Romance languages consists of demoting the grammatical subject of the corresponding active sentence. This active subject then may or may not be added as an adjunct by means of a preposition. This is quite common in the modern languages, (*The cake was eaten by my sister*), while in some of the older Germanic languages it seems to be limited to texts translated from Latin.

As far as the subject of passive sentences is concerned, the Germanic languages may again be divided into two groups. One group consists of languages with nominal case marking and which allow subjectless sentences. In these languages a passive sentence has a nominative subject only in those instances where the corresponding active sentence has an accusative direct object, as in (3b), derived from (3a). An object in any other case in the corresponding active sentence remains in the same case in the passive, as the dative in the Old Norse (4).

(3) a. *rak   hafr-a   heim*
       drove ram-PL.ACC home
    b. *Senn vár-u hafr-ar   heim rek-n-ir*
       soon were ram-PL.NOM home driven
       'Soon the rams were driven home'

(4) *Henni   var vel þakka-t*
    her.DAT was well thanked
    'She was well thanked'

This is the system found in Latin and all the Medieval stages of Germanic, as well as in modern German, Yiddish and Icelandic. In these languages, a distinction is made between structural and lexical case. Structural cases are nominative and accusative, lexical cases are dative, genitive, and accusative. The latter are assigned by lexical categories such as verbs, adjectives or prepositions, and cannot be changed through syntactic processes. Structural cases are assigned on the basis of their position in the sentence structure. An empty subject position in a passive sentence can be filled by another NP with a structural case. NPs with a lexical case cannot receive structural case in subject position, and they therefore remain in the same case form as in the active sentence. John Ole Askedal demonstrates clearly the significance of the two types of case assignment, structural and lexical, in the history and typology of Germanic.

The modern Romance languages still have special marking of indirect objects in the form of a preposition, French: *J'ai donné le livre à mon frère* 'I have given the book to my brother', and these arguments do not become subjects in the passive: *Mon frère a été donné le livre. But note the grammatical English translation: *My brother was given the book.* In Germanic languages without case marking of nouns, direct and indirect objects, as well as the complements of certain prepositional phrases can become subjects in the passive: *This bed has recently been slept in.* Thus it seems that at this stage the distinction between structural and lexical case has been abolished with the disappearance of the nominal case marking system in Germanic.

4.6 Ergativity

Although all Germanic and Romance languages throughout their known history are accusative type languages, some of them have developed a new type of ergative construction, unknown to Latin and older Germanic. This means that the sole argument of certain intransitive verbs may have the same position and (at least partly) the same syntactic properties as the direct object of transitive verbs. The Norwegian sentences in (5) both have a VP consisting of a verb followed by a complement NP and an adverbial:

(5) a. *Vi har [sett folk] heile tid-a*
we have seen people whole time-DEF
'We saw people all the time'
b. *Det har [komme folk] heile tida*
it came people whole time-DEF
'There came people all the time'

In Mainland Scandinavian, however, the class of verbs which can occur in this type of ergative construction, has been extended, and now exceeds the class of verbs that are usually considered unaccusative or ergative cross-linguistically. In Norwegian, a genuine intransitive verb, such as *arbeida* 'work', can be used in ergative constructions:

(6) *Det arbeider ein mann i hag-en*
it works a man in garden-DEF
'A man is working in the garden'

4.7 Implications

As can be seen from this survey, it is not only case marking and freedom of word order which characterize two types within the Italic/Romance and

Germanic branches of Indo-European. They differ also with regard to other morphosyntactic phenomena, such as the use of expletive subjects, promotion of NPs to subjecthood in passive sentences, and ergative constructions. There is thus no Romance or Germanic language with full case marking and expletive subjects in existential sentences. That would force the underlying subject to appear in the accusative. With the exception of Modern Faroese and some conservative mainland Scandinavian dialects, no Germanic or Romance language allows promotion of a lexically case marked NP to nominative subject in passive sentences. Normally, this kind of NP movement is permitted only for structurally case marked NPs, and can therefore affect other NPs than direct objects only in languages without case marking.

It is not likely that the differences between the two types would be due to pure chance. A common underlying factor should be sought. Such a factor could be the degree of grammaticalization of the subject and object roles. At the early stage, case marking was a means of identifying the roles of the nominal arguments in a sentence, while free word order took care of discourse functional requirements. Presumably, the topic function would most frequently coincide with the primary role (agent, or the highest role in the role hierarchy of the verb). The position filled by the NP with this dual function was reanalyzed as a grammatical subject position. The subject was then tied to a certain position in the sentence, and it was eventually felt as an obligatory part of it, which paved the way for the expletive, or dummy, subject. At this point, the case marking had become less distinctive, and subjects could have other semantic roles than that of agents, as in the modern passive sentence *My sister was given a prize*. This change of subject type is part of the process described for Danish by Lars Heltoft.

If the grammaticalization of subjecthood is not accompanied by a loss of case marking, a conflict may arise between case and position, in that a lexically case marked NP may be moved to a structural subject position. This is what seems to have happened in Icelandic, leading to the phenomenon called 'oblique subject'.

References

Chomsky, N.. 1995. *The Minimalist Program*. Cambridge, MA: MIT Press.
Faarlund, J.T. 1990. *Syntactic Change. Toward a theory of historical syntax*. Berlin: Mouton de Gruyter.

Feuillet, J. (ed.) 1998. *Actance et Valence dans les langues de l'Europe*. Berlin: Mouton de Gruyter [Empirical Approaches to Language Typology].

Greenberg, J. H. 1963. "Some universals of grammar with particular reference to the order of meaningful elements". In *Universals of Language*, J. H. Greenberg (ed.), 73–113. Cambridge, MA: MIT Press.

Harris, A. C. and Campbell, L. 1995. *Historical Syntax in Cross-linguistic Pperspective*. Cambridge: CUP.

Hawkins, J. A. 1979. "Implicational universals as predictors of word order change". *Language* 55: 618–648.

Keenan, E. L. 1976. "Towards a universal definition of 'subject'". In *Subject and Topic*, C. N. Li (ed.), 303–333. New York: Academic Press.

Lass, R. 1997. *Historical linguistics and language change*. Cambridge: CUP.

Lightfoot, D. W. 1979. *Principles of Diachronic Syntax*. Cambridge: CUP.

Lightfoot, D. W. 1991. *How to Set Parameters: Arguments from language change*. Cambridge, MA: MIT Press.

Lightfoot, D. W. 1999. *The Development of Language: Acquisition, change, and evolution*. Oxford: Blackwell.

Sapir, E. 1921. *Language*. New York: Harcourt, Brace & World.

Vennemann, T. 1975. "An explanation of drift". In *Word Order and Word Order Change*, C. N. Li (ed.), 269–305. Austin: University of Texas Press.

How far does semantic bleaching go?
About grammaticalization that does not terminate in functional categories*

Werner Abraham
Groningen-Vienna-Berkeley

According to influential work on grammaticalization, the route grammaticalizing changes take is from lexical to functional categories (Lehmann 1985, van Gelderen 1993). It will be demonstrated on two grammatical relations that this is a too specific assumption. First, modal particles in German and Dutch emerge from adverbials and conjunctions — obviously, semantically more complete elements -, but, on their route to non-adverbial particles, they do not arrive at any functional status in any minimal sense. Second, as regards the infinitival preposition (IPrep), IPrep in German as well as other Germanic languages, bleaches out semantically from an original adverbial without, however, ever reaching the functional syntactic domain (in terms of Minimalism). The third relevant characteristic to be mentioned in this context is the fact that, despite heavy semantic bleaching and arriving at new syntactic functions, the original lexical semantics remains 'shining through' in the case of modal particles (MPs) in German and Dutch. This allows us to reconstruct an LF-status of modal particles as a triple COMP mapping. The decision which of the three COMPs is instantiated by an individual MP depends on its original categorial status as diachronic pre-MP.

1. Introduction

According to influential work on grammaticalization, the route grammaticalizing changes take is from lexical to functional categories, i.e. the path from some X(P) to I^0/T^0 (van Gelderen 1993, Roberts 1993, both echoing prior work by H. Paul, É. Benveniste, Jerzy Kuriłowicz, and Chr. Lehmann). According to this canonic, definitory venue, the switch of categorial classification is always accompanied by semantic bleaching down to near-complete semantic depletion.

It will be demonstrated on two grammatical relations that this is too specific an assumption. The problem comes to the fore only if couched in terms of modern syntax. Not only is grammaticalization taken to be the pathway from a lexical element to a functional one (inflectional or derivative), but also from left (high or functional) to right (low or lexical) in the structural (right-branching) tree. It will be shown that neither is absolute: there is at least one notable structural instance of direction in grammaticalization from the structural right to left (from 'lower down' to 'higher up'). Furthermore, the telic goals of grammaticalization are by no means limited by head projections of the kind C, I, or T as is the canonic view in diachronic generative approaches, but that among the eventual landing sites of a lexical element exposed to grammaticalizing attrition may also be a likewise functional SpecVP — i.e. a node much lower, and in the lexical domain, of the representational structural graph.[1] Moreover, the conclusion (implicitly made or explicitly stated) that landing in a inflectional category presupposes total semantic bleaching will be contested in very general terms. It will be shown on material from German that despite clearly closing off a grammaticalization cycle, the category yielded is not bleached completely of semantic intension. Accordingly, we shall speak about 'semantic and syntactic legacies' of grammaticalized items clearly establishing 'family resemblances' throughout pathways of grammaticalization down to their terminal stages. It remains to be seen whether such family resemblances shown to hold for three independent phenomena of German diachronics provide instances of typological distinctions. It will be emphasized that in order to arrive at conclusive results about the nature of grammaticalization in the terms indicated above the grammaticalizing process needs to be described, and its triggers explained, in syntactic-morphological terms contesting, thus, any claims about the semantic or metaphorical nature of the process and its explanation.

These are the three areas where the indicated processes are pursued: *modal verbs* in German and their alleged evidential readings (Section 2); the growth and partial state of bleaching of *illocutive clausal particles* in German (Section 3); and the emergence of the *infinitival preposition* in the history of German (Section 4).There is a common characteristic about all of these grammaticalizing developments: none reached the status of a functional element (inflective or derivative, let alone bound, morpheme), and only one (the infinitival preposition, IPrep) has come to realize the status of an unbound grammatical morpheme. Is there the prospect that one of them will ever reach the status of a functional morpheme, which is the declared goal of grammaticalization? Or do we have to think about grammaticalization in totally different, and wider, senses? And, if so, which?

As for the terminology used throughout, I stick to the rather loosely defined, and yet amply described and illustrated, uses in the typology of languages and discussions of a more theoretical and methodological nature. In particular, 'evidential' describes forms of reference of hear-say and credibility with respect to a predicative expression (there is a host of other coinages; see below); quite similarly, epistemic (and, likewise, evidential) uses of verbs and predicative complexes (among which modal verbs) refer to a status of certainty or relative uncertainty of the predicative expression; and deontic modals (or, in the English terminological canon, 'root modals', since diachronically believed to be original — something which can be disputed) refer more narrowly to modal expressions in their 'modal' meaning (obligatoriness, necessity, permissiveness, etc.). There are authors which use 'evidential' and 'epistemics' on a par, while others wish to retain a distinction here. See Abraham (1999a) for one mode of distinction with reference to Baltic, Kartvelian and Finno-Ugrian languages as well as Germanic ones. In the remainder of this paper, epistemics and evidentials will be used interchangeably unless their precise distinction is called forth. The main reason for retaining just one encompassing concept does not only lie in their common 'hear-say' meaning. What is more, both appear to stem from original perfects or perfectives, at least in a strikingly frequent number of evidentials (Abraham 1999a) and, in any case and with the exception of *will* only, for modal verbs in Germanic. Thus, for ease of exposition, I will be using DMV (for the deontic, or root, meanings of modal verbs in Germanic) as well as EMV (for their epistemic uses) throughout in the remainder of this paper.

In a way, the title of this paper is somewhat incomplete. We do know that bleaching can go all the way so as to suspend every bit of lexical, referential meaning of the morpheme in question. What I have in mind to show, though, is how much farther the linguist's reconstructing arm reaches in the case that semantic attrition has left traces of semantic classifiability. The issue is thus a methodological one of diachronic linguistics as much as of synchronic description.

2. Modal verbs between root and epistemic readings

2.1 Evidentiality paradigms: The developemental perfect(ive)-imperfect(ive) cline

Despite the wide extension of the term *evidential*, there are subtypes other than the familiar *(ad)mirativity*. Thus, in Lithuanian there are two separate participial forms, the nominative active participle (NAP) denoting the 'report' or 'hearsay' type of evidential, and the neuter passive participle (NPP) 'inference on the basis of observable results' evidential. Both have different paradigmatically fully productive forms (Gronemeyer 1998:1).

(1) a. Šįanakt   lij-ę
       last-night rain-NAP.PAST.NT
       'I see it rained last night'
    b. Šįanakt   ly-ta
       last-night rain-NPP.PAST
       'Evidently, it rained last night'

No doubt, evidentiality has its morphological paradigm in its own right here. In the Western section of the Fenno-Ugric languages, and its subpart of the Baltic-Sea Fennic languages — i.e. in Finnish, Saami, Mordwinian, Cheremis, Votjakian and Syrjanian, the so-called Permic group — as well as in historical Hungarian, two types of fully productive paradigmatic pasts are distinguished: a paradigm for 'witnessing' and another for 'non-witnessing' (Bereczki 1992:72; according to Honti 1997:165f.). See (2) below.

(2) a. Witnessing paradigm   Non-witnessing paradigm
       Votyak   mįniz   mįnem   'has gone'
       Cheremis   mijəš   mijen
       Hungarian   mene   ment
    b. Votyak   mįne val   mįne vįlem   'went'
       Cheremis   mija əl'e   mija ulmaš
       Hungarian   megy vala   megy volt
    c. Votyak   mįnem val   mįnem vįlem   'had gone'
       Cheremis   mijen əlje   mijen ulmaš
       Hungarian   ment vala   ment volt

Notice that synthetic and analytic forms interchange according to tense or aspect, not with respect to the directness of witnessing. In other words, I am far from maintaining that evidential readings derive from, or are triggered by, perfects and/or perfectives only. According to Bereczki (1992:517; Honti 1997:168f.) the Hungarian periphrastic forms were *auditive* functions originally, which bleached due to the weakening Turkic linguistic contact in Modern Hungarian. The same holds for the periphrastic perfect and pluperfect in the dialects of Finnish (Itkonen 1966:282; Honti 1997:169). It is perhaps not superfluous to point out that the non-finite component in the periphrastic temporal complexes is not always a preterite participle, but occasionally also a gerund, as in Cheremis (Honti 1997:172), or more genally, a deverbal nominal as in Saami (Honti 1997:170). All of these render a statal property of the event referred to.

It has often been claimed, for example, that Bulgarian as well as Macedonian interlink the analytic perfect with the *auditive* (Horalek 1967:206; Honti 1997:175), which is held to be due to Turkic influence through centuries of close political and linguistic contact. One may want to investigate whether it is not the case that perfectness or perfectivity is at the bottom of evidentiality in these languages.

Whether one tries to avoid mutual areal influences or not, it is striking that one often speaks of the 'Old World *evidential* belt' covering Turkish, Kartvelian, Bulgarian-Macedonian and Albanian. This belt extends to include Georgian and the adjoining, only partly genetically related, Kartvelian languages ((East) Armenian, Laz, Mingrelian, Svan) as well as Turkish and Persian (Boeder 1998) or Estonian (Comrie 1976:86) and Lithuanian (Gronemeyer 1998), where the perfect has triggered a general evidential reading. See the following Georgian example, where the example in (3a) renders the evidential triggered by the perfect tense, whereas (3b) is the (narrative) aorist form (Boeder 1998:10, ex. (27)–(28)). (3c–d) are taken from Tschenkéli (1958:491f.).

Modern Georgian

(3) a. *tovli mosula*
    snow has.come
    'snow must have fallen'
   b. *tovli movida*
    snow came
    (as in a narrative irrespective whether or not the reporter has seen the snow falling)
   c. studenti   tserda   tserilebs
    the student wrote.IMPERF letter.PL
   d. student'ma datsera   tserili
    the student wrote.AOR the letter

e. student'ma dautseia   tserili
the student has.written.PERF the letter

Tschenkeli (1957:492) is very specific about the link between the perfect (as opposed to the 'imperfect' and the aorist) and what he calls the 'ungesehene, nicht wahrgenommene Tempus' or the 'anscheinende Zeitform', respectively. In Svan, the most archaic of the Kartvelian languages of the split ergative type, the perfect series is employed to express the evidential meaning of the verb (Sumbatova 2000:63). Within this series, there are both imperfective and perfective paradigms. See (4)–(5) for illustration of either evidential paradigm. The imperfective evidentials come in the form of a special participle and the copula in the present, past or subjunctive.

(4) a. (story about avalanches in the winter of 1986–1987 told by a young man from the village of Mulaxi)
amčikka mi mam xwardäs šwäns,   mare kämumbwex mäj xola
once   I not was   Svania.DAT but tell.AOR.3PL say bad
dwrew l<u>ǝmär</u>   mulaxs   i   mtlijänd šwäns
time be.IEVID.3SG Mulaxi.DAT and whole Svania.DAT
'I was not in Svania at that time, but they said it <u>was</u> a bad time for Mulaxi and the whole of Svania'

Notice the difference of aspect or tense on the Svan equivalents for *tell* (in the aorist) and, on the other hand, for the copula *to be* (in the perfect tense). The evidential meaning of the corresponding perfective paradigm demonstrates that the Svan perfect is essentially an evidential. In other words, in addition to the perfect meaning (if present in the first place), the meaning is that of indirect evidence, or mirativity, for the event reported. More generally and in the most neutral case: the meaning of the perfect is that of a completive action that was not observed by the speaker in the real world (Sumbatova 2000:66). See (5) below.

(5) a. active verbs: perfects are formed synthetically
miga
1SG.O-OV.build.PERF (O = 'object', OV = 'object version')
'I have apparently built'
b. passive verbs: perfects are formed periphrastically (passive participle + confix *lǝ__e*)
algēli (from *ad-lǝɹ-g-ēl-Le*)
PV.3SG.IO-OV.build.be.PRES.3SG (PV = 'preverb', IO = 'indirect object')
'(it) has apparently been built'

In what follows I will focus on evidentials that clearly connect to perfects or perfectives, and I will demonstrate that such a link is far from arbitrary. From this one can conclude that there may be more to what appear to be areal clusterings of this phenomenon due to language contacts.

2.2 The semantic evidentiality release behind the perfect (participle)

It follows beyond doubt from the small number of languages discussed above and totally unrelated to Germanic and unrelated even to Indo-European, that it is the perfect that triggers the development of evidentials. It has often been stated on the basis of extended empirical data sampling across languages that typical historical sources of evidentials are perfects and, more generally, resultative constructions (Willett 1988; Bybee & Dahl 1989). Comrie (1976: 110) sees the relation between perfects and evidentials (or 'inferentials') "in the fact that both categories present not an event in itself, but via its results [...]". Irrespective of whether the perfect is expressed synthetically (which often stems from a younger morphological fusion of an older participle morpheme into the copula) or periphrastically, the preterite participle is a perfect semantic and syntactic representative of a state category, and often resultative state, and, consequently, has adjectival properties (which restrict its subject to a non-Agent). Boeder (1998: 31, echoing Johanson 1996) coins the terms 'postterminal' and 'indirective' to get closer to an explanation, and he points out that results always imply a causal relation. The important issue in this relation is the distinction of an INTERNAL and an EXTERNAL type of causality (IC vs. EC). This is mirrored in the following examples (gleaned from Rutherford 1970; cf. Boeder 1998:31). Notice the enthymemic character of the link between the first and the second clause in (6b).

(6)   a.   he's not coming to class because I know that he's sick
           (EC: *X is the case because Y*)
   b.   he's not coming to class, [ENTHYMEME] because he just called from SD (IC: *I say X because Y*)
   c.   Mary isn't here because she has to work in her office   ... EC
   d.   Mary isn't here because I don't see her   ... IC

External causality can be rendered by the resultative perfect since both share the factual report that a present, unspecified state X is due to a past event Y, as in (7a) below. *Internal causality*, on the other hand, provides the reason for one's saying something. Witness (7) below, where the enthymeme of (6b) is made explicit.

(7) a. X because Y ... EC
     b. I say X because there is evidence Y for X ... IC

Note that the latter type of causality, IC, is not justified by the simple (7a) above. Rather, all sorts of justifications may apply (quite generally so, cf. Willett 1988:57). Compare (6b) above, which classifies types of IC according to the underlying intentions or capacities that may be involved on the part of the people reporting or involved as protagonists in the reported event. There may be sources like inference, hearsay, guessing, probability, surprise ('(ad)mirativity') etc., all of which the perfect as such and alone leaves unspecified, whereas they become specified in the case of the sub-specifying epistemic modal verbs (EMVs) in German rooted in the original, diachronically deontic predecessors as well as paradigmatically concomitant and diachronically co-existing deontic modal verbs (DMVs). It is not more than trivial, and yet quite enlightening, to say that there is a constant oscillating movement between the two modal variants — a change which is due to the participating semantic and syntactic characteristics of the clausal *actants* and *circonstants*. In a way, thus, (7b) above is the key to an understanding of evidentials and their relation to the (implicative) resultative perfect — where, beyond doubt, (6) above provides a clue to the types of 'evidence' to be supplied for the relation of causality on levels beyond that of the event syntax and semantics.

There is an important inference to be drawn from (7b), however: namely the valid conclusion that the performative definition in (7b) accounts for the fact that evidentials are normally restricted to finite assertions (cf. Boeder (1998: Section 5.7) on Georgian as well as for the present time meaning of the perfect). Recall, in this context, that model verbs in all Germanic are preterite presents, whose present tense meanings are derived from a perfective perfect with resultative purport (in the sense of the Latin inchoative verbal paradigm, as with *novi* and its implied perfective meaning 'I know' (from 'I have learned'), perfect of the present tense *nosco* 'I learn' (= 'I acquire/get to know')'). The inflection as well as the ablaut change between singular and plural of the Germanic modals are still witness to this origin.

2.3 The historical origin of evidentials as tied to specific forms

Boeder (1998:31ff.) speculates that the evidential meaning of the perfect in Modern Georgian is a reflex of the principally ambiguous usages of the resultative perfect all along from Old Georgian onwards. A similar conclusion is drawn by Sumbatova (1998:14; see also Natadze 1955 and Machavarani 1988 for identical conclusions, authors not mentioned by Boeder 1998). The perfect is fundamentally ambivalent. On the one hand, it refers to a completed (hence, past) event. On the other hand, the perfect implies some state resulting from the completion of this event. Emphasizing a connection between an existing result and a completed past action leads to evidentials whose meaning is triggered by inference from the state subsequent to the primary event.

It is interesting to see that in languages providing more than one perfect paradigm, the grammaticization may run through several steps of relaxing the aspectual resultative denotation of the preterite participle in the predicative evidential composite. (8) is gleaned from Sumbatova's investigation of the Kartvelian language of Svan (Sumbatova 1998: 16).

(8) LESS GRAMMATICIZED
⇓ 'true' resultative constructions
⇓ experiential (non-preverbal) perfect
⇓ perfective evidentials — retaining a resultative meaning: Georgian, Old Hungarian etc.
⇓ — 'pure', i.e. unconditioned evidentials (narratives):
⇓ imperfective evidentials — independent of perfect(ive) trigger: Svan, German (?)
MORE GRAMMATICIZED

The grammaticality cline in (8) is relevant for our next issue to be discussed. We will show that modal verbs in German project evidential meanings and that there is a clear dependency from the historical perfect and perfective.

Epistemic modal verbs (EMV) in Germanic and evidentials in general are seen to have in common both the contextual fit with respect to perfect and or perfectivity and predicative non-veridicality and inferentiality. Let us see to what extent German EMV and evidentials behave alike under closer scrutiny.

2.4 Systematic epistemic variation of German modal verbs

Given the many readings of what evidentiality is in the different languages (see our brief terminological discussion in the beginning) it may be interesting to see what the exact evidential background to each modal verb of German is. Quite clearly, the discussion of EMVs as relating to DMVs allows — or, rather, forces — a more concrete understanding of the retained lexical specifics despite the encompassing bleaching results, which are due to grammaticalization. In the following list of EMV-inferentials in German, the evidential meanings of each lexical are in some way weakly reflecting the original deontic meaning. Quite clearly, (9a,b) correspond closely to the *auditive*, possibly also to the *admirative*, while (9c,d) mirror more closely the concepts of *subjective* or *inferential*; all *subjective, vremya neočevidnogo deystviya, Nichtaugenzeugenschaftsmodus* and *epistemic* fit as cover concepts for the four meanings as a whole. Take the following illustrations from German modal verbs (MVs).

(9) Distinct epistemic readings of German modal verbs

German illustration of EMV	formal abbreviation in V2–structure	paraphrase	modal-epistemic distinction
X <u>will</u> stark sein	X [_{EMV} *will-*]+V	'X will/wants others to believe V'	'X pretends to V'
X <u>soll</u> stark sein	X [_{EMV} *soll-*]+V	'X soll/must be the case according to others'	'X refers with V to hear-say'
X <u>muß</u> stark sein	X [_{EMV} *muß-*]+V	'X muß/must be due to the accompanying facts'	'X's factual conclusion w.r.t. V is warranted'
X <u>mag</u> stark sein	X [_{EMV} *m?g-*]+V =	'X is capable of V-ing'	'X is possibly V-ing'

It is important to see that, other than for true evidentials whose occurrence is bound to the perfect or perfective paradigms, the epistemic readings of German MVs still echo in meaning their deontic brothers and, consequently, restrict their occurrences in contextual fit in a determining way. If there is something to the common ancestry of EMV in Germanic and evidentials, in the first place, then EMV appear to be highlighted today in an intermediate stage of their development. No doubt, much like for evidentials, there is a common source to this array of EMVs in German, i.e. non-veridical inferentiality. However, other than for evidentials cross-linguistically, none of them has bleached to the point where the original lexical source (deontic meaning) is depleted completely. There is no reason to assume that, in some future time, the four meanings will merge to one common evidential function: first, because the different meanings are meaningful distinctions upon the common reading of non-veridical evidentiality; and, second, because of the ever virulent principle of *one form, one meaning* in German.

We have seen that unconditioned evidential paradigms may stem from originally perfect(ive)-triggered evidential paradigms. Think of Svan in (8) above. We would like to assume that this is true for the history of German

EMVs also. In what follows we investigate this explanative venue further. In other words, it is assumed that EMVs were perfect(ive)-dependent at some point in the history of their emergence. If there is any deeper, motivating link between evidentials and epistemic modal verbs (EMVs) in Germanic, then there must have been a point in time where the 'finiteness gap' for EMVs did not exist yet.

2.5 The epistemic finiteness gap of German modal verbs

The fact that the occurrence of EMVs in German is limited to finite contexts, as opposed to the occurrence of DMVs, is puzzling. See (11)–(13) below. The fact that EMV have been canonically classified as raising verbs (for German see Abraham 1989) is but a consequence of the former fact; it cannot, however, serve as its explanation. For German, this distributional restriction has come to be called the 'finiteness gap of epistemic modals' (Reis 2000). There are two reasons why this gap comes unexpected: First, given the apparent relation between EMVs and evidentials under the common perfect and perfective origin, non-finiteness should not be excluded. After all, all synthetic perfects and perfectives provide also non-finite forms in the first place. Second, judging the emergence of temporal auxiliaries in Germanic languages as terminal developments of original deontic/root modal verbs (cf. English *will, shall* and, similarly, the other Germanic languages the only exception being German, which has come to use neither), the temporal usage appears to be preceded by the less deontic/root EMVs. However, it is strange to see that while deontics/roots and temporal uses of the identical modal forms provide finite forms, the intermediate forms are restricted to non-finite ones. Thus, while tri-functionality with the modal verbs appears to be the rule in the Germanic languages with the temporal function bleaching the deontic meaning in the most radical fashion, only the intermediate step represented by the EMVs shows the non-finite gap, not the inceptive stage nor the terminal one, however.

It has been shown in detail that, despite all parallels between evidentials and epistemic modal verbs (EMVs) in German on first sight, there are distinct properties. A list of the criteria for the distributional and diachronic emergence of epistemic modal verbs in German and evidentials across languages provides a clue as to what matters in the comparison of the two categories. See the generalization in (10).

(10)   German EMVs   Evidentials
   a. *in periphrastic perfects ≠ occur primarily in periphrastic perfects
   b. *in non-finite contexts   ≠ arise in non-finite contexts
   c. *in perfective contexts   ≠ occur primarily in perfective contexts

Notice that there does not appear to be a clue to the effect that evidentials in common do not arise in non-finite contexts (generally, evidential readings are presented in the morphological paradigms of the perfect or perfective, all numbers and persons; see Abraham 1999a). Thus, we appear to be forced to say that, at closer inspection, German modal epistemics and evidentials have no common grammatical triggering properties.

The puzzling finiteness gap for German EMVs is further spelled out in (11) and illustrated in (12)–(13) below. The illustrations in (12) and (13) testify to the generalization in (11).

['¬' = logical negator; ' ' = operator of logical possibility; in (13), '¬ ' thus means 'the specific reading is not possible', while ' ' means 'the specific reading is possible'; in (12), 'E' signifies 'epistemic reading', 'D' 'deontic reading'].

(11)   a. EMV dominates DMV (in SOV!): DMV [$_{FIN}$ EMV], but * EMV [$_{FIN}$ DMV]
   b. *EMV [$_{FIN}$ EMV]
   c. DMV [$_{FIN}$ DMV], unless disallowed semantically (for example, for 'horror aequi modi')

(12) Wenn sie dürfen(D/*E)   soll(D/E), aber nie   können(D/*E) will(D/E),
      if   she may   shall   but never can   will
      dann mag(D/E) sie auch nicht müssen(D/*E).
      then may   she also not   must
      Wenn sie aber   wollen(D/*E) dürfte(*D/E),
      if   she however will   might
      dann mag sie auch sollen, und dann kann sie auch müssen.
      then may she also shall   and then can she also must

(13)   a. daß das gehorsame Kind schweigen müssen[¬ EMV] wollte[EMV]
         that the obedient child silent be   must.NON-FINITE would.FINITE
      b. daß das gehorsame Kind schweigen wollen[¬ EMV]
         that the obedient child silent be   will.NON-FINITE
         mußte[EMV]
         must.PAST.FINITE

c. *daß er zuhause sein mußte*[EMV]
   that he at home be must.PAST.FINITE
d. *daß er zuhause sein hat müssen*[¬ EMV]
   that he at home be has must.NON-FINITE

Compare (13c,d) with (13a,b) above. With true evidentials we have no evidence of the finiteness gap, in contrast to epistemic modal verbs in German. With true evidentials, of course, the finiteness criterion never arose in the first place, in contrast to epistemic modal verbs in German.

How are we to explain the unexpected finiteness gap of EMVs, given the overwhelming and cross-linguistic common properties for EMVs and evidentials. What is it that makes just the epistemics with non-finite (and, thus, in German with periphrastic perfect) contexts. It appears that only two conclusions remain: one that evidentials and EMVs have nothing in common in the first place (meaning, more specifically, that it is pure chance that MVs were preterite presents and that evidentials are perfect(ive)-conditioned in a wide number of cases). I have called this the 'exclusion model' (Abraham 1999a) — I will not pursue this any further. The more interesting case is Alternative 2, which has to do with the 'finiteness parameter' in the history of the MVs in Germanic: If the finiteness parameter is historically younger than the aktionsart trigger of modal verbs, then we have a means to narrow in on the historical period of these two stages: on a prior stage where the finiteness constraint did not hold; and a consequent stage when, due to some influence, this constraint arose. If that were indeed the case, the investigation of the material in Old and Middle High German should allow an archeological *argumentum post quem* and *ante quem non*.

Is there reason to assume that there is some diachronic reality behind this conclusion? Much in distinction to the diachronic body of investigation on older stages of English (Denison 1993, as its last member in the chain), neither of the diachronic syntaxes by Behaghel and Paul can help one; the very notion of the distinction between deontic and epistemic readings of the modal verbs is inexistent. Fritz (1997), on the other hand, does not provide one single illustration for a double occurrence of modal verbs in Old High German or Middle High German. Nor is there any evidence in the general grammars of Middle High German about any change of the subcategorizing properties of modal verbs toward something like the finiteness parameter.

Another question that needs to be asked is whether there are epistemic uses, next to deontic ones, in the early phases of German and closely related languages. See (29). We shall therefore look into the older stages of English and German.

2.6 Early epistemic readings of modals and double occurrences

2.6.1 *Epistemic uses, next to deontic ones, in the early phases of German?*

Strikingly enough, there are no records to be found in Paul (1920) or Behaghel (1923). Yet, evidence for EMV-readings of the German equivalents of English 'may/can/must' can be found (according to Fritz 1997: 94–100; see also Fritz 1998: 128–129); examples are restricted to the earliest occurrences:

(14) a. thaz *mag* thes wanes wesan meist
    'this may have contributed the most to this idea'
    Otfrid II.7.50 (**863–871 A.D.**)
  b. wie *kan* gesein in deinr gewalt
    die hell und auch das himelreich
    'how may both hell and heaven be under your power?'
    Kaufringer, Sappler 1972, 3.426 (**15th cent.**)
  c. der (gekreuzigte) ist erstanden werlich/
    das *dorffen* mer (= "wir, die Soldaten am Grab") woil sagen sicherlich
    Alsfelder Passionsspiel 7392; DWbN 6, 1799 (**15th cent.**)
    'he has truly arisen, as we may say with certainty'
  d. min herre was biderbe gnuoc,
    aber jener der in da sluoc,
    der *muose* tiurre sin dan er [...]
    Hartmann, *Iwein* 2033–35 (**early 13th cent.**)
    'my master was good enough,
    but he who beat him,
    had to be even knightlier than him ...'

The picture that the historical attestation of German provides is somewhat discouraging. Let us see what is attested of historical material of English.

2.6.2 *The older stages of English*

If it is true that Old English modals behaved like Modern German modals (v. Kemenade 1992), we expect both epistemic readings and double occurrences of modals. Let us briefly illustrate this and then ask the question whether there was such a stage when non-finite uses of modals did not have to be root, but could also be epistemic. Are there such non-finite epistemic modals?

Epistemic modals, with and without subjects, are attested for Old English although none of them can be regarded as an established carrier of epistemic meaning (Denison 1993: 298). I restrict myself to just three samples from Denison's inventory (Denison 1993: 298ff.).

(15) a. Wel zæt swa *mæg*
         well that so may
         OE: *Bede* 2 1.96.23
         'that may well be so'
     b. wen   is, zæt hi us lifigende lungre *wyllen* sniome
         expectation is that they us living   intend   at once
         forsweolgan
         swallow up
         OE: *PPS* 23.2
         'It is likely that they will swallow us up at once'
     c. Wende ic zæt thu thy wærra   weorthan *sceolde*
         thought I that you the more-ware become should
         OE: *Jul* 425

By contrast, root meanings are quite common, and so are futural meanings, which are taken to have affinities with root as well as epistemic meanings (Denison 1993:304). While it is interesting to find early epistemic readings of modals in the first place, it is even more striking to find double or embedded occurrences, which — if we are to believe Denison (1993:310–311) — are instances of infinitival epistemic occurrences.

(16) a. And whan ye wole go withoute me   ye quite common
         and when you will go without me [sc. *Reason*] you
         shul wel *mown*   avaunte yow
         shall well be-able-to be-boastful
         ME: 1450 *Pilgr.L*(Cmb) 1.467
     b. I fear that the emperor will depart thence, before my letters *shall may* come unto yours grace's hands.
         1532 Cranmer *Let. In Misc.Writ.*
     c. some waye yⁱ appered at yᵉ firste *to mow* stande the realme in great stede
         1533 More, *Wks.* IX 84.4

There are even three verb clusters of the type 'modal+modal+V' (Denison (1993: 311) as well as (2000:114)).

(17) a. Also he *muste kunne*   evacuener him that is ful of yuel
         also he must know-how-to free   him that is full of evil
         humouris
         humours
         1400 *Lanfranc* 17.2

b. infantis mowe receive thi   sacrament of baptym eer   thei *mowe*
   infants may   receive your sacram.   of bapt.   before they may
   kunne   **worschipe** thee
   know-how-to worship   you
   1443 Pecock, *Rule* 375.2
c. if y se my neigbour goyng forto drenche him silf, y *oughte* forto
   if I see my neighbour going to   drown   him self I ought to
   wille **defende** him fro   drenching
   wish prevent him from drowning
   1454 Pecock, *Fol.* 129.5

2.7 Theoretical projection — and a provisional conclusion

Unless indeed EMV existed all along with DMV, as we have speculated, the break-down of DMV to EMV can only be envisioned as a process continuing over a considerable time span. We have no record of this development, neither in English nor in German. In other words, we do not know what exactly accompanied this break-down in terms of loss of lexical and/or morphological features. The main question to ask in this context is this: Why is it that EMV cannot surface in non-finite form? See Roberts (1986: 29) for the same question. An answer to (18) may be achieved by looking closely at the type of attrition EMV underwent. Notice that such attrition reflected upon for the diachrony of German may yield a clue also the type of attrition that English modals underwent on their way to Present Day English, since English modals have lost their deontic/root meaning to a great extent (i.e. totally except for *must*; cf. Abraham 1992). Now, what may seem to be missing with EMV as compared to DMV?

I will assume that in order for a verb to attain syntactic complement ('governed'; German 'regierten') status its subject will have to be theta marked (con Roberts (1986: 29)). This 'government' criterion excludes raising predicates since subjects of raising predicates do not project any semantic role. See the following illustrations in (18)–(19).

(18) ΘEr$_i$ *drohte/riet an*   *(jemandem)*$_j$ [ΘPRO$_{i/j}$ Θsich$_{i/j}$ *verachten zu*
     he threatened/promised someone   REFL despise   to
     wollen/$^{??}$müssen]
     will/must

(19) ΘEr$_i$ *will/muß/soll*   [ΘPRO$_i$ Θsich$_i$ *verachten wollen/$^{??}$müssen/können*]
     he will/must/shall   REFL despise   will/must/can

drohen/versprechen are canonical subject control verbs. Under their full lexical meaning, they assign a subject-Agent, while under the quasi-modal reading the subject gets the Theme or Experiencer role. Note that the root meanings of the modals in (19) and, likewise, the full lexical readings of *drohen/versprechen* in (18), with AG assigned for their subjects, do not yield meaningful readings. Rather, what renders some sense is where the subjects receive the status of an Experiencer or Theme. In other words, only the epistemic readings are available; the root meaning in (19), for example, would require the role of Agent for its subject, which is out for practical reasons.

According to Vikner (1988), in the case of verbal clusters as the ones under inspection, the subject may adopt, next to its main and strong thematic role assigned by the full lexical verb, one, but not more than one, extra and weak thematic role. See the following examples from Danish. Note that Danish, as each of the other Germanic Scandinavian languages, has two passives: a periphrastic one using *blive* 'become' as an Aux; and the synthetic *s*-passive. The crucial observation is that the two passives have different distributions with embedding under the two types of modals (German translations added because German is more telling than English).

(20) a. Hun *vil blive arresteret* ... *DMV, EMV
       he   AUX become arrested   ... participial passive
       German: '... *wird* verhaftet werden'   ... purely temporal
   b. Hun *vil arresteres*   ... DMV, *EMV
       he   *will* arrested (become)   ... reflexive passive
       German: '... *will* verhaftet werden'   ... voluntative-deontic

Since Vikner assumes that the Danish auxiliaries (auxiliary uses of) *blive, få* and *komme* assign extra semantic roles the subject in (20a) would collect three thematic roles (one for *vil*, another one for *blive*, and yet another one for *arresteret*) on *hun*, which is out irrespective of any specific assumption made with respect to assignment of semantic roles. This renders the deontic reading in (20a) ungrammatical. This is different in the case of EMV, which does not assign a semantic role of its own. Under the specific suspension of the strict Projection Principle ('each clausal constituent has only one semantic role'), (20a) receives an epistemic interpretation: *vil* in the function of an AUX (for German 'werden', not, however, 'wollen'!) does not assign the subject, *hun*, a third semantic role. In other words, (20b) also restricts the discharge of the semantic role on *hun* to two semantic roles, but different from that in (20a): one, under lexical government, executed by the participle of the main verb, *arresteres*, and a second, weaker one discharged by *vil*. So far the specific assumption made by Vikner (1988) and his attempt to account for the distinct distribution of the two Danish passives embedded under the specific modal readings.

The best evidence for our assumption that Mood does not project semantic roles for the respective subjects is provided also by the fact that subjunctive is never expressed on non-finite forms. Thus, in German there is no subjunctive infinitive. (21) below generalizes this empirical insight (see already Abraham 1992, 1995a: Ch. 6).

(21) *mood infinitive: *würden* (SUBJ.PRET), *seien* (SUBJ.PRES.),
*non-finite imperative

It has been claimed that root/deontic readings of MVs in German (but not in English!) are aspectual. From this follows that the scope relations for DMV are those in (22a), while those for EMV are reflected by (22b). Recall that V, the governing modal predicate in (22) below, projects a semantic selection grid for its governed modal verb, which is saturated in (22a), but not in (22b). As a consequence, EMV, whose subject is without a semantic role, has to raise to yield a syntactic position outside of any governed status. (22) formalizes in detail something like Roberts' (1986:29) 'Visibility Condition' for modals in much greater detail.

(22) a. $[_{CP} \ldots [_{IP} \ldots [_{VP\text{-aspect}} DMV_i [_{VP} t_i [V]]]]]$
b. $[_{CP} \ldots [_{IP} EMV_i [_{VP\text{-aspect}} t_i [_{VP} t_i [V]]]]]$

In (22a), deontic modality expressed by the lexical MV ranges over aspect expressed periphrastically by an AUX (German is right-headed, SOV, and therefore left-governing). The scope relations with an epistemic sentential operator as in (23b), however, are reverse to those with a deontic operator, epistemics ('inferential', 'subjective', 'conceptual') extending the widest scope covering even aspect. Recall with respect to (22b) above that in the dependent German clause, IP is in final position in accordance with the basic head-final projection of the German clause.

(22) symbolizes, in a structural manner, the requirement that any embedded verb — among which modal verbs in deontic reading — must project a strong thematic subject role. See the licensing condition in (23).

(23) SUBJECT SATURATION CONDITION:
a. A non-finite predicate must project a thematic role for its external argument.

b. (by replication to (23a))
An agreement relation between a finite predicate and its thematically empty lexical subject is licensed only if the predicate occurs finitely (i.e. in Infl).

If raising, in its early stages, was like (24) below, it must have restructured to yield (25) in the course of its loss of agreement through morphophonological attrition, its loss of the subjunctive, and due to loss of other paradigmatic identifiability, in English — but not in German.

(24) Raising modal/Aux (independent clause) subcategorized for (not governing!) CP_2 (the structure graph is highly abbreviated) — early stage:[2]

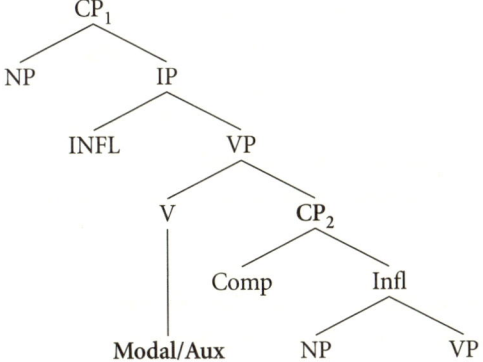

If raising verbs (German *scheinen*, *pflegen* etc., at least in their specific embedding-only usage) are subcategorized for CP_2 as in (25), the next diachronic step should provide DMV- subcategorization for a VP-complement (i.e. a governed verbal constituent as in South German dialects). The change from a morphological agreement system to a syntactic system was implemented by reanalysis in terms of AUX ((E)MV in (25) signifying 'EMV' in German, but MV in general in English since no deontic/root meanings are available any longer):

(25)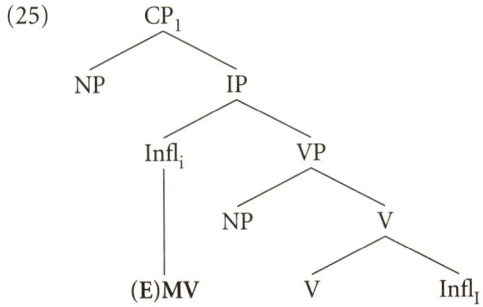

This is all we can provide, for the time being, in terms of evidence for the mere plausibility of our speculations on the 'German epistemic puzzle'. The spinn-off of the discussion of the syntactic behavior is that EMV may have split off from DMV diachronically by way of restructuring in terms of German (23)–(25). The alternative for that is that EMV-subjects had theta-rich readings in the early stages and lost those through attrition in the widest sense. This, in turn and in the absence of direct clues, confronts us with two more questions, whose solution may add indirect confirmation to the second alternative. Bear in mind as a background to this question the subject saturation factor in (23).

This is all we can provide, for the time being, in terms of evidence for the mere plausibility of our speculations on the 'finiteness gap of epistemic modal verbs' (the 'epistemic puzzle') in German and English. The spinn-off of the discussion of the syntactic behavior is that EMV may have split off from DMV diachronically by way of restructuring in terms of (24)–(25). The alternative for that is that EMV-subjects had theta-rich readings in the early stages and lost those through attrition in the widest sense. This, in turn and in the absence of direct clues, confronts us with two more questions, whose solution may add indirect confirmation to the second alternative. We have seen that there is no reason to exclude that there were indeed epistemic readings of MVs, both in English and in German. With that being so, the original parallel we drew between evidentials and EMVs is well motivated. At the same time, we have considered unlikely the case that EMV-readings in German will eventually arrive at a stage where the E-distinctions displayed in Modern German will no longer hold and be replaced by one common evidential reading for all 6 MVs. Thus, its bleaching process has stopped short of going all the way as in the case of the evidentials. On the other hand, grammaticalization did go through all the way in the case of all those modal verbs in Germanic which have arrived at a purely temporal function (foremost for *will* and *shall* in English and their lexical correlates in all Germanic languages — with the exception of German). This is what had to be shown in some detail.

3. Modal particles in German: Word classification and legacy beyond grammaticalization

The present Section deals with what has often been called an uncategorizable class of lexicals, the *illocutive, or modal, particles* (MPs) in German. They occur characteristically only in the continental West Germanic languages (German, Dutch, West Frisian, Yiddish, and overwhelmingly so in their substandards).

The data presented here are limited to German. The meaning of MPs is typically vague to indiscriminable, but their illocutive force and distributional constraints are nevertheless considerable and sharply delineated. The main goal of this Section is to delimit this non-category in distributional terms and explain the source of its specific illocutionary force and distributional behavior. As in the previous Section on the two types of modal verbs, it will be shown for modal particles that they have different underlying (logical) forms due to their historical sources and derivative pathways. Again, this Section contributes to a considerbale enrichment of the theory of grammaticalization and the diachronic changes word categories can be subject to.

3.1 Types of syntactically classifiable grammaticalization

In IJbema (1997), the following distinctions were made with respect to three fundamentally computational (= syntactic) types of grammaticalization in the area of verbal affixation.

a. one type of grammaticalization where a lexical element becomes a functional (= inflective) element, an affix, which is generated structurally in a *functional head* (e.g. the future tense affix *-ai* in French);
b. another type of grammaticalization involving a lexical element becoming a functional (inflective) element and structurally a head, but not an *affix* (such as the English 'infinitival preposition' *to*);
c. yet another type of grammaticalization where a lexical element becomes functional (inflective) and an affix, but does not end structurally as a functional *head*. The latter is illustrated by the 'infinitival preposition' *zu/te* in German/Dutch as well as prefixes such as German/Dutch *be-, ver-* (which have emerged from a prior adverbial status). See the following chart, (26).

(26) Syntactic types of affixation

affixal status ⇒ ⇓ lexical elements	bound (vs. unbound) morpheme	functional category: head (vs. Spec)
French future affix *-ai*	+	+
English *to*	−	+
German *zu*, Dutch *te*	−	−
German participial *ge-*; bare infinitival suffix *-e(C)n*	+	−

Notice that the English IPrep can be separated from the non-finite verb, while both German and Dutch do not allow for that (*to* hardly be able vs. *kaum fähig zu sein/(om) nauwelijks in staat te zijn*). Whether from this one may conclude that *zu/te* are in fact bound morphemes, just like the participial *ge-___t*, is hard to decide, in the face of the writing traditions in both languages. But this is not an important issue here. What matters is that *zu/te* are devoid of any lexical meaning (other than their prepositional homographs) and have attained functional Spec-status.

The characterization in (26) is straightforward and an essential step in the direction of restricting paths and results of grammaticalization. The present essay is meant to demonstrate to what extent the source category, the selection constraints it is subject to, and, finally, its categorial status (i.e. its status as a NP- or clause conjunction, or as a focus particle, to name just two of several possibilities) either continue, or change, in the course of grammaticalization and, if they change, what the order and extent of such a change can be and whether limitations on change can be detected. To pursue this course, two Sections are chosen in the history of grammaticalization *in statu nascendi* of present day modal particles in German: first, their logical classifiability on the basis of the source categories and meanings; and, second, their combinability, which is strongly constrained on the basis of their source status with different category belonging. Recall that modal particles are an ideal field of research for matters of grammaticalization since both uses, the pre-particle one and the particle one, are still extant side by side. Yet, they will hardly ever enter into the consciousness of the speaker as having anything in common with one another except their form. In essence, the present essay is also an attempt to illustrate that the *monogenetic hypothesis* (as opposed to the *polygenetic* hypothesis) may rightfully be assumed: i.e. that the methodological position that a homonym representing both a modal particle and another lexical category and meaning, derives its particle meaning and syntactic distribution from the stronger lexical representative (usually in the function of an adverb, a conjunction or coordination, or a focus particle). Opting for the *monogenetic hypothesis* saves one to assume two separate and unrelated entries in the lexicon, but saddles one up with the task to define and delimit the set of principles relevant and general enough to support such a derivative methodology.

It will be shown throughout that MPs do have meaning, albeit vague and syncategorical, which can be derived from the lexical meaning and behavioral syntasctic properties of their homonyms in syntactic distributions and with other categorial belongings. It will be demonstrated that the weak meanings and behavioral properties of MPs lend themselves to a threefold classification: there are MPs with a causal meaning, others with an adversative one, and a third class with a more or less clear veridical meaning. This will be summarized in Section 4.

(27) Legend for (i–iv) below: 'Topological field distribution in German'
COORD = coordination (such as English *however*); FF = fore field (comprising, in GB-terms, the structural space above TP or InflP (i.e. CP or SpecCP, respectively); 1st VB 'first verbal bracket' = T or Comp; MF 'middle field' = the structural space between T/InflP and the predicative; 2nd VB = V⁰ in a SOV-clause structure for German (Dutch, West Frisian, Yiddish); PF 'post field' = area of clause-extraposition; small caps denote clausal accent — other accent distributions beyond those provided below are possible; PART = (modal) particle]

| | | ⇐ | Thema ⇒ | | Rhema ⇒ | |
| | | | ⇐ | | | |
	COORD	FF	1st VB	MF	2nd VB	PF
(i)	–	*Du*	*kommst*	*aber* pünktlich!	–	–
		you	come	PART punctually		
(ii)	*Aber*	–	–	pünktlich	kommen!	–
	but			on time	come	
(iii)	–	*Wieso*	–	*denn aber* püntkl. kommen?	–	–
		how so		MP MP on time come		
(iv)	*Aber*	*wieso*	–	*denn* pünktlich	kommen?	–
	but	how so		MP on time	come	

Since the VP generally contains argument material which is rhematic in discourse-theoretical terms, it has been speculated that MPs operate as functors upon discourse referentially new material, or, in other terms, that MPs are at the scopally widest operator end of such material in the clause (Abraham 1989, 1995b). This speculation, no doubt crucial, awaits typological confirmation. It will not be the focus of the present discussion. Rather, we will address the question to which extent the syntactic, semantic, and systematically pragmatic properties of what we called the MP-homonyms — i.e. their homonymic lexicals with a full semantics and a clear syntactic categorization — are reflected in the behavior of the positionally and clause-typically heavily constrained MPs. In pursuing this question, this general line of investigation will be restricted to the occurrence of MPs in imperative expressions (cf. Abraham 1995b, where a similar investigation was pursued restricted to interrogative contexts). The goal of this presentation is thus to show that, indeed, the occurrence of a number of MP-lexicals in imperative contexts as well the exclusion of other MP-lexicals is rooted in the behavior and meaning of the lexical homonyms in non-MP functions.

Our overall methodological position is a 'monogenetic' interpretation of the status of MPs and their specific illocutive force. In other words, the illocutive force of MPs is a function of the interplay between the semantics and syntax of the MP-homonyms, on the one hand, and the specific distributional constraints that MPs are subject to. There is thus no need to have separate entries in the mental lexicon.

3.2 The scope of MP: original focus particles

Consider the following uses of *nur/bloß* (originally, as focus particles, 'only, just'). The idea is to show that MPs have scope over the VP or the predicate phrase. Compare (28a–c) with the clausal field chart in (27).

(28) a. *Bloß/Nur* [$_{VP}$ schön ruhig sein]!
   MP   nicely calm be
   only-MP nicely still be
   'Keep nicely quiet!'
   b. *Bloß/Nur* [$_{VP}$ die Türe nicht aufmachen]!
   MP   the door not (to) open
   'By all means, don't open the door!'
   c. *Aber* immer [$_{VP}$ Kindern den Vortritt lassen]!
   MP always   (to) kids   priority (to) give
   'Just let kids go first!'

Recall that 'Comp(lementizer)' in German identifies the clausal position of the subordinating conjunction as well as V2$_{finitized}$ in the main clause, whereas (28a–c) are non-finite. See (29).

(29)   FF   Comp   MF   2nd VB-V^0
   ad (28a)   ...   –   *Nur* [predicate]
   ad (28b)   ...   –   *Bloß* [$_{VP}$ DO (Neg) V]
   ad (28c)   ...   –   *Aber* [$_{VP}$ IO DO V]

What is the scope of the MPs in (28a–c)? Note first that MPs cannot contain in their scope the clausal subject, since in imperatives the subject is suspended, one can exploit this fact for the assumption that the MP-lexical occupies SpecAgrSP, where, according to its categorial status of [−N], it cannot be assigned nominative case and bars the theta-role from the structural mechanics.

3.3 MPs as a reflex of the semantics and syntax of the original homonymic lexicals

Consider (30a–c) with the attached illocutive forces. [FP = focus particle].

(30) a. FP-particle ranging over adjectival:
Sei *bloß* ruhig!
be MP still
'Be quiet for God's sake!'
b. FP-particle ranging over NP:
Sei *bloß* kein Ballermann!
'Don't be so grotesquely loud!'
c. FP-particle ranging over V or V':
Bloß die Augen zumachen!
'Let me just close my eyes!'

The question whether MPs reflect the semantics and syntax of the original homonymic lexicals in any interesting sense has not been the topic of previous discussions in any true sense (except for Abraham 1989 and, in a diachronic context, Abraham 1991). Generally, it is assumed that MPs are adverbials, since adverbials appear in identical positions in the middle field, i.e. to the left of verb-argument material. However, such an assumption does not lend full credit to the question what the categorial reflex of the original, pre-derivative, homonym is. The answer is trivial in such cases as *vielleicht* and *aber*, where quite clearly a sentential adverb and a coordinative lexical go to MP-status. The question is far from trivial, however, in the case of focus particles in the homonymic, pre-derivative, status. Take such MP-derived focus particles as *bloß* and *nur*, where the semantics of the pre-derived focus particle is such that it maps a scalar property, more precisely: the lower pole of this scale of value predications. For such a scalar property to be effective, however, the operated-upon category must be adjectival since only adjectivals have the property of being scalarly ranged. See the following illustrations for the scalar use of the focus particle (FP)-derived MP *bloß*. Notice that where an NP is the predicate it is generally a non-referential use of NP. In other words, in the canonical cases of the focus particle-derived MP operating upon ADJ- and NP-predicatives scalarity is clearly existant.

3.4 General constraints — 'grammaticalization legacy'

Other than adjectives and adverbs, MPs do not coordinate. See (31)–(32).

(31) *Das Kleid im   Schaufenster ist *doch* und *schon* schön.
     the dress in the window   is MP₁ and MP₂ beautiful

(32) *Das Kleid im   Schaufenster ist doch, schon schön.
     the dress in the window   is MP₁ MP₂ beautiful

However, certain MPs do combine under direct subjacency. Others clearly do not.

(33) Das Kleid im   Schaufenster ist *doch schon* schön.
     the dress in the window   is MP₁ MP₂ beautiful

(34) *Mach *eben aber* die Tür zu!
     do   MP₁ MP₂ the door closed

What we have to exclude furthermore are positions in which the MP-lexeme does not have MP-status. See (35a,b). [FP = focus particle]

(35) a. ⁇Was wolltest du *eigentlich denn* mit deinem Einwand erreichen?
         'What exactly did you want to achieve by your critical remark?'
         ... hardly acceptable
     b. Was wolltest du *denn eigentlich* mit deinem Einwand erreichen?
         ... MP-sequence
     c. Was *eigentlich* wolltest du *denn* mit deinem Einwand erreichen?
         ... FP — MP

We have to conclude that it is not the relative linear distance that plays a role. Rather, as delineated in detail in Abraham (1991:142), MPs fall into three distributional classes. See (36). [FP = focus particle origin of the lexical homonym; COORD = homonymic co-ordinator origin; ADV = homonymic adverb origin]

(36) Strict linear order of semantic MP-classes:

C1–COORD	C2–ADV	C3–FP
denn	*auch*	*bloß/nur*
	doch	*schon*
	eigentlich	*wohl*
aber	*etwa*	*auch*
	ja	

These linear constraints are reflected in the order in which the homonyms occur in clausal connection. Compare (37a–c).[5]

(37) Structural positions of the 3 semantic MP-types:
a. [_Coord _Nur_ [_Adv_- [_FP=CP_ [_Spec_ er [_C_ hat [_ja_   das Nötigste   getan]]]]]]
    only   he   has MP the most necessary done
b. [_Coord_ — [_Adv_ _Nur_ [_FP=CP_ [_Spec_–[_C_ hat er [_ja_ das Nötigste getan]]]]]]
c. [_Coord_ — [_Adv_–[_FP=CP_ [_Spec_ — [_C_ daß er [_ja nur_ das Nötigste getan hat]]]]]]

The linear gap in the ADV-slot in (37a) corresponds to a clear clausal prosodic pause. The same applies to the coordinators *denn, weil, aber* with V2-linearity. Now notice the following partial congruency between the semantic classification in (36) above and the syntactic-distributional classification in (37). What has been classified as 'veridical' has the lowest, or most rightward, syntactic position in any linear MP-combination, whereas the 'non-veridical' ones precede the veridicals. The two semantic classes turn out to have distinct, and convergent, linear distributions. This establishes yet another deeper link between the semantic properties of the homonymic MP-origins and the rather vague semantic, yet syntactically distinct behavior of MPs — which is what we intended to show in the first place and which is what we subsumed under the term 'grammaticalization legacies'.

Nothing of this type of link has been demonstrated in the literature on grammaticalization so far, to the best of my knowledge. I consider it important to the extent that it shows that many a syntactic base can be detected to what appears at first sight to be of purely semantic import. The latter perspective is by and large the leading perspective in the methodological study of modal particles.

3.5 Two methodological null hypotheses

To allow the derivation of MPs from their original full lexical homonyms the following two hypotheses need to be assumed (cf. Abraham 1997).

(38) **Specified syntactic Null Hypothesis:**
Modal particles come in three positional classes subdividing TopP: C1, C2, and C3.

What makes this hypothesis amenable? To answer this question let us formulate another hypothesis. See (39).

(39) Classification of an MP in C1, C2 or C3 depends on the syntactic selectional properties of the MP-homonyms as a legacy which has remained untouched throughout the diachronic grammaticalizing steps.

Let us spell out somewhat more concretely our empirical arguments in favor of these two assumptions. Take C3, which is the position for the sentential object conjunction *daß* 'that' derived diachronically from demonstrative *das*. Both the article and the demonstrative restrict their referential force to deixis. This rather content-vague denotation places C3 in immediate adjacency to the subordinated subject or object clause. Notice, furthermore, that in German C3 carries verbal features of agreement inflection of number and person. In Abraham (1995a: 590–92) it was argued that *daß* 'that' has an overwhelming affinity to the (finite) predicate in terms of verbal argumenthood. Apart from *daß*, C3 hosts MPs that derive from focus particles. What focus particles do, in general, is measuring out a local, direct scope of predicate properties much akin to deictic pronominal *das*.

C2, in turn, is characteristic of *wh*-question contexts, thus, more precisely in syntactic terms, of w-constituents. It attracts both the finite predicate and *wh*-words. In the case that the Specifier of C3 hosts topicalising projections what we have in Spec of C2 are *wh*-constituents. w-words basically represent clausal parts of speech such as subjects, objects, and adverbials. To all appearances, all MPs classified in C2 can be used as adverbs as well.

Finally, C1 is the most straightforward to classify. The MPs resorting to this position derive from coordinating adverbs throughout. They contain in their scope comparative conjunctions, which have been shown to belong to C2, or the verb-argumental content conjunction *daß* 'that'. See (40).

(40) a. *Und/denn/aber* WIE hat er das gesehen? *wh*-question context
'In which way is it that he has seen that?'
b. *Und/denn/aber* WIE daß er sie gesehen hat! *wh*-emphatic context
'No doubt, he has seen them!'

3.6 Conclusion

The main tenet of this investigation into the behavior of the typologically rare pseudo-category of modal particles in German was that, parallel to their semantics, MPs demonstrate a weakening of their syntactic inheritance of the homonymic lexical in pre-derived categorial status in terms of the range of selection properties. This proved to be the case to the extent that, what were semantically scalar focus particles originally, extended their selection to V, which is not a category lending its denotation to scalar and polarity ranking. We are, thus, confronted with a syntactic process of grammaticalization not only much akin to those semantic shifts so often claimed for grammaticalization, but, what is more, a possible and plausible source of the resulting semantic changes of intensional bleaching. This has been held to be principally the case also in the diachronic development of auxiliaries (Abraham 1995a). Given the fundamentally semantic horizon extended by researchers of sundry aspects of grammaticalization, this is a parsimonious methodological stance worth investigating further. Notice, furthermore, that, counter to the canonic assumption about the direction of category change in the clausal structure, adverbs in VP-adjunction positions (in the middle field) and focus particles within VP derive from layered categorial positions in the outer left field of the clause, $C_1(P)$-$C_3(P)$. Grammaticalization paths, thus, comprize also structural lowering processes in the course of which they bleach lexically, but are not completely deprived of illocutive intension and rather sharply delineated syntactic constraints.

4. The desemanticization of IPrep: Syntactic reanalysis or squishy metaphorization?

4.1 Some facts: squishes all over

There can be no doubt that on its path from N-selecting P to V-selecting P, the P-lexeme undergoes desemanticization. According to Haspelmath (1989) the following steps are run through in the grammaticalization of the preposition to reach the status of a selector of an infinitival clause. See (41).

(41) **Grammaticalization hierarchy with respect to IPrep-selecting predicates:**
allative → purposive → irrealis directive → irrealis potential → realis non-factive → (realis factive)

The gist of functionalist explanations such as in (41) is that the word class property with respect to the IPrep governing is extended by metaphorisation to reach the next, intensionally less concrete, semantic class. Establishing such hierarchical selective chains is the pervasive goal in functionalist accounts of grammaticalising phenomena (cf. Lehmann 1985; Heine *et al.* 1991; Demske 1994; Heine/Traugott 1995). The following examples from Old High German (OHG), (42)–(43)), Luther's Early Modern German, (44), and Modern German, (45)–(47), illustrate this gradual change.

(42) sie gertun al bi   manne inan zi rînanne
they desired all among men   him to touch.DAT
Hasp. [10]; Otfrid 11, 15, 7

(43) *es zimet dem   man ze lobene   wol*
    it befits the.DAT man to praise.DAT well
    Hasp. [11a]; *Tristan und Isolde*, 13

(44) *von   dem wird genommen auch das   er meint zu haben*
    from this is   taken   also that-which he means to have
    Hasp. [13]; Luther

(45) *Mutter versicherte fröh zu Hause sein zu wollen*
    mother claimed   early at home be to want
    Hasp. [15]

(46) ?*Sie stellte fest in einer schwierigen Lage   zu sein*
    she stated   in a   difficult   position to be
    Hasp. [16a]

(47) **Sie erfuhr ihm nicht mehr helfen zu können*
    she learned him no   more help   to can
    Hasp. [16b]

Both the starred and the question-marked versions are no longer fully acceptable in today's German, but were prior to the present stage. What is essential is the meaning of the embedding predicate, which mirrors Haspelmath's generalization about the step-wise semantic bleaching of IPrep in relation to the selecting predicate. The envisioned final step is that the IPrep *zu* loses its purposive attraction such that (48) is not acceptable any longer without the extra IPrep *um*, which is similar in function and remaining lexical meaning to English *for (to)*.

(48) *Er ging nach Amerika, *(um) Arbeit zu finden*
    he went to   America   for work to find
    Hasp. [17]

(48) without *um* was still acceptable at Goethe's time (1749–1832). Haspelmath also refers to Modern Dutch, which cannot but realise the second grammaticaliser corresponding to German *um* in steps on the chain in (41) not yet reached by today's German. Viz. Modern Dutch *om__te* in (49) vs. German (50).

(49) *Hij probeerde (om) werk te vinden*
    he tried   for work to find

(50) *Er probierte (, *um) Arbeit zu finden*
    he tried   for work to find

(51)   Moeder zei   (*om) vroeg thuis te zullen   zijn
       mother said   for   early back to become be

Dutch (51) illustrates the (bracketed) last step on the metaphorization hierarchy, (41), which is not yet realised, but is expected to in Dutch and, eventually, in German.

In the following attempt at an explanation of the historical development of IPrep such a semantic hierarchy has a heuristic task at best. What I will strive for is a description of the grammaticalization process in terms of syntactic categories leaving open, at this point, whether a scalar basis needs to be addressed.

4.2 The 'Relative economy constraint' for grammaticalization: German/Dutch vs. English

We discussed two approaches to the grammaticalization of prepositions to sentential complementisers: the functionalist word class extension by metaphorisation à la Haspelmath (1989, 1998); and the syntactic, step-by-step description of the diachronic change. It was argued that there is no need to generally envision a change of word class as drastic as that of 'P to Comp/Prep to Infl/Temp'. Rather, we have assumed two options: the verbal prefix as a small clause predicate under the matrix verb of the simple verb (see Abraham 1993 for German); or the conversion mechanics yielding the required result while preserving the original PP-projection. We felt strongly about the need to retain the diachronically original P-status. This pertains both to *um__zu* as well as *om__te/for__to* and *zu/te/to*. The constraint of word class change is all the more plausible if *um/zu* as well as *for_to* retain some weak semantics of its original P-lexical. It should perhaps be added at this point that one main critic of reanalysis as a explanans of the grammaticalization of IPrep in German, Haspelmath (1997: 12f.; as well as Ebert 1976 on a purely philological basis) maintains expressly that IPrep changes from P to a Complementizer.[3]

All this leads us to posit a number of generalizations, which we take as being novel to attempts made so far describing diachronic processes of grammaticalization in syntactic terms.

(52)   Relative economy constraint of word class change:
       Considerations of methodological economy as well as semantic considerations constrain the change of the categorization of a lexical element to a change of, and within, identical projection (i.e. from X^0 to Y^0 (i.e. small clause predicate) again) unless semantic bleaching has gone so far as to

totally empty the lexical element semantically. Not until such bleaching has occurred is it that recategorization as C/I/T can be assumed. This may appear trivial, but it needs to be stated clearly against the background of the category-projection theory.

(53) Prepositions appear to be subject to grammaticalizing to verbal particles before going any further, if ever, to a purely functional status in terms of C, I, or T. This is supported by the historical development in English, more precisely: from OE, where the situation is much like in Modern German, and Modern English, where the IPrep *to* and its distributional behaviour does not put it on a par with the German IPrep. Rather, it has been subjected to a much wider grammaticalization in terms of semantic bleaching and subordination to syntactic processes.

(54) It follows from the assumption that German *zu*/Dutch *te* is a lexical element binding the Θ-role of the lexically designated subject that IPrep must be subject to the binding mechanism, much in the sense this has been put to work for the passive morpheme (see Baker/Johnson/Roberts 1985). As such, it will naturally obey the chain condition (Reinhardt/Reuland 1993). It is natural and plausible to assume that the chain envisioned in our specific case is the one constituted by all argumental Θ-roles assigned by the predicate verb within VP. This can be seen to be in agreement with the constraint in (47) above. However, it may be also quite independent from the assumption of a status as small clause predicate for the verbal prefix. The close relation between *zu/te* and the passive morpheme holds only for its status as a verbal passive prefix as in German and Dutch, not, e.g., for English with its *to*-split.

(55) Relativization of the formalist position with respect to grammaticalization: The formalist claim that the grammaticalization of lexical elements involves invariably the raising to a functional domain ('reanalysis: from lexical to functional': see van Gelderen 1993, Roberts 1997) cannot be seen to hold without exception. The grammaticalization of P to a particle of V is a point in case.

4.3 Categorial reanalysis — or semantic-scalar, 'squishy' derivation? Old German vs. Modern German: The importance of being earnest about 'syntactic grammaticalization'

One must not fail to see the importance of the question whether there is a syntactic process behind the grammaticalization of IPrep, or whether some categorially squishy semantics is at the bottom of the development. It is for this reason that a not so brief diversion from our main topic is required.

The question whether or not reanalysis is at the bottom of grammaticalizing processes has been ardently discussed in recent publications (witness Haspelmath 1996, 1997; Abraham 1993; van Gelderen 1995; Roberts 1997). The core of the non-categorial, non-reanalysis, or 'squish claim' is as follows (Haspelmath 1996): there is a universal correlation between the inflectional and the derivational status of a transpositional affix and its syntactic properties, between which forms of squishy categorial status mediate. Forms which are more derivational behave syntactically as nominals, whereas more inflectional forms will take verbal complementation. Viz. (56) below.

4.3.1 *The derivational-inflectional squish category range*

Haspelmath (1996) claims that what is at the bottom of most grammaticalization routes is a blurring of the categories in the sense of (56).

(56)   Haspelmath's derivational-inflectional squish category range:

   ← +inflectional   +derivational →
   more preservation of internal syn-   less preservation of internal syntax
   tax (in other words: V and N hold   (in other words: V goes to N or
   their categorial status)   [–V], or it goes to [+V]

Under this perspective, an alleged scalar continuum, and consequently range of category squishes, allows for mixed constructions, where properties of both categories, N as well as V, are interwoven (i.e. 'squishes'). In Gaeta (1997) it is claimed that infinitival constructions in the history of German (from OHG to Modern German) support this theoretical claim for category squishes in the sense mirrorred in (57) (from Gaeta 1997:8). Notice that the gradual change illustrated in (57) does not exclude metaphorization as a driving force. Thus, we have to address two questions: that of metaphorization as involved in language change; and, likewise, that of categorial squishes and their status in language change.

(57)   for bare infinitivals ('Diachronic squish'):

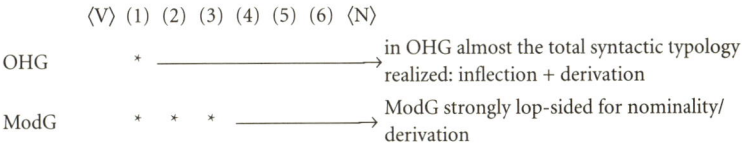

The numbers on the horizontal bar in (57), (1)–(6), refer to the distributional properties in (58) observed to hold for the two diachronic stages (cf. already

Abraham 1989). Gaeta (1997) regards (56) as evidence for his claim of a gradual shift, in which categorial overlap ('squish') is not excluded.

4.3.2 *The non-squishy nature of distributional properties*

Recall what lay at the bottom of Haspelmath's squish analysis: it was the correct empirical observation that distributional (or contextual, or selectional/ subcategorial) properties may change, while the changes of the coding properties need not keep step with the distributional changes. If this is to be contested it needs to be illustrated that the categorial status between nouns and verbs can be accounted for in terms of distributional ('behavioral') properties, while not a single of these leaves a shade of doubt as to its categorial belonging. Despite the distributional distinctions one cannot speak of categorial indifferences — which is what See (58).

(58) Surface forms in nominalizations from verbals:

		Status	O/MHG	ModG
(1)	nominative subject representation	IP/TP	–	–
(2)	accusative object representation	VP	+	– (?)
(3)	adverbial modification	VP/VP	+	– (?)
(4)	adverbial>adjectival modification	V/V	+	+
(5)	indefiniteness determination	Num/NP	+	+
(6)	definiteness determination	D/NP	+	+

The alleged scalar picture in (56) is enhanced if IPrep(+infinitive) is added to supplement the observational picture (cf. Gaeta 1997: 11). Witness (59) and (60), with the latter trying to instantiate Gaeta's claim made in the more general (59).

(59) Relative share and development of derivational vs. Inflectional properties (not a squish in the sense of (41) above!):
[ANC=action noun construction]

	⟨V⟩	(1)	(2)	(3)	(4)	(5)	(6)	⟨N⟩
ANC		*	*	*				
(*zu-*) infinitival					*	*	*	

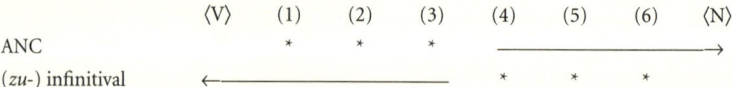

Let us exemplify the generalizations in (58) and (59). (1)–(6), inside (60), refer to the six constructional properties in (59) above.

(60) ANC (compare (59) above):

	in Modern German	in Old/Middle/Early New-High German	
(i)	*das Hannibal Zerstören Roms the H. destroy Rome.GEN	*	
(ii)	(*)das Türen Zuwerfen the doors closed-throwing	daz die lieben geste grüezen the the dear guests greeting *die lieben geste* is an accusative governed lexically by *grüezen*!	ENHG
(iii)	(*)das schnell Zuwerfen der Türe the quickly closed-throwing the door.GEN	mîn dort belîben my there staying	MHG
		ein michel ueben a much practising	MHG
(iv)	das schnelle Zuwerfen der Türe the quick closed-throwing the door.GEN	ir starkez arbeiten their strong working	MHG
(v)	sein die Türe Zuwerfen his the door closed-throwing	daz die lieben geste grüezen the the dear guests greeting	ENHG
(vi)	sein ?eine Türe/Türen Zuwerfen his a door/doors closed-throwing	vil michel liebe geste grüzen very much dear guests greeting	ENHG
		an ein strîten von den Tenemarke gân to a fighting of Denmark going	MHG

(60.1–6) are meant to give evidence to the general claim made in (58) and (59) that there is a principled distributional difference between inflectional vs. derivational functional categories. The underlying claim is that what was a stronger inflectional status of pre-Modern German stages has become derivational through recent development. Notice that, once we find acceptable Haspelmath's generalization on the basis of Old and Middle High German evidence as in (59), no appeal to metaphorization is required any longer. However, even this is a doubtful conclusion. Both the Modern German (iv)–(vi) (left column) in (59) and all direct glosses of the Middle High German (right column) above are correct in substandard variants (certainly in Southern German). Usually, dialectal evidence can be taken to be the more faithful linguistic evidence since it is uninhibited by grammarians. This makes the general validity of (57) very shaky, just like Gaeta's conclusions drawn from (58) and (59). At the same time, the syntax-distributional evaluation of (59) on the basis of the substandard varieties of German, obviates even the graduality picture in accordance with (57). No metaphorical explanation needs be appealed to.

The main patterns of infinitival usage in older stages of German, both with (cf. (59)) and without (see (56)) IPrep, are summarized in (61).

(61) verbal NPs:
   a. in thero ziti **des rouhennes**
      in the period of smoking
      des Rauchens; Tatian 2,3:definite determination — gerundial/ V-inflected
   b. **sînes bluates** rinnan
      his blood.GEN running
      ?*seines Blutes Rinnen*; Otfrid III, 25,36: subject genitive
   c. das versuochen **Christes**
      the seducing (of) Christ
      **das Versuchen*/^{OK}*die Versuchung Christi*; Konrad, Silv. 4000

(62) verbal PPs:
   a. er ward zi manne, bî zi irsterbanne
      he became man (there)with to die
      ^{??}*er wurde zum Mann mit ihnen zu sterben*;
   b. dî vlôch man unde wîp durch behalten den lîp
      who fled from man and woman for to remain alive
      Iw 7735–36
   c. wô der lantstrâze diu in (=3PL) ze rîten geschach
      where the road which (for) them to ride became
      Iw 3367 (B)
   d. die arbeit diu im ze Îdene geschach
      the task which (for) him on the Ides happened
      AH 293
   e. daz ez niemem kunde gesagen wô er im ze vindenne wart
      that it (to) no one could tell where he (for) him to find was
      Er 5574

Strikingly enough, the patterns displayed in (62c–e) have ergative features in the sense of Mahajan (1997): 'dative+ergative V' came to be replaced, without exception, by 'accusative+transitive *haben*' in Modern German.

The IPrep-construction (i.e. the infinitive with *ze/zi/zuo/zu*) shares with the bare infinitive the property of not forming a constituent with its subject argument. For the remainder, however, the IPrep-construction betrays both less inflectional and less derivational, and, thus, less verbal and less nominal, properties simultaneously. This places IPrep between the two poles of the noun/verb scale as shown in Gaeta's (59) (cf. Gaeta 1997:11).

Recall that the two alleged 'squishy' accounts of Old vs. Modern German, as in (60), on the one hand, and of the finite clause vs. the non-finite one, as in (61), hinge crucially upon the fact whether or not (60.2/3) above are really distinct in categorial terms as I characterized them. This is, no doubt, the case for written Standard German. It is not true, however, as mentioned, for the dialect, substandard varieties. Likewise, (58.2,3,5) above are fully grammatical as substandard variants. Thus, unless we restrict ourselves to a grammatical evaluation of the written standard, the two distinct areas with 'squishy', categorially transient periods in (60) coalesce and reduce to just one single distinct categorial difference: the suspended representation of the subject, which is shared by all stages of the historical development up to Modern German. No scalar category status, or transient section, is required any longer.

This leaves us with the 'squish' in (61)–(62)— which is of a different nature altogether to the extent that it compares two different types of construction: finite ones and non-finite ones. No change of one single catgeory is involved in the first place as was the case in (60). Thus, while (61)–(62) remains a valid comparison of two different construction types, the somewhat disconcerting category squish assumed for the diachronic development of German in (59) to all apearances is not the result of a natural historical process in the first place.

4.3.3 *Category status*

We conclude that there is little that speaks in favor of the category squish in (59), whereas the process-motivated explanation rendered by (61) appears to be well-founded. On the basis of this conclusion, there is even less motivation to assume a metaphorically based trigger of language change in Haspelmath's sense.

(63) It is claimed that infinitival *zu* is on a par with the participial prefix *ge-*, which occupies the subject position in a light verb structure, Specv^{max}, thus blocking, on the one hand, the subject-θ from surfacing at SS and raising to any higher functional position.

(64) It will be demonstrated how this step of accommodating the IPrep (as well as participial *ge-*) in Specv^{max}, affects the whole participial range between the passive preterite participle (only selected by *sein* 'be' and *werden* 'become-AUX') and the active preterite participle (in the selection of *haben* 'have'). It is assumed that what appears like a 'suspension' of the absorption of the external argument by the participial morpheme (*ge-*) (Haider 1986; Baker *et al.* 1993), is in fact a direct consequence of the fact that the auxiliaries *sein/werden*, and only those, are unaccusative predicates selecting only preterite participles where the internal argument surfaces as the

derived subject. By contrast, *haben* as Aux is a regular transitive verb (albeit without θ-assignment), thus selecting an external argument and an internal one. One substantial consequence of this *zu*-account is that control and raising construction are to be explained in terms of 'univerbation', i.e. a mapping procedure of the IPrep phrase onto the matrix phrase, which is meant to replace the PRO- and the raising account entirely. The theories of PRO and raising, thus, prove to be totally superfluous in the minimalistic scenario and come closer to traditional philological accounts.

Is it plausible to assume that what is clearly a head projection (like affix/suffix) should obtain the status of a Spec (i.e. the status of a word as Spec in vP as assumed originally by IJbema 1997). Is this a valid concern given that the projection theory appears to be violated?

I expressed the position that, since GB has assumed all along that the passive morpheme binds (and, consequently, 'absorbs') the theta-role of the external (agent) subject there must be a structural link between the subject syntax and the status of the head-morpheme of the passive participle. My conclusion was that in this specific case the IPrep *zu/te*, despite its apparent head status, can obtain the Spec position in (small) vP. Notice that the very fact that IPrep *zu/te* is seen to parallel the behaviour of the passive morpheme *ge-* is well founded given that it never occurs with the surfacing subject (just as the passive morpheme). The parallel need not, however, be drawn to the exhaustion of all properties of the two morphemes (free as regards *zu/te*, bound and grammatical (i.e. without lexical meaning) as goes for *ge-*).

If the above conclusion is indeed correct two conclusions follow: for one, the status of the verbal word would have to be suspended since the identical property of subject-suspension holds for what has traditionally been taken to be a separate word such as the IPrep (German infinitival *zu*, English *to*) and, likewise, the bound grammatical passive participle morpheme. Is this a problem? On which level is it one? The second conclusion is that there are at least two types of Spec-functions; those with head-status and those without, i.e. with a true constituent status. Question is: to what extent is the theta role, which appears to trigger the specific status of the janus-headed category of IPrep as well as *ge-*, part of a more general property responsible for this janus-like status of IPrep/*ge-*? To what extent can we assume that a Spec in vP is different of a Spec for any other full constituent — such that, e.g., filling the Spec of a vP is a thing different from any other Spec-filler?

The question whether the property 'a morpheme binds a theta-role' leads necessarily to the quality of this morpheme to fill Spec depends on the structural representation of lexicals. In Ackema (1999) it is assumed that heads have a structure identical to XPs. See Ackema?s structure for the perfective participle below (Ackema 1999). Cf. (65).

(65)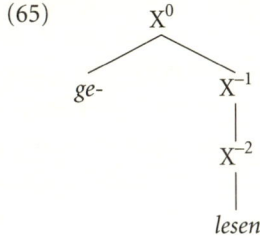

The idea of filling the SpecX⁰ is to avoid another theta role filling what otherwise is a theta devoid Spec (the technical implementation of 'theta-role absorption'). This is what we assume for *zu/te* to hold also. Notice that this implies that the subject role is provided by lexical implication ('lexical assignment') independent of its inflective form. The issue, however, is that particular inflective forms such as non-finites, which never take surface subjects, need be accounted for this syntactic lack despite the fact that the subject-**role** is always implied semantically.

What this analysis involves is the following: it makes a strong claim with respect to the *position* of a certain morpheme as well as its *function*. It is beyond doubt in the literature that the morpheme *ge-* 'absorbs' the external theta role if merged with the auxiliaries *sein* or *werden* (but it does not if merged with *haben*; cf. Abraham (1995a:Ch. 5)). Likewise, it is beyond doubt that this morpheme is bound in all languages under inspection which, on the basis of its distributional characteristic (suspension of the external theta role) can be placed in a morphological specifier to account for this behaviour. As goes for the position of IPrep, it is not treated alike in every language: German/Dutch *zu/te*, cannot be separated from the infinitival verb, while English *to* can. We might therefore say that English *to* with a different position also has a function different from German/Dutch. Note that also West Flemish has distributional properties different from those of German/Dutch. The value of the distinction between form (position) and function is that it allows one to test whether a difference in form/position coincides with a specific change in function.

As far as the mechanics of grammaticalization is concerned it is to be noted that any syntactic analysis will fall short of what is held to be one of the fundamental characteristics of German in semantic terms. It is common opinion that grammaticalization proceeds stepwise along a cline gradually losing lexical content and independence as a separate word, while acquiring more grammatical function (van Gelderen 1996). Both van Gelderen (1996) and Roberts (1997) assume that grammaticalization ends in a functional node. The question is whether this is always true.

Take the grammaticalization of Latin *habēre* to the French future affix *-ai/-as* etc. This can be taken as a standard case of what is held to be a lexical category (V, in the present case) grammaticalizing to a functional head — where this functional head is a ***bound*** morpheme. Take another example: according to van Gelderen (1996), OE *to*, just like OHG *zuo*, is a P assigning case to a nominal verb (the gerundial form of V), which is taken to be in AgrO. In ME, *to* grammaticalizes and acquires verbal features (specified as non-tense features). Moreover, the position of *to* changes such that it is generated in INFL. The evidence for this change is that *to* and the infinitival can be separated (*to not read*) and that the VP can be deleted (*Zoya tried to irritate Amir and Anji tried to also*; van Gelderen 1996: 118). Notice that the standard assumption of grammaticalization combines two properties: that of lexical attrition and that of grammatical boundedness (affixation). German/Dutch *zu/te* do not categorize under this twofold characterization of grammaticalization. There is no indication that the IPrep is about to lose its independence as a word, the main reason being that infinitival embeddings occur with or without the IPrep *zu/te* (*versuchen *(zu)* vs. *braucht nicht (zu) kommen* vs. *will (*zu) kommen*).

Within a general theory of grammaticalization, the above assumptions lead us to make the distinctions with respect to three fundamentally computational types of grammaticalization as in the chart in (26) above. We have seen in this chart, 'Syntactic types of affixation', that the participial morpheme *ge-* is of the third type, too, but that it is bound, which distinguishes it from the unbound IPrep morpheme, *zu/te* — something which is in line with our philological intuition in the first place.

One might wonder at this point whether a verbal prefix, such as *ge-*, taken usually to be much akin to the category of a head, is compatible with the specifier position, Spec*v*P, as assumed here. Notice, however, that affixes usually do not determine the category of the complex verb, as opposed to inflective morphemes, for example. The main reason to claim a Spec-Position for *ge-/zu/0__(C)n* is that the morpheme bears a theta role (AGENT, in our specific case). From this follows that the IPrep, *zu*, just as well as the participial circumfix, *ge-__t*, and the bare infinitival, *0__(C)n*, are not heads.

With respect to the diachronic changes in the categorial status of IPrep in German, here are some generalizations.

a. Whereas there is a rather squishy picture of categorization in all older stages of German (from OHG via MHG up to ENHG), the picture in Modern German clears to the extent that IPrep has all verbal properties. This is less so, however, for the bare infinitive, which still behaves along a number of criteria in accordance with the nominal-derivational status.
b. The fact that the categorial overlap area does not exist in the dialects of Modern German (cf. (60.ii) and (60.iii), which are grammatical, though not particularly frequent) diminishes the squishy picture of categorization between V and N at all historical stages. This is perhaps the most important result of our investigation: no category squish need be assumed in the diachronic and synchronic grammar of German.
c. It is considered premature, if ever possible at all, to decide whether or not language usage on the individual *or* reanalysis ambiguities holding between different generations in a language community trigger language change. Given our principled constraints on looking inside our brain the best we can do is remain agnostic as to this question. However, this does not imply that we should not consider intelligent, interesting, and meaningful ways of accounting for language change. The best we can probably do in such a methodologically difficult situation is to be circumspect of both empirical and methodological questions which are to accompany our work. This means minimally two steps: that we should not fall back behind the acribic methodological horizon drawn by contemporary formal grammar writing (distributional test patterns); and that we should try to evaluate those categories and complexes thereof which are amenable to intersubjective measuring to facilitate the most objective result. My guess is that semantic estimates range secondary in this respect to those about morphosyntactic data.
d. Everything we said about the IPrep so far and the participial derivative morpheme *ge-(__t)* has immediate consequences for the bare infinitive to the extent that non-finites suppress the subject from surfacing just as well. The phenomenon to account for are such bare infinitivals in ACIs ('ECM constructions') of the following type.

(66) a. *Ich sah **ihn** laufen*
       I saw him.ACC run
   b. *Ich hörte **sie** kommen*
       I heard her.ACC come
   c. *Ich spürte **den Onkel** mich streicheln*
       I felt the uncle.ACC me stroke

It is claimed that, counter to the main stream account in modern syntax, no PRO is required (see Abraham 1999, at some more length). Rather, I consider the accusative NPs *ihn/sie/den Onkel* to be governed directly by the matrix verb, while the infinitive is attached to it as an 'attributive predicate'. The constructional account is that of a small clause involving the accusative NP to be raised. (67) is all there is to say about this ACI ('ECM') in German.

(67) Ich [$_{VP}$ sah [$_{V'}$ ihn $_i$ [$_{SC=DO}$ t$_i$ laufen]]]

5. Conclusion

To the extent that the three independent phenomena described above range under the title of 'grammaticalization', they do not, or certainly not entirely, end up as functional morphemes (inflective or derivative) in any way. Thus, unless these phenomena are assigned a different status of language change, the definition of grammaticalization as the pathway from a lexical to a functional morpheme cannot be correct. This may be taken to be a purely terminological question. However, I doubt that it is. Notice that, if the development would have to go the decisive steps further along the alleged pathway of grammaticalization, one is at a loss to determine which functional nodes they would end up at:

a. the epistemic readings of the German modal particles with their clear evidential distinctions? Cf. (9) above. Notice that, despite their perfective descendence (as former preterite presents) and counter to the frequent typological interaction between synthetically marked perfect(ive) and evidentiality (Abraham 1999a), the modal verbs in German are neither on their way to inflectional markers, nor are they bleached enough semantically to become pure auxiliaries.
b. the German illocutive (modal) particle (MP), which is outside of VP, but clearly below any of the functional nodes in Minimalism (since, for sure, to the right of all definite objects)? This is very unlikely ever to happen, also given the remnant distinctive semantics and, linked to that, their distinct syntactic sources; recall (27) and (36)–(37) and cf. [$_{CP}$ [$_{C'}$*daß* [$_{AgrSubj=thema}$ *er* [$_{AgrDO=thema}$ *dies* [$_{ADV=MP}$ *eben/ja* [$_{VP=clausal\ rhema}$ *einen nassen Staub nennt*]]]]]
c. The IPrep in German, Dutch and West Frisian, *zu/te/te*, is a stable unbound morpheme despite the fact that it bears no semantics any longer and despite its absolutely low prosodic status; its distribution likens that of the inseparable participial prefix *ge__(t)*. See the illustration in (68).

(68) a. er hat das Boot ÜBER- **ge-** setzt
      he has the boat across   put
   b. er hat das Buch   Ø überSETZT
      he has the book   translated
   c. er hat das Boot ÜBER- **zu** setzen
      he has the boat across to put
   d. er hat das Buch   zu überSETZEN
      he has the book   to translate

This quite independent distribution of the IPrep *zu* does not qualify as a prospective bound functional (inflectional or derivative) morpheme. Given all this, would we want to stick to the definition of 'grammaticalization equalling from-lexical-to-functional'? I guess not.

All this may make us want to return to the original outline of grammaticalizing processes of language change devised by Lehmann (1989), i.e. the defining notion that lexical items lose syntactic independence (i.e. become 'syntactically bound", at least to a certain extent) thereby giving up their paradigmatic status in favor of a stronger syntagmatic status. After all, it remains totally opaque whether or not the processes described will ever continue to yield, eventually, functional (i.e. inflectional) categories. However, the more this accounts for the three processes of change described above, the less we may gain from this outline in terms of predictable force (which is what the generative attempts clearly were heading for). What is it that rests in this methodological aporia?

Notice that recently Janda (1999) has raised the fundamental doubt whether 'grammaticalization" should not been seen as 'actually an epiphenomenon which results from the intersection and interaction of other, independently motivated domains relevant for the synchronic and diachronic functioning of language [?].' (Janda 1999:1). Let us look at our three illustrtations in Janda's spirit. These are the points in case if we take the process of grammaticalization to be a mozaic of single, more or less independent processes as regards the three German cases.

(69) Grammaticalizing stages of MV, MP, and IPrep in German

	Epistemic Modals (Section 2)	Illocutive Particles (Section 3)	Infinitival Preposition (Section 4)
Partial semantic bleaching	+	+	+
Already functional morpheme	−	−	+
Reached syntactic specification on LF	Infl^0	C1^0/C2^0/C3^0	Spec$v$P
Bound	−	−	−
Reanalysis under cateory preservation (= no category squishes)	+	+	+
One-to-one relation between coding and context properties	+	+	−
Distance between historical source and yielded position	(?) from Asp^0 to Infl^0: considerable structural distance	From various functions left of VP to an underlying C1^0/C2^0/C3^0: considerable structural distance	From P to Spec$v$P: Considerable structural distance

Bleaching, at no point of the developments sketched above, has gone down all the way unto total depletion of meaning of the grammaticalized morphemes involved. It can only be speculated whether or not the German items in question will ever reach this point of total bleaching so as to yield purely grammatical morphemic status. But that is not the interesting issue. What is interesting, however, is the fact that the reconstruction of the syntactic behavior appears to depend crucially on the semantic structure of the original lexical morphemes which the bleaching process started out from. It remains to be seen whether any further prediction, or, for worse, if any interesting, historically telling reconstruction can be made without such semantic clues.

6. Typological speculation

It is reasonable to claim that morphological paradigms — the resulting forms of phonological attrition and reanalysis, i.e. of grammaticalization — (come to) exist under constant pressure by what in phylogenetic and ontogenetic research has come to be called 'synonymy avoidance principle' (amounting to something like 'let no two distinct forms come about, and/or exist, for one single, unique meaning or reference') and, at the same time, a counteracting principle that we would like to call the principle to give expression to 'family resemblance' (i.e. the non-suppression, or suspension, of semantic family belonging). It appears that languages can be evaluated typologically to which degree and, still sharper, whether or not, they observe these criteria. In the present article, I have excised, from three totally independent data ranges, pathways of grammaticalization in which the latter principle, i.e. 'family resemblance', was clearly adhered to. I am aware of the alternative account (disabling the typological implication to be made for languages such as German), i.e. that the grammaticalizing stages indicated are not completed yet such that family resemblance is still the result of uncompleted processes. On the other hand, each of the three phenomena has a considerable age down to the point where no, or hardly any, lexical-semantic component betrays its former source and where the 'legacy' is uncoverable only by means of syntactic reconstruction. Nevertheless, the family resemblance is quite overt: in the case of modal particles most clearly by way of the unique linear combinabilities; in the case of the infinitival preposition *zu* 'to' in the form of the 'allative' (futural) aspect; and in the case of the modal verbs both by their vague, yet indispensible, semantic distinction and the syntactic status of a raising verb (which the epistemic reading must have had all along in its historical development due to its clausal scope (in distinction to the scope over the verbal complex extended by the deontic meaning of the original preterite presents). The claim about observance of the principle of family resemblance in the history of German comes all the more convincing since not only does German adhere to this principle in its modern setup of paradigmatic (inflectional and derivational) forms; what is hardly less, it becomes more manifest also by a comparison with the development of the modal verbs in the history of English, where they are about to lose completely their deontic reading due to the loss of their original aspectual semantics (Abraham 1998). Given all that the speculation that we observe a distinct typological criterion with the principle of family resemblance does not appear too far-fetched.

Notes

* The present article has profitted from discussions with audiences at Vancouver, Antwerp, Berlin, Potsdam, Groningen, and Amsterdam. In particular, I would like to thank Elly van Gelderen (ASU), Tette Hofstra (Groningen), and Marga Reis (Tübingen/Berlin). In the final version I have heeded many an advice extended by the editor of the present volume, Jan Terje Faarlund.

1. It should be noted that the generative jargon about grammaticalization being movement from the low, lexical domain of the structural representation to a higher one, the functional domain, just echoes definitions of the term 'grammaticalization' against structural and philological backgrounds (É. Benveniste, J. Kuryłowicz, Chr. Lehmann, among many others). Thus, nothing new or linguistically estranging is involved except that the grammaticalizing processes can be checked in great detail against the formal structural background.

2. The fact that auxiliaries such as *(zu) haben, (zu) werden* and *(zu) sein* can be embedded, but *(zu) scheinen/pflegen/versprechen* (the latter only in the modal sense) cannot, implies that there are two types of what have been called 'Raising verbs' indiscriminately in the literature.

3. From a historical point of view, *zu* (when it appears with infinitive) developed from a very preposition-like morpheme to a very complementizer-like morpheme as it laboured its way into a growing number of constructions where only the bare infinitive or finite clause complements had stood before this stage.

References

Abraham, W. 1989. "Discourse particles in German: How does their illocutive force come about? Between a maximalistic and a minimalistic position". In *Discourse particles*, W. Abraham (ed.), 203–255. Amsterdam: John Benjamins.

Abraham, W. 1991. "The grammaticization of the German modal particles". In *Approaches to Grammaticalization*, Vol. 2., E. Closs Traugott and B. Heine (eds), 331–380. Amsterdam: John Benjamins.

Abraham, W. 1992. "The aspectual source of the epistemic-root distinction of modal verbs". Paper read at the Symposium on "Voice and Modality" at the University of California, Santa Barabara. (see also *Groninger Arbeiten zur germanistischen Linguistik* 30 (1989)).

Abraham, W. 1993. "Ergativa sind Terminativa". *Zeitschrift für Sprachwissenschaft* 12(2): 157–184.

Abraham, W. 1995a. *Deutsche Syntax im Sprachenvergleich. Grundlegung einer typologischen Syntax des Deutschen*. Tübingen: G. Narr.

Abraham, W. 1995b. "Warum stehen nicht alle Modalpartikeln in allen Satzformen?". *Deutsche Sprache; Zeitschrift für Theorie, Praxis und Dokumentation*. 23: 124–146.

Abraham, W. 1997. "The interdependence of case, aspect, and referentiality in the history of German". In *Parameters of Morphosyntactic Change*, A. van Kemenade and N. Vincent (eds), 29–61. Cambridge: CUP.

Abraham, W. 1998. "The aspectual source of the epistemic-root distinction of modal verbs in German". In *Sprache in Raum und Zeit. In memoriam Johannes Bechert*. [Beiträge zur empirischen Sprachwissenschaft 2], W. Boeder, C. Schroeder, K.H. Wagner and W. Wildgen (eds), 231–249.Tübingen: G. Narr.

Abraham, W. 1999a. "The morphological and semantic classification of 'evidentials' and modal verbs in German: the perfect(ive) catalyst". Paper presented at ICHL 15, Vancouver August 1999.

Abraham, W. 1999b. "The aspect-case typology correlation. Perfectivity and Burzio's generalization". In *Argument and case: Explaining Burzio's Generalization.* [Linguistik Aktuell/Linguistics Today 34], E. Reuland (ed.), 129–190. Amsterdam: John Benjamins.

Ackema, P. 1999. *Issues in Morphosyntax.* Amsterdam: John Benjamins [Linguistik Aktuell/ Linguistics Today 26].

Auwera, J. van der. and Plungian, V.A. 1998. "Modality's semantic map". *Linguistic Typology* 2(1): 79–124.

Baker, M. 1988. *Incorporation: A theory of grammatical function changing.* Chicago: The University of Chicago Press.

Baker, M., Johnson, K. and Roberts, I. 1985. "Passive arguments raised". *Linguistic Inquiry* 20(2): 219–251.

Behaghel, O. 1923. *Deutsche Syntax. Eine geschichtliche Darstellung.* Bd. I-IV. (1923–1932). Heidelberg.

Bereczki, G. 1992. "Türkische Züge in der Struktur des Syrjänischen und ihr Ursprung". In *Festschrift für Károly Rédei zum 60. Geburtstag,* S. Bakró-Nagy and P. Hajdú (eds), 71–76. Wien-Budapest.

Boeder, W. 1998. "Evidentiality in Georgian". To appear in *Evidentials in Turkic, Iranian, and neighbouring languages,* L. Johansson and B. Utas (eds). Berlin: Mouton de Gruyter.

Bybee, J. and Dahl, Ö. 1989. "The creation of tense and aspect systems in the languages of the world". *Studies in Language* 13(1): 51–103.

Chafe, W. and Nichols, J. (eds). 1986. *Evidentiality:The linguistic coding of epistemology.* Norwood, N.J.: Ablex.

Comrie, B. 1976. *Aspect.* Cambridge: CUP.

Conrad, R.J. and Lukas, J. 1995. "The assertion of high subjective certainty. Mufian (Papua New Guinea) oral narratives". In *Discourse Grammar and Typology. Papers in honor of John Verhaar,* W. Abraham et al. (eds) 103–118. Amsterdam: John Benjamins [Studies in Language Companion Series 27].

DeLancey, S. 1997. "Mirativity: the grammatical marking of unexpected information". *Linguistic Typology* 1(1): 33–52.

Demske-Neumann, U. 1994. *Modales Passiv und Tough Movement. Zur strukturellen Kausalität eines syntaktischen Wandels im Deutschen und Englischen.* Tübingen: M. Niemeyer [Linguistische Arbeiten 326].

Denison, D. 1993. *English Historical Syntax: Verbal constructions.* London: Longman.

Denison, D. 2000. "Combining English auxiliaries". In *Pathways of Change: Grammaticalization in English,* O. Fischer, A. Rosenbach and D. Stein. Amsterdam: John Benjamins [Studies in Language Companion Series 53].

Fritz, G. 1997. "Historische Semantik der Modalverben". In *Untersuchungen zur semantischen Entwicklungsgeschichte der Modalverben im Deutschen*, G. Fritz and T. Glonig (eds), 1–157. Tübingen: M. Niemeyer.
Fritz, G. 1998. *Historische Semantik*. Stuttgart: Metzler.
Gaeta, L. 1997. "The inflection vs. derivation dichotomy: the case of German infinitives". Paper presented at the XVI International congress of Linguists, Paris 20–25 July, 1997.
Gelderen, E. van. 1993. *From Agreement to Non-agreement*. Tübingen: M. Niemeyer.
Gelderen, E. van. 1996. The reanalysis of grammaticalised prepositions. Ms. ASU.
Gronemeyer, C. 1998. "The syntactic basis of evidentiality in Lithuanian". Paper given at 27th Annual Meeting of the Society of Linguistics in Europe at St. Andrews, 27–29 Aug. 1998, Workshop on Modality in Generative Grammar.
Guenchéva, Z. (ed.) 1996. *L'énonciation médiatisée*. Louvain-Paris: Peeters.
Haider, H. 1986. "Nicht-sententiale Infinitive". *Groninger Arbeiten zur germanistischen Linguistik (GAGL)* 28: 73–114.
Haspelmath, M. 1989. "From purposive to inifinitive — A universal path of grammaticisation". *Folia Linguistica Historica* X(1/2): 287–310.
Haspelmath, M. 1996. "Word class changing inflection and morphological theory". In *Yearbook of morphology 1995*, G. Booij and J. van Marle (eds), 43–66. Dordrecht: Kluwer.
Haspelmath, M. 1998. "Does grammaticalization need reanalysis?". *Studies in Language* 22(2): 315–352.
Heine, B., Claudi, U. Hünnemeyer, F. 1991. *Grammaticalization*. Chicago: University of Chicago Press.
Heine, B. and Traugott, E.C. (eds). 1994. *Grammaticalization*. 2 vols. Amsterdam: John Benjamins [Typological Studies in Language 19:1/2].
Honti, L. 1997. "Bloße Übereinstimmung oder kausaler Zusammenhang". *Incontri linguistici* 20: 159–181.
Horálek, K. 1967. *Bezevetés a szláv nyelvtudományba*. Budapest.
Itkonen, E. 1966. *Kieli ja sen tutkimus*. Helsinki.
IJbema, A. 1997. "Minimalismus und verb (projection) raising". *Groninger Arbeiten zur germanistischen Linguistik* 40: 229–248.
IJbema, A. and Abraham, W. 2000. "Die styntaktische funktion des infinitivischen *zu*". In *Deutsche Grammatik in Theorie und Praxis*, R. Thieroff; M. Tamrat; N. Fuhrhop and O.Teuber (eds), 123–136. Tübingen: Niemeyer.
Janda, R. 1999. "Beyond 'pathways' and 'unidirectionality': On the discontinuity of language transmission and the counterability of grammaticalization". *Language Sciences* 21 (special issue ed. by L. Campbell on cons and pros of 'grammaticalization theory').
Jászó, A. 1976. "Megjegyzések a participiumból alakult verbum finitumok mondattanához az északi osztjákban". *Nyelvtudományi Közlemények* 78: 353–358.
Johanson, L. 1996. "On Bulgarian and Turkic indirectives". In *Areale, Kontakte, Dialekte, Sprache und ihre Dynamik in mehrsprachigen Situationen. Beiträge zum 10. Bochum-Essener Symposium [...] vom 30.6.-1.7. 1995 an der Universität GH Essen*, N. Boretzky, W. Enninger, T. Stolz (eds), 84–94. *Bochum: Brockmeyer*.
Kemenade, A. van 1992. "The history of English modals: a reanalysis". Ms. University of Leiden.

Lehmann, C. 1985. "Grammaticalization: synchronic variation and diachronic change.". *Lingua e stile* 20(3): 303–318.
Lehmann, C. 1989. "Grammatikalisierung und Lexikalisierung". *Zeitschrift für Phonetik, Sprachwissenschaft und Kommunikationsforschung* 42: 11–19.
Lightfoot, D. 1979. *Principles of Diachronic Syntax.* Cambridge: CUP.
Machavarani, M.V.1988. "Stativ, rezultativ, passiv i perfekt v gruzinskom yazyke". In *Typology of resultative constructions,* V.P. Nedjalkov (ed.), 3–62. Amsterdam: John Benjamins.
Natadze, N.R. 1955. "K voprosu ob obrazovanii vremen I nakloneniy tret'yey serii v kvartel'skix yazykax". *Iberiysko-kavkazskoe yazykoznanie* 7: 99–100.
Palmer, F.R.1990 (1979). *Modality and the English Modals.* London: Longman [Longman Linguistics Library].
Paul, H. 1920. *Deutsche Grammatik.* Vol. 4. Halle: M. Niemeyer.
Reinhardt, T. and Reuland, E. 1993. "Reflexivity". *Linguistic Inquiry* 24(4): 657–720.
Reis, M. 2000. The functions of modal verbs in Modern German. Paper read at the Workshop on "Modalität" at the University of Tübingen, April 2000.
Roberts, I. 1986. *The representation of implicit and de-thematised subjects.* Dortdrecht: Foris.
Roberts, I. 1993. "A formal account of grammaticalization in the history of Romance futures." *Folia Linguistica Historica* 13(1): 259–278.
Roberts, I. 1997. Paper on Reanalysis. Workshop "Grammaticalization and reanalysis" at the ICHL 1997, September 1997, Düsseldorf.
Rutherford, W.E. 1970. "Some observations concerning subordinate clauses in English". *Language* 46: 97–115.
Sumbatova, N. 2000. "Evidentiality, transitivity, and split ergativity: Evidence from Svan." In *TAM and grammatical relation,* W. Abraham and L. Kulikov (eds), 63–96. Amsterdam: John Benjamins [Studies in Language Companion Series 50].
Sweetser, E. 1990. *From Etymology to Pragmatics. Metaphorical and Cultural Aspects of Semantic Structure.* Cambridge: CUP.
Traugott, E. Closs. 1986. "Pragmatic strengthening and grammaticalization". *Berkeley Linguistics Society: Proceedings* 14: 406–416.
Tschenkéli, K. 1958. *Einführung in die georgische Sprache.* Band 1/2. Zürich : Amirami Verlag.
Vikner, S. 1988. "Modals in Danish and event expressions". *Working Papers in Scandinavian Syntax* 39. Lund.
Willett, T. 1988. "A cross-linguistic survey of the grammaticization of evidentiality". *Studies in Language* 12: 51–97.

'Oblique subjects', structural and lexical case marking
Some thoughts on case assignment in North Germanic and German

John Ole Askedal
University of Oslo

The present paper is an attempt to give an integrated account of certain developments in North Germanic syntax: (1) Modern Icelandic and Faroese have so-called oblique subjects, i.e. dative, accusative or even genitive NPs with essentially the same distribution and syntactic rule properties as modern Mainland Scandinavian subjects. (2) Both Old and Modern Icelandic have a rather intricate system of lexical case assignment which differs from, e.g., the predominantly structural case assignment of Modern German. (3) Old Icelandic has DO-IO as well as IO-DO order, whereas Modern Icelandic, like non-case-marking Modern Mainland Scandinavian, to a greater extent has IO-DO.— On the basis of these data it is argued that after the North Germanic shift to SVO, the development has been in the direction of a modern topologically, not morphologically oriented syntax both in the non-case-marking and the case-marking languages. Among other things, this explains why case assignment has remained lexical and idiosyncratic in Icelandic instead of shifting to a simpler system of structural case assignment.

1. Preliminary remarks

In the present paper I shall discuss certain syntactic characteristics of old and modern North Germanic languages, for methodological and factual reasons with a certain emphasis on Icelandic, as compared with German. The phenomena dealt with are on the whole well-known and have received wide-spread attention in the literature. Hence I shall have few facts to add to what is already common knowledge. My aim is rather the more modest one of attempting to indicate certain comparative perspectives which have at least not been highlighted in the discussions known to me.

In particular, I shall deal with the following range of phenomena:
- the case assignment rules for subjects, direct and indirect objects (henceforth DO, IO) in Icelandic (and Faroese) and German, including the somewhat problematical distinction between 'stuctural' and 'lexical' case assignment[1]
- the so-called 'oblique subjects' of Modern Icelandic (and Faroese), i.e. dative, accusative or, in Icelandic, even genitive NPs with syntactic rule properties of subjects (as one special and spectacular aspect of case assignment)[2]
- the linear distribution of subjects, DOs and IOs in connection with the so-called 'configurationality' parameter[3]
- the traditional typological distinction between synthetic and analytic constructions, understood as different ways of coding syntactic relations, in connection with PPs as functional equivalents of IOs.

The above phenomena have attracted the attention of scholars working within synchronic as well as diachronic linguistics. With regard to diachronic perspectives, Faarlund (1990) deals with the transition from non-configurationality to configurationality; important work has also been done on the gradual acquisition of syntactic subject and object properties (e.g. Mørck 1994, 1995, 1998); and there is an intensive on-going debate concerning the age of the 'oblique subjects' of Icelandic (cf. Rögnvaldsson 1995; Haugan 1998; Faarlund, this volume).

In what follows I have one specific and one general aim. The first, specific aim concerns what I believe to be an omission in the by now extensive literature on so-called 'oblique subjects'. This literature has dealt in great detail with oblique subjects but has not sought to view oblique subject case assignment and lexical case assignment within the VP as systematically related phenomena.[4] Second, I shall argue, perhaps trivially, that both Insular Scandinavian (Icelandic, Faroese) and Mainland Scandinavian (Norwegian, Danish, Swedish) have syntactically more in common than one might believe at first glance when considering in isolation the morphological similarities between Insular Scandinavian and German as against the neutralization of Germanic case oppositions in Modern Mainland Scandinavian.

2. Case marking patterns

There can be no doubt that the modern languages in question have a Subject–Non-subject distinction in the sense that a NP constituent may be singled out as the basis or target of a number of syntactic rules which are not accessible to the other sentence elements (NPs and PPs) connected with the predicate. Such rules include, in particular, deletability in infinitival constructions and in the imperative, and the role of primary trigger of reflexivization and the pivot of categorial demotion and promotion in the passive (cf., e.g., Faarlund 1990:111). There are also coordination constraints to the effect that VP-external (nominative) subjects and other sentence elements (NPs) may not in general be coordinated. In this sense, 'subject' is here primarily understood as a syntactic category based on rule behaviour and only secondarily as a category coded in some specific manner. To the extent that one is dealing with more than one syntactic subject property, there is, synchronically, the logical possibility of different degrees of subjecthood and, diachronically, of gradual acquisition of subject properties (cf. Cole et al. 1980).

From this syntactic rule definition of subjects it follows that they need not be case-marked at all.[5]

Case-marking of subjects may come in two varieties, which may be labelled 'uniform' and 'non-uniform' case marking respectively. Uniform case-marking of subjects appears to be the more common type and is for instance exemplified by German and Latin. Consider the German examples (1)–(2), where non-nominative marking of an NP precludes the application of subject-specific rules:[6,7]

(1) a. Mir   fehlt das Geld   nicht.
        me.DAT lacks the money.NOM not.
        'I don't lack the money.'
    b. *Ich   hoffe,   das Geld   nicht
        I.NOM hope PRO the money.NOM not
        zu fehlen.
        to lack.INF
        'I hope not to lack the money.'
    c. Ich   hoffe, daß mir   das Geld
        I.NOM hope that me.DAT the money.NOM
        nicht fehlt.
        not   lacks
        'I hope that I shall not lack the money.'

(2) a. *Ihm   kommt die Hausarbeit   zu schwer*
him.DAT comes the homework.NOM too difficult
vor.
PART
'He finds the homework too hard.'
b. **Er   behauptet,   tüchtig zu sein,*
he.NOM claims   PRO clever to be
aber kommt die Hausarbeit   zu schwer
but _ comes the homework.NOM too difficult
vor.
PART
'He claims to be clever but finds the homework too hard.'
c. *Er   behauptet,   tüchtig zu sein,*
he.NOM claims   PRO clever to be
aber ihm   kommt die Hausarbeit
but him.DAT comes the homework.NOM
zu schwer vor.
too difficult PART
'He claims to be clever, but he finds the homework too hard.'

The prototypical example of non-uniform case-marking is morphological ergativity, where the subjects of transitive and intransitive verbs are marked differently but share syntactic rule properties (cf. Anderson 1976). Non-uniform case-marking appears to be rare in connection with morphological nominativity. However, as indicated initially, the common restriction to nominative subject-marking does not apply in modern Icelandic and Faroese (cf. Zaenen, Maling and Thráinsson 1990:99–106; Thráinsson 1994:175f.; Barnes 1986; Faarlund 1990:162–166; Faarlund, this volume). Nominative case-marking is more common and prototypical, but non-nominative marking occurs also. Icelandic and Faroese are thus instances of languages with non-uniform case-marking of subjects. Cf. for instance the Icelandic translational equivalents of German (1)–(2) in Modern Icelandic (3)–(4), where accusative (3) and dative (4) NPs display subject properties:

(3) a. *Mig   vantar ekki peninga.*
me.ACC lacks not money.ACC
'I don't lack money.'

b. Ég   vonast   til að   vanta ekki
I.NOM hope.REFL to to PRO lack   not
peninga.
money.ACC
'I hope that I shall not lack money.'

(4) a. Honum   finst   verkefnið
him.DAT finds.REFL homework-the.NOM
of þungt.
too hard
'He finds the homework too hard.'
b. Hann   segist   vera duglegur,
he.NOM says.REFL be   clever
en _ finst   verkefnið   of þungt.
but finds.REFL homework-the.NOM too hard
'He claims to be clever, but finds the homework too hard.'

Having established the two types of uniform and non-uniform case marking with regard to the subject side of the Subject–Non-subject dichotomy, one may ask whether a similar difference exists with regard to the Non-subject side of the dichotomy between Icelandic (and Faroese) and German. In order to investigate this, one has to look at case assignment rules pertaining to objects with two- and three-place verbs in these languages.

In modern German, all three oblique cases are used as the single object of two-place verbs, but with rather unequal frequency (5a). The accusative is the unmarked, default option (*sehen* etc.). Verbs governing a single dative object (*danken* etc.) form a much smaller class, and genitive coding of DO (*gedenken* etc.) is marginal.

With three-place verbs, only three — or four (cf. below) — combinations of case-marked objects exist, and again the patterns occur with very unequal frequency (5b). The unmarked case combination consists of A and D, of which two topological varieties exist. The more common variety by far has D preceding A as the basic serialization (*schenken* 'give' etc.), but in addition a few verbs (*aussetzen, unterwerfen* etc.) have A preceding D. Accusative coding of IO resulting in an A+A pattern is mainly restricted to three verbs (*lehren, abfragen, abhören*; cf. Askedal 1980). The A+D (*unterwerfen* etc.) and A+G (*beschuldigen* etc.) patterns do not appear to be amenable to a DO+IO analysis on a par with the D+A and the A+A patterns with regard to the prototypical realization of DO as [−Human] and IO as [+Human].[8] These object-coding patterns, given in (5a, b), combine with uniform subject coding to yield the case-marking hierarchy (5c) for the three basic syntactic relations subject, DO and IO in Modern German:

(5) a. Object-coding with two-place verbs:
 A > D > G
 b. Object-coding with three-place verbs:
 D+A > A+G > A+D > A+A
 c. Coding of syntactic relations:
 Subject: DO: IO:
 N A>D>G D>A

Modern Icelandic is systematically akin to modern German, but the patterns that are marginal in German appear to be somewhat less marginal in Icelandic, and with three-place verbs the object patterns differ in the two languages.[9]

As in German, all three oblique cases occur as the single object of two-place verbs. Two-place verbs with a genitive object are more common in Icelandic than in German and occur with predicates where the genitive has been long lost in German (*vænta* 'hope (for)', *krefjast* 'demand', *vitja* 'visit', *gá* 'look after', *leita* 'seek'). It should be noted that a prepositional complement is possible instead of the genitive with a number of the verbs in question (*leita eftir, gá að, til*). There is also a certain tendency to retain the genitive in more or less fixed locutions.[10]

The two-place pattern with a single dative object is basically comparable to its German counterpart, but certain differences exist. First, with a number of verbs Icelandic has a dative object where German has the more common accusative (*heilsa/grüßen* 'greet', *misþyrma/mißhandeln* 'mistreat', *refsa/ (be)strafen* 'punish', *spilla/verderben* 'spoil', *farga/ausrotten* 'eradicate'; *fresta/ aufschieben* 'postpone', *gleyma/vergessen* 'forget', etc.; cf. Kress 1982:215f.). Second, there exist in German productive word formation patterns with such prefixes as *ent-, zu-, nach-, entgegen-* (e.g. *entlaufen, zukommen, nachlaufen, entgegenkommen* etc.) for dative-governing verbs. Icelandic, on the other hand, has very few, and in general unproductive, prefix patterns with verbs.

Finally, Icelandic has the two-place A+A pattern[11] already illustrated in (3a) (Kress 1982:215), which is non-existent in German.

As to three-place constructions (cf. in general Zaenen, Maling and Thráinsson 1990:109–112, 119), Icelandic shares with Modern German the three-place pattern with dative IO and accusative DO (*gefa* 'give', etc) with the same basic D+A linearization and, in addition, a three-place construction with obligatory A+D linearization. In Icelandic, the latter pattern is found, first, with verbs with the prefix *sam-* 'together' (*samtengja eitthvað einhverju* 'connect something with something', *samlíkja eitthvað einhverju* 'compare something with something'; cf. Kress 1982:211). Second, it is found in a number of more or less fixed locutions (*firra/nema einhvern fjörvi* 'kill', *skirra einhvern vandræðum* 'save someone from trouble', *nema einhvern ráðum* 'deprive someone of liberty of action', *verja landið óvinum* 'protect the country from enemies') (Kress 1982:211). According to Kress (1982), the A+D pattern is in the latter cases no longer productive and has, as a productive pattern, been replaced by a D+PP or A+PP pattern with linear shifting of the thematic roles (cf. *stela einhverju frá einhverjum* 'steal something from someone', *leyna einhverju fyrir einhverjum* 'hide something from someone' etc. with D+PP and *taka eitthvad frá einhverjum* 'take something away from someone', *taka einhvern af lifi* 'take someone's life' with A+PP) (Kress 1982:211f.).

Like German, Icelandic also has an A+G pattern (*biðja* 'ask for', etc.). Associated with some verbs of this pattern there is a prepositional alternative without linear shifting A+PP (*hvetja einhvern einhvers/til einhvers* 'induce someone to something'). There are also instances of linear shifting from A+G to G+PP (← A) (*beiða einhvern einhvers* vs. *beiðast einhvers af einhverjum* 'ask something from someone').

Unlike German, Icelandic also has a D+D pattern (*heita* 'promise', *svara* 'answer') and even a D+G pattern (*óska* 'wish', *unna* 'be happy for something on someone's behalf', etc.) (Kress 1982:210–212). The Icelandic (N+)A+A pattern is largely restricted to co-predicative constructions (cf. Kress 1982:214) but is even found with other verbs (*kosta*, cf. Thráinsson 1994:177; and in locutions like *höggva einhvern banahögg* 'deliver the fatal blow to someone').

Given the possibility of oblique subjects also, there seems to correspond to the German summary in (5) the Icelandic one in (6) (cf. Thráinsson 1994:177):

(6) a. Object coding with two-place verbs:
     A > D > G
  b. Object coding with three-place verbs:
     D+A > A+D > A+G > D+D > D+G > A+A
  c. Coding of syntactic relations:
     Subject: DO: IO:
     N > D > A > G   A > D > G (?N)[12]   D > A

A few further comments are in order concerning Icelandic three-place constructions. As noted in connection with patterns involving two case-marked objects, there is a tendency to replace the dative or genitive following an accusative object by a prepositional complement. Besides, the IO–DO distinction does not seem equally applicable to all Icelandic genitive or dative objects in three-place constructions (cf. e.g. Mørck 1998: 368, with references). Furthermore, the status of the nominative in constructions with an oblique dative subject, as for instance (7) is assumed to be (Thráinsson 1994: 176), is a matter for debate:[13]

(7) Stelpunni   líka   hestarnir.
     girl-the.DAT like.3PL.PLUR horses-the.NOM
     'The girl likes the horses.'

With regard to two-place constructions, the fairly numerous instrumental datives (þekja hús (með) halmi 'cover the (roof of) the house with straw, thatch'; cf. Kress 1982: 225) are semantically autonomous and adverbial in nature (as is also evident from the alternatively possible prepositional construction).

On the whole, there seems to be a more clear-cut relationship between syntactic function and case marking in Modern German than in Icelandic. The subject appears uniformly in the nominative case in German, but in all four cases in Icelandic. The DO has the accusative as its prototypical manifestation in both languages, but the genitive is more common in Icelandic, and the dative is more clearly the case of IO in German than in Icelandic, where one even finds D+G and D+D object combinations, and in addition, at least in certain styles and environments, instrumental datives of a kind that were only residually present in the earliest Old High German and discarded about 1200 years ago (Dal 1966: 34). In this context it is also interesting to note that there were more verbs governing the dative in Middle High German than in the modern language (Van Pottelberge 1998: 453).

The Modern Icelandic case marking patterns in question are the continuation of corresponding Old Norse patterns. In the case of German, there is even in the oldest sources no indication of a D+D object construction. The functions of the accusative and the dative have on the whole remained fairly stable in German,[14] and there is no indication that the nominative has at any time been challenged by the oblique cases as the case of the syntactic subject. The main changes in the case-marking system are those found with the genitive (Donhauser 1990: 99[15]). Possibly due to a change in the aspectual system of the language (Leiss 1991), denotation of indefiniteness by the adverbal genitive (cf. Middle High German (8)) went out of use in the course of Early New High German,[16] although examples with a "partitive" genitive like (9) still occur with classical writers (cf. Dal 1966: 15f.):[17]

(8) sie   heten   noch des   goldes (Nibelungenlied)
    they.NOM had.SUB still the.GEN gold.GEN
    'They would still have gold.'
(9) es   schenkte der Böhme
    it.EXPL poured   the gypsy.NOM
    des   perlenden Weins   (Friedrich von Schiller)
    the.GEN pearling wine.GEN
    'The gypsy was pouring pearling wine.'

Similarly, the D+G pattern is attested as late as in the early 19th century, cf. (10), but is totally absent from the modern language (Dal 1966:20f.):

(10) Wie danke ich   euch   der   Gabe. (Johann Ludwig Tieck)
     how thank I.NOM you.DAT the.GEN gift
     'How do I thank you for your gift.'

Lexically conditioned, syntactically unproductive genitive objects are found in Modern German with a very small number of two-place verbs (*gedenken, bedürfen* and a few others) and a somewhat larger, but still restricted number of three-place verbs, some of which are reflexive, also governing an accusative object (*beschuldigen, sich annehmen* etc.).[18] In the modern language the constructions with a genitive object are often stylistically marked. The predominant function of the German genitive is now that of a marker of adnominal subordination (Donhauser 1998:69). Although some of the lexically governed genitives of Old Norse are supposed to be (if only derivatively) 'partitive' in meaning (Faarlund 1990:143), neither Old Norse nor Modern Icelandic has anything comparable to the older German aspectually conditioned 'partitive' genitive alternating with an accusative object.

It seems natural to describe the differences between Modern German and Modern Icelandic in terms of the distinction between 'structural' vs. 'lexical' case assignment.[19] 'Structural' in this connection should be construed as 'related to syntactic relation or function by a general rule' (which may again be associated with a specific position in syntactic structure).

For Modern German case assignments I propose, following Zifonun et al. (1997:1327),[20] the hierarchically ordered interpretation in (11):

(11) Subject:
        structural case →   N
     Object with two-place verbs:
        structural case →   A
        additional lexical case assignment →   D, G

Three-place verbs:
   structural case →   D+A
   additional lexical case assignment →   G as second object in A+G
                                                          D as second object in A+D
                                                          A as IO in A+A

For Modern Icelandic, I submit the following proposal (12) (the options not attested in German are underlined):

(12) Subject:
      structural case → N;
      additional lexical case assignment →   D, A, G
     Object with two-place verbs:
      structural case →   A
      additional lexical case assignment →   D, G
     Three-place verbs:
      structural case →   D+A
      additional lexical case assignment →   G as second object in A+G
                                                    D as second object in A+D
                                                    A as IO in A+A
                                                    <u>D+G</u>
                                                    <u>D+D</u>

On the face of it, the similarities predominate, but it is still evident that Icelandic has more lexical case assignment than Modern German. Icelandic has lexical case with subjects as well as with objects whereas lexical case assignment in German is restricted to objects. With three-place verbs German has IO in the accusative as a highly marked minor deviation, whereas Icelandic has two patterns — D+G, D+D — not found at all in Modern German but comprising a fairly large number of verbs in Icelandic. The charts (11) and (12) thus capture a general difference between German as a language with more structural and less lexical case assignment, and (Old and Modern) Icelandic as a language with more lexical ("quirky") and less structural case assignment. The more general conclusion to be drawn is that two fairly closely related languages with exactly the same set of case oppositions — N, A, D, G — may differ in a noticeable manner with regard to the distribution of lexical vs. structural case assignment.

    If one is correct in assuming a different distribution of structurally and lexically assigned case with Old Norse and Modern Icelandic verbs on the one hand, and Modern German verbs on the other, one might expect to find similar differences elsewhere in the grammar. In this connection mention has to be made of prepositions as another important category that assigns case. In Modern German, case assignment with prepositions is basically lexical, but in certain environments rules of a more strictly structural kind seem to apply. A case in point is the use of the dative instead of the genitive when the genitive cannot be given morphological expression, cf. (13):

(13)   *wegen der vielen Probleme* (GEN) —
       **wegen Probleme* (NOM/ACC/GEN) —
       wegen Problemen (DAT)
       'because of (the many) problems'

Here the dative may be considered a kind of default government marker and hence structurally motivated. Somewhat different is the productivity of the genitive with 'new' prepositions. Cf. for instance (14):[21]

(14)   (verbal participle of dative-governing verb)
       dem alten Gebrauch entsprechend →
       (reanalysis as dative-governing preposition)
       entsprechend dem alten Gebrauch →
       (more recent development of genitive government still not accepted by normative grammarians)
       entsprechend des alten Gebrauchs
       'in accordance with previous usage'

To my knowledge, there is nothing similar to this in Icelandic. This would seem to indicate that the principle of lexical assignment of case is in general more resistent to change in Icelandic than in German.

3. Topological patterns and constructional alternatives

There are indications that the case assignment differences between German and Icelandic noted in the previous section are to a certain extent correlated with differences concerning ordering possibilities and restrictions. There also exist ordering differences between Old Norse and Modern Icelandic (for a brief overview see Faarlund, this volume).

First it should be noted that all the examples of so-called 'oblique subjects' discussed in the literature have exactly the same topological properties as Icelandic nominative subjects and their functional counterparts in the modern Mainland Scandinavian languages, i.e. they are placed clause-initially or immediately after the finite verb (but not in later positions; cf. Mørck 1994: 177). Cf. e.g. (3a) and (4a), repeated here as (15a), (16a), and modern Norwegian (15b), (16b):

(15) a. Mig vantar ekki peninga.
me.ACC lacks not money.ACC
'I don't lack money.'
b. Jeg mangler ikke penger.
I.SUBJ lack not money.DO
'I don't lack money.'

(16) a. Honum finst verkefniðof þungt.
him.DAT finds.REFL homework-the.NOM too hard
'He finds the homework too difficult.'
b. Han finner hjemmeoppgaven for vanskelig.
he.SUBJ finds homework-the.DO too hard
'He finds the homework too difficult.'

In three-place constructions there exist certain intriguing linearization similarities, but also certain differences, between German and Icelandic.

As noted above, both languages have two kinds of double object construction with an accusative and a dative object, with different ordering of the two objects as D+A and A+D, respectively. In the latter, decidedly more marked case, neither language allows for reversed ordering of the objects (cf. German *seinen Körper der Sonne aussetzen/*der Sonne seinen Körper aussetzen* 'expose one's body to the sun', Icelandic *verja landið óvinum/*verja óvinum landið* 'defend the country against enemies' etc.). In the former, more productive linearization type, reordering is possible in German in accordance with theme-rheme structuring (or 'focus') requirements. Cf. e.g. (17):[22]

(17) a. Er hat seinem Freund das Buch
he.NOM has his friend.DAT the book.ACC
überlassen.
left.
'He left his friend the book.'
b. Er hat das Buch seinem Freund
he.NOM has the book.ACC his friend.DAT
überlassen.
left
'He left the book to his friend.'

c. *Er   hat das Buch   einem Freund*
      he.NOM has the book.ACC a   friend.DAT
      überlassen.
      left
      'He left the book to a friend.'
   d. **Er   hat ein Buch   dem Freund*
      he.NOM has a   book.ACC the   friend.DAT
      überlassen.
      left
      'He left a book to the friend.'

Reordering of this kind is possible in Modern Icelandic, too (Ottósson 1993: 371, 381–384; Holmberg and Platzack 1995: 189, 205–214). As in German, reordering appears to be possible when the accusative object is definite (thematic) and the dative object is indefinite (rhematic), or when both the dative and the accusative object are definite (thematic) or indefinite (cf. Holmberg and Platzack 1995: 206). Cf. for instance (17) and (18)–(19) (from Ottósson 1993: 381, 383):

(18) a. *Jón   gaf konunginum   ambáttina.*
        John.NOM gave king-the.DAT maidservant-the.ACC
        'John gave the king the maidservant.'
     b. *Jón   gaf ambáttina   konunginum.*
        John.NOM gave maidservant-the.ACC king-the.DAT
        'John gave the maidservant to the king.'

(19) *Ég   mun   gefa bókina*
     I.NOM shall.FUT give book-the.ACC
     einhverju bókasafni.
     some   library.DAT
     'I will give the book to some library.'

Object reordering is amply attested with corresponding double object verbs in Old Norse. Cf. (20), (21) (taken from Mørck 1998: 370f., cf. also 374f., with further references).

(20) *Hon   skyldi bera ǫl   víkingum.*
     she.NOM should carry beer.ACC vikings.DAT
     'She was to bring beer to the vikings.'

(21) *Nú   skulu vér   senda mann   Þórhalli ...*
     now shall we.NOM send man.ACC Thorhall.DAT
     'Now we shall send a man to Thorhall ...'

However, a certain tightening of positional requirements appears to have occurred as the indefinite A–definite D sequence in (21) is hardly possible in Modern Icelandic (or in Modern German) (cf. Ottósson 1993:383).

In a historical perspective, there has been a certain tightening of Modern Icelandic reordering rules in connection with subject and DO. Cf. the example for the Old Norse DO — subject order in (22a) (from Faarlund 1990:164) which is no longer available in Modern Icelandic but which still has parallels in Modern German, as in (22b):

(22) a. Skulu þessa gjǫld   dǿma tolf   menn.
         shall these fines.ACC fix twelve men.NOM
     b. Laut   Gesetz sollen die Geldbußen
         according law   shall the fines.ACC
         zwölf Männer   festlegen.
         twelve men.NOM fix
     a./b. 'Twelve [sworn] men shall fix the fines (according to the law).'

Concerning double object constructions with IO and DO, Sprouse (1995) has made the observation that the IO+DO — or, in case-marking terms, D+A — order should in fact be more favoured with SOV than with SVO languages under the assumption that the DO (A) is more closely connected with the verb than is the IO (D) (cf. also Ottósson 1993:371, 374; Holmberg and Platzack 1995:190–196). The order IO+DO (D+A) should also be universally preferred, as in fact it is irrespective of verb ordering (cf. Mallinson and Blake 1981:161–163), since it conforms to the universal tendency to have the category 'Human' take linear precedence over 'Non-human'. Given these general considerations, one might also expect SVO languages (like Nordic) to have less IO+DO (D+A) constructions than SOV languages (like German). On the other hand, the prototypical correspondence between SOV order and case marking (Greenberg 1966:96, Universal 41) should lead one to expect a more flexible ordering of dative IOs and accusative DOs than in non-casemarking SVO languages. Both suppositions are in fact borne out by Modern German vs. the Modern Mainland Scandinavian languages. Consider for instance the juxtaposition of German IO+DO constructions with their Norwegian counterparts in (23)–(28). In these examples, German has a dative IO where Norwegian has a PP. Concerning the more flexible ordering of IO and DO in German, consider (17b,c) and the DO-IO ordering of pronominal objects in (23a) and (27a):

(23) a. German:
Lichtenberg   mußte
Lichtenberg.NOM must.PRET
ihn   ihr   beschreiben.
it.ACC her.DAT describe
b. Norwegian (preposition *for* 'for'):
Lichtenberg   måtte
Lichtenberg.SUBJ must.PRET
beskrive det   for henne
describe it.OBL to her.OBL
a./b.   'Lichtenberg had to describe it to her.'

(24) a. German:
Er   mußte   ihm
he.NOM must.PRET him.DAT
eine Droschke holen.
a   cab.ACC fetch.
b. Norwegian (preposition *til* 'to'):
Han   måtte   hente en drosje
he.SUBJ must.PRET fetch a cab.DO
til ham.
for him.OBL
a./b.   'He had to fetch him a cab.'

(25) a. German:
Das   nahm ihm
that.NOM took him.DAT
den Mut   zum   Weiterreden.
the courage.ACC to-the.DAT further-talking
b. Norwegian (preposition *fra* 'from'):
Det   tok   fra ham
that.SUBJ took from him.OBL
motet   til å snakke videre.
courage-the.DO to to talk   further
a./b.   'That deprived him of his courage to go on speaking.'

(26) a. German:
Man   wird   ihm   das
one.NOM will.FUT him.DAT that.ACC
nicht zumuten   können.
not   expect.INF can.INF

    b. Norwegian (Preposition *av* 'of, from'):
       Man vil   ikke kunne   forlange
       one will.FUT not can.INF expect.INF
       det   *av ham.*
       that.DO of him.OBL
    a./b. 'One cannot possibly expect that of him.'

(27) a. German:
       Man   sieht es   ihm
       one.NOM sees it.ACC him.DAT
       an, ...
       PART
    b. Norwegian (preposition *på* 'on'):
       Man   ser det   på ham, ...
       one.NOM sees it.OBL on him.OBL
    a./b. 'One can tell from his appearance, ...'

(28) a. German:
       Und was soll   ich kochen,
       and what shall I   cook,
       rief   sie   ihm   nach, ...
       shouted she.NOM him.DAT PART
    b. Norwegian (preposition *etter* 'after'):
       Og hva   slags mat skal jeg lage,
       and what kind food shall I   cook,
       ropte   hun   etter ham, ...
       shouted she.NOM after him.OBL
    a./b. 'And what shall I cook, she shouted after him, ...'

In connection with the case-marking rules in Section 2 it was pointed out that in a number of instances Modern Icelandic shows a similar tendency to have PPs replace dative and genitive objects. A summary of the alternations and transitions in question is given in (29) (cf. also Kress 1982: 211f., 225; Holmberg and Platzack 1995: 205):[23]

(29) 1. G → PP: *leita einhvers* vs. *leita eftir*
      2. (instrumental) D → PP: *þekja hús (með) halmi*
      3. A+D → A+PP (with linear shifting of the thematic roles): *nema einhvern ráðum* vs. *taka eitthvad frá einhverjum*
      4. A+D → D+PP (with linear shifting of the thematic roles): *nema einhvern ráðum* vs. *stela einhverju frá einhverjum*

5. A+G → A+PP: *spyrja einhvern einhvers* vs. ... *um eitthvað*
6. A+G → G+PP (with linear shifting of the thematic roles): *beiða einhvern einhvers* vs. *beiðast einhvers af einhverjum*

According to Kress (1982), such replacements represent developments typical of the modern Icelandic language, but they are also attested in Old Norse (cf. Mørck 1998: 371). Consider for instance (30), (31):

(30) With the preposition *til* 'to':
Sendi hann   mann   til þeirra ...
sent he.NOM man.ACC to them.GEN
'He sent a man to them ...'

(31) With the preposition *fyrir* 'for':
Tók biskup   pá   at ... telja
took bishop.NOM then to   tell
fyrir hónum   stórmerki   guðs.
for him.DAT great-deeds.ACC God.GEN
'Then the bishop started to tell him ... about the great deeds of God.'

The examples (30), (31) form part of a more general system of oblique case/PP alternations in Old Norse. Cf. (32) which is based on the material presented in Nygaard (1905: 101–154):

(32) 1. G → PP: *vitja* (*til*) 'visit', *vána* (*til*) 'hope, wait for', *gæta* (*til*) 'heed', *geta* (*um*) 'mention, refer to', *kosta* (*til, við*) 'strive, long for', *leita* (*til, at, eptir*) 'seek, look for', *ørvænta* (*at, af*) 'give up the hope for', *minnast* (*á*) 'remember', *fýsast* (*til, á*) 'wish, long for', *girnast* (*til, á*) 'desire', *dirfast* (*til, at*) 'risk, venture'
2. D → PP: *heilsa* (*á*) 'greet', *treysta* (*á*) 'trust', *misfara* (*með*) 'mistreat', *una* (*við*) 'be content with', *hlíta* (*við*) 'content oneself with', *fagna* (*af, í*) 'enjoy, be pleased with', *hlýða* (*á, til*) 'listen to', *vægja* (*eptir, fyrir*) 'spare', *gremjast* (*við*) 'become angry with', *grimmast* (*við*) 'become angry with', *venjast* (*við*) 'accustom oneself to', *samneyta* (*við*) 'associate with', *samnægja* (*við*) 'stay content with', *reiðast* (*við*) 'be angry about', *hælast* (*af, um*) 'boast of'
3. A+D → A+PP: *líkja* (*eptir;* the dative is rare) 'render similar to', *samþykkja* (*við*) 'make conform to'; *auka* (*með* for the second 'instrumental' dative) 'increase'; certain verbs of deprivation or dispossession: *fletta, ræna, svipta* (*af*)
4. D+D → D+PP: *launa* 'reward', *bæta* 'pay, atone' (*með* for the second 'instrumental' dative)

5. A+G → A+PP: *minna* (*á*) 'remind'; *fylla* (*af*) 'fill'; *spyrja, frétta* (*at, eptir, um*) 'ask'; *fýsa* (*til*), *eggja* (*til, á*), *hvetja* (*til, at*) 'incite'
6. D+G → G+PP: *hefna* (*fyrir*; rare) 'avenge', *kunna* (*um*) 'reproach'

There are also certain genitive-governing adjectives which take a prepositional complement instead of the genitive. Cases in point are the following: *búinn* (*til*) 'prepared', *fullr* (*af*) 'full', *varr* (*við*) 'aware of', *skyldr* (*til*) 'obliged', *sannr* (*at*) 'convinced', *hlutlauss* (*af*) 'not involved, not a party to' (Nygaard 1905:148f.).

It seems that the instrumental dative mentioned in Section 2 tends to appear in fixed locutions or have a more or less archaic ring to it even in classical Old Norse prose (cf. Nygaard 1905:112–114, 117f.). Thus alongside of *hǫggva sverði* 'strike a blow with a sword' one also finds *hǫggva með sverði*. Besides, there exist a number of semi-lexicalized participial forms meaning 'decorated, equipped, furnished with' with an instrumental dative, for instance *tjǫldur* 'covered (with cloth)'. These participles alternatively take a PP with the preposition *með*, and the verbs from which these participles are derived normally take *með* (Nygaard 1905:107–108).

In addition, there are a number of dative-governing adjectives which allow for the use of a prepositional complement instead of the dative. These include adjectives meaning 'friendly' such as *blíðr, mjúkr* etc., most of which optionally take a prepositional complement with the preposition *við*, the adjectives *jafn* (*við*) 'equally good' and *sifjaðr* (*við*) 'related by marriage', and composite adjectives with *jafn-* (*við, sem*) (Nygaard 1905:104–106). Another case in point is adjectives that in conjunction with a dative mean 'quality in relation to', e.g. *blindr augum* 'blind on the eyes'. With such adjectives the alternatively possible PP (with *at, á, af, í* or *um*) is more commonly used (Nygaard 1905:123).

The dative also occurs in certain adverbial uses as an expression of cause, manner or price, where it competes with a PP (Nygaard 1905:114–120). In general, the PP is the more common option.

The example (30) and the three-place patterns in (32) show the common, unmarked object+PP order that accords with SVO expectations and which is also in conformity with the basic ... V N A order of Diderichsen's (1941/42) topological 'field analysis' that was in fact first established on the basis of 13th century Old Danish texts.[24]

4. Configurationality and the question of oblique subjects in Old Norse

According to the classical definition the following parameters define the general difference between configurational and non-configurational languages. Cf. (33):[25]

(33)	configu-rational	non-config-urational
1. flexible ("free") constituent order	–	+
2. rich morphological case system	–	+
3. discontinuous constituents	–	+
4. pronoun deletion ("pro-drop")	–	+
5. expletive elements	+	–
6. structure-changing NP-movements	+	–
7. VP constituent	+	–

In his pilot study Faarlund (1990: 84f.) argues, mainly on the basis of data pertaining to characteristic 7 (VP permutation, pronominalization, clefting), that modern Norwegian is configurational, and on the basis of data pertaining to characteristics 7 (likewise VP permutation, pronominalization, clefting), 3, 1, 4 (including coordination of relationally different arguments) and 5 (Faarlund 1990: 86–106) that Old Norse was non-configurational. Futhermore, Faarlund (1990: 160–166) indicates that certain non-configurational traits have been lost or weakened from Old to Modern Icelandic, in particular pertaining to discontinuity in PP and NP constitution (cf. characteristic 3 in (33)).

Faarlund's claims have not remained unchallenged.[26] Rögnvaldsson (1995: 5–21) argues that Faarlund at least overstates his case with regard to the alleged non-configurationality of Old Norse. Rögnvaldsson's own case is, however, only partly convincing. On the one hand, what Rögnvaldsson has to say about characteristics 1, 5, 6 (including 'oblique' or 'quirky' subjects[27]) in (33) and reflexivization hardly amounts to a refutation from an empirical point of view. On the other hand, his remarks on the discontinuity phenomena subsumed under characteristic 3, the VP as characteristic 7, and passive constructions represent noteworthy qualifications of Faarlund's views. As will appear, the arguments presented by Rögnvaldsson seem to indicate that Old Norse is somewhat less strongly non-configurational than Faarlund originally set out to prove.

Special attention is devoted to the question of subject/object asymmetry. Faarlund claims, to my mind convincingly, that the presence of a definable VP constituent in modern Norwegian implies a structurally defined subject, and, conversely, but perhaps less convincingly, that the absence in Old Norse of a VP implies the absence of a structurally defined subject (Faarlund 1990:110). According to Faarlund (1990:160–166) Modern Icelandic occupies an intermediate position. Consider first (34) (which in part represents an interpretation of Faarlund's claims):[28]

(34)

		ON	MN
1.	definiteness in discourse	±	+ > −
2.	characteristic position	−	(+)
3.	verb agreement	+ (−)	(−)
4.	uniqueness as reflexivization trigger	−	+
5.	omissibility of pronoun	+	−
6.	specific deletion in imperatives	−	+
7.	relational identity in coordination	±	+
8.	specific deletion in infinitives	+	+
9.	uniqueness as Raising trigger	+	+

If Faarlund's analysis is correct, it appears that the traditionally assumed nominative subjects of Old Norse have nominative case-marking parallel to Modern German nominative subjects, but that they have fewer or less specific syntactic subject properties, whereas Modern Norwegian subjects have in principle positional, not case marking, but — apart from verb agreement — in principle syntactic subject properties of basically the same kind that their case marked Modern German counterparts have (cf. also Faarlund 1990:132). Furthermore, Modern Icelandic is similar to Modern Mainland Scandinavian in allowing NPs with certain positional properties to be carriers of the subject-defining properties 8, 2, 4, 7, 9 in (34) (Faarlund 1990:162–166) irrespective of morphological case.

Here two claims are open to debate. First, one may question the contention that Old Norse had no subject/object asymmetry, i.e. no relational discrimination of subject and object categories. This contention is disputed by Rögnvaldsson (1995:18–21) with reference to reflexivization and certain other phenomena indicating a VP structure. On the whole, Rögnvaldsson's arguments make it seem unlikely that an adequate description of Old Norse can do without a VP or NP and PP categories.[29]

Second, concerning the question of 'oblique' or 'quirky' subjects in Old Norse, the facts referred to by Rögnvaldsson (1995:126–18, 1991), in particular the raising constructions, can hardly be taken as unequivocal evidence of the existence of 'oblique subjects' at this early stage, at least not if a complete set of defining syntactic rule properties like (33) is required. The basic claim that "only subjects can be raised" is in all probability a petitio principii in need of typological refinement. However, with regard to reflexivization, Maling (1998:224f.) points out that oblique NPs in what corresponds to the modern subject position ('non-nominative subjects' in her terminology) behave like nominative subjects in the same position. Haugan (1998:162f.) adds the further observation that in Old Norse a non-nominative is occasionally attested in coordination with a nominative subject. Cf. (35), (36) with the dative-governing verb *líka* 'please':

(35) *ðetta   líkar Þórdisi   illa*
this.NOM likes Thordis.DAT badly
ok   skýtur undan peningum.
and _ shoves away money-the.DAT
'This does not please Thordis at all and she shoves the money away.'

(36) *Ríður Kormákur   og   líkar heldur illa*
rides Kormak.NOM and _ likes rather badly
við Steingerði   en   verr   við Tintein.
at Steingerd.ACC and worse at Tintein
'Kormak rides and likes Steingerd badly and Tintein even less.'

There are also similar cases of pronoun deletion where no coordinating conjunction is present. Cf. (37):

(37) *Hví viltu   eigi flytja mig?*
why will-you.NOM not move me.ACC
Líkar eigi vel   við mig?
likes _ not well at me.ACC
'Why don't you move me over? Don't you like me?'

(37) seems intermediate between configurational conjunction reduction and non-configurational "pro-drop". Examples of this kind are problematic for the reason that syntactic relation does not in principle seem to be decisive for Old Norse co-referent pronoun deletion (Faarlund 1999, this volume).[30]

On the basis of topological similarity with Modern Icelandic and Mainland Scandinavian subjects, one might argue that the position of the dative between finite and non-finite verb in cases like (38) (from Haugan 1998:173) is indicative of (oblique) subject function in Old Norse too (cf. also Maling 1998:220):

(38) og voru þeim   gefin mörg langskip.
    and were them.DAT given many longships.NOM
    '... and they were given many longships.'

But this is no self-evident conclusion in view of the existence of sentences like (39):[31]

(39) að þar var manni   matur   deildur.
    that there was man.DAT food.NOM given
    '... that a man was given food there.'

where by parity of reasoning one would have to assume two subjects. Besides, one cannot in this context overlook the overall greater flexibility of Old Norse word and element order and the topological parallelism with Modern German sentences like (40), (41), where there is no possibility of assigning subject properties to the dative element:

(40) daß ihnen/den   Leuten   viele Langschiffe
    that them.DAT/the people.DAT many longships.NOM
    gegeben worden waren.
    given   been   were
    'that many longships had been given to them/to the people.'

(41) weil ihnen/den   Leuten   die Vorstellung
    because them.DAT/the people.DAT the performance.NOM
    sehr gut gefallen hatte.
    very good pleased had
    'because the performance had pleased them/the people very much.'

Haugan's (1998) other arguments for oblique subjects in Old Norse belong rather in the category of theory-internal stipulations and do not add much to the discussion.

Barðdal (1997) takes the same stand on the question of 'oblique subjects' in Old Norse as do Rögnvaldsson and Haugan. She considers the Old Norse data concerning conjunction reduction and reflexivization to be inconclusive (Barðdal 1997:30–31) and her remarks on raising constructions (Barðdal 1997:34–40) add nothing much to Rögnvaldsson's. Her remarks on word order and subject positions (Barðdal 1997:31–34) are open to the same kind of criticism as Haugan's views. In particular, she seems to imply that an oblique NP at the beginning of a clause must either be a topicalized object or an oblique subject, thus ignoring the possibility of unmarked early object position readily attested in Modern German. Her one example of "PRO-infinitive" (42) (Barðdal 1997:40f.) is dubious for philological reasons (cf. Faarlund, this volume):

(42) Þorgils   kvaðst   leiðast   þarvistin.
Thorgil.NOM said.REFL bore.INF.REFL there-stay-the.ACC
'Þorgils said he was bored by staying there.'

In his recent examination of the claims of Rögnvaldsson, Barðdal and Haugan, Faarlund (this volume) voices a number of critical comments of the kind adduced above, and in the main upholds his 1990 analysis.

To the outsider, the general conclusion would appear to be that Faarlund's original theoretical claims concerning Icelandic non-configurationality may have to be qualified with a view to VP, NP and PP constituency, but that his observations concerning empirical differences between Old and Modern Icelandic syntactic rule behaviour, including his scepticism with regard to assuming full-fledged 'oblique subjects' in Old Norse, are in the main correct and important.

There of course remains the question how the present-day 'oblique subjects' developed. In this regard two main hypotheses may be distinguished, which for ease of reference I shall dub the "revolution" and the "evolution" hypotheses, respectively. According to the revolution hypothesis, all syntactic properties characteristic of present-day 'oblique subjects' would have been acquired more or less simultaneously in the course of one radical upheaval, whereas according to the evolution theory their acquisition proceeded gradually. A comparative scrutiny of Rögnvaldsson's (1995) and Faarlund's (1990; this volume) data might lead one to assume for Old Norse the mere beginnings of an extended process of rule acquisition in conformity with the evolution hypothesis. The coordination pattern in (35)–(37) and the Old Norse reflexivization data (cf. Maling 1998) might perhaps be seen as a possible starting point for the development of 'oblique subjects'.[32]

On the other hand, the issue should be decidable where a more or less continuous tradition of written sources exists, as in the case of Mainland Scandinavian. However, there is a methodological problem here pertaining to the very concept of 'subject'. One cannot be sure on the basis of the topological pattern alone that Old Norse and Old Scandinavian oblique NPs occupying a position (or positions) similar to the position (or positions) of the subject in the modern languages are in fact subjects in a syntactic sense, but one can be reasonably sure on the basis of the syntactic rule evidence that the NPs of Modern Scandinavian in this position (these positions) are subjects. For this reason, the best thing to do would seem to be to investigate the syntactic rule behaviour, in different periods, of Old Norse and later nominative NPs, and of oblique NPs with the same linear distribution as modern (only residually case-marked) topological subjects. Mørck (1995) has undertaken an interesting investigation of this kind on the basis of the rather scanty Norwegian material. Here he takes into consideration older nominatives and their modern topological counterparts but, unfortunately, leaves out potential 'oblique subjects'.[33] According to Mørck (1995: 8–19), deletion in infinitivals and in the imperative, the ability to trigger Raising and the ability to embody the semantic patient role in the passive are subject specific properties in all the four historical periods to be assumed: Old Norse, Middle Norwegian (ca. 1350–1525), Early Modern (ca. 1525–1800), and Modern Norwegian. Quantifier Floating is restricted to subjects proper in Middle Norwegian times. In Early Modern Norwegian, uniqueness as antecedent of reflexive pronoun, relational identity as a condition on conjunction reduction, and insertion of the particle *som* in interrogative clauses with a subject complementizer (*hun spurte hvem som var kommet* 'she asked who had come' vs. *hun spurte hvem han hadde sett* 'she asked whom he had seen') follow suit. Non-omissibility of a subject complementizer in relative clauses was finally added to the list at the beginning of the modern period (cf. *mannen som var kommet* 'the man who had come' vs. *mannen (som) hun hadde sett* 'the man (whom) she had seen'). In a complementary diachronic study of DOs and IOs (Mørck 1998), it is shown that a similar process of gradual property acquisition may be observed with the object categories also. In particular, the IO–DO order was stabilized in Early Modern Norwegian (i.e. after ca. 1525).

Although it should be stressed that we are here dealing with another language and with periods of that language where case marking had disappeared or was disappearing, it seems highly unlikely that a totally different "revolution" model should be valid for the acquisition of subject properties in Icelandic, contrasting with the "evolutionist" pattern Mørck has detected for Norwegian.[34]

From a comparative point of view one may feel that the preoccupation with Old and Modern Icelandic provides one with somewhat less than a full perspective. It is an empirical fact that certain non-configurational traits of Old Norse — certain types of discontinuous constituent and pronoun deletion — are not attestable or were discarded in German at an early stage. Moreover, German has, as far as we can tell, at all times had its fair share of the kind of structure-changing NP-movements assumed to be characteristic of configurational languages and it has presumably also always had a VP constituent. Still, Modern

German with its relationally important morphology and its somewhat more flexible element order is more non-configurational in its basic clause structure than is Modern Icelandic. This analysis is presumably corroborated by the fact that German never had 'oblique subjects'.[35] The question of the dating of the onset of non-configurationality and the age of the 'oblique subjects' in Icelandic is of course of great interest for the history of that language and of the Scandinavian languages; but in a comparative perspective, the really important observation is rather that Icelandic and the Mainland Scandinavian languages have moved from what appears to have been a greater degree of non-configurationality than German to what is now clearly a greater degree of configurationality than that to be observed in Modern German.

5. Conclusions and perspectives

Summing up the results of Sections 2, 3 and 4, we have established the following:
- Modern Icelandic has more irregular, lexical case marking of subjects than Modern German ('oblique subjects'). The age of the Icelandic irregularity is uncertain, but it is highly improbable that Old Norse had anything like the full-fledged oblique subjects of Modern Icelandic (and Faroese). German never had 'oblique subjects'. Modern Mainland Scandinavian has lost case marking of non-pronominal subjects (and objects).
- Modern Icelandic has more irregular, lexical case marking of direct and indirect objects than Modern German. In the case of both languages, the case assignment rules pertaining to objects are the continuation of ancient patterns, but compared with Icelandic, German has in a diachronic perspective undergone a process of functional tightening of the rules for structural case assignment. When the earlier structural assignment of genitive case (Donhauser 1990) was lost with verbs,[36] only accusative and dative remained as structurally assigned object cases for DO and IO respectively. Modern Mainland Scandinavian has done away with case marking of non-pronominal objects and has only one oblique case for pronominal DOs and IOs alike, and hence only a residual system of case marking mainly based on position.
- In the unmarked case, Modern Icelandic has fixed D+A order corresponding to Modern Mainland Scandinavian IO+DO order. Still, Icelandic, like Modern German, allows for a certain amount of reordering, presumably attesting to the syntactic functionality of case marking.

– Icelandic shows a certain tendency to replace lexically case-marked NP objects by lexically governed PPs, and this tendency is probably stronger in Modern Icelandic than in Modern German. The ensuing Modern Icelandic PP patterns have parallels in both Modern Mainland Scandinavian and in Old Norse, thus attesting to a shared Scandinavian evolutionary propensity in accordance with the basic VO order.

These observations have a bearing on the typological characterization of the languages in question and our understanding of their historical relationships, in particular the often broached question whether, and in what way, German and Icelandic are morphosyntactically "conservative" languages. I suggest the following diachronic answers to these questions.

As noted in particular also by Faarlund (1990: 131f.), there is no way in which these various developments can be seen as initiated or triggered by low-level phonological or morphological attrition phenomena. The Ancient Nordic OV → VO shift precedes the loss of case morphology and the development of syntactic configurationality by hundreds of years.[37] This OV → VO shift presumably paves the way for syntactic configurationality, but the development of configurationality in North Germanic was hardly a unitary switching operation with instantaneous catch-all effects. Rather it was a complex process of fixation of element order followed by gradual subject rule aquisition by non-nominative NPs and later on loss of case morphology in Mainland Scandinavian.[38] The configurationality traits of Modern Icelandic provide abundant evidence that "loss of case marking and development of a configurational sentence structure with a hierarchically defined subject, should ... be seen as two separate and partly independent processes" (Faarlund 1990: 133).

As noted by for instance Ramat (1984: 394): "The shifting of SOV → SVO is consistent with a tendency synthetic → analytic." In this connection we may again refer to the numerous instances of dative or genitive object replacement by a PP. The more widespread use of a PP where less configurational and more synthetic German has a dative IO is a distinctive difference between Modern Mainland Scandinavian and Modern German verb valency (cf. (23)–(28)). The appearance of similar replacement relationships in Old Norse and to a greater extent in Modern Icelandic (cf. (32), (29), respectively) confirms Frans Plank's (1980: 290) observation that there is "empirical evidence that quite generally suggests that analytic coding increases prior to morphological decay".

From these observations several general conclusions follow. First, despite the superficial case-marking similarity between Icelandic, Faroese and German,

German still stands apart as the more conservative language with its Indo-European legacy of morphologically related syntactic rules. In North Germanic after the OV → VO shift the development has been in the direction of a topologically, not morphologically oriented syntax, both in the non-case-marking and the case-marking modern Scandinavian languages. In particular, Modern Icelandic (and Faroese) 'oblique subjects' and 'quirky case' with objects turn out to be two aspects of the same general phenomenon, i.e. the presence of more lexically assigned case in a syntactic rule system where topological ('configurational') relatedness has to a considerable degree ousted morphological relatedness. At the same time both Insular and Mainland Scandinavian show a tendency to replace case-marked NPs by more analytic PPs. In this perspective, the modern Insular Scandinavian languages (Icelandic and Faroese) are syntactically innovative but morphologically conservative. They thus occupy a rather natural intermediate position between Modern Mainland Scandinavian on the one hand and Modern German on the other. In a theoretical perspective, they represent a kind of disconnectedness of morphology and syntax which corroborates a theoretical approach stressing the modular autonomy of these two aspects of grammatical structure.

Notes

1. Cf. also n. 18.
2. Cf. e.g. Mørck (1994: 177–184) and the further references given there.
3. In what follows I shall use the term(s) 'configurational(ity)' in a fairly theory-neutral manner, as a convenient means of characterizing some rather striking empirical differences between languages (cf. Rögnvaldsson 1995: 4).
4. But cf. Zaenen and Maling (1990), who speak of 'quirky' case with regard to subjects as well as objects.
5. Or they may be only residually case-marked in accordance with position, as in the modern standard Mainland Scandinavian languages. Cf. Faarlund (1990: 150f.).
6. Cf. also Zaenen, Maling and Thráinsson (1990: 125–129 on German in contrast to 99–106 on Modern Icelandic).
7. In the linguistic glosses, the following abbreviations are used: NOM = nominative, ACC = accusative, DAT = dative, GEN = genitive, PLUR = plural, REFL = (originally) reflexive verb suffix, INF = infinitive, FUT = future, SUB = subjunctive, PRO = implicit subject of an infinitival construction. Deletion in coordination is indicated by a blank: _. In Modern Mainland Scandinavian the distinction between nominative, accusative and dative has been neutralized with all full nouns. With personal pronous, the distinction between the accusative

and the dative is also neutralized, but some pronouns still show a morphological opposition between a subject and a non-subject oblique form. Hence the following abbreviations are used instead of case terms: SUBJ = subject, OBL = oblique, DO = direct object, IO = indirect object. PART is used for any separable German verb prefix. In the valency patterns in the text (and in adjacent charts), the shorter abbreviations N, A, D, G are used for the nominative, accusative, dative and genitive, respectively.

8. At least in the case of the A+G combination, a DO+DO analysis might be suggested.

9. But cf. also the different analysis in Ottósson (1993:372). — In what follows I shall not deal with Faroese case assignment rules which form an altogether simpler system. The genitive is no longer used as the complement of a verb, but one does find the object patterns A, D, D+A, A+A as well as the equivalent of the Icelandic A+A pattern in (3a). Cf. Lockwood (1977:102–104), Barnes and Weyhe (1994:212–214).

10. Cf. e.g. Eisenberg et al. (1998:683) in comparison with (Kress 1982:220).

11. Where the first A has subject properties.

12. Cf. the discussion of (7) below. Similarly to what was assumed for Modern German, the genitive in three-place constructions with an A is presumably not to be categorized as an IO. It also seems natural to except the D+D and D+G combinations from an IO+DO analysis.

13. Perhaps one should here not opt for positive categorization as 'object' but rather for characterization as an element with partly subject (verb agreement), partly object (position) properties.

14. On the history of the German dative in relation to the accusative see Van Pottelberge (1998:437–453) and in general Willems and Van Pottelberge (1998).

15. "… denn in diesem Bereich [genitive objects] vollzieht sich in nachmittelhochdeutscher Zeit die wohl markanteste Veränderung in der Geschichte des deutschen Kasussystems: der weitgehende Rückzug des Genitivs aus seinen ursprünglich reichhaltigen adverbalen Funktionen, …"

16. Cf. also Donhauser (1990:106–109) on Old High German, and Kozmová (1998) for further Slavic perspectives. Cf. Donhauser (1998:70) for an empirical appraisal of the aspectuality hypothesis, which appears to be valid to a considerable extent with two-place verbs, but not with three-place verbs (Donhauser 1998:79–83), and, for somewhat more critical comments, Van Pottelberge (1998:426–437).

17. On the basis of the examples adduced in the contributions of Donhauser and others and in the standard handbooks, one might even suspect that there are two different stages, first an early stage in Old High German where aspectual determination of the adverbal genitive is important, and then a later Middle and Early New High German stage where the genitive alternating with the accusative is more clearly partitive.

18. Such unproductive lexicalized uses are also found in Old High German (Donhauser 1990:101–104, with references; 1998:82). Interestingly, Donhauser (1998:82–84) considers the "partitive" genitive with verbs to be 'structural', and the "non-partitive" genitive to be 'lexical'. This means that in Modern German the genitive has been altogether lost as a 'structural' object case (with primarily two-place verbs originally displaying an aspectual opposition) and that the number of instances of the genitive as 'lexical' case has been greatly reduced.

The "Genitivschwund" is thus due to two different processes, the most important result of which is a simplified system of only two 'structural' object cases — accusative and dative.

19. For a brief summary of problems relating to this distinction in the case of Modern German see Stubkjær (1994). 'Structural' or rather 'functional' case assignment in the sense intended here should not be construed as some sort of 'semantic case assignment' (cf. Faarlund 1990:138). The latter term is more apt in connection with less grammaticalized, more clearly 'adverbial' uses of case whereas the terms 'structural' (or 'functional') and 'lexical case' commonly refers to more highly grammaticalized, 'abstract' uses of case. Concerning these distinctions cf. also Zaenen and Maling (1990:139f.), who for 'lexical' case marking also use the terms 'idosyncractic' or 'quirky', and for 'structural' the term 'default' case marking. (Cf. also Zaenen, Maling and Thráinsson 1990:115, who use 'functional' for 'structural' case assignement.)

20. In particular, the dative marking of IOs is here considered to be structurally assigned, whereas Ottóson (1993:372) and Faarlund (1990:138) assume that Modern Icelandic IOs in the D–A pattern have lexical case (cf. also Zaenen, Maling and Thráinsson (1990:119, Table 1). For pertinent references and discussion see Holmberg and Platzack (1995:185f. et passim with regard to 'ordinary' and 'marked' case) and Molnárfi (1998:536 et passim) who like Zifonun et al. (1997) holds the view that dative IOs in Modern German have structural case. — In any case, a stricter definition of 'structural' case assignment excluding dative IOs would not affect the proportional relationship between the two languages compared here.

21. Concerning *entsprechend* cf. Eisenberg et al. (1998:384) and Berger et al. (1985:229f.). — There is also a third replacement pattern where the genitive is replaced by a PP with the preposition *von*: *innerhalb von zehn Tagen* 'within ten days' ← **innerhalb zehn Tage*, *aufgrund von Problemen* 'because of problems' ← **aufgrund Probleme*. This pattern is mostly used with recently developed prepositions of nominal origin.

22. Cf. e.g. Engel (1988:320–330). It should be noted that 'light' pronominal NPs precede full object NPs in the middle field and that in the domain of 'light' pronominal objects, the accusative precedes the dative, cf. e.g. (23a), (27a).

23. On the other hand, alternations of the kind $D_x + A_y \rightarrow A_y + PP_x$ ("Dative Shift") are rather rare in Modern Icelandic (cf. Ottósson 1993:372, with references, and Holmberg and Platzack 1995:188, 204f.), which in this respect goes rather with Modern German than with the Modern Mainland Scandinavian languages.

24. In (31) above, the position of the PP with a personal pronoun before the indefinite DO appears to be a more special case which is probably due to theme-rheme structure (focus) requirements.

25. For characteristics 1–6 see Fanselow (1987:32–48), Rögnvaldsson (1995:3), for 1–5 and 7 see Faarlund (1990:85f.).

26. For a brief summary of the ensuing discussion see Rögnvaldsson (1995:3f.).

27. Cf. also Rögnvaldsson (1991).

28. ON = Old Norse nominative, MN = Modern Norwegian NP preceding infinite verbs (topological subject).

29. Given the overwhelming text frequency of continuous PPs in Old Norse texts as against the comparatively rare occurrence of discontinuous PPs (cf. Rögnvaldsson 1995:8–10 vs. Faarlund 1990:95–100), the heuristic value of the latter cases should probably not be overestimated.

30. But cf. in this connection also Mørck (1994:170f.) who argues that "there is certainly a difference between nominative and ordinary oblique noun phrases with regard to ellipsis in imperative clauses", and he also suggests that "free ellipsis of subjectlike oblique noun phrases was impossible in Old Norse".

31. Cf. also Mørck (1998:376).

32. On the question of syntactic similarities between Old Norse nominatives and "subjectlike oblique noun phrases" cf. also Mørck (1994:178).

33. Concerning Mørck's terminology it should be noted that he calls Old Norse (Norwegian) nominative case and Modern Norwegian subject-defining position "distinctive subject properties", whereas subject-specific syntactic rules are in his terminology "non-distinctive subject properties". Concerning case marking and syntactic rule properties, it should rather be the other way around. However, Mørck's rather awkward terminology does not detract substantially from the value of his investigation.

34. Cf. also Mørck (1995:184–187) for a lucid comparison of Old Norse, Modern Icelandic, Modern Faroese and Modern Norwegian as four different synchronic states which may be seen as a sequence of consecutive diachronic stages.

35. Despite occasional — rather misguided — claims to the contrary; see Barðdal (1997:47, with references).

36. This species of structural case assignment may, however, only have been weakly developed, cf. Van Pottelberge (1998:431–437).

37. On Proto-Nordic verb order see in particular Braunmüller (1982:113–147) and Faarlund (1990:19–29). Despite the alleged relationship between OV and functional case-marking posited by Greenberg (1966:96, Universal 41), there is massive evidence from a number of languages to the effect that OV → VO change precedes the loss of case oppositions, cf. Faarlund (1990:51f.) with references.

38. However, Mørck (1994:191) makes the noteworthy suggestion that "The transition from the complex morphological system of Old Norse to the simpler system of Modern Norwegian may have taken place so quickly that the noun phrases in question at the very least had started to become morphologically indistinguishable from the subjects before they had aquired more than a few of the syntactic subject properties." This in fact means that the question of rule acquisition would have to be seen in connection with the typological development from morphological syntheticity to analyticity.

References

Anderson, S. R. 1976. "On the notion of subject in ergative languages". In: *Subject and Topic*, C. Li (ed.), 1–24. New York: Academic Press.

Askedal, J. O. 1980. "Über das Passiv von Verben mit zwei Akkusativergänzungen im Deutschen". In *Festschrift für Gunnar Bech. Zum 60. Geburtstag am 23. März 1980* M. Dyhr, K. Hyldgaard-Jensen and J. Olsen (eds), 1–18. Kopenhagen: Institut für germanische Philologie der Universität Kopenhagen [Kopenhagener Beiträge zur Germanistischen Linguistik, Sonderband 1].

Askedal, J. O. 1997. "Indirekte Objekte im Deutschen und im Norwegischen". In *Vergleichende germanische Philologie und Skandinavistik. Festschrift für Otmar Werner*, T. Birkmann, H. Klingenberg, D. Nübling and E. Ronneberger-Sibold (eds), 49–66. Tübingen: Max Niemeyer.

Barnes, M. P. 1986. "Subject, nominative and oblique case in Faroese". *Scripta Islandica* 37: 13–46.

Barnes, M. P. and Weyhe, E. 1994. "Faroese". In *The Germanic Languages*, E. König, and J. van der Auwera (eds), 190–218. London: Routledge.

Barðdal, J. 1997. "Oblique subjects in Old Scandinavian". *Working Papers in Scandinavian Syntax* 60: 25–50.

Berger, D. et al. 1985. *Duden. Richtiges und gutes Deutsch. Wörterbuch der sprachlichen Zweifelsfälle*. 3rd ed. Mannheim, Wien and Zürich: Dudenverlag.

Braunmüller, K. 1982. *Syntaxtypologische Studien zum Germanischen* Tübingen: G.Narr [Tübinger Beiträge zur Linguistik 197].

Cole, P., Harbert, W., Hermon, G. and Sridhar, S. N. 1980. "The acquisition of subjecthood". *Language* 56: 719–743.

Dal, I. 1966. *Kurze deutsche Syntax auf historischer Grundlage*. 3rd ed. Tübingen: Max Niemeyer.

Diderichsen, P. 1941/42. *Sætningsbygningen i Skaanske Lov. Fremstillet som grundlag for en rationel dansk syntaks*. Köbenhavn: Munksgaard [Acta Philologica Scandinavica 15].

Donhauser, K. 1990. "Moderne Kasuskonzeptionen und die Kasussetzung im Althochdeutschen. Überlegungen zur Stellung des Objektsgenitivs im Althochdeutschen". In *Neuere Forschungen zur historischen Syntax des Deutschen. Referate der Internationalen Fachkonferenz Eichstätt 1989*, A. Betten et al. (eds), 98–112. Tübingen: M. Niemeyer [Reihe Germanistische Linguistik 103].

Donhauser, K. 1998. "Das Genitivproblem und (k)ein Ende. Anmerkungen zur aktuellen Diskussion um die Ursachen des Genitivschwundes im Deutschen". In *Historische germanische und deutsche Syntax. Akten des Internationalen Symposiums anläßlich des 100. Geburtstages von Ingerid Dal, Oslo. 27.9. — 1.10.1995*, J. O. Askedal (ed.), 69–86. Frankfurt a.M.: Peter Lang [Osloer Beiträge zur Germanistik 21].

Eisenberg, P. et al. 1998. *Duden. Grammatik der deutschen Gegenwartssprache*. 6th ed. Mannheim, Leipzig, Wien and Zürich: Dudenverlag.

Engel, U. 1988. *Deutsche Grammatik*. Heidelberg: Julius Groos.

Faarlund, J. T. 1990. *Syntactic Change. Toward a theory of historical syntax*. Berlin: Mouton [Trends in Linguistics. Studies and Monographs 50].

Faarlund, J. T. This volume. "The notion of oblique subject and its status in the history of Icelandic".

Fanselow, G. 1987. *Konfigurationalität. Untersuchungen zur Universalgrammatik am Beispiel des Deutschen.* Tübingen: G. Narr [Studien zur deutschen Grammatik 29].

Greenberg, J. H. 1966. "Some universals of grammar with particular reference to the order of meaningful elements". In *Universals of Language.* 2nd ed. J. H. Greenberg (ed), 73–113. Cambridge, MA: MIT Press.

Haugan, J. 1998. "Passiv av norrøne dobbelt objekt-konstruksjonar og subjektspørsmålet". *Norsk Lingvistisk Tidsskrift* 16: 157–184.

Holmberg, A. and Platzack, C. 1985. *The Role of Inflection in Scandinavian Syntax.* Oxford: OUP.

Kozmová, R. 1998. "Interaktion der Kategorien Definitheit/Indefinitheit und der Kategorien Aspekt/Aktionalität in den germanischen und slawischen Sprachen". In *KontaktSprache Deutsch II. Germanistische Tagung Nitra — Passau Oktober '97,* W. Seifert, S. Pongó and H. Borsuková (eds), 29–43. Nitra and Passau: Universität Passau, Konstantin-Universität Nitra and Slowakische Landwirtschaftliche Universität.

Kress, B. 1982. *Isländische Grammatik.* Leipzig: Enzyklopädie.

Leiss, E. 1991. "Grammatische Kategorien und sprachlicher Wandel: Erklärung des Genitivschwundes im Deutschen". In *Proceedings of the Fourteenth International Congress of Linguists, Berlin/GDR, August 10-August 15, 1987,* W. Bahner et al. (eds), 1406–1409. Berlin: Akademie-Verlag.

Lockwood, W. B. 1977. *An Introduction to Modern Faroese.* 3rd Ed. Tórshavn: Skúlabókagrunnur Føroya.

Maling, J. 1998. Contribution to the discussion of Kristian Emil Kristoffersen's doctoral dissertation *Infinitival Phrases in Old Norse. Aspects of their Syntax and Semantics. Norsk Lingvistisk Tidsskrift* 16: 219–231.

Mallinson, J. and Blake, B. J. 1981. *Language Typology. Cross-linguistic Studies in Syntax.* Amsterdam: North-Holland [North-Holland Linguistic Series 46].

Molnárfi, L. 1998. "Kasusstrukturalität und struktureller Kasus — zur Lage des Dativs im heutigen Deutsch". *Linguistische Berichte* 176: 535–580.

Mørck, E. 1994. "The distribution of subject properties and the acquisition of subjecthood in the West Scandinavian languages". In *Language Change and Language Structure. Older Germanic Languages in a Comparative Perspective,* T. Swan, E. Mørck and O. Jansen Westvik (eds), 195–194. Berlin and New York: Mouton de Gruyter [Trends in Linguistics. Studies and Monographs 73].

Mørck, E. 1995. "Subjektets egenskaper i eldre nynorsk". *Norsk Lingvistisk Tidsskrift* 13: 3–21.

Mørck, E. 1998. "The development of direct and indirect object as distinct functional categories from Old Norse to Modern Norwegian". In *Historische germanische und deutsche Syntax. Akten des Internationalen Symposiums anläßlich des 100. Geburtstages von Ingerid Dal, Oslo. 27.9.-1.10.1995,* J. O. Askedal (ed.), 365–385. Frankfurt a.M.: Peter Lang [Osloer Beiträge zur Germanistik 21].

Nygaard, M. 1905. *Norrøn syntax.* 2nd ed. Oslo: Aschehoug. (Reprinted 1966).

Ottósson, K. 1993. "Double-object small clauses and reanalysis in Icelandic passives". In *The Proceedings of the Eleventh West Coast Conference on Formal Linguistics,* J. Mead (ed.),

371–387. Stanford: Stanford Linguistics Association, Center for the Study of Language and Information.
Plank, F. 1980. "Encoding grammatical relations: Acceptable and unacceptable nondistinctness". In *Historical Morphology*, J. Fisiak (ed), 289–325. The Hague, Paris and New York: Mouton [Trends in Linguistics. Studies and Monographs 17].
Ramat, P. 1984. "'Es war ein König in Thule (...), Dem sterbend seine Buhle ...': On the rise and transformations(s) of morphosyntactic categories". In *Historical Syntax*, J. Fisiak (ed), 393–415. Berlin: Mouton [Trends in Linguistics. Studies and Monographs 23].
Rögnvaldsson, E. 1991. "Quirky subjects in Old Icelandic". In *Papers from the Twelfth Scandinavian Conference of Linguistics*, H.Á. Sigurdsson (ed.), 369–378. Reykjavík: Institute of Linguistics, University of Iceland.
Rögnvaldsson, E. 1995. "Old Icelandic: A non-configurational language?" *NOWELE* 26: 3–29.
Sprouse, R.A. 1995. "The double object construction in the Germanic languages: Some synchronic and diachronic notes". In *Insights in Germanic Linguistics I: Methodology in*, I. Rauch and G.F. Carr (eds), 325–342. Berlin and New York: Mouton de Gruyter *transition* [Trends in Linguistics, Studies and Monographs 83].
Stubkjær, F.T. 1994. "Strukturelle und lexikalische Kasus". In *Sprachgermanistik in Skandinavien II. Akten des III. Nordischen Germanistentreffens, Mastemyr bei Oslo, 2. — 5.6.1993*, J.O. Askedal, H. Bjorvand and K.E. Schöndorf (eds), 163–173. Oslo: Germanistisches Institut der Universität Oslo [Osloer Beiträge zur Germanistik 16].
Thráinsson, H. 1994. "Icelandic". In *The Germanic Languages*, E. König and J. van der Auwera (eds), 365–385. London and New York: Routledge.
Van Pottelberge, J. 1998. "Aspekte der verbalen Rektion im Alt- und Mittelhochdeutschen". *Sprachwissenschaft* 23: 423–460.
Willems, K. and Van Pottelberge, J. 1998. *Geschichte und Systematik des adverbalen Dativs im Deutschen. Eine funktional-linguistische Analyse des morphologischen Kasus*. Berlin: Walter de Gruyter [Studia Linguistica Germanica 49].
Zaenen, A. and Maling, J. 1990. "Case and grammatical functions: The Icelandic passive". In *Modern Icelandic Syntax*, J. Maling ad A. Zaenen (eds), 137–152. San Diego: Academic Press [Syntax and Semantics 24].
Zaenen, A., Maling, J. and Thráinsson, H. 1990. "Unaccusative, passive, and quirky case". In *Modern Icelandic Syntax*, J. Maling ad A. Zaenen (eds), 95–136. San Diego: Academic Press [Syntax and Semantics 24]
Zifonun, G., Hoffmann, L. and Strecker, B. 1997. *Grammatik der deutschen Sprache*. Vol 2.. Berlin and New York: Walter de Gruyter [Schriften des Instituts für deutsche Sprache 7.2].

The notion of oblique subject and its status in the history of Icelandic*

Jan Terje Faarlund
University of Oslo

The term 'oblique subject' is used in recent descriptions of Icelandic about NPs that behave syntactically like subjects without having nominative case. Data in support of such an analysis can easily be found in Modern Icelandic. Various linguists have assumed that also Old Icelandic has oblique subjects. In this paper I first discuss the notion of oblique subject on a metatheoretical basis. My claim is that oblique subject is not an empirical entity, it is a result of a decision to use it as a descriptive device because it may yield a more economical or elegant description of certain facts about the language. The main body of the paper is a thorough examination of the kinds of data that have been used in support of an oblique subject analysis for Old Icelandic, supplemented by some of my own additional data. It turns out that the set of subject properties of Old Icelandic is different (smaller) than that of Modern Icelandic, and the result of this examination is that Old Icelandic does not exhibit data that call for an oblique subject analysis. The final section of the paper offers an account of the diachronic process that may have led to the kind of structure that justifies an oblique subject analysis of Modern Icelandic. This process is a reanalysis leading to a change in the possible content of the Specifier position of IP, whereby it has become an exclusive subject position. Non-nominative NPs in that position may have kept their oblique case, and become oblique subjects.

1. Introduction

The term 'oblique subject' refers to an NP that behaves syntactically like a subject without having nominative case, as illustrated by the data in (1)–(4) below. Like the term 'subject' itself — and most other syntactic notions for that matter — the notion of oblique subject is a theory internal term that exists as a result of a certain definition. It does not have a clear pre-theoretical extension;

it is not something that Icelandic "has". The term is, however, found to be useful in the description of certain syntactic phenomena in Icelandic, since there are certain empirical facts that can be accounted for in a more economical and elegant way by abandoning the traditional requirement that subjects be in the nomiantive case.

The term oblique subject is mainly used within a generative framework. The label 'oblique subject' attached to an oblique NP is therefore to be understood as a claim that the NP in question occurs in the position SpecIP (or whatever the canonical subject position might be).

2. Oblique subjects in Modern Icelandic

Oblique subjects are found with the following types of verbs: one-place experiencer verbs, such as *þyrsta* 'be thirsty'; verbs which take two oblique arguments and no nominative, such as *vanta* 'lack'; verbs which take a dative referring to a human experiencer, e.g. *líka* 'like' and *leiðast* 'be bored'; the passive of verbs take a dative or a genitive object, such as *hjálpa* 'help' and *sakna* 'miss'; and the passive of ditransitive verbs, where an oblique argument, typically the dative recipient, behaves like a subject, while the nominative theme is still an object.

In this section I summarize some of the facts that support the oblique subject analysis for Icelandic, based on Thráinsson (1994).

Subjects immediately follow the finite verb in direct questions.

(1) a. *Hefur strák-ur-inn aldrei séð pening-a?*
has boy-NOM-DEF never seen money-ACC
'Has the boy never seen money?'
b. *Hefur strák-inn aldrei vantað pening-a?*
has boy.ACC-DEF never lacked money-ACC
'Has the boy never lacked money?'

Subjects can serve as antecedents of reflexives, but never of other other personal pronouns in the same clause. In Icelandic, *sinn* is the reflexive possessive, *hans* is the non-reflexive, masculine pronominal possessive.

(2) a. *Strák-ur-inn$_i$ þarf pelann sinn$_i$/*hans$_i$*
boy-NOM-DEF needs bottle his
'The boy needs his bottle'
b. *Strák-inn$_i$ vantar pelann sinn$_i$/*hans$_i$*
boy.ACC-DEF lacks bottle his

Subjects can serve as antecedents for reflexives across clause boundaries (long distance reflexives), whereas objects cannot.

(3) a. *Marí-a$_i$ er leið yfir því að þú skulir aldrei heilsa sér$_i$*
María-NOM is sorry over that that you should never greet herself
'María is sorry that you never greet her'
b. *Marí-u$_i$ leiði-st   að þú skulir aldrei heilsa sér$_i$*
María-DAT bothers-REFL that you should never greet herself
'It bothers María that you never greet her'
c. **Ég sagði Marí-u$_i$ að þú hefðir aldrei heilsað sér$_i$*
I told María-DAT that you had never greeted herself
'I told Maria that you had never greeted her.'

Subjects can be deleted in the second conjunct in coordinated sentences if it is coreferential with the subject in the preceding sentence.

(4) a. *Harald-ur$_i$ gaf Marí-u   hamstur og [_$_i$] bauð henni svo í bíó*
Harald-NOM gave María-DAT hamster and   asked her   then in
cinema
'Harald gave Maria a hamster, and then invited her to the movie.'
b. *Haraldi$_i$ geðjast vel að Marí-u og [_$_i$] býður henni oft   í bíó*
Harald-DAT likes   well to María and   asks her   often to
cinema
'Harald likes Maria and often invites her to the movie.'
c. **Harald-ur gaf Marí-u$_i$ hamstur og [_$_i$] bauð honum svo í bíó*
Harold-NOM gave María-DAT hamster and   asked him   then in
cinema
'Harald gave Maria a hamster, and then she invited him to the movie.'

3. The notion of oblique subject

Metatheoretically and methodologically it is important to note that the dative phrase in e.g. (4b) is not a subject because it is in SpecIP, but it is postulated to be in SpecIP because it has certain subject-like syntactic properties, such as triggering conjunction reduction. The fact that a given NP can be placed in SpecIP is therefore not a proof that it is a subject. Rather, the fact that such an analysis allows for interesting generalizations is evidence that it is a plausible analysis.

Oblique subjects never trigger agreement for person or number on the finite verb. The use of this term therefore represents a decision to ignore the traditional morphological subject criteria, case and verb agreement. This choice may be well founded if it turns out that it allows for interesting generalizations, which no doubt is the case for Modern Icelandic. Another language with a morphological system similar to that of Icelandic, is German, which of course also is genetically closely related. In Modern German, however, oblique NPs do not exhibit the same syntactic subject properties as in Icelandic. The verb *grauen* 'fear' takes the experiencer in the dative, but this dative cannot be deleted under identity with a preceding subject.

(5) *Ich_i verliess ihn, und [−]_i graute davor,   sein Vertrauen zu missbrauchen
    I   left   him, and   feared there.for his trust   to abuse
    'I left him, and I was afraid to abuse his trust.'

Like in Icelandic, the German verb *helfen* 'help' takes its object in the dative, but unlike Icelandic, the German dative NP does not behave like a subject in the passive.

(6) a. *Er kam, und *(ihm)   wurde geholfen* (German)
        he came and   him.DAT was   helped
    b. *Hann kom, og (honum) var hjálpað* (Icelandic)

Neither do facts from other Indo-European languages with rich morphology, such as e.g. Russian, seem to support an oblique subject analysis. It is of course problematic to determine whether extinct languages have oblique subjects, since the decision to some extent must depend on negative data, as in (2), (3c), (4c), (5) and (6a) above.

In the remainder of this paper I will try to find answers to the following question: did Icelandic acquire oblique subjects during its modern period, or did even Old Icelandic have oblique subjects? In accordance with the discussion above, this question should be rephrased as: does Old Icelandic exhibit syntactic constructions that call for an analysis involving oblique subjects?

Several researchers have presented such data (Rögnvaldsson 1991, 1995, 1996; Barðdal 1999, 2000; Haugan 1998, 2000), but as can be expected for an extinct language, the data are not conclusive. Very often they are ambiguous, allowing alternative analyses. The more or less explicit assumption of the three researchers just mentioned, is that there is a minimal difference between Old and Modern Icelandic, and as long as there are no data that speak up loudly against the same analysis of the two stages, they must be similar. Other researchers, besides myself (Faarlund 1990), Juntune (1992), Mørck (1992) and Kristoffersen (1994), have argued against the oblique subject analysis for Old Icelandic, and Falk (1997) also for Old Swedish.

The fact that oblique subjects do not seem to be a characteristic feature of Indo-Europan languages, indicates that at some point in the history of Icelandic or North Germanic, certain subject-like oblique NPs aquired subject properties. This development may of course also have taken place in other languages, followed by a subsequent change from oblique to nominative case, as described by Cole et al. (1980).

In Section 4 I will examine data presented by the above mentioned researchers, along with other data, to see to what extent the alleged oblique subjects of Old Icelandic should be analyzed as such. This examination will show that very few of the data presented favor the oblique subject hypothesis. In a final section, I will sketch an account of the introduction of oblique subjects in Icelandic.

4. Subject properties in Old Icelandic

The first task is to determine what phenomena can be considered subject properties in Old Icelandic. Many attempts have been made to establish a universal set of subject properties. The best known is Keenan 1976. A certain subset of these are relevant for Germanic languages. Sigurðsson (1992) presents a list of 17 subject properties for Icelandic. It is doubtful whether all of these can be considered subject properties except statistically or stylistically. In any case, many of them are applicable only if we have access to native speakers or large statistical material.

Considering subject as a morphosyntactic category, I will disregard semantic criteria from the outset. And as we are discussing oblique subjects, morphological criteria such as case marking are of course also excluded. The only other morphological criterion, verb agreement, clearly goes against the existence of oblique subjects, both in Old and Modern Icelandic, since the verb never agrees with an oblique subject. In the Modern Icelandic sentence (7a) the initial dative phrase is claimed to be the subject, but the finite verb and the participle agree with the nominative object. A similar pattern is found in Old Icelandic (7b).

(7) a. *Hon-um vo-ru gefn-ir pening-ar-n-ir*
him-DAT were-3PL given-PL.NOM money-PL.NOM-DEF-PL.NOM
'He was given the money'
b. *fjórir hleif-ar brauð-s er-u hon-um*
four loaf-MASC.PL.NOM bread-GEN are-3PL him-DAT
fǿrð-ir hver-n dag
brought-MASC.PL.NOM every-ACC day.ACC
'Four loaves of bread are brought him every day' (Ólafs saga helga)[1]

The relevant subject properties, then, are syntactic properties. They can be divided into two types, behavior with respect to certain syntactic phenomena, and distribution, that is position in the sentence. In Section 4.1. we will look at the behavioral properties, and in Section 4.2. word order and subject positions will be examined. In embedded non-finite clauses known as accusative with infinitive, subjects undergo various syntactic and morphological processes, which will be considered in Section 4.3.

4.1 Behavioral properties

The following behavioral properties have been discussed for Old Icelandic by the authors cited in Section 3.

Subject-to-subject raising
Subject-to-object raising
Cliticization
Subject PRO in infinitival clauses
Clause-bound reflexivization
Long distance reflexivization
Conjunction reduction
Quantifier float

These are all subject properties in modern Mainland Scandinavian languages (Faarlund 1992), and (as far as I know with the exception of quantifier float) they have all been used to support the notion of oblique subjects in Modern Icelandic. This does not mean that they can all be taken to be subject properties in Old Icelandic. If they can be shown to be properties of non-subjects as well, the question of whether they apply to subject-like oblique NPs, that is potential oblique subjects, will of course be irrelevant.

In order to avoid a circular argumentation, we need to be able to contrast the behavior of oblique NPs that are clearly not subjects to oblique NPs that might potentially be analyzed as oblique subjects. We will assume that an oblique NP governed by an active verb which also takes an agent nominative NP is not a potential oblique subject. This kind of NPs, henceforth referred to as 'object', is exemplified in (8).

(8) a. *Nú tekr han-n hest-in-n*
now takes he-NOM horse-DEF-ACC
'Now he takes the horse' (Hrafnkels saga)
b. *þeim reið Goðgest-r konung-r*
it.DAT rode Godgest-NOM king-NOM
'King Godgest rode (on) it' (Heimskringla)

On the other hand, if Old Icelandic does have oblique subjects, they would typically be the recipient dative of ditransitive verbs in the passive, as in (9a), or the dative experiencer with *þykkja* 'seem', (9b), or an oblique argument (typically a human experiencer) with verbs that do not usually take a nominative argument, as in (9c). Such NPs will be referred to as 'potential oblique subjects', while the term 'subject' will be used to refer to nominative subjects only.

(9) a. *var þeim gefin-n dagverð-r*
was them.DAT given-MASC.NOM lunch-NOM
'They were given lunch' (Heimskringla)
b. *þótti hon-um hon vel haf-a gert*
seemed him-DAT she.NOM well have-INF done
'He thought that she had done well' (Heimskringla)
c. *Ragnhild-i dróttning dreymdi draum-a stór-a*
Ragnhild-ACC queen.ACC dreamt dream.PL.ACC great.MASC.PL.ACC
'Queen Ragnhild had great dreams' (Heimskringla)

In what follows I will examine each of these subject properties in relation to subjects, objects and potential oblique subjects. Subject-to-object raising and cliticization, will be treated in Section 4.3.

4.1.1 *Subject-to-subject raising*
This is found first of all with the verb *þykkja* 'seem' and its synonyms. The subject of the embedded clause is raised and becomes the subject of *þykkja*.

(10) a. Hon   þótti   mér   þat   vel þekkj-a-st
       she.NOM seemed me.DAT that.NEUT.ACC well accept-INF-REFL
       'She seemed to me to accept it' (Gunnlaugs saga)
    b. brátt   þótti   mér   örn-in-n   ýf-a-st
       suddenly seemed me.DAT eagle.NOM-DEF-MASC.NOM anger-INF-REFL
       mjök
       much
       'Suddenly it seemed to me that the eagle became very angry.'
       (Gunnlaugs saga)
    c. þótti   hon-um   hon   vel haf-a   gert
       seemed him-DAT she.NOM well have-INF done
       'He thought that she had done well' (Heimskringla)

In (10c) *hon* is the surface subject of *þótti*, while in Deep Structure it is the external argument of *gert*, the main verb of the embedded clause. It has thus been raised from the lower to the higher sentence. There is no example of a similar raising of an object or of a potential oblique subject. If that were to take place, the NP, which would be in an oblique case in the lower clause, would appear in the nominative in the raised construction, since *þykkja* takes a nominative subject on the surface. (This is not begging the question, because when the embedded verb otherwise takes a nominative subject, this invariably appears as a nominative with *þykkja*, as in (10).)

Rögnvaldsson (1995 and 1996), followed by Barðdal (2000), use examples like (11) as evidence of raising of potential oblique subject in Old Icelandic.

(11) Árn-a   kvað-st   þat   illt þykkj-a
     Árni-DAT said-REFL that.ACC bad seem-INF
     'Arni said that he found this bad' (Svínfellinga saga)

The verb *kveða* takes a nominative subject. Being the surface subject position of *kveða* therefore means having nominative case. Here *Árna*, which is the underlying dative experiencer of *þykkja*, remains in the dative, and can therefore not have been raised into the subject position of *kveða*. Admittedly, (11) is still a strange sentence, since the matrix verb lacks a subject expressing the agent. But it does not become less strange by analyzing the dative NP as a subject, since there is general agreement among all who believe in oblique subjects, that they cannot be agents (e.g. Barðdal 2000). Most probably, (11) and the very few similar examples found are due to some kind of contamination.[2] They are also ungrammatical in Modern Icelandic (Kjartan Ottósson, p.c.). The normal construction with *kveða* and an embedded *þykkja*-clause is for the dative of *þykkja* to remain in the dative, while there is a nominative agent of the matrix verb *kveða*. If the two are identical, the dative has the form of a reflexive, as expected. Example (12) is from Juntune 1992.

(12) Gretti-r$_i$ kvað sér$_i$ þat   betra þykkja en
      Gretti-NOM said himself.DAT that.ACC better seem than
      bak-elda-gørð-in
      baking-fire-making-DEF
      'Gretti said that seemed better to him than building a baking fire'
      (Grettis saga)

If the dative of *þykkja* were really treated as a subject of the embedded clause, we would at least expect it to be cliticized to the matrix verb *kvað*, as in other accusative with infinitive constructions, (cf. 4.3). In (12) the accusative subject of the infinitival clause is *þat* 'that', which corresponds to the nominative of the equivalent finite sentence. There is thus no evidence of raising to subject of a potential oblique subject in Old Icelandic.

4.1.2 *Subject PRO*

In infinitival clauses, the non-expressed argument is always the subject. That is, the subject is represented by PRO, the object never is.

(13) a. Han-n   heitr   at gef-a   þeim   bæði ríki   ok fé
         he-NOM promises to give-INF them.DAT both power and wealth
         'He promises to give them both powe and wealth.' (Heimskringla)
     b. Kjartan   kaus   heldr at ver-a með konung-i en   far-a til
         Kjartan.NOM chose rather to be   with king-DAT than go-INF to
         Ísland-s
         Iceland-GEN
         'Kjartan would rather stay with the king than to go to Iceland'
         (Laxdøla saga)

I have not been able to find any example of a potential oblique subject represented by PRO in infinitival clauses. Nor has any of the proponents of oblique subjects in Old Icelandic presented any convincing data.

Haugan (2000) analyzes the following sentence as containing PRO:

(14) tek-r   þá   nú at þyrst-a   mjök
      take-3SG them.ACC now to thirst-INF much
      'They are now beginning to be very thirsty' (Flóamanna saga)

But the accusative pronoun *þá* is not an argument of *tekr*, which would take a nominative agent. It must therefore have been moved out of the infinitival clause, leaving a trace, not PRO in the subject position of the infinitive. I have argued above that this movement is not raising, since that would have required a change into nominative. It is therefore A-bar movement to SpecIP. This kind of movement can be argued for also on other grounds, cf. Section 4.2. The structure of (14) is therefore (15a) instead of (15b).

(15) a. $_{CP}$[tekr $_{IP}$[þá$_i$ $_{VP}$[at þyrsta t_i]]
 b. *$_{CP}$[tekr $_{IP}$[þá$_i$ $_{VP}$[at PRO$_i$ þyrsta]]

Barðdal (2000) also concludes that Old Icelandic has non-nominative PRO, but her only evidence are sentences like (16), where the subject of the infinitive is the reflexive clitic -*st* on the verb *kvaðst*.

(16) Þorgils$_i$ kvað-st$_i$ leið-a-st þar-vist-in
 Þorgils.NOM said-REFL bore-INF-REFL there-stay-DEF.NOM
 'Thorgils said that he was bored by staying there' (Flóamanna saga)

This can be analyzed in two ways. Either -*st* may be cliticized without movement; in that case this clitic is the subject of the infinitive, and there is no place for a PRO. Or the reflexive subject is moved out of the embedded clause before cliticizing; in that case the subject of the infinitive is a trace rather than PRO. Sentence (16) is, however, very interesting for another reason, and I will return to it in Section 4.3.

4.1.3 Clause-bound reflexivization

A subject binds a reflexive in the same clause, both a reflexive pronoun and a reflexive possessive determiner. This is the normal pattern.

(17) a. Flosi$_i$ bjó sik$_i$ aust-an
 Flosi.NOM prepared himself.ACC east-from
 'Flosi got ready to go west' (Njáls saga)
 b. han-n$_i$ ger-ir sér$_i$ bø í dal þeim
 he-NOM makes himself.DAT farm in valley that.DAT
 'He builds himself a farm i that valley' (Hrafnkels saga)
 c. sá mað-r$_i$ kom skip sín-u$_i$ til Íslands
 that.NOM man-NOM came ship-DAT his-DAT to Iceland
 'That man came with his ship to Iceland' (Hrafnkels saga)

d. *hon-um   gaf han-n$_i$ alla hina beztu grip-i   sína$_i$ halfa*
    him-DAT gave he-NOM all   the   best   treasure-PL.ACC his half
    við   sik$_i$
    with himself
    'He gave him half of all his most valuable things' (Hrafnkels saga)

The antecedent of the reflexive may also be a potential oblique subject. The following examples are from Rögnvaldsson 1996: 53.

(18) a. *ef hon-um$_i$ þykk-ir   sér$_i$ þat nokkut fullting*
         if him-DAT seem-3SG himself.DAT that some   help
         'If he thinks that this is of any help to him' (Egils saga)
    b. *ok   er þat eigi kynlegt at   slíkum mönn-um$_i$ þykk-i*
        and is that not strange that such   men.PL.DAT seem-SUBJ.3SG
        all-t   lákt hjá   sér$_i$
        all-NEUT.NOM low with themselves
        'And it is not surprising that such men find everything humble with themselves.' (Laxdøla saga)
    c. *en   er   hann sá   bréf þetta, virðist   hon-um$_i$ þat bréf*
        and when he   saw letter this   seemed him-DAT that letter.NOM
        fjör-ráð   við sik$_i$
        murder-plot with himself
        'And when he saw this letter, he thought that it was a plot to murder him' (Íslendinga saga)

A reflexive may, however, also be bound by an object. Examples (19) are from Juntune (1992: 76).

(19) a. *Ólaf-r   konung-r þakkaði henni$_i$ vel orð   sín$_i$*
         Ólaf-NOM king-NOM thanked her.DAT well words.ACC hers
         'King Ólaf thanked her well for her words' (Heimskringla)
    b. *Börk-r svarar   svá, at   han-n   myndi gjalda hon-um$_i$*
        Börk answers so   that he-NOM would pay   him-DAT
        föðurarf   sin-n$_i$
        inheritence.ACC his-ACC
        'Börk answered that he would give him his inheritance' (Eyrbyggja saga)
    c. *Þorkell auðgi ferr þá   til fundar við Gísla$_i$ ok sagði hon-um$_i$*
        Þorkel rich   goes then to meeting with Gísli and said him-DAT
        sekt   sín-a$_i$
        banishment.ACC his-ACC

'Thorkel the Rich then went to meet Gisli and told him about his banishment' (Gísla saga)

d. [*Guðleikr fór um sumarit í Austrveg til Hólmgarðs ok keypti þar pell ágætlig*]
'Gudleik travelled in the summer east to Holmgard and bought there excellent cloth'

er han-n ætlaði konung-i$_i$ til tígnar-klæða sér$_i$
which he-NOM intended king-DAT for stately-clothes himself.DAT
'which he intended for the king for his robes of state' (Ólafs saga helga)

According to Zaenen et al. (1985) this kind of binding yields ungrammatical sentences in Modern Icelandic. In most cases the object binds the reflexive possessive. As expected, binding of a reflexive pronoun by the object is relatively rare, since that would require two identical non-subject NPs in the same sentence. In (19d), however, there is a reflexive pronoun, but significantly it is a possessive dative.

The reflexive possessive can even occur in the subject, bound by an object. The reflexive pronoun has no nominative form, and is of course excluded from the subject role.

(20) a. en þó varð honum$_i$ sín$_i$ vón at hegoma
but still became him-DAT his hope.NOM in vain
'But still his hopes were vain' (Barlaams saga)

b. eigi mátti frjalsa han-n$_i$ frá dauða öll sín$_i$ konungleg sæla
not could save him-ACC from death all his royal bliss.NOM
'All his royal bliss could not save him from death' (Barlaams saga)

c. en því váru David-i$_i$ léttari sínar$_i$ sakar
but therefore were David-DAT lighter his-PL.NOM charges.PL.NOM
fyrir guði
before God
'But therefore David's charges before God were less serious for him' (Konungs skuggsja)

The data in (19) and (20) show that examples of potential oblique subjects binding a reflexive, as in (18), do not in and of themselves support the oblique subject hypothesis.

4.1.4 Long distance reflexivization

In modern Icelandic, a reflexive in a subordinate sentence may be bound by the subject of the matrix sentence if the verb in the subordinate sentence is in the subjunctive.

(21) Jón₁ upplýsti hver   hefð-i   barið sig₁
     Jón revealed who.NOM had-SUBJ hit   himself
     'John revealed who had hit him'

Nygaard (1905: 342) states that long distance reflexives occur only exceptionally. Personal pronouns are the rule. Nygaard's three examples of long distance reflexives all have a nominative subject as their antecedents. I offer just one example here.

(22) Sigmundr₁   biðr þá,   at   þeir   mundu hjálpa sér₁
     Sigmund-NOM asks them.ACC that they.NOM should help   himself.DAT
     'Sigmund asks them to help him' (Flateyjarbók)

Rögnvaldsson (1995: 19) states that "[l]ong-distance reflexivization is rare in Old Icelandic [...]; but when it occurs, it always appears to have a subject antecedent". He offers no examples or no other substantiation of this claim. In a later work he quotes three examples of long distance reflexivization with oblique antecedents, and adds that "Ég hef í fljótu bragði ekki fundið fleiri dæmi en þessi þrjú. [I have so far not been able to find more examples than these three.]" (Rögnvaldsson 1996: 64).

(23) a. ok   er   konung-r frétti þat þá   líkar hon-um₁ eigi þarvist
         and when king-NOM heard that then likes him-DAT not presence
         þeirra ok þykkir eigi örvæntat   at   þeir muni   þar
         their and seems not unexpected that they will.SUBJ there
         efl-a-st   ætl-a   til móts   við sik₁
         strengthen-INF-REFL intend-INF in opposition with himself
         'And when the king heard this, he did not like their presence and he did not consider it unexpected that they would gather strength against him' (Geirmundar þáttr)
     b. ok   þótti   hon-um₁ sem fóstr-a   sín-um₁ mund-i
         and seemed him-DAT as   fosterfather-DAT his-DAT would-SUBJ
         mein at verða
         harm to become
         'And it seemd to him as if his fosterfather would be harmed' (Ljósvetninga saga)
     c. hina næstu nátt eptir er   Gest-r var skírðr   dreymdi han-n₁
         the next night after that Gest   was baptized dreamed him-ACC
         at   Bárðr faðir   sin-n₁   kæm-i   til hans₁
         that Bárd father.NOM his-NOM came-SUBJ to him
         'The next night after Gest was baptized, he dreamed that his father Bárd came to him' (Bárðar saga)

These data can of course be interpreted either way: Old Icelandic long distance reflexivization can only be bound by subjects, and the oblique antecedents in (23) are oblique subjects; or, Old Icelandic long distance reflexivization can also be bound by objects, and the antecedents in (23) are not subjects. The low frequency of long distance reflexivization in Old Icelandic and the scarcity of examples of oblique antecedents leaves the decision to guesswork or personal preference. In any case, such reflexivization is not obligatory, as shown by (23c), where both the anaphor *sinn* and the non-anaphoric pronoun *hans* are bound by *hann* in the higher sentence.

4.1.5 Conjunction reduction

In Modern Icelandic, as in English and in Mainland Scandinavian, a subject in the second conjunct may be deleted under identity with the subject of the first conjunct. In these languages the deletion itself in the second conjunct as well as the triggering of the deletion are therefore subject properties. Such deletion is found also in Old Icelandic.

(24) a. þá   brá   han-n$_i$ sverð-in-u   hart ok títt   ok hljóp [_$_i$]
        then drew he-NOM sword-DAT-DEF hard and often and ran [NOM]
        í   stofu-na
        into room-DEF
        'Then he suddenly drew the sword and ran into the room'
        (Ólafs saga helga)

   b. við fors-inn   var [otr   ein-n]$_i$ ok hafði [_$_i$]   tekit
        by waterfall-DEF was otter.NOM one-NOM and had [NOM] taken
        lax   ór   fors-inum
        salmon out.of waterfall-DEF
        'By the waterfall there was an otter and it had taken a salmon out of the waterfall' (Snorra Edda)

   c. reið Illugi$_i$ þá heiman   skjótt ok keypti [_$_i$]   skip halft
        rode Illugi.NOM then home.from quick and bought [NOM] ship half
        'Illugi then rode from home and bought one half of a ship'
        (Gunnlaugs saga)

A subject may also be deleted under identity with a potential oblique subject.

(25) a. Hon-um$_i$ líkar illa   ok fer   [_$_i$]   á fund   Guðmund-ar
        him-DAT likes badly and goes [NOM] to meeting Guðmund-GEN
        'He does not like this at all and goes to meet Guðmund'
        (Ljósvetninga saga)

b. [þeim svein-i]ᵢ var nafn   gefit ok [_ᵢ]   kallað-r
   that boy-DAT was name.ACC given and [NOM] called-MASC.NOM
   Þorleik-r
   Þorleik-NOM
   'That boy was given a name and called Þorleik' (Laxdøla saga)
c. þat líkaði henniᵢ   allvel,   ok þakkaði [_ᵢ] hon-umⱼ
   that liked her.DAT very.well and thanked [NOM] him-DAT
   stórmennsk-u   sínaⱼ
   generosity-ACC his-ACC
   'She liked it very much and thanked him for his generosity'
   (Laxdøla saga)

In (26) a potential oblique subject in the second conjunct (the dative *honum* 'him') is deleted under identity with the subject of the first conjunct.

(26) var sáᵢ   vatn-i   ausinn ok [_ᵢ] nafn   gefit ok
     was that.MASC.NOM water-DAT poured and [DAT] name.NOM given and
     kallað-r   Egil-l
     called.MASC.NOM Egil.NOM
     'He was baptized and given a name and called Egil' (Egils saga)

However, in Old Icelandic objects as well may trigger the deletion.

(27) a. Guð-in   gerðu brúᵢ   til himins af jörðu, ok heitir
        god-PL.NOM.DEF made bridge.ACC to heaven off earth and is.called
        [_ᵢ]   Bifröst
        [NOM] Bifröst
        'The gods made a bridge to Heaven from the Earth and called it
        Bifröst' (Snorra Edda)
     b. þá   lét Óðinn bera inn í höll-ina sverðᵢ,   ok váru [_ᵢ]
        then let Odin bring in to hall-DEF sword.PL.ACC and were [NOM]
        svá björt   at...
        so bright that
        'Then Odin had swords brought into the hall, and they were so
        bright that ...' (Snorra Edda)
     c. síðan   skaut Ásmundr at Ásbirni selsbana spjótiᵢ,   ok kom
        afterwards shot Ásmund at Ásbjörn Selsbani spear-DAT and came
        [_ᵢ]   á hann miðjan
        [NOM] at him middle
        'Afterwards Ásmund attacked Ásbjörn with a spear, and it hit him in
        the middle' (Ólafs saga helga)

Also, objects may be deleted under identity with subjects as well as with objects and other constituents in the preceding sentence.

(28) a. *síðan fluttu [þeir Þorgils]$_i$ líkit$_j$ upp með*
afterwards moved they.NOM Þorgils.NOM corpse.DEF.ACC$_i$ up with
á-nni ok grófu [_$_i$] [_$_j$] þar niðr
river-DEF and buried [NOM] [ACC] there down
'Afterwards Þorgils and his men moved the corpse up along the river and buried it there' (Heimskringla)

b. *[Einarr Þambarskelfir]$_i$ fór með [lík-i Magnús-s*
Einar-NOM Þambarskelfi-NOM went with corpse-DAT Magnús-GEN
konung-s]$_j$ ok með honum [all-r þrøndaher-r]$_k$ ok
king-GEN and with him all-NOM Thronder.army-NOM and
fluttu [_$_{i+k}$] [_$_j$] til Niðaróss
moved [NOM] [ACC] to Niðaros
'Einar Þambarskelfi brought King Magnus' corpse to Niðaros, and the whole Thronder army followed him' (Heimskringla)

c. *hon-um$_i$ var fengin leynilega harpa$_j$, ok sló hann$_i$ [_$_j$]*
him-DAT was gotten secretely harp.NOM and struck he.NOM [ACC]
með tá-num
with toes-DEF
'He was secretely given a harp, and he played it with his toes' (Snorra Edda)

In (28a) both the subject and the object are deleted in the second conjunct, under identity with the subject and the object, respectively, in the preceding sentence. In (28b) the object is deleted under identity with a complement of a preposition in the preceding sentence. Here, too, the subject is deleted under identity with a (rather complex) subject in the preceding sentence. In (28c) the object is deleted under identity with a preceding nominative subject, but note that the potential oblique subject (*honum*) does not trigger deletion of *hann*, which would be expected of a "real" subject.

This kind of data shows that facts about coreference deletion in conjoined sentences cannot be used as subject criteria in Old Icelandic, and deletion of, or deletion triggered by, potential oblique subjects do not support the oblique subject hypothesis.

4.1.6 Quantifier float

A quantifier or the word *sjalfr* 'self' may move out of the NP to which it belongs, and into another position in the sentence, in Old Icelandic either the topic position or the position of the sentence adverbial.

(29) a. *all-ir   váru   þeir   efniligir   menn*
       all-MASC.PL.NOM were they.MASC.PL.NOM promising men.PL.NOM
       'They were all promising men' (Gunnlags saga)
    b. *ok þessir menn,   er   nú eru nefndir,   váru*
       and these men.MASC.PL.NOM who now are mentioned were
       all-ir   uppi á einn tíma
       all.MASC.PL.NOM up   at one time
       'And these men, who have now been mentioned, all lived at the same time' (Gunnlaugs saga)

In his thorough and detailed study of subject properties in Old Norse, Mørck (1992) has also found quantifier float from potential oblique subjects.

(30) a. *han-n   fjarar al-lan   at þurru*
       him-ACC ebbs all-MASC.ACC at dry
       'It (=the fjord) became all dry at low tide'
    b. *þá skipan   sem   yðr   mætti sjölf-um   vel líka*
       that arrangement which you.PL.DAT might self-PL.DAT well like
       'That arrangement which you might like well yourselves' (Diplomatarium Norvegicum V 46)

But quantifiers may also be moved out of objects. Mørck's examples are all from Old Norwegian, but there is no reason to assume that Old Icelandic was any different in this regard.

(31) a. *ef vit skulum hana   glósa   all-a*
       if we shall   her.ACC explain all-FEM.ACC
       'If we are to explain it all' (Konungs skuggsjá)
    b. *því   at syndir mínar eru svá margar at   mér   eru sjölf-um*
       that.DAT that sins mine are so many   that me.DAT are self-DAT
       útalligar
       countless
       'Because my sins are so many that I cannot count them myself' (Konungs skuggjsá)

Mørck notes that quantifier float is much more frequent from subjects than from objects or from potential oblique subjects. The latter two seem to be equally rare. The fact that we find sentences like those in (30) is therefore no argument in favor of the subject status of the oblique NPs in those sentences.

4.2 Subject position

As shown in Section 2 above, distributional criteria are important for identfying the subject in Modern Icelandic. In this section I will examine the subject positions found in the Old Icelandic material to see whether they are exclusive subject positions, or whether they may also host objects and other types of constituents. One type of argument in favor of the oblique subject analysis for Modern Icelandic, is the fact that only subjects can appear in a position between the finite and the non-finite verb, that is in SpecIP.

(32) a. *Hafði Sigga   aldrei hjálpað Harald-i?*
       had   Sigga.NOM never helped Harald-DAT
       'Had Sigga never helped Harald?'
    b. **Hafði Haraldi aldrei hjálpað Sigga?*
    c. *Hefur henni   alltaf þótt   Ólaf-ur   leiðinlegur?*
       has   her.DAT always seemed Ólaf-NOM boring
       'Has she always found Ólaf boring?'
    d. **Hefur Ólafur alltaf þótt henni leiðinlegur?*

The nominative subject in (32a) and the dative subject in (32c) may appear immediately after the finite verb, while the dative object in (32b) and the nominative object in (32d) may not. Similarly, subjects occupy the position immediately after the complementizer in subordinate clauses (Barðdal 2000).

(33) a. *Ég kaupi bók-ina   ef þú   elskar hana*
       I buy   book-DEF if you.NOM love   it.ACC
       'I will buy the book if you love it'
    b. **Ég kaupi bókina ef hana elskar þú*
    c. *Ég skila bók-inni ef þér   leiði-st   hún*
       I return book-DEF if you.DAT bore-REFL it.NOM
       'I will return the book if you are bored by it'
    d. **Ég skila bókinni ef hún leiðist þér*

These facts are taken to show that even oblique NPs may appear in SpecIP. Since structural position is such a strong subject criterion in Modern Icelandic, arguments in favor of oblique subjects in Old Icelandic have also been based on position in the sentence. It is a well known fact, however, that Old Icelandic exhibits certain word order patterns that are no more acceptable in Modern

Icelandic. Distributional criteria for Old Icelandic must therefore be based on the syntax of Old Icelandic itself, independently of the modern language. In this section I will present a survey of possible positions for the nominative subject in Old Icelandic. Then I will demonstrate that each of these positions is also available for objects.

In most cases the subject moves to the specifier position of IP. If no further movement of the subject takes place, it appears in the position immediately following the finite verb, which may then be considered the base position of the subject.

(34) a. þá   gekk Sigurð-r   konung-r til
        then   went Sigurd-NOM king-NOM to
        'Then King Sigurd came' (Ólafs saga helga)
    b. nú   tekr   han-n   hest-in-n
        now   takes he-NOM   horse-DEF-ACC
        'Now he takes the horse' (Hrafnkels saga)
    c. síðan   fluttu   þeir   Þorgils   lík-it   upp með
        afterwards moved   they.NOM   Þorgils.NOM   corpse.DEF.ACC   up   with
        á-nni
        river-DEF
        'Afterwards Þorgils and his men moved the corpse up along the river' (Heimskringla)

In subordinate sentences, this corresponds to the position immediately following the complementizer.

(35) a. at   skip   kom   af hafi
        that ship.NOM came   off sea
        'that a ship came from the sea' (Gunnlaugs saga)
    b. er land   var allt alheiðit
        as land.NOM   was all   all-heathen
        'as all the land was heathen' (Gunnlaugs saga)

An object may precede the subject. This object is then typically a pronoun, while the subject is an indefinite NP. (Example (36a) is from Haugan 2000; (36b–d) are from Christoffersen 1993.)

(36) a. Mund-u   þat   sumir menn   mæl-a   í   mínu landi
        would-3PL   that.ACC some men.PL.NOM   say-INF in my   country
        'Some men would say so in my country' (Finnboga saga)

b. *ok má því engi mað-r skipt-a*
      and may that.DAT no man-NOM change-INF
      'And nobody may change it' (The Law of Magnus Lagabøti)
   c. *ok finn-a han-n aðrir menn á djúpi*
      and find-3PL him-ACC other men.NOM on deep
      'And other men find it in the deep' (The Law of Magnus Lagabøti)
   d. *þá skal sín-um₁ husum hvar₁ ráð-a*
      then shall his house.PL.DAT each.NOM rule-INF
      'Then each shall decide over his own house' (The Law of Magnus Lagabøti)

The structures in (36) may be analyzed as having the subject *in situ*, that is it remains in SpecVP instead of moving to SpecIP (Haugan 2000: 174).

The subject is the constituent that is most often topicalized, that is moved to SpecCP.

(37) a. *Hallfreð-r setti bú saman*
        Hallfred-NOM set home.ACC together
        'Hallfred set up a home' (Hrafnkels saga)
     b. *Þorbjörn átti fé líti-t*
        Þorbjörn.NOM owned money.ACC little-NEUT.ACC
        'Þhorbjörn had little money' (Hrafnkels saga)
     c. *kastali var fyrir austan sund-it*
        castle.NOM was for east sound-DEF
        'There was a castle east of the sound' (Ólafs saga helga)
     d. *kona ein var við vatn-it*
        woman.NOM one was by water-DEF
        'There was a woman by the lake' (Hrafnkels saga)

Heavy or complex subjects, or subjects carrying new information, may appear at the end of the sentence. They can then be considered extraposed, that is right-adjoined to CP or IP.

(38) a. *þar var á skip-i kona hans ok son*
        there was.3SG on ship-DAT wife.NOM his and son.NOM
        'His wife and son were there on board the ship' (Hrafnkels saga)
     b. *en áðr þrælar höfðu matazt, þá vár-u*
        but before slaves had eaten then were-3PL
        komnir til Orms margir menn ór
        come.PART.PL.MASC.NOM to Orm many men.PL.NOM from

bygð-inni,   er   hann hafði orð   sent
settlement-DEF that he   had word sent
'But before the slaves had eaten, many men from the settlement had come to Orm, (men) whom he had sent for' (Ólafs saga Tryggvasonar)

c. *Þar vár-u   ok falln-ir   af Hrafnkatli tolf*
there were-3PL also fallen-PL.MASC.NOM from Hrafnkel twelve
menn
men.PL.NOM
'Twelve of Hrafnkels men had also fallen there' (Hrafnkels saga)

d. *en eigi þykki mér   meira vert   dráp   Eyvind-ar ok*
but not seems me.DAT more worthy killing.NOM Eyvind.GEN and
mann-a   hans
men.GEN his
'But I do not find the killing of Eyvind and his men more worthy' (Hrafnkels saga)

The subject may appear in object position, as a complement of V. This is first of all found with passive verbs.

(39) a. *ok var fluttr   varnað-r   þeira til skips*
and was moved goods-NOM their to ship
'And their goods were moved on board the ship (Gunnlaugs saga)

b. *er dreginn belg-r   á   höfuð hon-um*
is pulled skin-bag-NOM on head him-DAT
'A skin-bag is pulled over his head' (Gísla saga)

The difference between (38) and (39) is that the subjects in (39) cannot be considered extraposed or right-adjoined to CP/IP, since they are followed by constituents which belong inside VP. These subjects remain in their original object position although the verb is in the passive.

Even in active sentences the subject may be found in object position.

(40) a. *hefir hér setit svala   ein við glugg-inn*
has here sat   swallow.NOM one by opening-DEF
'There has been a swallow sitting here by the opening' (Egils saga)

b. *var þá   sigit blóð   fyrir augu þeim*
was then sunk blood.NOM before eyes them.DAT
'Then the blood sank down before their eyes' (Hrafnkels saga)

c. *hér er kominn Böðvar-r   bróðir hans í   dal*
here is come   Böðvar-NOM brother his in valley
'Here Böðvar his brother has come to the valley' (Valla-Ljóts saga)

The verbs in these sentences are typical ergative or inaccusative verbs, which means that the surface subject is base generated in object position (Perlmutter 1978, Faarlund 1991, Haugan 1999: 201f). So here, too, the explanation may be that the subject has not been moved out of its D-structure object position.

To sum up, we can identify five different subject positions in Old Icelandic. In terms of surface linear order (Phonologocal Form) and structural position (S-Structure) they can be characerized as follows:

(a) PF: first position
SS: SpecCP
Example (37)
(b) PF: following finite verb or complementizer
SS: SpecIP
Example (34), (35)
(c) PF: following other constituents, preceding non-finite verb
SS: SpecVP
Example (36)
(d) PF: following non-finite verb
SS: ComplVP
Example (39), (40)
(e) PF: final position
SS: Right-adjoined to CP or IP
Example (41)

Position (d) is obviously also an object position. Position (c), SpecVP, is the external argument position. Here we of course do not expect to find objects; neither do we expect to find potential oblique subjects, since they are never agents or external arguments. Verbs that take potential oblique subjects are mostly ergative or passive verbs. Position (a), the topic position, is of course also a position for objects.

(41) a. *Fjór-a menn   sendi hon   fjögurra vegna   í bygð-ina*
       four men.ACC sent she.NOM four   directions in district-DEF
       'Four men she sent in four different directions in the district'
       (Heimskringla)
   b. *Ásu   dóttur   sín-a   gipti   han-n   Guðrøð-i   konung-i*
       Ása.ACC daughter his-FEM married he.NOM Gudrød-DAT king-DAT
       'His daughter Ása he gave in marriage to King Gudrød'
       (Heimskringla)

    c. *fé   þat all-t   gaf han-n   liðsmönn-um   sín-um*
       money.ACC that all-NEUT gave he-NOM follower-PL.DAT his
       'All that money he gave to his followers' (Heimskringla)

Position e), final extraposition, is available to objects as to other constituents.

(42) a. *Baugi   kallaði ilt   fjárhald   si-tt*
          Baugi.NOM called bad.NEUT.ACC money.keeping his-NEUT.ACC
          'Baugi called the administration of his money bad' (Snorra Edda)
     b. *ok réðu   þar til hlunns skip-i   sín-u*
          and arranged there to log   ship-DAT their-DAT
          'and pulled up their ship there' (Gunnlaugs saga)

This leaves us with SpecIP, the canonical subject position. There is no doubt that we find potential oblique subjects in this position.

(43) a. *þat   líkaði Eyólf-i   illa*
          that.NOM liked Eyólf-DAT badly
          'Eyólf did not like it at all' (Ljósvetninga saga)
     b. *sá   kostr líka-r   mér   vel*
          that.NOM choice like-3SG me.DAT well
          'I like those terms' (Fóstbrøðra saga)
     c. *var þeim   gefinn dagverð-r*
          was them.DAT given lunch-NOM
          'They were given lunch' (Heimskringla)
     d. *austmaðr spurði, hvat   han-n   hefði dreymt*
          eastman asked what.ACC him-ACC had dreamt
          'The man from the East asked him what he had dreamt'
          (Gunnlaugs saga)

However, objects are also found in the immediate post-verbal position, cf. the examples in (36), repeated here.

(36) a. *mund-u þat   sumir menn   mæl-a í   mínu landi*
          would-3PL that.ACC some men.PL.NOM say-INF in my   country
          'Some men would say so in my country' (Finnboga saga)
     b. *ok má því   engi mað-r   skip-ta*
          and may that.DAT no   man-NOM change-INF
          'And nobody may change it' (The Law of Magnus Lagabøti)
     c. *ok finn-a   han-n   aðrir menn   á djúpi*
          and find-3PL him.ACC other men.NOM on deep
          'And other men find it in the deep' (The Law of Magnus Lagabøti)

d. *þá skal sín-um*$_i$ *husum hvar*$_i$ *ráð-a*
   then shall his-PL.DAT house.PL.DAT each.NOM rule.INF
   'Then each shall decide over his own house' (The Law of Magnus Lagabøti)

These sentences may be analyzed as having its subject remaining in SpecVP, while the object is moved to SpecIP. Likewise, in subordinate sentences an object or another type of constituent may appear between the complementizer and the finite verb.

(44) a. *at þess-a jörð hefi ek haft*
     that this-FEM.ACC land.ACC have I had
     'that I have owned this land' (The Law of Magnus Lagabøti)

   b. *en ef þat mælir nökkur-r*
      but if that.ACC says someone-NOM
      'but if someone says so' (The Law of Magnus Lagabøti)

   c. *ok er þeim gaf byr*
      and as them.DAT gave wind.ACC
      'and when they had sailing wind' (Gunnlaugs saga)

   d. *en Þorstein-i var sagt, at falln-ir væri buðarvegg-ir hans*
      and Þorstein-DAT was said that fallen-PL.NOM were boothwall-PL.NOM his
      'And Þorstein had been told that the walls of his booth had fallen down' (Gunnlaugs saga)

   e. *til bøjar þess er at Grenj-um heitir*
      to farm that which at Gren-PL.DAT is.called
      'to the farm called Gren' (Gunnlaugs saga)

   f. *sem nú hefr þú upp tekit*
      which now have you.NOM up taken
      'which you have taken up now' (Fljótsdøla saga)

It appears that the specifier position of IP is not a unique subject position in Old Icelandic. In Modern Icelandic, it seems to be reserved for the subject, nomintiave or oblique.[3] It may be argued that some of the examples in (44) are instances of stylistic fronting, whereby a head is moved to a position in front of I. This is very common in Modern Icelandic, and it is not a subject property neither in Old nor in Modern Icelandic. There is no generally accepted description of stylsitic fronting, but the fact that it is (by definition) head movement, does not make it plausible to treat it as movement to SpecIP. Rather, it has been suggested by Holmberg & Platzack (1995) among others that stylistic fronting involves cliticization to I. But note that at least (44a) and (44e) cannot be stylistic fronting in this sense, since the moved elements are maximal phrases. The only plausible account, therefore, is movement to SpecIP.

If objects, predicate complements, and adverbials can move to SpecIP, then certainly potential oblique subjects must also be expected to move there, whithout that making them subjects. There is thus no evidence from word order in favor of the oblique subject hypothesis for Old Icelandic.

4.3 Accusative with infinitive

Data from accusative with infinitive constructions have been used extensively in the debate about oblique subjects. Accusative with infinitive constructions are non-finite clauses with the subject in the accusative and the verb in the infinitive.

(45) a. *opt hefi ek heyrt* [*yðr   þat mæl-a*]
       often have I heard you.ACC that say-INF
       'I have often heard you say that' (Heimskringla)
    b. *þá sá ek* [*fljúg-a ofan frá fjöll-unum   örn*
       then saw I   fly-INF down from mountains.DEF eagle.ACC
       mikin-n]
       big-MASC.ACC
       'Then I saw a big eagle fly down from the mountains' (Gunnlaugs saga)
    c. *Þorstein-n   kvað* [*hana   haf-a   vel gört*]
       Þorsteinn-NOM said her.ACC have-INF well done
       'Þorsteinn said that she had done well' (Gunnlaugs saga)

The fact that the subject undergoes case shift, is a potential subject criterion.

Accusative with infinitive constructions are sometimes referred to as involving subject-to-object raising, the assumption being that the subject of the lower verb is raised into the object position of the higher verb, where it receives accusative case from it. A more recent generative analysis is the "Small Clause" analysis, first proposed by Stowell (1981), whereby the embedded subject remains *in situ*. But since this is a position that is governed by the higher verb, it receives accusative case from it (Haegeman 1994: 171f). A problem with both of these analyses is that there is at least one verb which may take an accusative with infinitive, without otherwise assigning accusative case to its object, namely *geta* 'guess, mention', which regularly takes a genitive object. Compare (46a) with an accusative with infinitive construction and (46b) with a NP object.

(46) a. ek get   hér verit haf-a   Gunnar
       I guess here been have-INF Gunnar.ACC
       'I guess Gunnar has been here'
    b. bað   hon Hjalta   aldri get-a   þess mál-s   fyrir
       asked she Hjalti.ACC never mention-INF that matter-GEN for
       konungi
       king
       'She asked Hjalti never to mention the matter to the King'

Unless we are dealing with two different verbs *geta*, it is hard to explain where the accusative *Gunnar* comes from if it is dependent on the matrix verb.[4]

This need not concern us here, however. No matter where the accusative comes from, we are faced with the problem of identifying the subject of the infinitive in the accusative with infinitive constructions. All we know is that this is the NP that corresponds to the subject of the equivalent finite sentence. However, since most objects also are in the accusative case, the subject of an accusative with infinitive construction cannot be identified by means of its case alone. We need to look for additional criteria to identify the subject in accusative with infinitive constructions. We will consider these criteria in turn.

As already noted, subjects change into the accusative in accusative with infinitive constructions, as in (45). Accusative objects remain in the accusative, and are thus indistinguishable from subjects on the basis of case alone. Dative or genitive objects do not change:

(47) þeir kváðu han-n   ráð-a   mund-u   því   við Svía-konung
     they said him-ACC procure-INF should-INF that.DAT with Swede-king
     'They said he would procure that with the Swedish king' (Heimskringla)
     (From Kristoffersen 1996: 138)

Nor are there any certain cases of potential oblique subjects changing from the dative or the genitive into the accusative (except possibly under cliticization, see below). Consider (12), repeated here, with the dative *sér* as a potential oblique subject of the infinitive *þykkja* 'seem'.

(12) Grettir$_i$ kvað sér$_i$ þat   betra þykkja en
     Gretti-NOM said himself.DAT that.ACC better seem   than
     bak-elda-gørð-in
     baking-fire-making-DEF
     'Gretti said that seemed better to him than building a baking fire'
     (Grettis saga)

Rögnvaldsson (1991:373) presents three other sentences with an accusative with infinitive construction containing a dative. Since he uses them to support the claim that these datives are subjects of the accusative with infinitive construction, we need to take a closer look at each one of them.

(48) a. *Gunnar-r   sagði sér   þat   ver-a nær skapi*
       Gunnar.NOM said himself.DAT it.ACC be   near mood
       'Gunnar said that this was what he wanted to do' (Njáls saga)
   b. *Ingólf-r   sagði þeim   ver-a mál at setj-a-st um kyrrt*
       Ingolf-NOM said them.DAT be   time to sit.REFL on still
       'Ingolf said that now it was time for them to settle down'
       (Flóamanna saga)
   c. *Þórð-r   kvað Þorgeir-i   mjök missýn-a-st*
       Þórð-NOM said Þorgeir-DAT much mistake-INF-REFL
       'Thord said that Thorgeir was much mistaken' (Ljósvetninga saga)

Rögnvaldsson does not state explicitly what the evidence is that the dative NPs in these accusative with infinitive constructions are subjects, but from the context we may surmise that what he has in mind is their position before the infinitive. He admits that "the exact analysis of these constructions may be controversial" (p. 373), but his implicit claim is nevertheless that the dative phrases in (48a–b) are oblique subjects. Let us therefore examine these constructions a bit more closely. The accusative with infinitive constructions correspond to the following (constructed) finite sentences:

(49) a. *mér   er þat   nær skapi*
       me.DAT is that.NOM near mood
   b. *þeim   er mál at setj-a-st   um kyrrt*
       them.DAT is time to sit-INF-REFL on still
   c. *Þorgei-ri   missyn-i-st   mjök*
       Þorgeir.DAT mistake-3SG-REFL much

In (49a) the verb is *vera* 'be', with the nominative *þat* 'that/it', followed by the predicate complement *nær* 'near'. There is no obvious reason why the dative should be analyzed as the subject here, rather than the nominative *þat*. And if *mér* is the subject, it is unclear what *þat* would be. (49b) is a similar type of sentence. It also has a good subject candidate other than the dative phrase, namely the infinitival clause *at setjast um kyrrt*. In addition there is a complement NP in the nominative, *mál*. If the dative *þeim* is the subject, what then are the syntactic functions of the infinitival clause and the NP *mál*? The phrase

Þorgeiri in (49c), however, is a more likely candidate for a potential oblique subject. But since we have reason to reject the subjecthood of the dative phrases in (49a–b), we have to conclude that the preverbal position in accusative with infinitive constructions is not a subject position, and thereby the argument for the subjecthood of the dative phrase in (49c) and in the accusative with infinitive construction in (48c) falls apart as well.

It is easy to show that the preverbal position in accusative with infinitive constructions is not an exclusive subject position, consider (50). ((50a–b) are from Kristoffersen (1996)).

(50) a. *þá hugði han-n [þar mund-u far-a Hákon jarl]*
then thought he.NOM there would-INF go-INF Hákon.ACC earl.ACC
'Then he though that Earl Hákon might be going there' (Heimskringla)

b. *nú ætla ek [oss mun-u léttara falla at eiga um við Svein jarl einn saman]*
now think I us.DAT will-INF easier fall to deal with Svein earl one together
'Now I think it will be easier for us to deal with Earl Svein alone' (Heimskringla)

c. *hugði-st$_i$ han-n$_i$ [konung mund-u mýkj-a meg-a]*
thought-REFL he-NOM king.ACC would-INF soften-INF may-INF
'He thought he might soften the king' (Heimskringla)

In (50a) the adverbial *þar* 'there' is in the preverbal position, while the subject follows the verb. In (50b) the dative *oss* 'us', which by no stretch of imagination can be analyzed as a subject, is in the preverbal position. In (50c) *konung* is the object of *mýkja*, but still precedes the verb. We can conclude therefore, that the preverbal position in an accusative with infinitive construction is not a unique subject position. And since change of case does not affect potential oblique subjects, there is so far no evidence from subject-to-object raising in support of oblique subjects in Old Icelandic.

There is, however, one other phenomenon which seems to select subjects in accusative with infinitive constructions. If the subject of the embedded clause, that is of the infinitive, is coreferential with the subject of the higher clause, it is cliticized to the matrix verb.

(51) a. *austmað-r$_i$ kveð-st$_i$ á þat hætta mund-u*
       eastman-NOM says-REFL at that dare should-INF
       'The man from the East said that he would take the risk'
       (Gunnlaugs saga)
   b. *ok kvað-st$_i$ han-n$_i$ vilj-a   far-a   útan*
       and said-REFL he-NOM want-INF go-INF out.from
       'He said he wanted to go abroad' (Gunnlaugs saga)

It does happen, although rarely, that a reflexive accusative subject is not cliticized:

(52) *Svasi$_i$ kvað sik$_i$ ver-a þann   Finn-in-n*
     Svasi.NOM said himself.ACC be-INF that.ACC Finn-DEF-ACC
     'Svasi said that he himself was that Finn' (Heimskringla)

The reason why *sik* is not cliticized in (52), may be that it is emphasized. An object in the embedded clause which is coreferential with the matrix subject is never cliticized. A potential oblique subject may or may not be cliticized. Compare (53a–c) and (53d,e).

(53) a. *Grettir$_i$ kvað sér$_i$ þat   betra þykkja en*
       Gretti-NOM said himself.DAT that.ACC better seem than
       bak-elda-gørð-in
       baking-fire-making-DEF
       'Gretti said that seemed better to him than building a baking fire'
       (Grettis saga) (=12)
   b. *at   eigi segði han-n$_i$ · sik$_i$ þyrst-a*
       that not said he-NOM himself.ACC thirst-INF
       'that he did not say that he was thirsty' (Egils saga)
   c. *Aron$_i$ kvað sik$_i$ dreymt haf-a   at   ...*
       Aron.NOM said himself.ACC dreamt have-INF that
       'Aron said that he had dreamt that ...' (Islendinga saga)
   d. *Auðun-n$_i$ setti-st   niðr við ár-bakka-n   ok kvað-st$_i$*
       Auðun-NOM sat-REFL down with river-bank-DEF and said-REFL
       þyrst-a
       thirst-INF
       'Auðun sat down by the riverbank and said he was thirsty'
       (Sturlunga saga)
   e. *Hrafn$_i$ kvað-st$_i$ sýn-ast   at   haldinn væri*
       Hrafn.NOM said-REFL seem-INF that held   was
       'Hrafn said he thought he was being held' (Hrafns saga)

(Example (53b) is from Haugan 2000, and (53c–e) are from Rögnvaldsson 1995 and 1996). The fact that the dative appears with the clitic form -*st* is not an argument in favor of its changing from the dative to the accusative, since the same form -*st* is also used for dative reflexives in other contexts:

(54) a. *þeir snúa skip-um   sín-um*
       they turn ship-PL.DAT their-PL.DAT
       'They turn their ships around' (Jómsvikinga saga)
   b. *Ólafr$_i$ sný-st$_i$ nú austr*
       Ólaf-NOM turns-REFL now east
       'Ólaf now turns East' (Ólafs saga helga)

However, since objects do not cliticize to the matrix verb, sentences like (53d,e) do present strong evidence in support of oblique subjects in Old Icelandic. There is nevertheless a clear difference between subjects and potential oblique subjects in this regard. Reflexive subjects that fail to cliticize, as in (52), are extremely rare, according to Nygaard 1905.[5] On the other hand, full form reflexives as potential oblique subjects seem to be more common than cliticized ones.

Rögnvaldsson (1996: 60) quotes two examples of accusative with infinitive constructions where a nominative NP remains in the nominative while a potential oblique subject is cliticized.

(55) a. *Þorgils$_i$ kvað-st$_i$ leið-a-st   þar-vist-in*
       Þorgils.NOM said-REFL bore-INF-REFL there-stay-DEF.NOM
       'Þorgils said that he was bored by staying there' (Flóamanna saga)
   b. *Þórð-r$_i$ kvað-st$_i$ þykkj-a   tvennir kost-ir   til*
       Þórð-NOM said-REFL seem-INF two   choice.PL.NOM to
       'Þórð said that he felt that two possibilities existed' (Þorgils saga)

The finite counterparts of these accusative with infinitive constructions would have a dative and a nominative NP. In the accusative with infinitive constructions in (55), the dative has been cliticized, while the nominative remains in the nominative. This would be the only type of construction that would clearly call for an oblique subject analysis in Old Icelandic. But they are probably not from Old Icelandic at all. Sentence (55a) does not occur in the main editions of the Flóamanna saga. It comes from an addition in a manuscript from the 17th century. About this manuscript (AM 515,4°) Finnur Jónsson says:

> Den således istandbragte tekst er nu ikke i alle henseender helt pålielig, ti Þórður kunde ændre noget i det, han afskrev.

[The text thus established is not in all respects quite reliable, because Þórður [the scribe] would change some of what he copied.] (Jónsson 1932: iv–v)

Then Jónsson goes on to give examples of such changes, including changes into modern Icelandic usage, such as adding the word *líka* in the meaning 'also'. In a discussion about the 17th century copies of Medieval manuscripts, Jørgensen (1998) says the scribes from that period would concentrate on the content of the texts, rather than the linguistic form.

> Med avstanden i tid tilbake til foreleggets tilblivelse øker faren for misforståelser som leder til forvanskninger, og for skrivemåter og andre endringer som skyldes nyislandsk påvirkning.
>
> [The greater the distance in time is between the original and the copy, the greater is the risk of misunderstandings leading to orthographic and other changes due to *influence from Modern Icelandic* (italics added, JTF)] (Jørgensen 1998: 185).

Sentence (55a) therefore represents 17th century Icelandic, and not necessarily Old Icelandic.

Sentence (55b) also has a different form in other editions. Þorgils saga is part of the Sturlunga saga, and in other editions of the Sturlunga saga, based on the most reliable manuscript, the Króksfjarðarbók (e.g. Vigfusson 1878), the corresponding sentence has the dative form *Þórði* (cf. footnote 3) in stead of the nominative as in Rögnvaldssons example. This sentence then has the same form as (11) above, and it must also be a contamination of two structures. The equivalent direct speech would be (56).

(56) *mér   þykkj-a   tvennir kost-ir   til*
      me.DAT seem-3PL   two   choice.PL.NOM   to

When this sentence was embedded under *kvað*, the writer "forgot" to express the experiencer of *þykkja* as a nominative agent of *kveða*, and at the same time he "forgot" to change the nominative *tvennir kostir* into the accusative.

4.4 Summary of subject properties

This examination of subject properties can be summarized in this table:

Property	Subject	Pot.OBL.SUBJ	Objekt
Subject raising	+	−	−
PRO	+	−	−
Reflexive	+	+	+
LD reflexive	+	+	?
Conjunction reduction	+	+	+
Quantifier float	+	+	+
Position	+	+	+
Position in AcI	+	+	+
Clitic	+	+	−

The table shows that potential oblique subjects side with objects with respect to the two properties subject-to-subject raising and PRO in infinitival clauses. With respect to clause-bound reflexives, conjunction reduction, quantifier float, position in finite clauses, and position in accusative with infinitive constructions, there is no difference between subjects and objects, so that these properties do not consitute subject criteria.

This leaves us with two kinds of evidence that might support an oblique subject analysis for Old Icelandic: long distance reflexivization and cliticization in accusative with infinitive constructions. The question is then whether these two criteria are sufficient to support the oblique subject analysis.

Let us take a look at them again. Long distance reflexivization is extremely rare in the Old Icelandic material. The only data we have are (23a–c), three sentences with potential oblique subject antecedents. We have no way of knowing whether other antecedents are also possible. Long distance reflexivization should therefore be ruled out as possible evidence of oblique subjects.

The other criterion is more interesting. Cliticization seems in fact to be a subject criterion which also includes potential oblique subjects, cf. (53d,e), repeated here.

(53) d. *Auðun-n$_i$ setti-st niðr við ár-bakka-n ok kva-st$_i$*
Auðun-NOM sat-REFL down with river-bank-DEF and said-REFL
þyrst-a
thirst-INF
'Auðun sat down by the riverbank and said he was thirsty'
(Sturlunga saga)

e. *Hrafn*ᵢ   *kva-st*ᵢ   *sýn-ast*   *at*   *haldinn væri*
   Hrafn.NOM said-REFL seem-INF that held   was
   'Hrafn said he thought he was being held' (Hrafns saga)

There is, however, a marked difference in frequency between cliticized subjects (close to a hundred percent) and cliticized potential oblique subjects (probably less than fifty percent). The fact that sentences like (53d,e) do occur, can of course not be ignored in this context. But since they are the only possible evidence of oblique subjects in Old Icelandic, and since non-cliticized forms occur as often, I would consider them as early evidence of an incipient development towards the Modern Icelandic structure, rather than proof of oblique subjects in Old Icelandic.

Here I take the opposite stand from that of Barðdal (2000), who places the burden of proof on those who deny the existence of oblique subjects in Old Icelandic. Instead I will claim that the language (Old Icelandic) is innocent (of hosting oblique subjects) until the opposite has been proven. I have two reasons for this skepticism. First, oblique subjects seem to be such a rare species in the grammatical jungle, that we need some very clear and unambiguous testimony to admit that it is there. Second, the fact that they exist in Modern Icelandic but not in Old Icelandic can be given a very plausible explanation, to which I now turn.

5. The history of the Icelandic subject

The Germanic languages past and present can be conveniently divided into two types, predominantly synthetic and predominantly analytic (for details, cf. Faarlund 1998 and forthcoming). All the "Old" and "Middle" stages belong to the first category, and so does Modern High German. English, Dutch, Afrikaans, Frisian, and Mainland Scandinavian belong to the latter type. Since all the ancestors of this latter group belonged to the synthetic type, they have all undergone a change. Rather than going into details about syntactic change in West Germanic, I will describe briefly a syntactic change in Mainland Scandinavian, before placing Icelandic in this scenario.

Assuming that Old Scandinavian is like Old Icelandic as far as subjecthood goes, this language (dialect, rather) is characterized by a SpecIP position that can host different kinds of constituents, not only subjects, although subjects are the most frequent type of constituent in that position. Through reanalysis, the SpecIP position was specialized as a subject position. (A similar development is described in more detail in Faarlund 1990: 177f). Sentences with objects and adverbials in that position then became impossible, and sentences such as (57a) became ungrammatical. As the nominal case marking in Mainland Scandinavian was lost, potential oblique subjects in that position became regular subjects. (57b) has the Modern Norwegian form (57c). As a consequence, pronouns, which still maintain their case inflection, changed to the nominative, so that (57d) changed to (57e).

(57) a. *mund-u þat sumir menn mæl-a í mínu landi*
would-3PL that.ACC some men.PL.NOM say-INF in my country
'Some men would say so in may country' (Finnboga saga) (= 36a)
b. *þat líkaði Eyólf-i illa*
that.NOM liked Eyólf-DAT badly
'Eyólf did not like it at all' (Ljósvetninga saga) (= 43a)
c. *Det lika Eyolf dårleg*
that liked Eyolf badly
'Eyolf did not like that at all'
d. *sá kostr líka-r mér vel*
that.NOM choice like-3SG me.DAT well
'I like those terms' (Fóstbrøðra saga) (= 43b)
e. *Det vilkåret likar eg godt*
that term like I.NOM good
'I like those terms very well'

In Icelandic (and Faroese) basically the same development took place. SpecIP was specialized as a subject position, but the case system remained more or less intact. The syntax of modern Icelandic is very similar to that of a typically analytic language, but the synthetic type morphology has been maintained. As a consequence, a potential oblique subject in SpecIP was reanalyzed as a subject, and acquired syntactic subject properties, without losing its oblique case marking. This led to a change in the inventory of possible surface structures in Icelandic, and it is precisely this new inventory that justifies the use of the notion of oblique subject in that language.

Exactly when this happened, is of course impossible to determine. The language generally referred to as Old Icelandic, or Old Norse, was spoken for about seven centuries over an area stretching from Norway to Greenland. What is usually called classical Old Icelandic, the language of the sagas, is assumed to represent the language in Iceland of the 13th century. This language is remarkably uniform, but it is hardly surprising that it may show some variation pointing towards the subsequent development into Modern Icelandic.

Notes

* Thanks are due to Trygve Skomedal and Kristian Emil Kristoffersen for suggestions and comments to an earlier version of this paper.

1. In the Old Icelandic examples I use the standardized Old Norse spelling regardless of the spelling used in the sources quoted.

2. Trygve Skomedal (p.c.) wants to analyze *kveðjast* as some kind of an auxiliary verb, whereby all the NP arguments in the sentence still get their case and theta-role from the embedded (main) verb. On such an analysis, the initial dative phrase has the same function in (11) as it would in the corresponding sentence without the auxiliary: *þat þykkir mér illt*, and the arguments for or against its subjecthood would be the same.

3. Holmberg & Platzack (1995: 115) argue that SpecIP is an A position in Modern Icelandic, while Rögnvaldsson & Thráinsson (1990) argue that SpecIP may be used as a landing site for A-bar movement, as is obviously the case in Old Icelandic.

4. Similar AcI constructions are found in Latin, where they can even serve as subjects.

Ionia-m   in servitute Pers-arum   esse   probr-um   est
Ionia-ACC in slavery   Persian.PL.GEN be.INF disgraceful.NEUT.NOM is
'That Ionia is under Persian slavery is disgraceful'

This makes it even less likely that the accusative is assigned by a governor in the matrix sentence (for a possible solution, see Faarlund 1995).

5. Nygaard (1905) quotes only two examples from what he terms "popular style". Then he has a few more examples from "learned style", most of which involve matrix verbs that do not usually take an Accusative with Infinitive in the popular style, e.g.

kenn-i   mað-r$_i$ sik$_i$ svá   haf-a   ást   gud-s
know-SUBJ man-NOM himself.ACC thus have-INF love.ACC god-GEN
'May man know that he thus has the love of God' (Norwegian Book of Homilies)

Nygaard's definitions of the two styles in question are as follows:

Den folkelige stil har sit forbillede i den daglige tale og det mundtlige foredrag, saaledes som dette havde udviklet sig i offentlig forhandling og i sagamændenes fortælling. Den lærde stil følger i en viss udstrækning, tildels paa en paafaldende maade, analogier fra fremmed sprogbrug, især fra latin. [The popular style is patterned on everyday speech and oral performance, the way it had developed in public affairs and in the narratives of the saga men. The learned style follows to some extent, partly in a remarkable way, analogies from foreign usage, especially from Latin.] (Nygaard 1905: 1)

References

Barðdal, J. 1999. "Argument structure, syntactic structure and morphological case of the impersonal construction in the history of Scandinavian". *Scripta Islandica* 1–13.
Barðdal, J. 2000. "Oblique subjects in Old Scandinavian". *NOWELE* 37: 25–51.

Christoffersen, M. 1993. *Setning og sammenheng. Syntaktiske studier i Magnus Lagabøters landslov.* Kristiansand: Agder distriktshøgskule.

Cole, P., Harbert, W., Hermon, G., and Sridhar, S. N. 1980. "The acquisition of subjecthood". *Language* 56: 719–743.

Faarlund, J. T. 1990. *Syntactic Change. Toward a theory of historical syntax.* Berlin: Mouton de Gruyter.

Faarlund, J. T. 1991. "The unaccusative hypothesis and configurationality". In *Papers from the 27 Annual Regional Meeting of the Chicago Linguistic Society,* L. Dobrin et al. (eds), 141–154. Chicago: Chicago Linguistic Society.

Faarlund, J. T. 1992. *Norsk syntaks i funksjonelt perspektiv.* Oslo, Bergen, Tromsø: Universitetsforlaget.

Faarlund, J. T. 1995. "Diachrony, typology, and universal grammar: From 'Classical' European to Modern Western European". In *Papers from the 31st Annual Regional Meeting of the Chicago Linguistic Society,* A. Dainora et al. (eds), 153–170. Chicago: Chicago Linguistic Society.

Faarlund, J. T. 1998. "L'actance des langues germaniques". In *Actance et valence dans les langues de l'Europe. Empirical Approaches to Language Typology.* J. Feuillet (ed.), 789–809. Berlin: Mouton de Gruyter.

Faarlund, J. T. (Forthcoming). "From ancient Germanic to modern Germanic languages". In *Language Typology and Language Universals,* M. Haspelmath et al. (eds). Berlin: Mouton de Gruyter [Handbooks of Linguistics and Communication Science].

Falk, C. 1997. *Fornsvenska upplevarverb.* Lund: Lund University Press.

Haegeman, L. 1994. *Introduction to Government and Binding Theory.* 2nd edition. Oxford and Cambridge, Mass.: Blackwell.

Holmberg, A. and Platzack, C. 1995. *The Role of Inflection in Scandinavian Syntax.* Oxford: OUP.

Haugan, J. 1998. "Passiv av norrøne dobbelt objekt-konstruksjonar og subjektsprørsmålet". *Norsk Lingvistisk Tidsskrift* 16: 157–184.

Haugan, J. 2000. *Old Norse Word Order and Information Structure.* Trondheim: NTNU.

Jónsson, F. 1932. *Flóamannasaga.* København: Samfund til udgivelse af gammel nordisk litteratur.

Juntune, T. W. 1992. "Subject and reflexive in Old Icelandic". In *Recent Developments in Germanic Linguistics,* R. Lippi-Green (ed.), 69–79. Amsterdam: John Benjamins.

Jørgensen, J. G. 1998. "Om verdien av sagaavskrifter fra 1600-tallet". *Collegium Medievale,* 175–192.

Keenan, E. L. 1976. "Towards a universal definition of 'subject'". In *Subject and Topic,* C. N. Li (ed.), 303–333. New York: Academic Press.

Kristoffersen, K. E. 1994. "Passiv i norrønt og nyislandsk — ei samanlikning". *Norsk Lingvistisk Tidsskrift* 12: 43–69.

Kristoffersen, K. E. 1996. *Infinitival phrases in Old Norse. Aspects of their syntax and semantics.* Oslo: University of Oslo.

Mørck, E. 1992. "Subjektets kasus i norrønt og mellomnorsk". *Arkiv för nordisk filologi* 107: 53–99.

Nygaard, M. 1905. *Norrøn syntax.* Oslo: Aschehoug.

Perlmutter, D. M. 1978. "Impersonal passives and the unaccusative hypothesis". In *Proceedings of the Fourth Annual Meeting of the Berkeley Linguistic Society*, J. J. Jaeger et al. (eds), 157–189. Berkeley: Department of Linguistics, University of California.
Rögnvaldsson, E. 1991. "Quirky subjects in Old Icelandic". In *Papers from the twelfth Scandinavian conference of linguistics*, H. Á. Sigurðsson (ed.), 369–78. Reykjavík: University of Iceland.
Rögnvaldsson, E. 1995. "Old Icelandic: A non-configurational language?" *NOWELE* 26: 3–29.
Rögnvaldsson, E. 1996. "Frumlag og fall að fornu". *Íslenskt mál og allmenn málfræði* 18: 37–69.
Rögnvaldsson, E. and Thráinsson, H. 1990. "On Icelandic word order once more". In *Modern Icelandic Syntax*. J. Maling and A. Zaenen (eds), 3–40. San Diego: Academic Press [Syntax and Semantics 24].
Sigurdsson, H.Á. 1992. "The case of quirky subjects". *Working Papers in Scandinavian Syntax* 49: 1–26.
Stowell, T. 1981. *Origins of Phrase Structure*. Cambridge, MA.: MIT.
Thráinsson, H. 1994. "Icelandic". In *The Germanic Languages*, E. König and J. van der Auwera (eds), 142–189. London: Routledge.
Vigfusson, G. 1878. *Sturlunga Saga*. Oxford: The Clarendon Press.
Zaenen, A., Maling, J., and Thráinsson, H. 1985. "Case and grammatical functions: The Icelandic passive". *Natural Language and Linguistic Theory* 3: 441–483.

Towards personal subjects in English
Variation in feature interpretability*

Elly van Gelderen

> The paper examines the well-known change from impersonal to personal subject from the point of view of a slight person split in Old and Early Middle English: third person pronouns remain impersonal longer than first or second person. This split is shown to be linked to the different rates of disappearance of morphological Case in the first, second, and third person paradigm by arguing that the change from impersonal to personal involves the loss of inherent/lexical/semantic Case and the introduction of structural Case. Both changes are indicative of a larger typological change from synthetic to analytic, which can be seen as a change from Interpretable to Uninterpretable features.

1. Introduction

It is well-known that Old and Middle English have impersonal constructions, where the highest thematic argument, in this instance the Experiencer, is not assigned nominative Case. One could also refer to these as morphologically ergative constructions. The traditional account (e.g. van der Gaaf 1904; Jespersen 1894; Lightfoot 1979) is that, due to the decline of Case marking in Middle English, the Experiencer is reanalysed as Agent, with a nominative rather than a dative Case. This change coincides with changes that rigidify the word order, e.g. the introduction of modal auxiliaries. The two changes are related and, in this paper, I account for both in terms of changes affecting the features. The focus is on syntactic ramifications of the reanalysis of Experiencer to Agent, namely the activation of the Spec IP to check Case.

Sections 2, 3, 4.1, and 5 are written from a (more or less) theory-neutral perspective; 4.2 uses a Minimalist account. In 2, the data are described in detail for *Beowulf*, an Old English text, and in 3, a person split is argued for. In 4, I present an account in terms of Minimalist features, and in 5, changes in the Middle English situation are examined.

2. Impersonal, possessive, and passive

Constructions such as (1) are numerous, as is well-known (cf. Jespersen 1894, Van der Gaaf 1904, McCawley 1976, Lightfoot 1979, Fischer & van der Leek 1983, von Seefranz-Montag 1983, and Allen 1995 to name but a few). As Denison (1993) mentions, there is a lot of confusion around the term 'impersonal'. I will use it for those constructions where the 'highest' argument (on a thematic hierarchy such as Causer > Agent > Experiencer > Location > Theme) does not have nominative Case. This highest argument may be a person, animate, or inanimate, and hence, the term 'impersonal' is not a very good one but used for convenience. To give an idea of the variety, I list a few of the impersonals in *Beowulf*. The glosses indicate number and Case only when relevant to determining subjecthood:

(1) Beo 687
   swa him gemet þince
   so him find thing
   'as he sees fit'.

(2) Beo 1252
   swa him ful oft gelamp
   as them very often happened-S
   'as happened to them often'.

(3) Beo 1718–9
   hwæþere him on ferhþe greow / breostord blodreow
   however, him on spirit grew thought cruel[1]
   'However, cruel thoughts came to his mind'.

(4) Beo 1736–7
   ne him inwitsorh / on sefan sweorceð
   not him sorrow on mind darkens
   'sorrow does not darken his mind'.

(5) Beo 1878–9
ac him on hreþre hygebendum fæst / æfter deorum men dyrne
but him in heart/mind heart-strings constant after dear man much
langað
longs
'but he longs much for the dear one in his heart/mind held by his heart-strings'.

(6) Beo 2043
him bið grim sefa
him be bitter hart
'he will be angry'.

The question now arises whether or not the impersonal subject is a real subject. In none of the sentences from *Beowulf* does the impersonal subject trigger verbal agreement. Thus, in (2) above, (7), and (8), the verb is singular even though the impersonal subject is plural:

(7) Beo 1921
næs him feor þanon
not-was.SG them far from-there
'they would not have to go far'.

(8) Beo 1103
þa him swa geþearfod wæs
which/though them need was-SG
'which they were of necessity forced to do'.

The verb sometimes agrees with the 'object', as is shown in (9):

(9) Beo 639
Þam wife þa word wel licodon
the-DAT woman-DAT the-NOM words well like-P
'The woman liked those words', or 'Those words were pleasing to the woman'.

Faarlund (this volume) uses a number of criteria to show that Old Icelandic does not have an oblique subject whereas Modern Icelandic does, for instance, subject raising, long distance reflexives controlled by the impersonal subject, coordinate reduction. The sentences above and below display none of those characteristics. Reflexives are not available and, in English, are not necessarily subject controlled. Coordinate reduction is often claimed to occur with the impersonal controlling the deleted subject, but checking all instances of impersonals in *Beowulf*, I find no convincing ones. The possible candidates are (10), (11), (12) and (13):

(10) Beo 2098–2100
   hwæþre him sio swiðre swaðe   weardade / hand on Hiorte ond he
   whether him the right   remained behind   hand in Heorot and he
   hean   ðonan / modes geomor meregrund   gefeoll
   wretched thence mood sad   lake-bottom fell
   'However, his right hand remained in Heorot and he threw himself in the lake'.

(11) Beo 755
   Hyge   wæs him hinfus   wolde on heolster   fleon
   heart/courage was him ready (to depart) wanted to hiding-place flee
   'He lost his courage and wanted to flee'.

(12) Beo 1876–80
   [W]æs him   se man   to þon leof ... / ac him   on hreþre   hygebendum fæst /   æfter deorum men dyrne langað
   was him-DAT the man-NOM to that dear   but him-DAT in heart/mind heart-strings constant after dear   man much longs
   beorn wið blode.
   'He held the man so dear ... but he longs much for the dear one in his heart/mind held by his heart-strings'.

(13) Beo 2180–1
   næs   him   hreoh sefa / ac he   mancynnes mæste
   not-was him-DAT angry   heart but he-NOM mankind's   highest
   cræfte
   power-DAT
   'he was not angry but he with mankind's highest power ...'

In (10), *he* is not deleted but would have resulted in coordination reduction controlled by the impersonal. Deletion would not have violated alliteration. In (11), the subject of *wolde* has been left out but one cannot tell whether that is under identity with *him* or because a pronoun has been left out (Old English has pro-drop, see van Gelderen 2000). In (12), an impersonal subject is repeated after *ac*, and (13) is like (10). Hence, the impersonal subject need not be in Spec IP. The one strange fact is (14), where the modifying *self* is inflected for nominative, not dative, which would be *selfan*:

(14) Beo 1839
   þæm   þe him   selfa   deah
   him-DAT that him-DAT self-NOM is capable
   'who himself is a capable person'.

This may suggest *him* is in Spec IP with dative Case with *selfa* getting nominative.

Possessives, as in (3) and (4) above and (15), are similar to experiencer constructions, since the possessor is higher on the thematic hierarchy than the Theme and has dative Case. They are therefore included with impersonals, even though the term ergative would be better here. From Old to Middle English, there is change away from a use of the verb *to be* towards the verb *to have*. Hence, constructions such as (15) become (16):

(15) Beo 1873
 Him wæs bega   wen
 him was both-GEN probable
 'He thought both possible'.

(16) Beo 3000
 ðæs   ðe   ic wen   hafo
 that-GEN that I belief have
 'therefore I believe'.

As mentioned, constructions such as (1) to (15) are often referred to as impersonals, or psych-verbs as in Belletti & Rizzi (1988). I will not argue in favor of one division over the other (many have been suggested). Their experiencer subject, even though it is not marked nominative and does not agree with the verb, is said to be the subject. The dative Experiencer is thus the pivot (cf. Dixon 1994). Evidence for this is provided in Lightfoot (1979), namely the coordination facts, as in (17), where the second personal subject is deleted under identity with the preceding impersonal subject. (This argument of course crucially depends on whether or not Old and Middle English have pro-drop):

(17) Chaucer, CT A 785
 us thoughte it was noght worth to make it wys, And — granted him withouten moore avys
 'We did not consider it worthwhile to hold off, and granted him without more council'.

Allen (1986) develops this more and shows that subjects of the second conjunct are only freely deletable if the first occurrence is a nominative or a preposed dative. The data in *Beowulf* discussed above are inconclusive, however. In this paper, the main emphasis will not be on whether or not the impersonal is a real subject, but on the changes involving Case. For impersonal subjects, I assume the Case is theta-related, and not checked in Spec IP, but possibly moved there for other reasons. For personal subjects, Case is checked in a structural position, possibly Spec IP.

Apart from impersonals such as (1) to (14), and possessives such as (15) above, 'passives' such as (18) to (23) can be added as well since the highest argument is not assigned nominative. These are all the passives with *him* in *Beowulf* but *him* can be analysed as Experiencer:

(18) Beo 140
ða   him gebeacnod   wæs
which him indicated (by means of a sign) was
'which he was shown'.

(19) Beo 1192
Him wæs ful boren
him was cup carried
'He was brought a cup'.

(20) Beo 1269
þær him aglæca   ætgræpe wearð
here him monster grabbed became
'here he was grabbed by the monster'.

(21) Beo 2682
Him þæt gifeðe ne wæs (þæt...)
him that given not was
'He wasn't granted that'.

(22) Beo 2696
swa him gecynde wæs
so   him taught was
'as he had been taught'.

(23) Beo 2983
ða   him gerymed wearð-S
then them allowed were
'when they were allowed'.

In this section, I have provided examples of impersonal constructions in *Beowulf*. The evidence on whether they are real subjects, i.e. in Spec IP, is hard to come by and not the focus of this paper. What is important is that their Case is not related to Spec IP but to the theta-marking of the verb. In the next section, I show there is a person split, before going on to Case and an account of the changes.

3. Person split

As for the possessives and impersonals with third person, there are different ways of showing the person split: (a) the ratio of impersonally used first person pronouns out of all the dative first person instances as opposed to the same ratio with third person ones, and (b) the percentage of first person impersonals out of the total of first person personal subjects as opposed to the percentage of third person ones. Regarding (a), there is a total of 200 occurrences of singular and plural *him*, and 42 are used impersonally (=21%). Adding passives, 50 are used impersonally (=25%) with third person as opposed to 8 out of 65 (=12.3%) with first person singular and plural. The results are given in Table 1. Statistically, the difference between 1SG and 3SG (χ^2 is 5.342, $p<.05$), and between a combination of 1SG and 2SG versus 3SG (χ^2 12.018, $p<.001$) is significant, but not between 1SG and 2SG, which is expected. Only for third person is number statistically relevant. As can be seen, the percentages for plural are quite similar for the different persons. This means plural is changing before singular, but I will not go into that here.

Table 1. Impersonal versus personal uses of first, second and third person dative pronouns

	impersonal		personal	Total
1SG	7	(= 12.7%)	48	55
1PL	1	(= 10%)	9	10
2SG	3		41	44
2PL	1		5	6
3SG	47	(= 28%)	120	167
3PL	3	(= 9%)	30	33

Regarding (b), there is a total of 353 third person nominative pronouns (singular and plural; figures from Klaeber 1922), as compared to 50 impersonal ones (=14%). The total number of first person singular pronouns used in a personal construction is 181, as compared to 7 impersonal uses (=3.7%). Thus, first person is used less in an impersonal construction than third person is. The results are given in Table 2. The difference between 1SG and 3SG (χ^2 is 14.269, $p<.001$), and between 1SG/2SG versus 3SG (χ^2 17.285, $p<.001$) is significant, but, as above, again not between 1SG and 2SG. Again, only for third person is number statistically relevant:

Table 2. Impersonal dative versus personal nominative

	impersonal		nominative	Total
1SG	7	(= 3.7%)	181	188
1PL	1	(= 6.7%)	24	25
2SG	3		62	65
2PL	1		12	13
3SG	47	(= 14.3%)	282	329
3PL	3	(= 4%)	71	74

If Old and Middle English are changing into 'personal' languages, this slight person split is not unexpected and provides insight into the transition of languages from (somewhat) ergative to non-ergative, and perhaps explains why ergative languages often display a person split. The instances with first person are listed here, and their renderings in Modern English are interesting, in that most have become 'personal':

(24) Beo 316
Mæl is me to feran
time is me to go
'I have to go'.

(25) Beo 473
Sorh is me to secganne on sefan minum
Grief is me to say   in heart my
'I am sorry to say'.

(26) Beo 1853–4
me þin   modsefa /   licað leng   swa wel, leofa Beowulf
me your spirit/character like longer so well dear Beowulf
'I like your character better and better, dear Beowulf'.

(27) Beo 2651
þæt me is micle leofre þæt ...
that me is much better
'That I had much rather'.

(28) Beo 2653
Ne þynceð me gerysne þæt ...
Not seems me right   that
'I don't think that is right'.

(29) Beo 555
hwæþre me gyfeþe wearð
whether me given was
'I was granted ...'.

(30) Beo 3088
þa   me gerymed wæs
which me was   cleared
'which for me was cleared'.

With second person plural *eow*, the total numbers are perhaps too small to have any significance. There is 1 impersonal, as in (31), out of a total of 6 occurrences with *eow*. The numbers are also small with first person plural (1 impersonal in 10):

(31) Beo 1987
Hu lomp   eow on lade, leofa Biowulf
how happened you on trip dear Beowulf
'How was your trip, dear Beowulf'?

These figures suggest that plurals change before singulars.

The second person singular has more instances and it patterns with the first singular in that the percentage of impersonally used ones is very low. Out of 44 instances of *þe*, 3 are impersonal (= 6.8%), as in (32):

(32) Beo 660
Ne bið þe wilna gad
not be you willing lack
'You shall lack nothing'.

There might be a slight number split as well. The number of plural impersonal constructions (sentences (2), (7) and (8) above) out of all plurals is 3 (i.e. 9%), whereas the number of singular impersonals is 47 (i.e. 28%). The plural specially marked accusative is also lost before the singular one, and in the next section I argue these are related. For instance, in *Beowulf*, of the 200 instances of 'him', 33 are plural and 167 are singular.

In other Old English texts, the split is similar, as I show in van Gelderen (2000). In conclusion, it can be argued that third person pronouns continue to appear in impersonal constructions longer than first or second person. In the next section, I will show that third person pronouns have morphological Case longer. NPs with thematic or inherent Case need not move to a Specifier of a functional category to check Case. Morphological Case is lost for third person in Early Middle English. The two texts that have third person morphological Case are *The History of the Holy Rood Tree* and Layamon. In these the person split continues somewhat, but it does not continue in the later Middle English texts such as *Gawain* and Chaucer that lack a morphological distinction between dative and accusative, and that have evidence for overt functional categories such as I(nflection), where nominative can be checked.

4. Account

In 4.1, I argue that Old English has morphological Case. Hence, impersonal constructions are not unexpected since these involve NPs with Case based on the theta-role of Experiencer. The person split is also not unexpected since morphological Case first disappears on first and second person pronouns. In 4.2, I argue such a person split can be accounted for in a Minimalist framework if one argues that morphological Case is Interpretable, and that cross-linguistic variation is caused by the difference in Interpretability of features.

4.1 Morphological Case and the person split

Old English is a synthetic language: grammatical relations are indicated through both agreement and Case. As expected in a synthetic language, pronominal subjects (and objects) are more optional, auxiliaries are rare, prepositions are mainly spatial and temporal, and subordination is not as common as in Modern English. As the inflection disappears, grammatical relations become encoded through word order and through the use of auxiliaries and prepositions.

One way of looking at the change towards an analytic language is as a change from morphological to structural licensing, as in e.g. Kiparsky (1994; 1995). Morphological Case is theta-related (e.g. a Goal or Experiencer is assigned dative Case), distinguishes between a number of different Cases through endings, and is not lost after movement. Chomsky (1986: 193) puts it in the following way: "[w]e distinguish the 'structural Cases' objective and nominative, assigned in terms of S-structure position, from the 'inherent Cases' assigned at D-structure ... Inherent Case is associated with [theta]-marking, while structural Case is not". Rather than use the term inherent Case, I will refer to this as theta-related or morphological Case.

The German dative is an instance of morphological Case. German distinguishes between nominative, genitive, dative, and accusative. Dative and genitive

Case are assigned to objects depending on the theta-roles of the objects. Once the morphological Case is assigned, the NP can move without losing the Case (possibly to Spec CP in (34)). For example, *helfen* 'help', as in (33), assigns a dative to its object that has a Goal theta-role (cf. Haider 1985, who uses the term 'lexical Case'). In these cases, passivization retains the dative Case, as (34) shows:

(33) *Sie hilft ihm*
she-NOM helps him-DAT
'She helps him'.

(34) *Ihm/*er wurde geholfen*
him-DAT/he-NOM was helped
'He was helped'.

Thus, morphological Case is assumed if a language distinguishes morphologically between the different Cases. In Old English, this is certainly so. Instances of some of these in *Beowulf* are the accusatives *mec* and *þec*, dependent on *niman* 'take' in (35), and *oferswyðan* 'overpower' in (36); the datives *me* and *þe*, in (24) and (32) above; the dative *him* in (15), and the accusative *hine* in (37):

(35) Beowulf 447
gif mec   deað nimeð
if me-ACC death takes
'If death seizes me'.

(36) Beowulf 1768
þæt ðec   dryhtguma   deaþ oferswiþeþ
that you-ACC mighty-ruler death overpowers
'that death overpowers you, mighty ruler'.

(37) Beo 1799
Reste hine þa rumheort
rested him the big-heart
'The big-hearted one rested himself'.

Old English third person pronouns distinguish between nominative, genitive, dative, and accusative, but first and second person dative and accusative forms merge quite early on. In *Beowulf*, an early text, the first and second person singular specially marked accusative forms *mec* and *þec* occur somewhat frequently. There are 55 instances of *me* and 16 of *mec* (hence, 22% of the total number of accusative and dative pronouns is the specially marked accusative); and 44 instances of *þe* and 8 of *þec* (=15%). However, these forms are restricted in that they occur with a very limited set of verbs: for instance, *mec* occurs with *nyman* 'take', as in (35), 6 times. Instances of the specially marked third person are more frequent. There are 200 instances of *him* (1 of *hym*), of which 167 are masculine singular dative (cf. Klaeber's glossary), and 73 of *hine/hyne* (=30%) which are masculine singular accusative. First and second person plural are disappearing: there are 4 accusative first person plurals (against 13 dative ones) and 2 second person accusatives (against 10 datives). Therefore, first and second person accusative forms stop appearing (putting the numbers of first and second together and comparing them with third, the difference is statistically relevant), with the second person being less frequent than the first.

Apart from different morphological forms, a second piece of evidence for the presence of morphological Case is that Case is related to the theta-role of a verb as in Chomsky (1986:193). Thus, in (38) to (41), objects such as *þæm feonde*, *him*, and *sæmannum* are dative because verbs such as *ætwendan* 'escape', *forscrifan* 'proscribe', and *onsacan* 'strive against' assign Goal theta-roles (cf. Visser 1963; Mitchell 1985 for lists with genitive, dative, and accusative objects):

(38) Beo 143
se   þæm   feonde   ætwand
who-NOM the-DAT enemy-DAT escaped
'he who had escaped the enemy'. (Visser 284)

(39) Beo 106
siþðan him scyppend forscrifen hæfde
since him creator banned had
'since the creator had banned him'. (Visser 292)

(40) Beo 2353
ond æt guðe   forgrap Grendeles   mægum
and at battle [he] seized Gendel-GEN kinsmen-DAT
'and he crushed Grendel's kinsmen to death in battle'.

(41) Beo 2954
þæt he sæ-mannum onsacan   mihte
that he sailors-DAT strive-against might
'that he might strive against the sailors'. (Visser 395)

A third piece of evidence for morphological Case is that, as in the German (34), Case in Old English does not depend on a structural position. Impersonal constructions are good examples of that. They have dative Case on the basis of their Experiencer theta-role, but need not be in a particular position to check this Case. There are other constructions, generally analysed as passives that I will also analyse as having Experiencers. Unlike in Modern English, passives occur where the Experiencer bears a dative Case, as in (18) to (23) above (Note that it is sometimes hard to determine if the participle is an adjective or a verb). Second, the passives that appear to be the same as those in Modern English, e.g. (42), can in fact be argued not to be derived from an active construction:

(42) Beo 1539
þa he gebolgen wæs
then he angered was
'then he became angry'.

The occurrence of passives such as (18) above indicates that morphological Case, and not structural objective Case, is assigned to the object since the Case is not dependent on the structural position of an element, in this case the subject position, but on the thematic relationship. The dative marked NP seems to bear an Experiencer theta-role, in the same way as in the constructions discussed in this paper. Not much hinges on analyzing them this way though.

So far, I have shown what is meant by morphological Case and have argued that Old English has this. The person split discussed in Section 3 can be accounted for since Case distinctions, i.e. morphological Case, with first and second person pronouns disappear before third person ones.

4.2 Interpretability: Morphological vs. structural Case

I now turn to structural Case which is independent of theta-relations, and is checked in certain structural positions. For instance, in Modern English, Case, tense, and agreement features are present in functional categories such as I(nflection) and must be checked through movement of NPs and V to I (cf. Chomsky 1995; etc). For instance, in (43), *she* checks its Case with the (finite) I, and *has* checks its tense and agreement features in I (the Case of *Bela* and inflection on *been* are ignored here):

(43)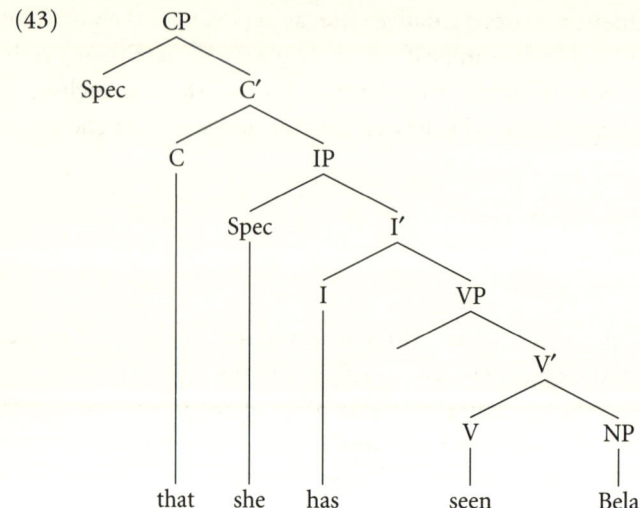

This checking accounts for the rigidity in word order. At the time that morphological Case disappears (in Early Middle English), auxiliaries and infinitival markers appear (cf. van Gelderen 1993) that activate the functional category where both Case and agreement are checked, namely the IP (or the expanded IP, as in Pollock 1989). Modals such as *may*, *do*, and *to* are argued to be in I (cf. Akmajian, Steele & Wasow 1979). Once the I is introduced, it can then be used for checking, as long as the features are Uninterpretable. The position also becomes obligatory and if an NP is not present, it needs to be filled with pleonastic *it* or *there*. Before the activation of the IP in Middle English, Case was either related to theta-roles, or assigned under government by C (see Platzack & Holmberg 1989: 44 for this claim in other languages; van Gelderen 1997: 56).

In a Chomsky (1995) framework, I argue that both the change in Case, from morphological to structural, and the introduction of (checking in the) IP can be seen in terms of a change where Interpretable features become Uninterpretable ones. There are two levels in a syntactic derivation: the PF representation gives information to the Articulatory-Perceptual system and the LF one to the Conceptual-Intentional system. Legibility must be ensured at these interface levels (Chomsky 1998: 119). Features are therefore divided as to whether they are phonetic, i.e. not allowed at LF, or semantic, i.e. not allowed at PF. Thus, a derivation splits into two parts, one part going to LF and one part to PF. There are, however, features in language that are neither phonetic nor semantic, thereby violating legibility. These features are Uninterpretable and do not "enter into interpretation at LF" (Chomsky 1995:277); they exist "to force movement, sometimes overtly" (p. 278) to a higher functional category.

Uninterpretable features trigger movement but Interpretable ones do not. Interpretable features are relevant at LF and do not erase or delete but can be 'used over'. Uninterpretable features explain several phenomena treated as separate before the introduction of the Minimalist framework; for instance, (a) an NP has one and only one Uninterpretable Case feature, and (b) the features justify the inclusion of functional categories such as IP in the numeration to enable checking. In the generative framework, movement has always been seen as problematic. As Chomsky (1998:42) puts it, "[w]hy language should have this [movement] property is an interesting question, which has been discussed for almost 40 years without resolution". Verbal agreement and Case are problematic as well since they are not relevant to the interpretation in Modern English. Chomsky (1998:42–8) proposes to connect both of these problems: the 'offending' Uninterpretable Case and agreement are eliminated through movement.

Case in Modern English (43) is Uninterpretable but, as seen in the previous section, Case in Old English is not dependent on a structural position. That is why it can be assumed to be Interpretable; it is related to the meaning of the verb and related to its theta-role. As a result, functional categories play less of a role in Old English. Languages can differ as to whether their features are Interpretable or not. I next give another example of feature variation.

According to Chomsky (1995:283), the person and number, i.e. φ-, features of Nouns are Interpretable because they can be reused, i.e. used twice in checking. The example given by Chomsky is (44) where *John* moves to the subject of the IP to check its Case, checking φ-features along the way:

(44)   John is [*t* Agr [*t* intelligent]].

However, in (44), there is no agreement between *intelligent* and *John*, and Agr may not have been activated. Thus, there is no empirical evidence that the φ-features are Interpretable. In languages other than English, there is such evidence since the number features appear twice, both on the verb and on the adjective or past participle. An instance is French where the number features in (45) appear on both the finite verb *sont* 'are-3PL' and the past participle *parties* 'left-FP'. The person features are only marked on the finite verb and the gender features only on the past participle:

(45)   *Les femmes sont   parties*
         the women are-3PL left-FP
         'The women have left'.

Thus, it can be argued that languages and different stages of the same language differ as to which features are Interpretable. In Modern English, Case features and the person and number features of verbs are Uninterpretable. In other languages, number features on nominals are Interpretable, but not person, and so on. Structural Case features are Uninterpretable in Modern English but Interpretable in Old English. The status of features ultimately accounts for differences in word order, Case and agreement across languages, and for whether a language is synthetic or analytic.

The change from impersonal constructions to personal ones can be accounted for in terms of a change from Interpretable (i.e. morphological) to Uninterpretable (i.e. structural) Case. I limit myself to impersonal pronominal subjects. The subject of the 'impersonal' construction has Interpretable features in Old English but Uninterpretable ones in Middle English. I show that different person and number features change at different paces. This is not unexpected and can be seen in a number of other phenomena as well, e.g. reflexives, agreement, and pro-drop (cf. van Gelderen 1999a,b, 2000).

5. Early Middle English: The demise of the person split and the introduction of structural Case

If the person split in impersonal constructions is due to third person pronouns retaining morphological Case longer, there should be a correlation between finding a person split and the presence of both dative and accusative third person pronouns, and no split and the absence of both dative and accusative. This is indeed the case: Layamon is a good instance of the former whereas Chaucer is of the latter. For instance, especially in the earlier version of Layamon's *Brut* (10th century), *hine* 'him-ACC' as in (46) is quite frequent, but this often disappears in the later version, as (47) shows:

(46) Caligula 2442
7 hine fæire on-feng
'and received him heartily'.

(47) Otho, idem
and onderfeng him deore.
'and received him well'.

In Chaucer, *hine* has disappeared. Above, I have also claimed that there is a relationship between structural Case and checking in functional categories.

Again Layamon and Chaucer are good examples: in Layamon, there is little evidence for an overt IP whereas in Chaucer there is. First, I will examine the person split.

The person split continues up to Early Middle English and is found in Layamon's *Brut* (13th century). In the first 6000 lines of the Caligula version of Layamon, there are 137 instances of impersonal *him*, as in (48) to (50), out of a total of 534 occurrences of *him* (= 26%), whereas there are 26 instances of impersonal *me* out of a total of 194 (= 13.4%):[2]

(48) Caligula 4
 sel þar him þuhte
 splendid there he thought
 'Splendid it seemed to him'.

(49) Caligula 6
 Hit com him on mode
 it came him on mind
 'It came to his mind'.

(50) Caligula 161
 Wa wes him on liue
 woe was him in life
 'He was anguished in life'.

So, since Layamon's Caligula version has morphological Case with third person, as (46) shows, one expects a construction that uses it more with third person. This is indeed the case. Also expected is an absence of evidence for an overt IP and for checking of nominative in I (instead of in C). The evidence for the absence of I is the behavior of modals as main verbs, absence of 'dummy' *do*, dependence of *to* on the infinitive (see van Gelderen 1993), and the absence of clear pleonastic subjects such as *there* indicating that Spec IP need not be filled (see van Gelderen 1997:95). Hence, Layamon is still C-oriented, rather than I-oriented.

The person split is lost in the 13th century. This correlates with the loss of morphological Case and the introduction of overt elements in functional categories such as I. In *Gawain and the Green Knight*, Chaucer, and Gower, both the split and separate dative and accusative forms are absent. For instance, in the first 7000 lines of the *Canterbury Tales*, 30 of the roughly 250 instances of *me* are impersonal (=12%) and 35 of the 320 instances of *him* are impersonal (=11%). In Gower's *Confessio Amantis* (1390s), there are 96 instances of *me* and 16 are used impersonally (=17%) and the numbers are roughly the same for *him*, where 40 impersonals appear out of a total of 220 (=18%). Neither the difference in Chaucer nor that in Gower is significant, as expected if the split has disappeared.

The loss of morphological Case goes hand in hand with the introduction of an I-position. The evidence for the use of an I is the appearance of sentences such as (51) and (52) in the late 14th century. In (51), *do* occupies I and in (52), an expletive *there* appears in Spec IP:

(51) Reeve's Tale, I, 4025
what do ye heer?

(52) Knight's Tale, I, 2043
And over his heed ther shynen two figures

Since the dative in Old and Early Middle English is optionally assigned to the Experiencer (cf. Belletti 1988) and since it is assigned on the basis of a theta-role (Experiencer) rather than of a particular structural position, it is morphological. In terms of Minimalist features, the optionality means they are Interpretable and need not be deleted by LF, at least as features of the nominal expression. As structural Case is introduced in the 13th century, these Case features become Uninterpretable and must be checked in a higher functional category, such as C or I.[3]

The loss of the specially marked accusative forms, such as *mec* 'me-ACC' and *þec* 'you.SG-ACC', is indicative of the loss of morphological Case. The latter forms disappear earlier (by the 13th century) than the ones for third person such as *hine* 'him-ACC'. As mentioned, in *Beowulf*, first and second person specially marked accusative forms, such as *mec* and *þec*, are not as frequent in relation to dative forms as third person ones are. There are 55 instances of *me* and 16 of *mec* (=23%); 167 instances of *him* (1 of *hym*) and 73 of *hine/hyne* (=30%). First person accusatives may already be weaker (not in statistically relevant ways though). The first and second person ones disappear throughout Old English. In Caligula, *hine* is still quite strong. The absolute numbers of singular third person masculines are 1235 instances of *him* and 682 of *hine* in Caligula, but the special first and second person pronoun forms have disappeared. In *Gawain and the Green Knight*, Chaucer, and Gower, *hine* ceases to occur and so do first and second person special forms. In Old and Early Middle English, the demise of impersonals and the loss of morphological Case are related because, in both cases, first and second person pronouns are the first to experience the loss.

6. Conclusion

In conclusion, I argue that Old and Early Middle English have impersonal constructions that display a (slight) person split. Thus, third person is more likely to appear in morphologically Case marked positions. In a Minimalist framework, this means third person Case remains Interpretable longer. The same person split occurs in the loss of the specially marked accusative/dative forms. The split is accounted for if first and second person pronouns lose morphological Case before third person ones do. This loss is shown in both their morphology and in their function as 'ergative' subject. With the introduction of an IP, it becomes possible to check Case in the Spec of IP.

The data discussed in this paper present some challenges for 'traditional' Minimalism. How can one deal with tendencies? The change is not absolute and takes several centuries to complete. One can argue that words such as *me* 'me-DAT' were in the lexicon with Interpretable and Uninterpretable Case. Forms such as *mec* 'me-ACC' were only Interpretable. Interpretable features need not be checked in functional categories. As morphological Case disappears, functional categories are added. Thus, in Minimalist framework, the main difference between synthetic and analytic languages is that (53) can be understood in the latter but not in the former:

(53) Him saw me

Notes

* Many different hierarchies have been suggested and, in some (cf. e.g. Dixon 1994: 6–7), thematic roles are not seen as primitives but as related to event structure. As in Pesetsky (1995), I assume that the theta-role of the subject of verbs such as *annoy* and *worry* is Causer, and hence, their appearance in the subject position rather than the Experiencer:

i. That argument annoyed him.

1. In both (3) and (4), I assume that possessor raising renders *him* into an argument and *on ferhþe* and *on sefan* into adverbials.

2. The difference between ergative use of *him* and of *me* is significant ($p < .001$). Adding 270 instances of *hine*, the percentage would be 17% and the difference would no longer be statistically significant.

3. Cf. Rice & Saxon (1995) for a similar idea in Athabascan languages. Mahajan (1997:47) mentions the person split in certain languages and argues that those "will require some mechanism by which P assignment is blocked ... when the subject is a 1PL/2PL pronoun". In a note he suggests that first and second persons are 'higher' than third persons.

References

Akmajian, A, Steele, S. and Wasow, T, 1979. "The Category of AUX in Universal Grammar". *Linguistic Inquiry* 10.1: 1–64.
Allen, C. 1986. "Reconsidering the history of *like*". *Journal of Linguistics* 22: 375–409.
Allen, C. 1995. *Case Marking and Reanalysis*. Oxford: OUP.
Belletti, A.1988. "The case of unaccusatives". *Linguistic Inquiry* 19(1): 1–34.
Belletti, A. and Rizzi, L. 1988. "Psych-verbs and è-Theory". *Natural Language and Linguistic Theory* 6: 291–352.
Chomsky, N. 1986. *Knowledge of Language*. New York: Praeger.
Chomsky, N. 1995. "Categories and transformations". In *The Minimalist Program*. Cambridge: MIT Press.
Chomsky, N. 1998. "Some observations on economy in generative grammar". In *Is the Best Good Enough?*, P. Barbosa, D. Fox et al. (eds), 115–127. Cambridge: MIT Press.
Denison, David 1993. *English Historical Syntax*. London: Longman..
Dixon, R. 1994. *Ergativity*. Cambridge: CUP.
Faarlund, J. T. This volume. "The notion of oblique subject and its status in the history of Icelandic".
Fischer, O. and Leek, F. van der. 1983. "The demise of the Old English impersonal construction". *Journal of Linguistics* 19: 337–68.
Gaaf, W. van der 1904. *The Transition from the Impersonal to the Personal Construction in Middle English*. Heidelberg: Carl Winter.
Gelderen, E. van 1993. *The Rise of Functional Categories*. Amsterdam: John Benjamins.
Gelderen, E. van 1997. *Verbal Agreement and the Grammar of its 'Breakdown'*. Tübingen: M. Niemeyer.
Gelderen, E. van 1999a. "Pronominals as anaphors in the history of English". In *Reflexives: Forms and functions*, Z. Frajzyngier (ed.). Amsterdam: John Benjamins.
Gelderen, E. van 1999b. "Binding theory and minimalist features". *WCCFL 18 Proceedings*.
Gelderen, E. van (2000). *A History of English Reflexives*. Amsterdam: John Benjamins.
Haider, H. 1985. "The case of German". In *Studies in German Grammar*, J. Toman (ed.), 65–101. Dordrecht: Foris.
Jespersen, O. 1894. *Progress in Language*. London: Allen & Unwin.
Kiparsky, P. 1994. "The rise of positional licensing in Germanic". Talk Amsterdam..
Kiparsky, P. 1995. "Indo-European origins of Germanic syntax". In *Clause Structure and Language Change*, A. Battye and I. Roberts (eds), 140–169. Oxford: OUP.
Klaeber, F. (ed.). 1922. *Beowulf*. Boston: D.C. Heath [1950 edition].
Lightfoot, D. 1979. *Principles of Diachronic Syntax*. Cambridge: CUP.
Mahajan, A. 1997. "Universal Grammar and the Typology of ergative languages". In *Universal Grammar and Typological Variation*, A. Alexiadou and T. Hall (eds), 35–57. Amsterdam: John Benjamins.
McCawley, N. 1976. "From OE/ME 'impersonal' to 'personal' constructions: What is a 'subject-less' S?". In *Papers on the Parasession on Diachronic Syntax*, 192–204. Chicago: CLS.
Mitchell, B. 1985. *Old English Grammar*. Oxford: OUP.

Pesetsky, D. 1995. *Zero Syntax*. Cambridge: MIT Press.
Platzack, C. and Holmberg, A. 1989. "The Role of AGR and Finiteness". *Working Papers in Scandinavian Syntax* 43: 51–76.
Pollock, J.-Y. 1989. "Verb movement, UG and the structure of IP". *Linguistic Inquiry* 20: 365–424.
Rice, K. and L. Saxon 1995. "The subject positions in Athapaskan languages". Unpublished ms.
Seefranz-Montag, A. von 1983. *Syntaktische Funktionen und Wortstellungsveränderung*. München: Wilhelm Fink Verlag.
Visser, F. 1963–1973. *An Historical Syntax of the English Grammar*. Vol I-IIIb. Leiden: Brill.

Focus and universal principles governing simplification of cleft structures*

Alice C. Harris

Harris and Campbell (1995: Chapter 7) propose specific universals governing processes that simplify biclausal structures, including the simplification of focus clefts to monoclausal focus constructions. In particular, it is claimed there that after a biclausal construction is reanalyzed as monoclausal, the main verb governs the syntax of the single-clause structure, even though conservative coding rules (e.g. case marking, agreement, word order) at first make it appear that the derived auxiliary governs those constituents that originated in its clause.

Since the writing of that book, another example has come to light. Synchronic data on the typology of focus in North East Caucasian (NEC) languages by Konstantine Kazenin (1994, 1995, 1996) provide the basis for the present study of diachronic development of biclausal and monoclausal focus structures in these languages and make it possible to test the claims referred to above. It is argued in the present paper that some NEC languages have a focus cleft and/or a monoclausal focus construction, historically derived from (1). It is shown that the derived monoclausal structures in various NEC languages have the range of properties predicted in Harris and Campbell (1995). Additional data show a different development of biclausal focus in Udi, a NEC language not treated by Kazenin.

1. Introduction

Harris and Campbell (1995) propose the following specific universals governing the simplification of focus clefts.

(1) *Stage I*: The structure continues to have all of the superficial characteristics of a biclausal structure and none of the characteristics of a monoclausal one.
Stage II: The structure has some characteristics of a biclausal structure and some characteristics of a monoclausal one.

Stage III: The structure has all of the characteristics of a monoclausal structure and no characteristics of a biclausal one.
(2) After reanalysis
    a. The two clauses of the cleft construction become a single clause in surface structure.
    b. The highlighted constituent is realized in the grammatical relation that the clefted constituent bore in the content clause in the input.
    c. A discourse marker [focus marker] is formed from some combination of (i) the copula, (ii) the relativizer, and the (iii) expletive pronoun.
Harris and Campbell (1995: 166–167)

Harris and Campbell (1995: 191–194) also propose more general universals governing all processes of simplifying biclausal structures, together with universals that interact with these processes. However, it seems to be more useful to examine the more specific universals cited in (1–2), which apply only to clefts.

Since Harris and Campbell (1995) was written, another example has come to my attention. Synchronic data on the typology of focus in North East Caucasian (NEC) languages by Konstantine Kazenin (1994, 1995) provide the basis for the present study of diachronic development of biclausal and monoclausal focus structures in these languages and make it possible to test the claims referred to above. Although some of the focus phenomena in the various NEC languages had been previously described (see especially Xajdakov 1986), traditional sources called focus by such terms as 'emphasis' and 'logical stress', making it impossible to identify it with the phenomenon now more commonly called focus. Work by Kazenin, together with work by Haspelmath (1993) on the Lezgi language, and my own on Udi (Harris 1996), has established the connection between the phenomenon widely referred to as focus and these phenomena in NEC languages.

The purpose of the present paper is to examine the NEC facts from a diachronic perspective to determine whether they support the universals proposed in Harris and Campbell (1995). I will show that the developments of focus in NEC languages do support the universals proposed in Harris and Campbell (1995).

Before I go on to the development of the focus cleft, I need to describe the NEC family and comment on the origins of the cleft construction in this family. A structured list of the members of the family is found in the appendix, and alternative names for some languages are listed in parentheses. Although it is agreed that Khinalug is a member of the family, there is doubt about its exact affiliation, though most believe it to be a member of the Lezgian subgroup. The existence of NEC as a family is widely accepted, though it has not yet been possible to develop a consensus on the sound system of PNEC and to reconstruct that language. In Nikolayev and Starostin (1994), it is proposed that the NEC family and the North West Caucasian family are daughters of a single ancestor. Although that theory has found support among some Russian linguists, most western linguists have found it unconvincing (see Nichols 1997; Schulze 1997). I therefore treat NEC as a family without further affiliations.

Although the focus cleft has been identified in a number of languages of the NEC family, it cannot be reconstructed to the proto-language (PNEC), both because still too little is known of the constructions in these languages, and because clefts are so easily borrowed. Thus, we must accept that at least the following possibilities exist: (i) that the cleft existed in PNEC and was inherited by many of the daughters, (ii) that after the break up of the family, the construction was borrowed from a contact language outside the family, such as Russian, Armenian, Azeri, a Kartvelian language, an Iranian language, or a member of the North West Caucasian (NWC) family, (iii) that the cleft was a development of one or more daughter languages and was subsequently borrowed from within the family, or (iv) that there was independent, parallel development of the focus cleft.

Lastly, it must be pointed out that neither Harris and Campbell (1995) nor the present paper claims that all focus constructions originate as clefts. This paper examines only those that clearly do so. Many of the NEC languages have a variety of means of marking focus, and it is by no means claimed here that all are reflexes of clefts.

I discuss the stages of change, (1), in Section 2 below and return to this in Section 3. In Section 2 I discuss the universals listed in (2).

2. Stages I–III

It is, of course, not surprising to find that NEC languages are at various stages from among those represented in (1). For example, on the basis of the data available, it appears that Chechen is at Stage I, that is, that no reanalysis has been made. Nichols (to appear) shows that Chechen has a focus cleft, (3b), but apparently it lacks monoclausal focus.

(3) a. ḣa   v-o:γ-i: txüöca? [Nichols, to appear]
       you.ABS CM-go-Q   us.INSTR
       'Are you going with us?'
   b. ḣa   v-u-j   txüöca   vo:γurg?
       you.ABS CM-is-Q   us.INSTR go.PART
       'Are you going with us?' 'Is it you [who are] going with us?'

Like other languages of the family, Chechen has ergative-absolutive case marking; that is, subjects of transitives are in the ergative case, while subjects of intransitives and direct objects are in the absolutive case. 'You' is in the absolutive case in (3a) because it is subject of the intransitive verb 'go'; in (3b) it is subject of 'be'. This structure is shown in (4).

(4) [$_S$ FocC$_i$ Copula-Agmt$_i$ [$_S$ ... Verb]]
       SUBJ   PARTICIPLE

(4) also indicates that the focused constituent (the FocC) conditions agreement on the copula. In the inherited agreement system, still retained by most of the languages, the verb agrees in gender-class with the nominal in the absolutive case; in (3b) this is represented as the *v-* prefix, glossed as CM. Universally, the embedded clause in the focus cleft has the structure of a relative clause, and in NEC languages the inherited structure for the expression of the relative clause involves a participle. We see the participle in *voγurg* in (3b), and we will see participles in the clefts of other languages of the family. Thus, following Nichols' analysis, Chechen has a focus cleft, and I assume that the structure has not been reanalyzed.[1]

For the expression of focus, literary Dargi has syntactic doublets — one construction at Stage I, and a second at Stage II. I begin with the Stage I construction, a focus cleft. Kazenin (1994) adduces the following sentences in his synchronic study.[2]

(5) a. x'o-ni   uzbi   arkul-ri[3]
       2SG-ERG   brothers.ABS bring.PAST-2SG
       'You brought the brothers.'
   b. x'o   sa-j-ri   uzbi   arku-si
       2SG.ABS   FM[COP-CM-2SG]   brothers.ABS bring-PART.SG
       'YOU brought the brothers.' 'It is YOU, having brought the brothers.'
   c. *uzbi x'o saj-ri arku-si

(5a) is a simple sentence without focus, while in (5b) 'you' has been focused.[4] (5b) has all the characteristics we would expect of a focus cleft: (i) The focused constituent, *x'o* 'you', is in the absolutive form (Xajdakov 1985:83), as is appropriate for the subject of the copula or for the predicate nominal. (ii) the copula *sa* 'be' agrees with *x'o* 'you' in person and number (*-ri*) and in gender-class (*-j*) as appropriate for its subject. (iii) the verb *arkusi* 'bring' is expressed as a participle, the inherited form used for relative clauses. (iv) The participle agrees with *x'o* 'you' in number (*-si*) as its head (e.g. Abdullaev 1971:87). (v) As Kazenin (1995) shows, *x'o sajri* 'you are, it is you' is a constituent, and *uzbi arkusi* 'brought [the] brothers' is a separate constituent. (5c) is ungrammatical because the former constituent cannot break up the latter.[5] The pattern represented by (5b) is thus at Stage I as a focus cleft.

In contrast, the other focus construction found in literary Dargi, (6), represents Stage II.

(6) b. *x'o-ni   sabi   uzbi   arku-si*   [Kazenin 1994, 1995]
2SG-ERG FM[COP] brothers bring-PART.SG
'YOU brought the brothers.'
 c. *uzbi   x'o-ni   sabi   arku-si*
brothers.ABS 2SG-ERG FM[COP] bring-PART.SG
'YOU brought the brothers.'

The cleft pattern of (5b) has been reanalyzed as a monoclausal structure, illustrated by (6); yet it retains some characteristics of its biclausal origins. I assume that it has the structure shown in (7).

(7) [$_S$ [$_{FP}$ FocC -FM] ...... Verb]
                          PART

Its monoclausal features include the following: (i) The focused constituent, *x'o-ni* 'you-ERG' is in the ergative case; this shows that its case is determined by its status as subject of the transitive verb *arkusi* 'bring', no longer by its status as subject of the copula. (ii) The copula, now reanalyzed as a focus marker, no longer agrees with the focused constituent, *x'o-ni* 'you', but with the direct object, *uzbi* 'brothers'. This is ordinary for the auxiliary in a periphrastic construction with transitive verbs in Dargi; the form *sa-bi* agrees with the direct object in person and number (*-bi* third person plural is the same for all gender-classes). (iii) As Kazenin shows in (6c), *uzbi arkusi* 'brought brothers' does not form a single constituent that cannot be broken up.

The reanalysis of the pattern in (5b) as a monoclausal structure has not been completely actualized. It retains the following characteristics of the biclausal structure out of which it developed: (i) The main verb continues to be expressed as a participle. (ii) The participle continues to agree with the focused constituent, though that is no longer its head. Although the one-time copula now agrees with the direct object, not with the focused constituent, it is surprising that it agrees at all. That is, we would instead expect that it would be frozen. I return to this issue below.

In this section I have shown that a construction may be at Stage I, having characteristics of a cleft, or at II, mixing characteristics of a cleft with ones of a monoclausal structure, as discussed by Harris and Campbell (1995). In Section 3 I return to the issue of Stage III.

3. Universal features

The point of the claim in (2) is that the three features coincide. Clearly, in a short paper such as this I cannot show that each characteristic of (2) is met in every NEC language that has entered Stage II (there are too many). I continue therefore with Dargi; additional data to support the same points from additional NEC languages is available in articles by Kazenin and in Xajdakov (1986).

Concerning (2a), in the pattern illustrated by (6b), that is after reanalysis, the structure is monoclausal, as shown by the fact that the transitive verb 'bring' has as its subject *x'o-ni* 'you', expressed in the ergative, and has as its direct object *uzbi* 'brothers', expressed in the absolutive.

Concerning (2b), in the reanalyzed pattern, the focused constituent, *x'o-ni* 'you' bears the grammatical relation — transitive subject — that it bore in the subordinate (i.e. 'content') clause in the input structure (5b). That is, in (5b) the role of 'you' in the embedded clause is subject of the transitive verb 'bring'. And this is its role also in the reanalyzed sentence, (6b).

(2c) lists three potential components of the reanalyzed focus marker: the copula, the relativizer, and the expletive pronoun. It allows also for various combinations of these. In literary Dargi, exemplified above, we find the copula (including, of course, the agreement markers, which are bound morphemes).

In other NEC languages we find some variations. For example, in Bagvalal and Botlikh, both in the Andian subgroup, the copula is invariant *ida*, and the invariant focus marker *da* is derived from it (Gudava 1971: 155–156; 1962: 154).

On the other hand, in Udi, a member of the Lezgian subgroup, the copula is usually zero in the present tense; the agreement markers which we may assume were once associated with it (see Section 3) now serve also as focus markers.

Neither a relative pronoun (comparable to English *who*) nor a relative particle (comparable to English *that*) is characteristic of NEC languages; there the inherited construction for the relative is the participle. Indeed Dargi, like some of its sister languages, retains the participle as part of the focus construction, though it is difficult to think of it as a focus marker.

Expletive pronouns are likewise uncharacteristic of these languages, yet we find what could be evidence of one in the focus construction in the Tsudakhar dialect of Dargi. Here a demonstrative pronoun preceding a constituent indicates that it is in focus.

(8) a. *dale belk'unda kayar* [Khazhal-Makhi subdialect]
I.ERG wrote   letter.ABS
'I wrote a letter.' [Xajdakov 1986: 90]

b. *ez dale belk'unda kayar*[6]
this I.ERG wrote   letter.ABS
'I (FOC) wrote a letter.'

(9) a. *du vač'ibda*
I.ABS arrived
'I arrived.'

b. *ez du vač'ibda*
this I.ABS arrived
'I (FOC) arrived.'

I have shown in this section that in the Dargi pattern illustrated by (6b), all of the features of (2) are met. Additional variation with respect to feature (2c), the form of the focus marker, is found in other NEC languages.

4. Udi

Udi, a member of the Lezgian subgroup, has undergone a great deal of change in all areas of its grammar, and it therefore differs greatly from its sister languages. As described in greater detail in Harris (1996 and to appear, Chapter 3), focus is marked by clitics that also serve as agreement markers. In content questions, a different clitic, *-a* (glossed 'Q'), replaces the agreement marker. These are illustrated with the question-answer pairs in (10)–(11).

(10) a. *merab-en šu-x-a bes-e*
Merab-ERG whom-DAT-Q ask-AORII
'WHO did Merab propose to?'

b. *q'onšin xinär-ä-ne bes-e*
neighbor girl-DAT-3SG ask-AORII
'He proposed TO THE NEIGHBOR GIRL.'

(11) a. *xinär-en ek'a-a   yamaluɣ-b-esa?*
girl-ERG what.ABS-Q mend-DO-PRES
'WHAT is the girl mending?'
b. *xinär-en partal-le   yamaluɣ-b-esa*
girl-ERG clothing.ABS-3SG mend-DO-PRES
'The girl is mending CLOTHING.'
c. *xinär-en partal   yamaluɣ-ne-b-sa*   (No focus)
girl-ERG clothing.ABS mend-3SG-DO-PRES
'The girl is mending clothing.'

Though the contemporary construction illustrated in (10)–(11) is monoclausal, there are traces of a cleft structure in Udi recorded in the 19th century. (The pattern of (10)–(11) already existed in the 19th century and was, in fact, the prevalent pattern.) Note that a focused constituent must immediately precede the verb in the contemporary language; (12) illustrates ungrammatical alternatives to (11b).

(12) a. **partal-le   xinär-en yamaluɣ-b-esa*
clothing.ABS-3SG girl-ERG mend-DO-PRES
'The girl is mending CLOTHING.'
b. **xinär-en yamaluɣ-b-esa partal-le*
girl-ERG mend-DO-PRES clothing.ABS-3SG
'The girl is mending CLOTHING.'

However, in the 19th century, focused constituents were sometimes separated from the verb, as illustrated in (13–14).

(13) *un-nu   lek'er-ax   ba-sak-e*   [Sf xv: 22]
you-2SG container-DAT in-push-AORII
'YOU pushed the container (here, bucket) in, ….'
(14) *Ili-in   ạyel-ụx   or-q'un čal-la   laxo lay-c-i*   [Sf xvii: 5]
Ilia-GEN child-PL.ABS how-3PL fence-on on up-LV-AORI
'[He saw] HOW Ilia's children climbed up on the fence.'

Given the prevalence of focus clefts in languages of the same family, the word order of (13)–(14) suggests that they may be reflexes of a cleft pattern (cf. 'It was you [that pushed the bucket in]', '…how it was [that Ilia's children climbed up on the fence].')

If this inference is correct, the focus construction of contemporary Udi, (10)–(11), is in Stage III, with no evidence at all of the focus cleft. First, the focused constituent in (10b) is in the dative case, governed by the verb *bes-* 'ask, request'; if it were in a cleft, we would expect the focused constituent to be in the absolutive as subject of the copula. Second, agreement is with the subject of the main verb, as for example in (12), not with the focused constituent, which would have been subject of a copula. (Agreement in Udi is entirely innovative in character, and its trigger is the subject, not the absolutive-nominal.) Third, the main verb is expressed as a finite form, not as a participle; it does not agree with the focused constituent. Lastly, the focused constituent is able, indeed is required, to break up the rest of the sentence; the latter does not form a constituent. Thus, the focus construction is entirely monoclausal and no longer shows any signs of having been biclausal. It is inferred here that this is because the reanalysis and its actualization have been completed.

5. Conclusion

Harris and Campbell (1995) propose two sets of universals relating to the transition from biclausal focus cleft to a monoclausal focus construction; these are stated in (1) and (2). In Section 1 I showed that one construction in Dargi and apparently also one in Chechen are at Stage I, while a second focus construction in Dargi is at Stage II, with some characteristics of a biclausal structure and some of a monoclausal structure. In Section 3 I showed that the focus construction in Udi is at Stage III, with no characteristics of the biclausal structure remaining.

In Section 2 I showed that the monoclausal focus structure of Dargi has all of the features of (2). I showed further that various other NEC languages fulfill (2c) in other ways. Thus, it has been shown that the derived monoclausal structures in various NEC languages have the range of properties predicted in Harris and Campbell (1995).

Much more work is needed on focus constructions in these languages. From a diachronic point of view, there are two anomalies in some of the languages: (i) The copula, which seems to be a reflex of the copula of the main clause of the cleft, seems at the same time to be involved as an auxiliary in the tense-aspect-mood system of some languages (see Kazenin 1996 on Godoberi). (ii) It seems odd that focus in so many of the languages involves agreement, either with the subject or with the absolutive-nominal, depending on the language; we might expect instead that agreement would be with the focused constituent. While these anomalies are not relevant to the issue addressed in this paper, they are important ones for further research.

Abbreviations

The following abbreviations are used:
ABS	absolutive case
AORI,II	aorist I, II
CM	gender-class marker (agreement with the absolutive-nominal)
COP	copula
DAT	dative
ERG	ergative case
FM	focus marker
FocC	focused constituent
FP	focus phrase
INSTR	instrumental case
PART	participle
PRES	present
Q	question marker
SG	singular
SUBJ	subject

Appendix: North East Caucasian Family

Nakh (Vainakh)
    Chechen
    Ingush
    Tsova-Tush (Bats, Batsbi)
Daghestanian
    Avar-Andi-Tsez
        Avar
        Andian subgroup
            Andi
            Botlikh
            Godoberi
            Karata
            Chamalal
            Tindi
            Bagvalal
            Akhvakh

    Tsezian subgroup
        Tsez (Dido)
        Hinukh
        Khvarshi
        Bezhta
        Hunzib
Lak-Dargi
    Lak
    Dargi (Dargwa)
Lezgian subgroup
    Lezgi (Lezgian)
    Tabasaran
    Aghul
    Rutul
    Tsakhur
    Budukh
    Kryts
    Archi
    Udi
    Khinalug (?)

Notes

* This material is based upon work supported by the National Science Foundation under Grant No. SRB-9710085 and by the International Research and Exchanges Board under the ACLS-Academy of Sciences Exchange with the Soviet Union (1989). I am grateful to both organizations for their support. The research on Udi could not have been completed without the patient help of my consultants, Luiza Nešumašvili, Dodo Misk'ališvili, Nana Agasišvili, Caco Čik'vaiʒe, Valya Broyani, Alvina Mat'ilian-Barxudarašvili, Simon K'isbabašvili, and Zina Silik'ašvili. Many other people helped me in my fieldwork in various ways, including P'ap'i Šarabiʒe, Malxaz Šarabiʒe, Tina Misk'ališvili, Nugzar K'isbabašvili, Sandro P'ač'ik'ašvili, Šorena Jeiranašvili, Važ Šengelia, Marina K'isbabašvili, Tamrik'o Misk'ališvili, Mamuli and Nana Nešumašvili, and the P'ač'ik'ašvili family, with whom I stayed in 1975.

1. Nichols states (to appear, p. 45) that the cleft structure "is used when a word other than the verb is questioned." She does not state or imply that the cleft is used only in this situation.

2. If I understand Kazenin (1995) correctly, he feels that (5b) and sentences of this type are not clefts because the copula determines the case of the focused constituent — absolutive. If I understand correctly, he claims that this is not characteristic of clefts. However, that would be incorrect; in unreanalyzed clefts, the focused constituent is subject of the copula, and this grammatical relation determines its case, in this instance absolutive (see, for example, Harries-Delisle 1978). Because I am not certain of whether Kazenin views this Dargi construction as a cleft, I have provided my own analysis.

3. The [x'] is a pharyngeal voiced spirant.
4. I follow Lambrecht (1994) in assuming that every sentence has focus, but for the purposes of the present paper, "focus" includes only argument-focus in Lambrechet's terms.
5. See also Xajdakov (1986:88) on the order of words.
6. On the demonstrative pronoun in this dialect, see Xajdakov (1985:87).

References

Abdullaev, Z.G. 1971. Očerki po sintaksisu darginskogo jazyka. Moskva: Nauka.
Gudava, T'. 1962. *Botlixuri ena* [The Botlikh language]. Tbilisi: Ak'ademia.
Gudava, T'. 1971. *Bagvaluri ena* [The Bagvalal language]. Tbilisi: Mecniereba.
Harries-Delisle, H. 1978. "Contrastive emphasis and cleft sentences". In *Universals of human language*, Vol. 4, J.H. Greenberg, et al. (eds),419–86. Stanford: Stanford University.
Harris, A.C. 1996. "Focus in Udi". In *Linguistic Studies in the Non-Slavic Languages of the Commonwealth of Independent States and the Baltic Republics*, H.I. Aronson (ed.), 2 201–220. Chicago: Chicago Linguistic Society.
Harris, A.C. To appear. *Endoclitics and the Origins of Udi Morphosyntax.* Oxford: Oxford University Press.
Harris, A.C. and Campbell, L. 1995. *Historical Syntax in Cross-Linguistic Perspective.* Cambridge: Cambridge University.
Haspelmath, M. 1993. *A Grammar of Lezgian.* Berlin: Mouton de Gruyter.
Kazenin, K.I. 1994. "Focus constructions in Daghestanian languages and the typology of focus constructions". Unpublished ms., Moscow State University.
Kazenin, K.I. 1995. "Focus constructions in North Caucasian languages". Unpublished ms., Moscow State University.
Kazenin, K.I. 1996. "Focus constructions". In *Godoberi*, A.E. Kibrik, et al. (eds), 227–236. München: Lincom Europa.
Lambrecht, K. 1994. *Information Structure and Sentence Form: Topic, Focus and the Mental Representation of Discourse Referents.* Cambridge: Cambridge University.
Nichols, J. 1997. "Nikolayev and Starostin's *North Caucasian etymological dictionary* and the methodology of long-range comparison: An assessment". The Tenth International Non-Slavic Languages Conference. Chicago.
Nichols, J. To appear. "Chechen (with notes on Ingush)". In *Languages of the Caucasus: Indigenous Languages and Their Speakers*, A.C. Harris and R. Smeets (eds), Richmond, England: Curzon Press.
Nikolayev, S.L. and Starostin, S.A. 1994. *North Caucasian Etymological Dictionary.* Moscow: Asterisk.
Schulze, W. 1997. Review of Nikolayev and Starostin 1994. *Diachronica* 14: 149–161.
Xajdakov, S.M. 1985. *Darginskij i megebskij jazyki: principy slovoizmenenija.* Moskva: Nauka.
Xajdakov, S.M. 1986. "Logičeskoe udarenie i členenie predložnija (dagestanskie dannye)". In *Aktual'nye problemy dagestansko-nakhskogo jazykoznanija*, 79–96. Maxačkala: Dagestanskii filial Akademii nauk SSSR.

Recasting Danish subjects
Case system, word order and subject development

Lars Heltoft
Roskilde University

The present article is an attempt to construct a scenario for the typological change of the subject in the Scandinavian languages, Danish, Norwegian and Swedish, from nominative subjects to categorical subjects. This change must and will be seen in the context of the rise of the so-called subordinate clause word order. Most of the material will be taken from three stages of Danish. In addition to Modern Danish, the 13th century is represented by the language of the Scanic Law and the mid 15th century by the Danish Lucidarius.

The background is the Copenhagen version of functional grammar, as presented by the papers in Engberg-Pedersen et al. (1996), and the topological theory of Paul Diderichsen (1941, 1943). No specific knowledge of these traditions is presupposed.

1. Introduction

Subjects in Old Scandinavian differ markedly from subjects in the Modern Scandinavian languages. Apart from being inflectionally marked as nominative, they were to a large extent optional and could occur in any position. In (1) a nominative subject follows even the non-finite verb and occurs — as I shall say — in the postfield of the sentence.

(1) Æn vm thæt wil dylia   arfui   hans. at hanum døthum.
     but if this will contest heir-N his   at him   dead
     'but if there is an heir of his who wants to contest this after his death'
     SkKl 8

This positional option is no longer a part of Danish, Norwegian and Swedish syntax. For Danish, the modern situation for main clauses is shown in (2).

Grossly, subjects are obligatory and have fixed positions. They must occur either sentence initially or as the third constituent.

(2) a. *Odysseus ville   ikke tage   sin bedste bue   med.*
      Ulysses would not bring his best   bow along
   b. *Så   ... gjorde Odysseus sig   parat.*
      then   made Ulysses REFL ready
      'then U. equipped himself'
   c. *Men sin bedste bue   ville   han ikke tage   med.*
      but his best   bow would he   not bring along
      'but his best bow he would not bring along'
      VS Odys 9

As we shall see below, these differences reflect a major typological change, also with respect to the coding of Scandinavian syntax.

1.1 Assumptions about subjecthood

For the present purpose, we do not need to recapitulate international discussions on subject typology in full, a few major points will suffice.

Languages that have subjects ascribe a privileged status to an NP, the primary NP. Subjecthood is this privileged status. Subject typologies concern the domains, structures and limits of this primacy.

In the discussions following Keenan (1976) two sets of subject criteria have been laid down, in Schachter's (1977) terms role related and reference related criteria. I shall mention only those selected by Faarlund (1989: 195):

- Role related criteria: verb agreement, addressee of imperative (role dependent), raising, role dependent equi-deletion.
- Reference related: Control of reflexives (dependent on referential identity), leftmost occurrence (givenness), coreference deletion in coordinated sentences.

Typologically, I shall claim that subjecthood cannot be handled in full in terms of this dichotomy only. Other domains may very well grammaticalize as subjects. For synchronic and diachronic descriptions of the Scandinavian languages we shall need the concept of a *modal subject*. A modal subject is a subject that grammaticalizes speaker-related content distinctions. The relevant expression systems are inflection, position, or both, the relevant content distinctions are those of illocutionary frame (such as declarative vs. question), or of subjectivity vs. objectivity.

Subjects, then, will be assumed to draw their codings from three main semantic domains, namely those of semantic roles, predicational structure and illocution/subjectivity.

1. A classical example of subjects encoding semantic roles is the unmarked nominative subjects of older Indo-European languages.
2. Subjects encoding predicational structure we find in categorical subjects, the subject as a grammaticalized topic (Lehmann 1976), or 'the entity predicated about' (Sasse 1987). Categorical structure grammaticalizes the aboutness-relation, the subject's complementary constituent is the VP.
3. Subjects with modal or illocutionary structure are illocutionary subjects (German term 'Aktualsubjekt', the subject as part of the — in modern terms — illocutionary frame system (Paul Diderichsen 1941, 1943)). Or they are modal subjects in a narrower sense, encoding distinctions of subjectivity vs. objectivity (Heltoft and Falster Jakobsen 1996).

1.2 Assumptions about syntax, content and expression

We shall not need lengthy discussions of the particular differences between functional and formal approaches, nor of internal differences between functional schools. However, to avoid misreadings, a few characteristic features will be made explicit. For detail, see above all Harder (1996ab) and Engberg-Pedersen (1996).

Being exactly a functional theory, Copenhagen functional grammar insists that all syntax has a content aspect. All syntactic constructions are coded, and so are all word order options, see further 7.2.

And all codings are at least to some degree language specific. There is no simple mapping from cognitive universal content to syntactic 'form'.

It follows that all syntactic changes are content changes as well. A distinction between deep structure change and semantic change as presupposed by Harris and Campbell (1995) is simply not relevant. There is no deep structure, nor is there an autonomous syntax, but syntax operates at two levels, the level of expression syntax and the level of content syntax.

The notion of grammaticalization employed will be a wide one. It is not restricted to the cline from lexical or dialogical item to inflectional element. Word order changes are also the results of grammaticalization processes, provided that they result in paradigms, that is, limited sets of coded options. Thus, the concept of grammaticalization employed here will include syntactic restructuring processes — as already hinted at by Meillet (1921), and thus not be restricted to the widely used traditional one (Meillet 1921; C. Lehmann 1985,

1992; Hopper and Traugott 1993, and many others). For details and for the concept of a paradigm employed, see Heltoft (1996).

1.3 The empirical issue. Overview of the phenomena discussed

The attested development of the three Scandinavian languages Danish, Norwegian and Swedish documents a major typological change, comprising:

1. A change of subject type, from coding of semantic roles to coding of predication structure. The change from a nominative subject of the classical Indo-European type to a categorical subject, 'the entity predicated about'. Correspondingly, the development of a VP, the syntactic organization of a complex rhematic constituent predicated about the subject.
2. A massive reduction of the case system to a minimal distinction between nominative and oblique in a handful of personal pronouns.
3. A change of word order coding. Old Scandinavian subjects were not positionally bound, they were sensitive to a general iconic coding system of word order as an information structural system. In Modern Scandinavian this principle has been superseded by the well-known positionally expressed division of labour between valency governed constituents: subjects are always preverbal in relation the non-finite verb, either sentence initial or in subject position, cf. (2); objects and bound PPs are in specific postverbal positions.
4. A change of the subject towards an active role in the illocutionary frame system of the sentence.
5. The coding of the indefinite subject as a modalized subject, a development specific to Danish and Dano-Norwegian.
6. A reinterpretation of V2-structure, resulting in main clause word order expressing assertive (constative) illocutionary frame. The general typological pattern for main clauses is P^1VSO, meaning that if the subject is not plainly sentence initial, it will immediately follow V2. (P^1 is Simon Dik's open initial position (1989), the fundamental field of Scandinavian topological tradition (Diderichsen 1941, 1943, 1946 and elsewhere).
7. The rise of unmarked Scandinavian subordinate clause word order, plainly SVO, but insisting on preverbal positions for sentence adverbials and negation: SAVO.

It remains a mystery why the change to categorical structure should be accompanied by the change referred to in 7. Not only are subordinate clauses in

Modern Danish, Norwegian and Swedish firmly SVO, but they display the markedly different adverbial order that creates an alternative to V2 in some contexts, namely SAVO: Subject > sentence adverbials and negation > verbal constituent > objects etc. I shall offer a possible solution to the question of how the processes are related by delving into the changes of the 14th and 15th centuries, a period that has been largely neglected.

The initial state referred to by developments 1–4 may be illustrated by (3), (3a) repeating (1). Old Danish subjects could occur in any non-verbal position. The word order rules of Old Scandinavian did not express subject functions and object functions, but were sensitive to textual and informational factors. Just as much as objects and adverbials, nominative subjects acquired textual coding through position:

(3) a. *Æn vm thæt wil dylia   arfui   hans. at hanum døthum.*
      but if   this will contest heir-N his   at him   dead
      SkKl 8
    b. *Warthær thræli   hand   af hoggin bøte..*
       is   thrall-D hand-N off cut..   pay as compensation..
       'if a thrall has his hand cut off, he (who did this) must pay as compensation..'
       SkL 122

In example a. *arfui hans* is a nominative subject; it is a new discourse referent, not a contextually given referent. An adequate translation would be 'an heir (of his)', not 'his heir'. Quite unlike Modern Danish, Old Danish and Old Scandinavian in general could mark this status positionally, by postverbal position.

Example (b) exemplifies subject focus. The nominative subject is the second NP, preceding the non-finite verb, itself being preceded by a dative NP. A subject in this position — given certain modifications — will express the focus of the sentence, as would indeed any other constituent — NP or adverbial — in this position. I shall speak of this mechanism as iconical focus — in a sense to become explicit below.

We cannot presuppose that NP-VP structure is common syntactic organization principle for Old and Modern Scandinavian, let alone a universal structure. I shall side with Jan Terje Faarlund (1990) in assuming that NP-VP structure reflects a syntactic subtype, and as such a language specific phenomenon. It follows that there is no a priori reason to assume oblique subjects for Old Scandinavian, including Old Icelandic. Although I shall not be concerned directly with oblique subjects, the evidence that I shall present for other analyses, would seem to go against the NP-VP analysis of the oblique subject, also in its disguised forms, the IP-Spec analysis or Comp-Spec analyses.

Faarlund (1989, 1990) contrasts Old Norse and Modern Norwegian as an illustration of the difference between a role encoding language and a reference encoding language — in my terminology, between a case language of the Indo-European type and a language with categorical structure. By tracing the same development for Danish subjects, I shall suggest a chain of reanalyses that will match other syntactic changes in Danish (and probably Mainland Scandinavian in general). In addition, it will demonstrate the need for the concept of a modal subject.

2. Categorical aspects of Modern Danish subjects

I shall employ a set of traditional, but fairly clearcut tests to set up the conditions for identifying categorical structure. We cannot here discuss the relations between distributional approaches to constituent structure and the dependency approach that I shall use. I shall presuppose that syntactic categories and their structural potential must be found on the basis of dependency relations, whereas positional analyses must rely on distributional tests.

The basis for both dependency tests and distributional tests is the commutation test as employed and defined by Hjelmslev (1943). No category will be needed that does not convey content distinctions. No content distinction will be needed that does not find its own mark at the level of expression.

One way dependency relations (hypotaxis) will not suffice. In the vein of Jespersen and Hjelmslev I shall employ two way dependency relations as well (nexus or cataxis). The relations between subject, finite verb and object are the aim of our analysis and simple enough to serve as our example, too.

Dependency relations can be seen as abstract relations of governance between syntactic categories, in the terminology of Peter Eisenberg as categorial governance (Kategoriale Rektion, Eisenberg 1989), or as lexical governance (Lexikalische Rektion). Viewed at the level of abstract categorial dependency or governance, the relation between subject and finite verb is cataxis, the relation between finite verb and direct object is hypotaxis:

(4) Subject   Verb   Object

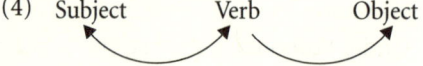

The subject-finite verb relation is the abstract formulation of the fact that subjects are obligatory in a clearcut categorical language like Modern Danish. Verb and subject form a catatagm or nexus, verb and object a hypotagm. Objects are verbal modifiers. Where a full NP subject is not available, the subject slot is filled by formal, pronominal subjects, or in certain constructions, even by situative adverbials, see examples (16a) and (17a).

Following the view of Sasse (1987), I shall take categorical sentence structure to refer to the content aspect of the structure in (4). The subject expresses the entity predicated about, the VP the syntactically construed complex predicate applied to this entity. In cases where this content structure is not found, for instance in thetic constructions like (16a), we shall assume that categorical structure has been generalized at the level of expression.

Lexical governance, on the other hand, is found in relations between **stems** and syntactic categories. These are valency relations. It will thus be perfectly meaningful to say that (4) is (5) at the level of valency relations, since valency deals with the presence and identity of subjects, objects etc., in so far as this is determined by the verb-stem and is not a general construction principle of the language in question.

(5)   Subject   Verb-stem   Object

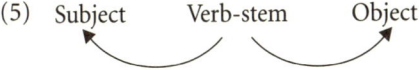

Furthermore, dependency relations are found between inflectional categories. According to tradition, Danish shows catataxis between the subject nominative (where available) and the tense of the finite verb, the oblique case being the default case to apply in all other situations. This situation — applying neatly to Danish of the 16th and 17th centuries — is an inflectional parallel to the catataxis between syntactic categories in (4). At both levels, syntactic dependencies parallel categorical content structure.

2.1 Case in Modern Danish

In present day Danish a change of the case system has taken place, the result of which is the abolishment of catataxis between nominative and tense.

A reinterpretation process which Swedish and Norwegian do not seem to partake in, has been on its way for at least 150 years in Danish. Danish nominatives (found in personal pronouns only) are reinterpreted in 3rd person pronouns such that the nominative is now the purely anaphorical subject, the oblique case the default form. Non-anaphorical subjects are in the oblique form (Heltoft 1997).

(6) a. *ham/*han der står på hjørnet, er fra uropatruljen.*
he-A/*he-N who is standing on the corner is from the riot squad
'he who is standing on the corner, is a policeman'
b. *ham/*han på hjørnet er fra uropatruljen.*
he-A/*he-N on the corner is from the riot squad
'the one on the corner is from the riot squad'

3rd person pronominal subjects modified by a parenthetical relative clause are pure anaphors and take the nominative; those modified by a determinative relative clause are not pure anaphors, but are made identifiable by way of the relative clause. They take the oblique case, and (7a–b) is a clear contrast.

(7) a. *han, der har boet her altid, er en oplagt kandidat.*
he-N who has lived here always is an obvious candidate
'he is an obvious candidate, having lived here for so long'
b. *ham der har boet her altid, er en oplagt kandidat,*
he-A who has lived here always is an obvious candidate
nytilflytteren er ikke.
the newcomer is not
'he who has lived here always is an obvious candidate, the newcomer isn't'

Swedish and Norwegian continue on the track already laid, tending to abolish case also in 3P pronouns. Danish, however, rearranges its case structure to fit with prototypical, categorical subject traits, a prototypical categorical subject being given: definite or anaphorical. Instead of abandoning role related criteria by losing case altogether, Danish adds reference related coding, or better: textual coding, to the old case distinction, thus showing an alternative way for a language to comply with type C criteria (Faarlund 1989).

2.2 Coding of information structure in Modern Danish

Modern Danish information structure has developed to fit categorical structure, namely to comply with the limited positional freedom of subjects and their inherent coding as the entity predicated about, henceforth the thematic constituent — or straighforwardly, the theme.

Presupposed here is a critical examination of Halliday's (1967, 1996) concepts of information structure. Space will not allow much detail, and we cannot discuss English here, either. The main point, however, is Halliday's confusion of the initial token of the clause with the initial position, in a structural sense. Subjects are coded syntactically as themes, they may in Danish be in the first position (Simon Dik's P^1, 1989); since they are already coded syntactically as themes, they are the obvious candidate for unmarked P^1-filling. P^1, however, may host constituents from the VP as well, see Figure 5 below. We shall therefore need to distinguish between the constituent in P^1, in Danish tradition the fundament of the clause, and the theme of the clause, which is always the subject. The concept of a theme is used here in a deliberately non-Hallidayan sense as 'the base, the thing put there, the entity predicated about', that is, as a content description of the subject. In the unmarked case, the subject is both the fundament and the theme.

The VP — including the valency bound constituents of the clause, except the subject — will be called the rheme, the extended predicate. (In Danish topology, the VP is hosted by the so-called content field, the field for the semantic information of the sentence).

The focus is the most important part of the message, the constituent or part of a constituent that the speaker invites the hearer to deny the truth of or the relevance of in the message in question. The focus is a contextually bound phenomenon, an element of *la parole*, and theoretically, it is a pragmatic notion. Actual foci must be interpreted as such in context by the hearer.

Languages may grammaticalize the focus to various extents. Some languages have specific positional rules for pointing out the focus, we shall see that Old Scandinavian had such rules. A categorical language like Modern Danish will have an open focus domain, in Danish the VP, inside which the hearer will normally have to search for the focus, when interpreting the utterance.

A prototypical definite subject is not normally the bearer of the focus — the focus must fall inside the VP. We shall speak of the subject as the antifocus, the VP as the (open) focus domain.

Making the subject the focus will require something extra, normally a

Coding of subject in Modern Danish (from Heltoft 1997)

Expression	Subject position Subject	Content field positions VP: Other valency bound constituents
Content	Entity predicated about ('thematic constituent') Antifocus	Rhematic constituent Potential focus

specific construction. A thetic construction (the *der*-construction, see below (16a) and (17a)) turns the subject into a content field constituent that carries the focus. This is well known, so let me draw attention to a topological mechanism that includes the subject into the focus domain, making it a potential focus bearer. (8a) is the normal situation, but a sentence adverbial preceding the subject will include the subject in the focus domain, (8b) will normally mean that it was now the king's turn to face the facts.

(8) a. *Dernæst måtte kongen jo bøje sig for kendsgerningerne.*
next must the king for sure accept the facts
'next, you see, the king must accept the facts'
b. *Så måtte jo kongen bøje sig for kendsgerningerne.*
then must for sure the king accept the facts
'next, you see, *the king* must accept the facts'

3. Old Danish sentence structure

Given the importance I have ascribed to dependency relations as the basis of syntactic structure, it follows that Old Scandinavian does not have categorical structure, since its subjects are not obligatory. This principle is valid for both subjects, objects and prepositionally governed NPs. All such relations are hypotactic.

Up to the mid 13th century, or in some contexts even later, subjects were structurally optional, even in indicative sentences. Such features belong to the role related subject features, cf. the role related properties listed for Old Norse by Faarlund (1990). The following example[1] shows both role related gapping and zero subjects.

(9) *Hauir man sløkefrithu børn. oc æræ æy thingliusd.*
has man children by a concubine and are not registered at the thing,
tha scal arf æy tæka æftir thæt um thæt ær døt.
then must heritage not take after it if it is dead
'If a man has children by a concubine, and (they) are not legally registered, then if one is dead, he is not entitled to inherit it'
SkL 61 GO

For direct objects and prepositionally adjoined objects I quote:

(10) ⟨Ræfua unga ma ængin man grafua vp. af annars marko. oc æy af scoge.
      'a fox's young may no man dig up from another's field and not from
      vtan han bøte siax øra. ællar sæli siata mans eth fore.
      wood unless he gives six ores as compensation or six men's oath'⟩
      Æn ma han swa taka at   han graui   æy at.
      but can he so   take that he dig-PRES.SUBJ not after
      tha taki   han sacløst.
      then take-PRES.SUBJ he   free of trial
      'but can he take (them) in such a way that he does not dig after (them),
      then he may take (them) without any legal consequences.'
      SkL 202

The priority given to the subject in a language like Old Scandinavian must be understood in terms of its unmarked case and the relations of agreement between verb and subject. It is not reflected in the constructional principles for its syntactic categories. It follows that arguments for a VP in such a language are sparse. I shall side with Faarlund 1990 in assuming that there is none.

4. Modal aspects of Modern Danish subjects

Danish grammatical tradition stresses the modal character of the Danish subject. Paul Diderichsen (1941, 1943 and later) speaks of the subject in Danish not only as the predication base (*to hypokeimenon*), but also as an 'Aktualsubjekt', a precondition for the predication to attain reality value (German *Realitätswert*). In modern terms we could speak of illocutionary frame, the coding at sentence level of the abstract domains within which the listener is to pin down the actual illocutionary value of the utterance.

4.1 Illocutionary frame

Danish contrasts declarative P^1 V^2 (S) order with Zero V S order, the word order for yes-no questions and conditionals. An empty P^1 is a necessary, but not sufficient condition for yes-no questions or conditionals to arise. The subject must be filled in. In this sense, inversion is an integrated part of the system of illocutionary frame.

(11) a. *hun kommer*
          she comes
          'she comes'

b. Ø kommer hun
    comes she
    'does she come' or 'if she comes'

Trivially, an empty P^1 does not in itself trigger questions and conditionals. Marked styles such as diaries and pastiches thereof in fiction allow empty P^1's in assertive utterances, the omitted subject being the speaker.

(12) Handler i hvert fald som en luset opportunist dagen efter, går med i
     acts   admittedly as   a lousy opportunist the day after joins
     demonstrationstoget   til Fælledparken sammen med Katrin og
     the demonstration parade to F.   with   K.   and
     Alexander, men sælger ikke billetten til alle dem,
     A.   but do not sell the ticket to all those
     der står og gerne vil købe.
     wanting to buy one
     H-J N Fodbold 15

4.2 Coded assertive meaning

In Modern Danish, a P^1 filled in by any constituent is coded for assertive illocutionary frame, an empty P^1 is coded to become a question or a conditional. Compared to the older language, V^2 has become specialized to code assertive meaning.

This coding applies to declarative main clause word order in Danish, and also to declarative main clause word order in subordinate clauses, or embedded V^2, as others have it (Vikner 1995, Holmberg and Platzack 1995). The main clause word order system was partially illustrated in (11), and since declarative main clause order is $P^1 V^2$, both V^2 and subject position will precede a sentence adverbial and a negation, see (13a).

In fact, embedded V^2 forms the optimal basis for an analysis of this coding. Take (13) as an example of main clause V^2.

(13) a. han gider ikke arbejde.
        he cares not work-INF
        'he does not care to work'
     b. det er klart at han gider ikke arbejde.
        it is clear that he cares not work-INF
        'it is clear that he does not care to work'

c. *det er klart at   arbejde   gider han ikke.*
   it is clear that work-INF cares he   not
   'it is clear that working is not what he cares to do'
d. *det er klart at   han ikke gider arbejde.*
   it is clear that he not cares work
   'it is clear that he does not care to work'

The clue is the relationship between the coded content of the V² construction and the semantics of the matrix verbs (Heltoft 1999). Given a grammar that recognizes that syntactic constructions are signs and have meaning, the following principle should render superfluous all talk about bridge verbs, as in e.g. Vikner (1995):

> V² is coded in Modern Danish as assertive illocutionary frame. It follows that when embedded, it will comply to verbs with compatible semantic restrictions on their *at*-clause. In all cases, lack of the V² option is due to inconsistency between the demands of the construction (assertive illocutionary frame) and the demands of the matrix verb.

(14) a.   P¹=S V   Neg V
     **det er trist at* han gider   ikke arbejde.*
     it is a pity that he   care-PRES not work
   b.   P¹=V V   S Neg
     **det er trist at* arbejde gider   han ikke.*
     it is a pity that work care-PRES he not
   c.   P¹=S Neg V   V
     det er trist at han ikke gider   arbejde.
     it is a pity that he not care-PRES work
     'it's a pity that he does not care to work'

(15) a.   P¹=S   V   Neg V
     **de bestred   at vidnet   kunne ikke læse.*
     they contested that the witness could not read
   b.   P¹=V V   S   Neg
     **de bestred   at læse kunne vidnet   ikke.*
     they contested that read could the witness not
   c.   P¹=S   Neg V   V
     de bestred   at vidnet   ikke kunne læse.
     they contested that the witness not could read
     'they contested that the witness was illiterate'

This construction reveals the modern joint venture between a categorical subject and a modal subject, formed during the 16th and 17th centuries. The categorical, prototypically definite subject of Modern Danish is, for one thing, coded as the thematic constituent, the entity predicated about, it is therefore the unmarked P^1 filler. At the same time, cf. (11)–(12), it is integrated into the assertive system, an Aktualsubjekt in Diderichsen's terms (1943), an interpersonal subject in Halliday's (Halliday 1967, 1996). See Heltoft (1999) for more detail and examples.

4.3 Subjective vs. objective indefinite subjects

Prototypical Modern Danish subjects are definite. Indefinite NPs, however, may very well occur as subjects in subject positions, but they are then modally marked, cf. Heltoft and Falster Jakobsen (1996). Simple descriptive indefinite subjects trigger the thetic sentence construction: the semantic role that would occur in subject position or in P^1 in a categorical sentence, if attached to a definite NP, is a positional object in the thetic construction, *der/her* 'there, here' being inserted in subject position. Quite meaningfully, Danish tradition speaks of this phenomenon as a content subject manifesting object expression features. An indefinite subject in P^1 or subject position is found in (16b).

(16) a. *der var faldet* en sten *ned fra taget.*
there was fallen a tile down from the roof
'a tile had fallen down from the roof'
b. en sten *var faldet ned fra taget.*
a tile was fallen down from the roof
'a tile had fallen down from the roof'
(Both from Heltoft and Falster Jakobsen 1996).

Such clauses are not free variants. Provisionally, (16a) is a description of a factual situation, whereas (16b) is a kind of narrated scenario; many native speakers identify (16b) as fiction. Similarly for (17b).

(17) a. *Der kommer* en mand *gående ud fra Bellevue*
there come-PRES.ACT a man walking out from Bellevue
Strandhotel.
Beach Hotel
'a man comes walking out of the B.S.' or 'there is a man walking out of the B.S.'
b. En mand *kommer gående ud fra Bellevue Strandhotel.*
a man come-PRES.ACT walking out of Bellevue Beach Hotel
'a man comes walking out of the B.S.'

This use is clearly modal. Similarly, such indefinite subjects appear in normative or generic statements, but not in plain descriptive utterances.

(18) en ræv *spiser* ikke gulerødder
 a fox eat-PRES.ACT not carrots
 'a fox does not eat carrots'

Such modalized indefinite subjects are typical of Danish and (at least) Dano-Norwegian, but they are unknown in Swedish. For more detail about the content of these subjects and their intimate relationship with a modal reanalysis of the *s*-passive in Danish, see Heltoft and Falster Jakobsen (1996).

4.4 Summary

The subject in Modern Danish, then, is modal in these two senses: it contributes to the illocutionary frame system of Modern Danish V^2; it provides prototypical, definite categorical subjects for this system, and finally, it provides a modal option, whenever the subject is indefinite.

Modal and categorical subject properties run along together very well.[2] An exact chronology of this development would demand further empirical research, but its roots are at the end of the 15th century, its full development belongs to the 16th century, possibly extending into the 17th century as well.

5. The historical forerunner: The free subject

The positionally free subject type as shown in (3ab) was retained at least until the end of the 15th century. The manuscript AM 76,8° of the Danish Lucidarius — dating from the 1460s — still shows many examples, now typically marked as indefinite (informative):

(19) a. vthæn thæn stund ther the i skiærs eeld æræ tha
 but the hour that they in purgatory are then
 kommer til tøm ænglæ oc andræ hæliæn (..) oc hw swolæ tøm
 come-SG to them angels and other saints   and soothe   them
 'but at the time they are in Purgatory, then angels and other saints come to them and soothe them'
 Luc 66r

b. *Thet gyuæ   oss then herræ ther   iek mynæ talæ   met burdæ*
   that give-SUBJ us this Lord whom I   my speech with began
   'May the Lord I spoke about at the beginning, grant us this'
   Luc 51v

c. *Sithen gangher   ther vthen   om allæ wegnæ   en eldh mwr*
   then go-PRES.SG there around at all directions a fire wall
   'Then there is a wall of fire all around it'
   Luc 53r

d. *vorder   tha noghet falk   til   i verdæn*
   become-PRES then any   people existing in the world
   'will there then exist any human beings in the world?'
   Luc 68r

6. OV and VO characteristics and codings: Iconic focus

The change to categorical structure from nominative structure is normally taken to be a structural reaction to the decay of the case system, but to my mind, it is time for second thoughts about this view. The clue to the development of categorical structure in Danish is not to be found among the role features of Old Danish, but it is to be found in the contrast between extant OV-features and VO-features, since these are the features that provide the ground for a sensible reanalysis of the codings of word order. Before pursuing this line of thought, however, we shall need a brief analysis of the codings of OV vs. VO-order. (I shall draw on Heltoft 1995, but most of my views are compatible with the description of Old Norwegian by Marit Christoffersen 1993).

Where the non-finite verb is concerned, Old Scandinavian retains systematic OV options, alternating with VO options, with regard to both NPs, i.e. objects and to PPs and other adverbials. The finite verb is not involved, since this is fixed to the second position.

Again, being at a transitional stage from OV to VO order does not prevent Old Danish from turning this distinction into a grammaticalized, semantic contrast. Old Scanic codes its clausal OV word order iconically, iconic to be understood in the sense of diagrammatic isomorphism, cf. Engberg-Pedersen 1996. The position to the very right of the negation marks an OV constituent as the focus. Negational scope is expressed by contiguity. Constituents to the left of negation are sheltered from its scope, excepting the finite verb itself. As originally pointed out by Pedersen (1993), in (21) the indirect object *bondanum* is backgrounded by way of its prenegational position, similarly for *thæn harm* in (22).

Again: the order Negation > X > V marks the X (subject, object or whatever) as the iconic focus (20)–(22), categories preceding negation are sheltered from its scope (21)–(22). A sheltered NP is very often the nominative subject, but need not be. (21) has both a sentence initial anaphorical subject and a backgrounded object, a dative NP.

	P1	V2	X..	NEG	X..	V
			background		focus	

Figure 1. Iconic focus and background

(20) Warthær hanum sac   gifuin. At han hafuir **sumt** reth. oc æy
     is   he-D accusation given that he has   some paid and not
     alt. witi..
     all witness
     'If accused that he has only paid some and not all, he must witness..'
     SkKl 20

(21) at han giorthe <u>bondanum</u> æy **mera** schatha j   thy af   hoggi
     that he did owner-D-DEF.D not greater-A loss in this-D cut-D
     'that he did not inflict on the owner a greater loss'
     SkL 125

(22) Julianus gat   <u>thæn harm</u> æy **længær** thold
     Julianus could this insult no longer stand-PERF.PART
     oc gaf   thæn dom   at hænnæ tungæ skuldæ af skæræs
     and pronounced the sentence that her tongue be   cut off
     St. Christina, Cambridge fragment, GL p. 285

In the format of a topological frame, reconstructed on the basis of Paul Diderichsen (1941), Figure 4:

	P1	V2	X..	NEG	X..	V
			background		focus	
at	han	hafuir			sumt	reth.
oc				æy	alt.	
at	han	giorthe	bondanum	æy	mera schatha	
	Julianus	gat	thæn harm	æy	længær	thold

Figure 2. Topological frame for Scanic

I shall resume the analysis of (3) as (23), explaining more of its context:

(23) *Warthær   thræli   hand   af hoggin.. bøte..*
become-PRES thrall-D hand-N off cut   pay as compensation
'if a thrall has his hand cut off, he (who did this) must pay as compensation.'
SkL 122

Since this example is not negative, the focus function of the subject is not positionally marked, but must be reconstructed from the context. (We could in fact be facing two backgrounded constituents.) But the text is very clear. We are dealing with compensations for blows and injuries inflicted on thralls. Other parallel rules specify other parts of the body or total loss. Moreover, this example is a nice illustration of the way a role related language employs its voice opposition[3] (cf. Faarlund 1989), for agent demotion only, without promoting any particular constituent and thus without any reshuffling of the relationship between morphological case and semantic roles.

Free adverbial adjuncts follow the same principle. Example (24) deals with millowners' obligations to stop or reduce output in the spring in order not to flood farmers' meadows. Their drawdoors must be lifted. For those who refuse, a legal procedure is described, including a final legally fixed term. This day is the focus of example (24):

(24) *Wil han æy at them stæfnu   dagi sith stiborth   vp taka.*
will he not at that   meeting day his draw-door up take
bøte   spial   ofna ængium.
compensate for-PRES.SUBJ damage upon the meadows
oc til   siax øra.
and in addition six ores
'will he not even at this legal meeting day take up his draw-door, he must compensate for the damage upon the meadows and pay six ores in addition.'
SkL 214

This iconic system is active as late as the 15th century. Again, the Lucidarius text will provide the material:

(25) *Thaa ær monyn fwll æn førstæ solæns lywsen kan ey **fullælich** skynæ aff*
'then the moon is full but the first light of the sun cannot fully shine back
monyn. Tha worthær monyn i mynnæ oc mynnæ
from the moon. Then the moon grows ever smaller.'
Luc 62v

(26) a. *Hwy moo man æy **thaa** see monyn.*
　　　why can one not then see the moon?
　　　'Why can't one then see the moon?'
　　　Luc 63r
　　b. *hwy mwæ ey **diæfflæ** frælsæs aff theræs pinæ*
　　　why can not devils save-PASS from their torment
　　　'Why cannot devils be saved from their toement?'
　　　Luc 75v

In questions a former focus is retained, along with the added question focus. The question foci in these questions are of course the interrogative *Hwy* (for *hwī*) 'why', but the scope of this 'why' is not why the moon is not seen, but why it is not **then** seen.

(27) *D(iscipulus). huelkæ lund skal man sinæ synder **rætælegæ** bædræ*
　　D. In what ways should one his sins in the right way improve?

(28) a. *M(agister). særlegh thwænæ lund thet førstæ at syndæn skal aldræ **saa***
　　　M. Especially two ways, the first one that sin must never so
　　　***lønligh væræ** ællær saa vquem legh væræ ællær saa manig fold væræ*
　　　coveted be or so unsuitable be or so manyfold be
　　　*ath vi skullæ ey **gernæ** siæ vor skrefftæ fadær tøm.*
　　　that we would not willingly tell our confessor (about) them.
　　b. *Thet annæt ær at syndæn skal aldræ **saa gaffnlegh væræ** til værælszæns*
　　　The second way is that sin must never so much to the benefit be of the
　　　*gaffn oc aldræ **saa løstælegh** til legæmet at føluæ at vi skullæ ey hauæ*
　　　world and never so lustful for the body to follow that we will not have
　　　*then hw ath vi villæ **thøm** aldræ thydræ øræ.*
　　　the intent that we shall them never again do
　　　Luc 70v-71r

In fact, this iconic system is fully alive in present day Danish, but only with free adverbials (manner adverbials, place and time adverbials). Subjects and objects are no longer accessible to iconic focus — only free adverbials are.

For ease of exposition, let us speak of free space and time adverbials only, these have their unmarked position at the end of the clause, but they may occur interverbally, in the actualization field of Paul Diderichsen's sentence frame. Traditional descriptions leave it at that and ignore the alternative positions relative to negations, let alone their codings:

(29) a. *Jeg skal ikke her gennemgå rapportens.. mange spændende resultater.*
'I shall not here go through this report's.. many exciting results'
Berl T 280698 1 17
b. *det kan jeg da   ikke i dag   stå   her og   bestride*
that can I   surely not today (stand here and) deny
'I surely cannot be denying this here today'

(29ab) imply 'I may very well be willing to do so on other occasions, but not here/today', respectively. English translations are hard to squeeze into the right information pattern.

(30) *der vil i denne sag ikke i øjeblikket blive skredet ind over for ham*
'there will not at the moment be taken any measures against him'

Example (30) implies that 'measures are possible at a later stage, but not right now'. Free time and place adverbials can be sheltered from negation to form a kind of secondary or auxiliary topic. Thus, (31) is about the police and something that often happens. Even if they may normally be successful in suppressing details, these have a tendency to leak during critical phases.

(31) *politiet kan ofte ikke under efterforskningens mest kritiske fase*
the police can often not during the most critical phase of the
mørklægge centrale detaljer man ikke ønsker frem
investigation suppress central details they do not wish to become publicly known

The following template will provide an overview.

	Adv. topic	Neg	Focus	V...
det kan jeg da		ikke	i dag	stå her og bestride
der vil	i denne sag	ikke	i øjeblikket	blive skredet ind..
politiet kan	ofte	ikke	under efterforsk- ningens.. fase	mørklægge..

Figure 3. Iconic adverbial focus in Modern Danish.

The fact that this old system is still preserved in restricted, but well-defined contexts, is in itself a strong argument for the adequacy of the iconic principle. The drastic historical change to Modern Danish can be described as a reinterpretation of the nucleus (the verb + its valency bound satellites) to categorical structure, while the free adverbials retain the old structure.

We are now in a position to approach this reinterpretation process. I shall attempt to show that the development of categorical subjects and the decay of iconic focus in Danish must be understood as one process. The rise of modern subordinate clause word order results from a generalization of the iconic background-focus system to positions preceding the finite verb.

7. From nominative structure to categorical structure

The reduction process of the Scandinavian case system is already well on its way from the outset of Danish as a historically recorded language. It is normally assumed that word order replaces the dismantled case system, but such ambiguous statements are in need of clarification and qualification. It is striking to see iconic word order at full bloom in the mid fifteenth century, some 150 years after the de facto dismantling of case in the central Zealand dialect. I shall assume that the creation of categorical structure and categorical subjects cannot be viewed as a direct consequence of the reduction of the case system. This reduction process is to a large extent a generalization of syncretisms common to all Old Scandinavian dialects.

7.1 Briefly on the dismantling of the case system

We need not go into details about the original system. The nominative is the unmarked role marker, open to whatever semantic role the verb will assign to it. I assume that the accusative is not neutral in this sense, but (as is Modern Danish) inaccessible to the agentive role (-Ag). The originally partitive-negative genitive has been shunted off from the case system to form a new modifier-paradigm (Hansen 1956, Heltoft 1996b, and also Norde (this volume). By 1300 the originally polysemous dative had lost at least two senses, namely its instrumental-sociative reading and its locative reading, retaining only recipient and experient readings:

(32) ...*the gamblæ skra   thær ærchebiscup æskil oc biscup absalon... gafæ*
     the old   statutes that archbishop Eskil and bishop Absalon   gave
skanungum.
Scanians-D
'the old statutes that archbishop Eskil and bishop Absalon gave the Scanians'
Addition 1300 to ms. AM 37,4° of the Scanic Law

(33) *sæms them æy. ær scoga ago. at swin gange samman.*
agree-SG they-D not who woods own that the pigs may come together
'if the woodowners do not agree that the pigs may come together'
SkL 2066

(34) *En man i sin ytarste tima. tha thøkte honum som en stor sten ofvir*
A man in his utmost hour, then thought he-D/A as a big stone above
honum hængde. oc vilde vpa honum falla.
him hang and would upon him fall
'A man, in his utmost hour, felt as if a big stone was hanging above him and would fall down upon him'
SjT p. 95

By the time of the Lucidarius text this language retains only a distinction between a nominative and an oblique case — and only for seven personal pronouns. Still, remnants of role related criteria can be found. The nominative is the subject marker, neutral to role; the oblique form occurs elsewhere, notably also with mental process verbs to mark an experient role.

(35) *Mig haabes ath i ere icke for den skyld komne hid ath i wille gøre nogen iomfrw wanheder.*
'Me hopes that you have not come hither because you want to dishonour any maid'
KM p. 278

In Modern Danish–and Swedish and Norwegian as well — few traces are left of the experient case role as a grammaticalized phenomenon. The disappearance of the experient function would leave only the coding subject vs. non-subject for the nominative vs. oblique distinction. In most cases, this distinction is already fully covered by the modern positional rules for subjects, see further below.

7.2 Word order patterns as paradigms

Word order options are grammaticalized systems, that is, they are organized in closed paradigms with stable content contrasts (Heltoft 1996b). I shall sum up the word order paradigms already discussed and introduce the critical generalization of OV order that forms the paradigmatic basis for the reinterpretation of Danish to categorical structure.

Old Scandinavian is firmly verb second, both in main clauses and in subordinate clauses, meaning that the finite verb never occurs in positions later than the second position. We may disregard empty P¹'s as continuative markers and take into account only empty P¹'s as markers of questions and conditionals.

7.2.1 *The paradigms for the Scanic Law*
The paradigms for the Scanic Law are the following:

		I		II		III
Paradigm 1.	(C) P1 V2	XX..	V	XX..	V	XX..
	(C) Ø V2	XX..	V	XX..	V	XX..
Paradigm 2.	XV vs. VX					
Paradigm 3.	X NEG V vs. NEG X V					

Figure 4.   Word order paradigms for the Scanic Law.

Paradigm 1 applies to both subordinate clauses and main clauses. Old Scandinavian does not distinguish between clause types by way of word order. Contrary to the modern situation, the Old Scandinavian word order paradigm has no specific position reserved for the subject. The nominative subject is undoubtedly the most frequent constituent to appear in P¹ or in immediate postverbal position, but this is not due to its positions being coded, but to contextual factors. Unmarked subjects (agents in many cases) turn up as the normal backgrounded constituent, but this is not a coded nor obligatory phenomenon.

Paradigms 2 and 3 summarize the focus system as described above. Paradigm 2 is a generalized formulation of the OV vs. VO paradigm, paradigm 3 the focus vs. background system.

7.2.2 *Generalizing the OV-pattern after certain conjunctions*
We find in manuscripts from the 14th and 15th centuries a generalization of the OV rules so as to apply also in relation to the finite verb. This reinterpretation does away with verb second order by analyzing the topological space between C and finite verb in a way quite analogous to the space between finite verb and non-finite verb in paradigm 1. The result is the creation of a specific pattern for subordinate clauses, on the basis of topological patterns already available in paradigm 1.

The Lucidarius ms. (app. 1460) adds paradigm 4 to paradigms 1–3.

		I		II		III
P¹	V$_{fin}$ (V2)	XX..	V	XX..	V	XX..
	C	XX..	V$_{fin}$	XX..	V	XX..

Figure 5.   Reanalysis of C-position as V2-position

This reanalysis equals the position for verb second with the position for conjunctions. Some conjunctions, especially conditionals, causal and temporal conjunctions, are lexical indicators of the semantic reality value (*Realitätswert*) of the clauses they govern. This is probably the semantic background for the rise of Scandinavian subordinate clause word order: Sets of conjunctions — lexical markers of reality — are reanalysed to positionally match the finite verb in verb second conjunctionless clauses, since this position is also an essential part of a reality system, the illocutionary frame system.

This idea is of course substantially influenced by the analysis of verb second in government and binding theory over the last 15 years, but I know of no predecessors where the historical analysis is concerned, nor of its consequences for subordinate clause word order. The positions for V2 and C are identified, and the topological space between C and the finite verb is reanalysed to the effect that P^1 is abolished and that the iconic background-focus system is now found between C and the finite verb, not only between finite and non-finite verb.

Paradigm 4. is documented in examples (36)–(37):

(36)   Rel. S   Adv.   Finite V
thet samme legæmæ Ø   mænæskæ førræ hadæ
that same body   men   before had
thet fongæ the igen.
that have they back
'men have back that very same body as they had before'
Luc 68r

(37)   Rel. S   Adv. Finite V
thet barn ther hun thaa fødhæ   thæt skulæ fanghæ manghæ lydhæ.
the child that she then bore   that would have many   defects
'the child that she gave birth to then, that was to have many defects'
Luc 56v

(38)   C   S   DO   Finite V
the louæ guth.. oc æræ saa gladæ / at the hans ænlædæ see / at..
they praise god (..) and are so joyous that they his face   see that..
Luc 72r

(39) a.   Rel.   S   Adv. Finite V
        the   æræ thry stædæ ther   mænnæskæ   nw   skal
        these are three places where men   now   shall
        plauæs   i.
        be tormented in
        'these are three places where men will now be tormented'
        Luc 75v
    b.   Rel. S   Adv.   part. Vfin
        eet ær thet Ø   iek athæns aff   sade.
        one is that   I   earlier of   said
        'one is the one I have already told of'
        Luc 75v

As shown in (40) this rule applies also to form sentences with postverbal subjects, showing that the preverbal obligatory subject position of modern times has still not been formed.

(40)   ath følgæ the syndher oc mangæ andræ ondhæ syndher meth teres lecomæ.
       to follow such sins and many other evil sins with their body
       Rel. Neg. Pred.   Finite V subject infinitive
       ther æi   quemt   ær   aff at syæ owenbarligh.
       that not   suitable are   about to tell in public
       'that are not suitable for public mention'
       Luc 57r

This process can in fact be traced back to earlier stages, but there are to my knowledge no examples in the Scanic Law. The fragment of the Christina Legend quoted here is originally part of ms. K 48 dating back to 1300.

(41)   C   S DO Fin.V S   DO   Fin.V
       West thu æi thæt ac thic føddæ oc   thu minæ spænæ dithæ.
       know you not that I   you bore   and you my breasts   sucked'
       'dost thou not know that I gave birth to you and you sucked my breasts'
       St. Christina fragment, GL p.285

The positional model for the creation of paradigm 4 is probably the relative clause construction traditionally called the 'wedge', an obligatory filling of P^1 in subject relative clauses by a non-subject constituent, an idea already pointed to by Paul Diderichsen (unpublished notes). The wedge is illustrated from the Scanic Law in (42) and from Lucidarius in (43).

(42)   Rel. DO Finite V Adv. Perf. ptc.
vtan vfritha man æri thæn ær skip hafuir   thær brutith.
unless outlaw be-SUBJ he that ship has   there wrecked
'unless the man who has wrecked his ship there should be an outlaw'
SkL 165

(43)   Rel. Pf.ptc.   Finite V
syer mek..hwar then deel ær skapt ther bygther   ær   aff verdhen.
tell me.. where that part is created that inhabited is   of the world
'tell me.. where the inhabited apart of the world was created'
Luc 51v

(44) a.   Rel. DO   Finite V
       Siætæ er ormæ ther tøm   æder   bodæ bag og foræ.
       sixth is snakes that them eat   both back and front
       'the sixth one is snakes that eat them from both sides'
       Luc 66v
 b.   Rel. Neg. adv. Finite V
       fiardæ er then grad   ther aldri   ændæs.
       fourth is the weeping that never   ends
       'the fourth one is the weeping that never ceases'
       Luc 66v

(45) tha   talæthæ hans son ther længæ hauthæ thæyd (= thiæd).
      then spoke   his   son who long   had   kept silent
      'the spoke his son who had for a time time remained silent'
      Rydårb. I, 75, 20

For the modern Dane, examples with free adverbial wedges like (44b) and (45) can be structurally mistaken for modern subordinate clause word order, but in the framework of the stage found in Lucidarius — as shown by structures (42) through (44a) — they can be mistaken for field-I constituents of paradigm 1. Given the reanalysis of C as V2, they appear as just a special case of field I with only one constituent.

The creation of paradigm 4. leads to the prediction that contrary to the ordinary picture of OV changing into VO, we should expect OV frequency to increase again with the rise of C/V2. The rise of OV in the 14th and 15th centuries has been claimed by Diderichsen (unpublished notes), and recently, a detailed count and statistics on the basis of Old Swedish material has led Lars-Olof Delsing (1999) to the same conclusion. In the sense of offering a set of motivated reanalyses, paradigm 4 is an explanation of this mystery.

Not only does this reanalysis offer an explanation of the OV pattern, it also paves the way for an understanding of the odd outcome of subordinate clause formation. Paradigm 4 allows any constituent type to occur in field I: NPs, nonfinite verbs and adverbials.

Notice that paradigm 4 is optional. V^2 is maintained in the alternative paradigm 1, including still the iconic focus system, as seen in (46).

(46) at de folk dræbe hvert annet ey.
that those peoples kill each other not
'that those nations do not kill each other'
Luc 56r

Most examples of paradigm 4 have backgrounded examples, and clear focus examples with explicit negation are scarce. (40) was one, taking the predicative adjective *quemt* 'suitable' into the scope of negation.

(40′) Rel. Neg. Pred. Finite V subject infinitive
ther æi quemt ær aff at syæ owenbarligh.

The outcome is a system for subordinate clauses that allows verb positions different from V2. Thus, paradigm 4 may be viewed as an optional marker of subordinate clause status.

7.3 Abandoning OV

OV is replaced by VO by reinterpretation to categorical structure. This process is easier to isolate in subordinate clauses, the word order of which is not bound up with illocution. I have nothing definitive to say about the details here, except that subjects — statistically dominant in P^1 and in post finite position, cf. Christoffersen (1993) — are now semantically reinterpreted as the entity predicated about, that is, the grammatically identified backgrounded constituent. Its new syntactic counterpart is the VP. The new subject regains a formal, this time positional marker as the NP next to the reality marker V2/C:

	P1	V2/C	Subject position
Main Clauses:	S	V	–
	X	V	S
	Ø	V	S
Subordinate clauses:		C	S

Figure 6. Outcome of the reinterpretation to categorical subject

Cf. paradigm 5, distributing subjects and all other valency bound constituents to field I and fields II-III, respectively. Subjects obtain their specific position by being interpreted as the constituent immediately following the reality marker V2/C.

		I			II		III
Paradigm 5.	C P1	V2	S A NEG A	V	O.. A..	V	A
		C	S A NEG A	V	O.. A..	V	A

Observe that the introduction of categorical structure affects only valency bound constituents. All objects, verbs and predicatives and bound adverbials are relegated from field I, this being interpreted as the subject field. Free adverbials retain their positions in field I, that is, they retain their free, iconic information structure, as shown in (29)–(31), cf. appendix 1. The attractiveness of this analysis is of course the understanding of Scandinavian subordinate clause word order as a residual product of other interpretations. We no longer face the task of substantiating an isolated emergence of preverbal adverbial positions, since the SC-order SAVO now follows from other well motivated developments.

Especially attractive is the historical meaningfulness of the analysis. Given the reinterpretation of C-position as analogous to V2-position and the generalization leading to paradigm 4, free adverbials represent a continuation of the old iconic word order. They were turned into a peripheral phenomenon, as predicational structure became the basic organization principle. Still, in Modern Danish the two systems coexist.

7.4 The assertive frame compromise

Space will only allow a brief mention of the new status ascribed to V2 in Modern Danish.

In Modern Standard Danish P^1 is coded as the option of abstract illocutionary frame. A P^1 filled in by any constituent is coded for assertive illocutionary frame, an empty P^1 is coded to become a question or a conditional. Old Scandinavian was less firmly coded; suffice it to say that verb second did not code assertive frame, since verb second coexisted with all semantic types of conjunctions. In (47) the main clause is assertive, not due to its word order, but rather to its indicative mood and to the absence of conjunctions saying otherwise; the subordinate clause is a conditional, marked only by the conjunction *utæn* 'unless'. The word order is verb second here, too, so this pattern has no assertive coding,

(47)   æn kirkæ ran   ma thæt æy hetæ   utæn han wil æy repæ.
       but church open theft can it not   be called unless he will not use ropes
       'but this cannot be called open theft from a church, unless he will not
       measure land with ropes..'
       SjKl 6

as against (48a), absolutely impossible and inconsistent in Modern Danish:

(48)   a. *hvis han vil ikke måle sin jord op.
           'if he does not wish to measure his lands'
       b. han vil ikke måle sin jord op.
           'he does not wish to measure his lands'

Again, the background for the reinterpretation of V^2 is the rise of the neutral subordinate clause order. The creation of an alternative order to V^2 facilitates the specialization of this pattern to manifest assertive illocutionary frame.

8. Summary of the changes

This overview of the main subject related changes from Old Danish to Modern Danish draws on a chart in Heltoft 1995. The present version splits the changes into two phases by adding the results of this article. This split should enable us to see how subject reinterpretation and word order change interact.

The picture emerging is in fact surprising, in comparison to the traditional view. The definitive typological innovations lie in the period from Lucidarius to Modern Danish, not in the 13th century. The decay of the case system in the 13th century (12th for the Zealand dialect) — however prominent in the mind of the traditional, inflectionally oriented grammarian — seems to have no direct impact on the word order system. Instead, the reinterpretations that lead to radical changes take place in the information structural system, thus paving the way for a massive redesign of this system.

Scanic Law		Lucidarius
case expresses semantic role		case expresses semantic role (see next)
impersonal verbs taking oblique case		impersonal verbs taking oblique case
distinct mood		distinct mood
nominative subject	>	no case distinction in nouns
topic constructional	>	extraposition (dislocation)
optional definite article	>	fully developed paradigm for definiteness
optional subject	>	few instances of subjectless sentences
free position for subject		free position for subject
no VP		(probably) no VP
interverbal positions open		interverbal positions open
fixed focus position		fixed focus position
fixed background position		fixed background position
subject focusable through position		subject focusable through position
wedge	>	iconic focus generalized to wedge
C position and V2 position distinct	>	C position = V2 position
iconic focus only in non-finite OV	>	iconic focus generalized to finite OV
general V2 order	>	finite V possible later than V2

Lucidarius		Modern Danish
case expresses semantic role	>	remnants of case express subjecthood and anaphoricity
impersonal verbs taking oblique case	>	no impersonals with oblique case
distinct mood	>	rudimentary mood, tense is modal
few instances of subjectless sentences	>	obligatory subject
free position for subject	>	fixed subject position
no illocutionary subject	>	illocutionary subject
non-modal indefinite subject	>	modal indefinite subject
(probably) no VP	>	rise of VP
interverbal positions open	>	objects and bound adverbials in VP
fixed focus position	>	open focus domain
fixed background position	>	enclitical position for light constituents
subject focusable through position	>	subject focusable through construction, esp. *der*-construction
general V2-order	>	assertive V2 vs. neutral SC-order (SAVO)

Appendix. Overview of word order paradigms

			I		II		III
Paradigm 1.	K	P1 V2	XX..	V	XX..	V	XX..
	K	Ø V2	XX..	V	XX..	V	XX..

Paradigm 2. XV vs. VX
Paradigm 3. X NEG V vs. NEG X V

		I		II		III
Paradigm 4. P¹	V2	XX..	V	XX..	V	XX..
	K	XX..	V	XX..	V	XX..

		I		II		III
Paradigm 5. P1	V2	S A NEG A	V	O.. A..	V	ZZ.. A
	K	S A NEG A	V	O.. A..	V	ZZ.. A

In a process not dealt with in the present article, the third verbal position is reinterpreted as the position for non-verbal predicates, P, resulting in paradigm 6, the sentence frame for Modern Danish.

Paradigm 6. K P1	V2	S A NEG A	V	O.. A..	P	BA.. A
	K	S A NEG A	V	O.. A..	P	BA.. A

Notes

1. The full manuscript text adds a pronominal subject:

> Hauir man sløkefrithu børn. oc æræ æy thingliusd. tha scal han [*late hand above line, app. 1430*] arf æy tæka æftir thæt um thæt ær døt.
> SkL GO 61

The critical readings *oc æræ æy thingliusd*; *tha scal arf æy tæka* are supported by two old, independent manuscript traditions, namely A³ (B74, app. 1250, the oldest extant ms. of this text, belonging to tradition A) and by E (E don.var. 136, 4°, app. 1430, still reflecting an older linguistic stage).

2. Nothing prevents further compromises between categorico-modal structure and nominative subject structure. In the terms of the present article, Modern Icelandic retains its old nominative subject, while at the same time establishing a modal and categorical subject that may serve as a reflexive antecedent. Modern Icelandic subject structure is a compromise between nominative structure and illocutionary-categorical structure as found in Modern Central Scandinavian languages. The oblique form in (i)–(ii) *henni* is the so-called oblique subject, the form *Ólafur* the nominative subject.

(i) a. Hefur henni alltaf þótt   Ólafur leiðinlegur?
       has   she-D always thought Olav-N dull?
       'has she always found Olav dull?'
    b. Ólafur hefur henni alltaf þótt leiðinlegur
    c. *Hefur Ólafur henni alltaf þótt leiðinlegur?
(ii) Henni$_i$ þykir bróðir sinn$_i$/*hennar leiðinlegur
     she-D thinks brother REFL   dull

3. This formulation is preferred in order to avoid claims that Old Norse had passives, cf. Dyvik 1980.

Sources

B 74	Codex Holmiensis B 74, quoted from GL.
B 74 GO	Codex Holmiensis B 74, quoted from transscription by Finn Delager for Gammeldansk Ordbog [Old Danish Dictionary project], 1995.
BerlT	Berlingske Tidende [a Copenhagen daily newspaper].
DgL	Danmarks gamle Landskabslove I. Ed. by Johs. Brøndum-Nielsen et al. Copenhagen 1933.
GL	Gammeldansk læsebog [Old Danish Reader], ed. by Nelly Uldahler and Gerd Wellejus. Copenhagen 1968.
H-J N Fodbold	Hans-Jørgen Nielsen 1979. *Fodboldenglen. En beretning.* Copenhagen: Tiderne Skifter.
KM	*Karl Magnus Krønike*, ed. by Paul Lindegård Hjorth. Universitets-Jubilæets Danske Samfund. København: Schulz. 1960. Christiern Pedersen's 1534 translation.
Luc	A Danish Teacher's Manual from the Mid-Fifteenth Century (COD. AM 76,8°). S. Kroon et al. (eds), Lund: Lund University Press, 1993.
SjKl	Zealand Ecclesiastical Law, after Codex Holmiensis C 69, as printed in GL.
SjT	Siæla Trøst, ed. by Niels Nielsen. Universitets-Jubilæets Danske Samfund. Copenhagen: Schulz. 1937–52.
SkKl	Scanic Ecclesiastical Law, after Codex Holmiensis B 74 and Codex AM 37,4°. Text as in GL.
SkL B 74	The Scanic Law, after Codex Holmiensis B 74, text — if not otherwise stated — from GL.
SkL B 69	The Scanic Law, after Codex Holmiensis B 69, as printed in DgL, text II.
VS Odys	Villy Sørensen 1988. *Den berømte Odysseus.* Copenhagen: Gyldendal.

References

Bjerrum, A. et al. (eds) 1966. *Paul Diderichsen. Helhed og Struktur. Udvalgte sprogvidenskabelige Afhandlinger.* Copenhagen: C. E. G. Gads forlag.

Christoffersen, M. 1993. *Setning og sammenheng. Syntaktiske Studier i Magnus Lagabøters Landslov.* Kristianssand.
Delsing, L-O. 1999. "Från OV-ordföljd til VO-ordföjd". *Arkiv för nordisk filologi* 114: 151–232.
Diderichsen, P. 1941. *Sætningsbygningen i skaanske Lov.* Copenhagen: Ejnar Munksgaard.
Diderichsen, P. 1943. "Logische und topische Gliederung des Satzes im Germanischen". Reprinted in Bjerrum et al.
Diderichsen, P. 1946. *Elementær dansk Grammatik.* Copenhagen: Gyldendal.
Dik, S.C. 1989. *The Theory of Functional Grammar. Part 1. The Structure of the Clause.* Dordrecht: Foris.
Dyvik, H. 1980. "Har gammelnorsk passiv?" In *The Nordic Languages and Modern Linguistics.* In *Proceedings of the Fourth International Conference of Nordic and General Linguistics in Oslo 1980,* E. Hovdhaugen (ed.), 81–107. Oslo: Universitetsforlaget.
Eisenberg, P. 1989. *Grundriss der deutschen Grammatik.* 2. überarbeitete und erweiterte Auflage. Stuttgart: Metzler.
Engberg-Pedersen, E. et al. 1996. *Content, Expression and Structure. Studies in Danish Functional Grammar.* Amsterdam: John Benjamins.
Engberg-Pedersen, E. 1996. "Iconicity and arbitrariness". In Engberg-Pedersen et al. 1996, 453–468.
Faarlund, J.T. 1989a. "Discourse functions and syntax". In *CLS 25. Papers from the 25th Annual Regional Meeting of the Chicago Linguistic Society. Part Two: Language in Context,* B. Music et al. (eds) 30–40. Chicago Linguistic Society.
Faarlund, J.T. 1989b. "A typology of subjects". In *Studies in Syntactic Typology,* M. Hammond, E. Moravcsik and J. Wirth (eds) 193–207. Amsterdam: John Benjamins.
Faarlund, J.T. 1990. *Syntactic Change. Toward a theory of historical syntax.* Berlin: Mouton de Gruyter [Trends in Linguistics. Studies and Monographs 50].
Halliday, M.A.K. 1967. "Language structure and language function". In *New Horizons in Linguistics,* J. Lyons (ed). Harmondsworth: Penguin.
Halliday, M.A.K. 1996. *An Introduction to Functional Grammar,*2. ed. London: Edward Arnold.
Hansen, A.. 1956. "Kasusudviklingen i dansk". In *Festskrift til Peter Skautrup,* S. Aakjær et al. (eds), 183–193. Aarhus: Universitetsforlaget i Aarhus.
Harder, P. 1996a. *Functional Semantics. A theory of meaning, structure and tense in English.* Berlin: Mouton de Gruyter.
Harder, P. 1996b. "On content and expression in syntax". In *Proceedings of the 13th Scandinavian Conference of Linguistics,* L. Heltoft and H. Haberland (eds), 83–92. Department of Languages and Culture, Roskilde University.
Harris, A.C. and Campbell, L. 1995. *Historical Syntax in Cross-linguistic Perspective.* Cambridge: CUP.
Heltoft, L. 1995. "Grammatikaliseringsprocesser i dansk syntakshistorie". In *Sproghistorie i 90erne,* B. Holmberg (ed.), 124–168. Copenhagen: Selskab for Nordisk Filologi.
Heltoft, L. 1996. "Paradigms, word order and grammaticalization". In E. Engberg-Pedersen et al. 1996, 469–494.

Heltoft, L. 1997. "Hvem opslugte hvo — et bidrag til beskrivelsen af det danske kasussystems udvikling". In *Ord, Sprog oc artige Dict. Festskrift til Poul Lindegård Hjorth*, F. Lundgreen-Nielsen et al. (eds), 227–256. Copenhagen: C.A. Reitzel.

Heltoft, L. 1999. "Hierarki og rækkefølge — skandinavisk ledstilling i funktionel grammatisk belysning". In *Sætningsskemaet i generativ grammatik*, P.A. Jensen and P. Skadhauge (eds), 31–62. Kolding: Institut for Erhvervssproglig Informatik og Kommunikation, Syddansk Universitet, Kolding.

Heltoft, L. and Falster Jakobsen, L. 1996. "Danish passives and subject positions as a mood system". In E. Engberg-Pedersen et al. (eds), 199–234.

Hjelmslev, L. 1943. *Omkring Sprogteoriens Grundlæggelse*. Copenhagen: Københavns Universitets festskrift.

Holmberg, A. and Platzack, C. 1995. *The Role of Inflection in Scandinavian Syntax*. Oxford: OUP.

Hopper, P.J. and Traugott, E. Closs. 1993. *Grammaticalization*. Cambridge: CUP.

Keenan, E. 1976. "Towards a universal definition of 'subject'". In C. Li 1976, 303–333.

Lehmann, C. 1985. "Grammaticalization: synchronic variation and diachronic change". *Lingua e Stile 20*: 303–18.

Lehmann, C. 1992. "Word order change by grammaticalization". In *Internal and External Factors in Syntactic Change*, M. Gerritsen and D. Stein (eds), 395–416. Berlin: Mouton de Gruyter [Trends in Linguistics. Studies and Monographs 61].

Lehmann, W.P. 1976. "From topic to subject in Indo-European". In C. Li 1976, 446–456.

Li, C. (ed.) 1976. *Subject and Topic*. New York: Academic Press.

Meillet, A. 1921 [1912]. "L'Évolution des formes grammaticales". In *A. Meillet, Linguistique historique et linguistique générale*, 130–148. Paris: Edouard Champion. Orig. *Scientia (Rivista di Scienza), vol. XII*, 1912, No. XXVI, 6.

Pedersen, K.M. 1993. "Letledsreglen og lighedsreglen — novation, ekspansion og resistens". In *Jyske Studier*, K.M. Pedersen and I.L. Pedersen (eds), 199–218. Copenhagen: C.A. Reitzel.

Sasse, H.-J. 1987. "The categorical vs. thetic distinction revisited". *Linguistics* 25: 511–567.

Schachter, P. 1977. "Reference-related and role-related properties of subjects". In *Grammatical Relations. Syntax and Semantics* 8, P. Cole and J. Sadock (eds), 279–306. New York: Academic Press.

Vikner, S. 1995. *Verb Movement and Expletive Subjects in the Germanic Languages*. Oxford: OUP.

Ergative to accusative
Comparing evidence from Inuktitut*

Alana Johns
University of Toronto

This paper examines the case of different dialects of Inuktitut which appear to vary in their distribution and function of the antipassive construction. It is hypothesized that a difference in grammatical restrictions on this construction will coincide with a quantitative difference in occurrence, i.e. some dialects have moved further along the continuum toward a nominative-accusative typology. However, it is shown that counting the number of tokens of the case marker in question does not show any statistical significance, due to the fact that this case marker has functions independent of object marking and that these functions appear to vary in inverse proportion to the degree to which it is used as an accusative marker.

1. Alternation and syntactic change

Central to our understanding of diachronic change in syntax are synchronic facts involving alternation. The term alternation here refers to instances in the syntax where more than one syntactic construction is generally but not specifically feasible. In other words, although there are no optional operations in the syntax (see Chomsky 1995), there are often two syntactic constructions possible. For example, where the transitive clauses is possible, it is usually also possible to have a passive clause instead. The question remains as to the properties that condition the presence of each alternative. As will be shown in this article, which examines two constructions in Inuktitut, the transitive and the "antipassive", the conditioning features can change, and such changes can lead towards a change in the typology of the language, in this case from an ergative/absolutive system towards a nominative/accusative one.

Syntactic change can not be abrupt and linguists, especially historical linguists and sociolinguists, look for an explanation of change which will allow the linguistic system to maintain itself coherently, at the same time allowing for change. As an example of a coherent change, Johns (1999b) argues that the grammaticalization of a volitional morpheme to a future morpheme in Inuktitut does not move directly from a volitional to an epistemic, which would be incoherent, i.e. non-logical. Instead, the grammaticalization crucially involves a stage where the lexical semantics of the morpheme in question results in a deontic interpretation, but that depending on the animacy of the independent subject, this deontic interpretation will be interpreted as either inanimate deontic or volitional (animate deontic). It is the surface ambiguity (Harris and Campell 1995), resulting solely from contextual interpretation (and not any inherent ambiguity) which creates the conditions by means of which the next stage of grammaticalization can take place. Likewise Bejar (1999) singles out ambiguity deriving from context, e.g. structural or other features, as the crucial element in the conflation of the genitive and plural morphemes in Old English. Central to these approaches is the idea that it is necessary for there to be some sort of ambiguity or alternation in order for change to take place. In effect, the alternation/ambiguity introduces some semblance of dynamism to the system (when in fact there is none).

This paper explores some methodological issues in using comparative data as evidence for a change in a language's grammatical system. Using different dialects, we will compare evidence for a grammatical change based on differing grammatical restrictions to evidence based on statistical findings. The change in question involves a varying use of ergativity between the dialects. As a consequence, one of the central aspects of this paper is the issue of typological shift from an ergative/absolutive to a nominative/accusative language (see also Dixon 1994 and Dorleijn 1996). Ergativity refers to a property of a language where the object of the transitive verb patterns similarly to the intransitive subject, e.g. in case or agreement, while the subject of the transitive verb has distinct patterning. In contrast, in a nominative-accusative language, the subject of the transitive verb and the subject of the intransitive verb pattern in a similar fashion, while the object of the transitive verb has distinct patterning.

Ergativity has been discussed extensively in linguistic literature and many proposals have been put forward to explain it (see Dixon 1994; Bittner and Hale 1996; Woolford 1997). It is well-known that ergativity comes in various guises in different languages (see Dixon 1994). In the paper that follows, the syntactic explanation for ergativity in Inuktitut is left aside (see Johns 1992 for one proposal); instead the focus is on identifying and characterizing features involved in the typological shift. Ultimately the results of this research should benefit our understanding of ergative systems. At the very least, this research supports the position taken in Johns (1999a) that typological shifts from ergative to nominative-accusative take place incrementally (see also van Gelderen this volume).

2. Two types of object constructions

Inuktitut[1] is a language which is spoken from Alaska to Greenland. It is a dialect continuum where speakers of neighbouring dialects usually, but not always, can understand one another, and where speakers of dialects geographically distant often cannot fully understand one another, although they can usually get the gist of the other's speech . The dialects spread generally from west to east, so that more conservative properties are largely found in the west and more innovative properties to the east. In particular, the western dialects are phonologically conservative in contrast to the eastern dialects (see Dorais 1993). Naturally, there are likely to be exceptions to these generalizations, i.e. that some properties in the western dialect may be innovative and others in the eastern dialects conservative.

In Inuktitut, there exist two different syntactic constructions in which the argument equivalent to the direct object in English can appear. I will use the term DIRECT OBJECT throughout this paper, but the reader should understand that it refers to an argument (semantically the theme or patient of the action) rather than to any single syntactic position or grammatical relation. In fact, I have argued elsewhere (Johns 1992) that one type of these "direct objects" discussed below is syntactically a subject, in the sense of being an argument which is syntactically associated with a verbal element through a predication relation.

We see an example of this type of direct object in the example below from the Qairnirmiut dialect, shown in (1). I will call this construction the ergative/absolutive or E/A construction.[2]

(1) *anguti-up **arnaq*** *taku-ja-a* [Qairnirmiutut]
 man-REL woman.ABS see-TR.PART-3SG.3SG
 'The man sees the woman'

The NP expressing the direct object in this construction gets absolutive (null) case and agrees with the verb. The agent of the action gets relative (ergative) case and also agrees with the verb. The E/A construction is characterized in main clauses by the obligatory presence of the transitive mood morpheme.

The direct object is also found in another construction which I will call here the nominative/accusative or N/A construction (see Kalmar 1979a; Bok-Bennema 1991) but which is also sometimes referred to as the antipassive construction, shown in (2).

(2) *angut   nanur-mik   taku-juq*   [Qairnirmiutut]
    man.ABS polar.bear-MOD see-INTR.PART.3SG
    'The man sees a polar bear'

In this second construction, we see that the direct object has a different case on it, the modalis case (which is sometimes referred to as the instrumental — see below). The agent of the action is in absolutive case and only the latter agrees with the verb. The mood morpheme is now intransitive. A final characteristic of this construction is that certain verb stems require an obligatory antipassive morpheme immediately following. Verbs of perception, such as that in (2) either do not require this morpheme or it is null.[3]

Finally both these constructions contrast with the intransitive construction shown in (3).

(3) *angut   pisuk-tuq*   [Qairnirmiutut]
    man.ABS walk-INTR.PART.3SG
    'The man is walking'

The intransitive greatly resembles the N/A construction except that it never requires additional morphology and does not take a direct object. Note the ergative patterning in examples (1) and (3), since the direct object and the intransitive subject both receive absolutive case, while the transitive subject gets distinct (ergative) case.

While both constructions shown in (1) and (2) are in use in dialects across the arctic, the basis of the alternation has been a matter of some contention within the field of Inuktitut linguistics. Kalmar (1979b) argues that the E/A is used for a given entity while the N/A is used for a new entity. Bittner (1987) argues against this account in favour of a scopal account. We leave aside this important issue in order to examine more superficially the distribution of this alternation in a number of dialects. In other words, we expect that comparative evidence will shed light on this question.

3. Syntactic restrictions: A typological shift?

It is clear that languages can change from nominative-accusative to ergative and vice-versa (see Chung 1978 and Dixon 1994: 193–203). These changes seem to vary in nature cross-linguistically, however, in some cases involve a reanalysis/grammaticalization of passive (nominative-accusative to ergative) or antipassive (ergative to nominative-accusative).

Johns (1999a) claims that there is typological shift underway in eastern dialects of Inuktitut, in particular Labrador Inuttut, such that it has become more nominative-accusative and less ergative-absolutive. Note that this describes a degree of ergativity, not any absolute state, under the assumption that ergativity is an epiphenomenon (Johns 1992). This shift towards nominative-accusative is demonstrated by the fact that in Labrador Inuttut, the restrictions on the use of the N/A (antipassive) construction are more relaxed than in western dialects. Although there has not been enough change in order to conclude that Labrador Inuttut is what might be typologically classified as nominative-accusative, it is clear that some change has taken place on the level of ergativity in this dialect. In the following section, I review the differences in dialect restrictions which show that the N/A construction is more highly favoured, and the E/A less favoured in Labrador Inuttut. This latter finding is somewhat surprising, as the status of the E/A construction could have preserved its *status quo*.

3.1 Restrictions on accusative

In this section, I show that western dialects exhibit more syntactic restrictions on the use of the N/A construction than are found in eastern dialects. In the western Siglit (or Inuvialuit) dialect, spoken in Tuktoyaktuk and other communities in the Mackenzie delta, the most striking restriction on the N/A construction is that it cannot be used with names, but only with common nouns. As was seen above, the modalis singular case marker on the direct object in the N/A construction, is -*mik*. This case cannot be added to a name without the entity being changed in meaning from a unique individual to one of a set of individuals with this property, as shown in (4), which is marked as marginal as a result of the bizarre interpretation.

(4) ?*Alana-mik* [Siglitun]
 Alana-MOD
 'someone dressed up as Alana'

The second major restriction in Siglit is that there are very few, if any, antipassive morphemes in this dialect. There is no mention of any in the most definitive grammar on this dialect, that of Lowe (1985). That antipassive morphemes are absent or few may be considered a restriction, since we will interpret multiple types of antipassive morphemes to be suggestive of greater use of the construction in the language. In other words, we will consider it surprising, if not impossible, for there to be a marginal construction with many different morphemes associated with its presence.

Finally the most compelling evidence that the N/A construction is restricted in this dialect is the fact its use as a pure N/A construction is virtually undiscussed in grammars of western dialects. The absence of discussion shows that the construction is minimally not central to the grammar of the language. Recall, that in (2) we have shown that the direct object is marked with the modalis case -*mik* in the N/A construction. In the discussion of the use of this case in his grammar of the Siglit dialect of Inuktitut, Lowe (1985) gives 26 examples of constructions exemplifying the use of the modalis -*mik*; however only one is a direct object in the sense we use here, i.e. patient/themes of verbs which have no other complicating grammatical factor (to be discussed below). Instead of the N/A, the discussion of the use of the modalis case is centred around a number of other important constructions in the language: the instrumental, the double object construction and noun incorporation. Lowe (1985: 63) describes the use of the modalis case in this dialect as "unquestionably the most difficult syntactic function to describe". He summarizes it generally as indicating "the mode of actualizing or realizing an event" (p. 66). We see this property in the instrumental construction in (5).

(5) *nirrivik   allarun-mik salumma-gaa*   [Siglitun] Lowe (1985: 64)
     table.ABS cloth-MOD   clean-TR.PART.3SG.3SG
     'He/she cleaned the table with a cloth'

Notice that the verb has double agreement, and that there is a direct object *nirrivik* 'table' in absolutive case, i.e. the construction is in all respects E/A. These same two factors are also found in the double object construction, shown in (6), where the -*mik* case is also found.

(6) *aitqating-nik aittu-gaa*   [Siglitun] Lowe (1985: 66)
     mitts-MOD.PL give-TR.PART.3SG.3SG
     'He gave her a pair of mitts'

Although the absolutive goal is not overtly present, it is implied by the double agreement morphology on the verb. Thus in both these constructions, the use of modalis case is associated with the E/A construction and is found on NP's, usually non-human, which are in addition to the direct object. Note that although most Inuit dialects have a dative alternation, the unmarked case is for the goal to agree with the verb, as in (6), thus necessitating the use of the modalis on the theme (Johns 1985).

Finally the modalis case is also found on stranded modifiers of incorporated nouns, as shown in (7).

(7) *qatuqtu-**mik** atigi-ruaq-tuaq*
     white-MOD   parka-have-INTR.PART.3SG
     'He has a white parka' [Siglitun] Lowe (1985:65)

Although the incorporated noun is not strictly speaking the direct object of the action (Johns 1999c), we see that the modalis case is once again found as a supplementary case. It licenses an extra syntactic element, in this case the modifier, which otherwise would not be grammatically possible.

In summary, we see that in dialects such as Siglit, the N/A construction is largely subsumed (perhaps to the point of absence[4]) by the use of the modalis case in constructions which are either E/A or involve noun incorporation.[5] Thus we may hypothesize that the normal form for a simple transitive verb in Siglit is E/A, and the N/A construction is highly marked if not ungrammatical.

In contrast to what we have just seen with respect to a western dialect of Inuktitut, Labrador Inuttut, an eastern dialect spoken in Labrador on the north Atlantic coast of North America, shows many differing properties. To begin with, as discussed in Johns (1999a) names can appear as direct objects marked with modalis case in the N/A constructions, as in (8).[6]

(8) *Margarita   Kuinatsa-i-juk   Ritsati-**mik***   [Labrador Inuttut]
     Margarita.ABS tickle-AP-INTR.PART.3SG Richard-MOD
     'Margarita is tickling Richard'

Names do not pose a problem as direct objects in this construction but they do in more western dialects, as was seen above in (4), and as is reported by Johnson (1980) and discussed in Manning (1996).[7]

In addition to names being possible with modalis case, there are numerous forms of antipassive morphemes found in the N/A construction in Labrador Inuttut. I provide some examples from Beaudoin-Lietz (1982) in (9), where the antipassive morphemes are in bold.

(9) a. *milu-tsi-vuk* [Labrador Inuttut]
throw-AP-INTR.IND.3SG
'That person threw and hit something'
b. *kivi-si-vuk*
lift-AP-INTR.IND.3SG
'He lifts it up'
c. *kata-i-vuk*
drop-AP-INTR.INDIC.3SG
'He dropped it'
d. *pi-kKu-ji-vuk*
do-ask-AP-INTR.IND.3SG
'He told him to do something'
e. *apu-nni-vuk*
bump-AP-INTR.IND.3SG
'He did bump it'
f. *tili-tli-vuk*
command-AP-INTR.IND.3SG
'He tells someone to do something'

As discussed above, we interpret numerous types of this morpheme to be indicative of a wider usage. The distribution of these morphemes, also discussed in Bittner (1987), has not received an explanation to date.

In summary, the overall picture of Labrador Inuttut as compared with more western dialects is that of a dialect where any direct object can freely appear in the N/A construction and where there are numerous morphological devices to instantiate this construction. From this perspective, the N/A construction is a true competitor to the E/A construction, unlike in Siglitun, where we saw that the N/A construction plays only a small role (if any) in the grammar. It should be noted that although the modalis case is not used for instruments in Labrador Inuttut, it still has an auxiliary role, being found in double object construction and on elements modifying incorporated elements, similar to what we observed in the Siglit example in (7). Thus, while the interpretation of the modalis case as an accusative morpheme is more likely in Labrador Inuttut, it cannot be exclusively interpreted as such.

3.2 Restrictions on ergative

In the previous sections we have seen that the grammar of the eastern dialect Labrador Inuttut is more accommodating to the N/A construction, affording it a prominent place in the grammar. The evidence for this was fewer restrictions on its usage and more morphemes to create it. In this section we will see that alongside of this favouring of the N/A, we find a subtle but distinct disfavouring of the E/A construction in this dialect. The subtlety of this evidence is that a small subset of possible E/A constructions is disallowed

In most Inuit dialects, a morphological causative may attach directly to an inherently transitive verb stem, i.e. one which would otherwise be obligatorily E/A. An example is given in (10) from the western Qairnirmiutut dialect.

(10) *kunik-ti-taa* [Qairnirmiutut]
kiss-cause-TR.PART.3SG.3SG
'He/she makes someone kiss him/her'

Nevertheless, according to Smith (1982), in Labrador Inuttut, a causative morpheme may not attach directly to such a verb stem, as shown by by the hypothesized example in (11).

(11) **kuni-tti-tanga/vauk*[8] [Labrador Inuttut Hypothetical example]
kiss-cause-TR.PART.3SG.3SG/TR.IND.3SG.3SG
'He/she makes someone kiss him/her'

The restriction is not between the causative morpheme and the ergative construction. If the verb root is semantically intransitive to begin with, the causative can appear in an ergative construction, as shown in (12).

(12) *ani-ti-tanga* [Labrador Inuttut]
go.out-cause-TR.PART.3SG.3SG
'He/she made him/her go out'

Smith (1982) calls this restriction the Detransitive Complement Constraint. This is given in (13).

(13) *The Detransitive Complement Constraint*   Smith (1982)
Complement sentences of affixal verbs are detransitivized prior to verb raising.

Whatever the explanatory basis of this restriction, the significant fact here is that it entails that a certain class of possible E/A constructions, such as that in (11), are effectively eliminated as possible derivations in the grammar. Instead, passive or antipassive morphology must be added to sentences such as (11) in order to create a legitimate construction, as discussed in Smith (1982). This restriction not only eliminates some of the E/A possibilities which are found in other dialects, it also increases the likelihood that the theme of a lower transitive verb will be in modalis case. The latter effect results from the addition of antipassive morphology.

As we see from the above discussion, in all of the changes which Labrador Inuttut has undergone in comparison to other dialects, the grammar favours N/A over E/A. Not a single one of these changes favours E/A. The strongest version of this finding is to state that we do not expect to find a dialectal innovation in Labrador, comparable to that in (13), which entails that the E/A construction must be used. Thus we can interpret the overall tendency of the grammar of this eastern dialect as a shift toward a pattern where N/A predominates, i.e. a nominative-accusative system. Languages switch in typology and here we see a dialect which is part-way in terms of this switch. In the following section, we examine the link between this shift in grammatical restrictions and frequency.

4. Statistical evidence: Frequency

The frequency with which a particular grammatical pattern appears in a language variety is an integral part of the study of language change. Lightfoot (1999:84) discusses the fact that a particular construction may increase in frequency within a grammar but that this fact does not in itself constitute a change in grammar. Nevertheless, as he points out, a statistical change does affect the input data of the next generation of speakers. It is the reinterpretation of input by the children which leads to change, and here the key issue, as Lightfoot states, is learnability.

Kalmar (1979b) reports that of the first ten texts of Rasmussen (1930), 117 out 123 clauses with objects are ergative, while only 6 are antipassive, i.e. 4.8% N/A. In Kalmar's own elicitation notes, 57.1% of randomly picked translations were N/A. As Kalmar's data was from a later time, we might construe this difference (4.8% vs. 57.1%) as an indication that N/A is gradually taking over. But a number of caveats are in order here. First, as Kalmar suggests, text materials may differ stylistically from elicitation notes. Generally texts and elicitation involve major differences in discourse factors, e.g. previous discourse, which is available in texts but rarely in elicitation. The other possible problem with Kalmar's figures is that Rasmussen's texts may have been in a different dialect from that of Kalmar's elicitations.

On the basis of the grammatical restrictions discussed above, Johns (1999a) predicts that eastern dialects should show a distinct difference in the frequency of N/A as opposed to E/A. This prediction is given in (14).

(14) *Frequency Inferential Principle* (Johns 1999a)
Increased Restriction(s) → Decline ($X^n → X^{n-m}$)
Decreased Restriction(s) → Incline ($X^n → X^{n+m}$)
where *m* can be any number greater than 0

This claim makes a prediction regarding the correlation of statistical frequency and grammatical restriction. If this correlation can be substantiated, then we may infer a difference in statistical frequency from simply observing a difference in the number of grammatical restrictions. Equally were we first to observe a difference in grammatical frequency, we could infer that grammatical restrictions had changed. In fact, under the latter view we may revise the arrows in (14) to bidirectional arrows (↔). We now turn to an examination of the frequency of the N/A in a number of texts from different dialects. All of these texts are narratives, however the age of the speakers varies slightly. With the exception of one speaker, all are over 50 years old.

The initial strategy was to establish the total number of *-mik* tokens, i.e. use of modalis case, and compare it with the total number of words per texts. The thinking here was that even though there are other uses of *-mik,* that these other uses will remain stable so that an overall increase in the use of *-mik* will be observed in those dialects where restrictions on the N/A have loosened. For this reason, the total number of tokens of *-mik* (and its plural form *-nik*) were counted and compared with the total number of words as a percentage. The results are shown in Table 1. Note that in some texts, there were English words inserted for various reasons, e.g. relating English discourse quotation, etc. These words were not included as part of the total.

Table 1. displays dialect results from the most westerly dialect Siglit on the far left to the most easterly dialect Labrador on the far right.

Table 1. Percentage of *-mik* tokens per dialect text

	S	A	Q	M	L
-mik total	27	1	10	41	20
word total	291	63	180	1,301	409
% *-mik*	9.28	0	5.5	3.1	4.9

S = Siglit; A = Ahiarmiut; Q = Qairnirmiut; M = Mittimatalik; L = Labrador

Instead of the expected overall increase in the use of -*mik* from west to east, we see that the results are rather mixed, with the largest percentage of -*mik* tokens actually found in the most western dialect Siglit. How can this be? Recall that the assumption underlying the initial counting was that the non-N/A uses of -*mik* would remain more or less stable across dialects. The motivation in counting -*mik* tokens rather than grammatical constructions is that -*mik* tokens are easily found in a computer search of a text, while grammatical constructions must necessarily be identified and labelled before counting. The relatively small number of -*mik* tokens in Labrador Inuttut may be explained by the fact that its auxiliary use in other constructions has diminished in this dialect. As discussed above, in Siglit, -*mik* is used for the following constructions.

(15) a. object case of non-names (possibly only with a partitive interpretation).
 b. instrumental
 c. theme argument of double object constructions
 d. modifiers associated with incorporated nouns.

In contrast, in Labrador Inuttut, the -*mik* case is used as follows.

(16) a. object case of nouns.
 b. modifiers associated with incorporated nouns.
 c. double object constructions.
 (There is no instrumental case, instead the goal -*mut* case is used).

Counting frequency is not always a straightforward methodology. Dresher (2000, 67), based on joint research done with Aditi Lahiri, concludes that in counting sometimes "The number of tokens is less important than the number of types of words." Thus numerical total is not necessarily the ultimate factor, but the range of entities which appear can be significant in some instances. From this perspective we may view the Labrador dialect as decreasing the range of constructions that use -*mik* at the same time as the -*mik* case has become a direct alternative to the absolutive of the E/A construction. This decrease in types may be the source of fewer overall tokens.

It is interesting to note that this issue of distinguishing between constructions types was not part of Kalmar's procedure. For example, Kalmar (1979b: 142) states that his minimum requirement for a clause to be counted as antipassive is that it contain a subject in absolutive case and a noun with -*mik* case. Consider the example in (17) from Kalmar (1979b: 125), which he gives from Rasmussen (1930).[9]

(17) tuga-alu-Ø-gøøq   nErlEr-mik
raven-the.fool-Ø.CASE-it.is.said goose-MOD
nuliArtaa-tla-pip-p-øq-Ø
take.wife-INT-INT-IND-MONO-3
'The foolish raven married a goose'

In this example, although the object of marriage is indeed a goose, syntactically the construction involves noun incorporation of the noun *nuliAr* 'wife'. Since the vast majority of noun incorporating affixes obligatorily require intransitive (or single agreement) verbs, the only way in which the noun meaning 'goose' can be added to the construction is via the modalis case. In addition, the relation of 'goose' to 'wife' is not independent but one of kind, i.e. it modifies the incorporated noun. In other words, the syntax of this construction makes the E/A alternative unavailable. Counting constructions such as these will only give us the number of these constructions, not the number of true antipassive alternatives. Thus we may conclude that counting antipassives should involve only constructions where a) there is a noun in *-mik* case which is semantically the theme argument of the verb and b) that there is no other NP in the sentence to compete with this NP, i.e. no goal object nor incorporated noun.[10] This involves a more sophisticated means of counting, since each verb form must be evaluated as to whether or not the conditions are such that in principle the other construction could be available. Even so, things are not always clear. Consider the following example from the Ahiarmiut dialect.

(18) niri-gjua'-tua-rumaaq-mat   hikhing-mik
eat-a.lot-a.lot-will-CAUS.3SG ground.squirrel-MOD
'He will eat a big meal of ground squirrel'

In this example the noun *hikhik* 'ground squirrel' meets the requirements a) and b) above. The noun is in modalis case and there is no second NP "object" which has eliminated the option for the first to be absolutive (and hence E/A). Nevertheless, the translation of the sentence opens up some doubts. It does not mean that he will eat a lot of some ground squirrel or another but instead that his meal will consist of ground squirrel (multiple or not). This recalls Lowe (1985)'s definition of the semantics of the modalis case as actualizing an event. Thus the noun in modalis case is not a clear case of canonical object. From this, we can summarize our conditions for counting an argument as a canonical object across dialects. These are as in (19).

(19) *Canonical object properties*: To be a canonical object, the argument must be:
  i. an individuated argument.
  ii. there must be no absolutive goal argument in sentence.
  iii. the argument must be external to the verb.
  iv. no other argument may be morphologically attached to verb (i.e. no noun incorporation).
  v. the argument must bear the theme (i.e. patient) role with respect to the action.

5. Conclusions

In conclusion, we have seen that mere counting of the -*mik* case forms does not suffice to show a change in grammatical typology. The forms must be counted according to the grammatical contexts in which they are found, i.e. whether they are on a canonical object or not. Yet we have also seen that this is no easy, nor non-arbitrary task. It is made difficult by the fact that each construction must be evaluated as to whether or not the ergative-absolutive form is a real alternative to the nominative-accusative form. It may be arbitrary to eliminate partitive objects from consideration.

Nevertheless, the grammatical restrictions discussed in this paper indicate that we are dealing with a robust change in grammatical usage, possibly a change from inherent case in the western dialects to structural case in Labrador Inuttut (see also van Gelderen this volume). One of the more interesting patterns which emerges in this change is that the overall usage of the modalis case remains more or less the same, even as it becomes something equivalent to an accusative case. Auxiliary functions of the case disappear from a grammar where the case has assumed a more central syntactic role. We might see this in terms of a conservation of usage.

This drift towards nominative-accusative can only take place where there exists two alternative constructions (the E/A and the N/A). Yet, as we have seen, in each grammar these constructions are not truly alternatives, but depend on substantive grammatical restrictions within each dialect. Clearly for the changes to take place, a generation of young speakers must reinterpret these restrictions. The fact that both are superficially possible makes this reinterpretation more likely.

Notes

* This paper was first presented at the International Conference on Historical Linguistics held in August 1999 at the University of British Columbia in Vancouver. The research was made possible through SSHRC funding (grants 410-94-570 and 410-97-0493) and a travel grant from the Dean of Arts and Sciences at the University of Toronto. Thanks to Elan Dresher and Charles Nuligaq for discussion. All errors are mine.

1. The name Inuktitut is used to refer to the language in most of Canada, except in the west where speakers prefer the term Inuvialuktun. Outside of Canada, Inuit is sometimes used to refer to the language, although literally it refers to the people.

2. Grammatical abbreviations used in this article are: ABS = absolutive case (phonetically null); REL = relative case, i.e. ergative; MOD = modalis case (also called instrumental in the literature); TR = transitive, i.e. double agreement; INTR = intransitive, i.e. single agreement; PART = participial mood (a type of declarative); IND = indicative mood (a type of declarative); CAUS = causative mood (used as either a dependent mood or a presuppositional declarative (see Gillon 1999); SG = singular; PL = plural; AP = antipassive; PERF = perfective; D.PST = distant past; DR = disjoint reference; CONJ = conjunctive mood (similar to gerund); PASS = passive. I give the dialect name in square brackets to the right of each example.

3. In fact, antipassive morphemes can appear with perceptive verbs, but with an inceptive meaning (see Bittner 1987 and Seigle 1998).

4. More research is needed on the question as to whether an antipassive even exists in this dialect. Of all the examples in Lowe (1985)'s discussion of the modalis case, only one is clearly a simple object construction, and this example contains a perception verb, therefore no (overt) antipassive morpheme is expected.

5. Noun incorporation is obligatory depending on the verb type, so there is no question of either E/A or N/A being a possibility with such a verb.

6. While (8) is an elicited example, examples from texts involving names in modalis case are reasonably easy to find in the Labrador dialects. See Johns (1999a) for an example from a narrative text in the Rigolet dialect of Labrador. More recently, I found the following in a Labrador magazine.

i. *Sivuli-lau-kKuk*   *O'Brien-imik KI* (Fall 1999: 6)
   lead-D.PST-IND.3SG   -MOD
   taku-ti-tlu-gu   *Kima-tau-sima-ju-mik*
   see-DR-CONJ-3SG abandon-PASS-PERF-INTR.PART.-MOD
   'He led O'Brien, showing him the abandoned site' [translation modified]

7. Manning (1996:94) says that Michael Fortescue doubts the acceptability of a name in modalis case in Kalaalisut (West Greenlandic) cited in Bittner (1987). If such examples are indeed not possible in this dialect, it may have something to do with the fact that in Kalaalisut the modalis *-mik* is used quite a bit as the instrumental, similar to what we saw in the Siglit example in (5). In Labrador Inuttut, on the other hand, the case used for the instrumental is often *-mut*, normally found on goals. Clearly, there is much work to be done on dialectal case system comparisons and their link with syntax. A final note — Kalmar

(1979b: 123) gives an example from the Igloolik dialect (central eastern) with a name in modalis case.

8. This example is hypothesized based on the grammatical restriction described in Smith (1982). It is not clear at this time whether in fact this restriction holds for all varieties of Labrador Inuttut. Further research is needed on this question.

9. I leave the transcription and gloss as in Kalmar (1979b, example 22). Ø.CASE stands for null case (absolutive). MONO stands for single person agreement (intransitive), and INT stands for intensifiers.

10. The notion of competition recalls Bittner and Hale (1996).

References

Beaudoin-Lietz, C. 1982. *Aspects of Certain Intransitivizing Postbases of a Transitivizing Postbase in Labrador Inuttut.* M.A. thesis, Memorial University of Newfoundland.

Bejar, S. 1999. "Genitive, plural and the loss of the definite adjectival inflection in English". Talk presented at ICHL XIV, Vancouver.

Bittner, M. 1987. "On the semantics of the Greenlandic antipassive and related constructions". *International Journal of American Linguistics* 53: 195–231.

Bittner, M. and Hale, K. 1996. "The structural determination of case and agreement". *Linguistic Inquiry* 27: 1–68.

Bok-Bennema, R. 1991. *Case and Agreement in Inuit.* Foris Publications. Dordrecht.

Chomsky, N. 1995. *The Minimalist Program.* Cambridge: MIT Press.

Chung, S. 1978. *Case Marking and Grammatical Relations in Polynesian.* Austin: University of Texas Press.

Dixon, R.M.W. 1994. *Ergativity.* [Cambridge Studies in Linguistics 69]. New York: Cambridge University Press.

Dorais, L.-J. 1993. *From Magic Words to Word Processing: A History of the Inuit Language.* Iqaluit: Arctic College [Available through Inuksiutiit Katimajiit, Laval Québec.]

Dorleijn, M. 1996. *The Decay of Ergativity in Kurmanci.* [Studies in Multilingualism 3]. Tilburg:Tilburg University Press.

Dresher, B. E. 2000. "Analogical levelling of vowel length in West Germanic". In *Analogy, levelling, markedness: Principles of change in phonology and morphology,* A. Lahiri (ed.), 47–70. Berlin: Mouton de Gruyter.

Gillon, C. 1999. "When WH-words move and why: A case study of Inuktitut". M.A. forum paper, University of Toronto.

Harris, A. C. and Campell, L. 1995. *Historical Syntax in Cross-linguistic Perspective.* Cambridge: Cambridge University Press.

Johns, A. 1985. "Dative 'Movement' in Eskimo". *Papers from the Parasession Lexical Semantics,* 162–172. Chicago Linguistic Society, Chicago, Illinois.

Johns, A. 1992. "Deriving Ergativity". *Linguistic Inquiry* 23(1): 57–87.

Johns, A. 1999a. "The decline of ergativity in Labrador Inuttut". In *Papers from the Workshop on Structure and Constituency in Native American Languages*. MITWPL 17: L. Bar-el, R.M. Déchaine and C. Reinholtz (eds), 73–90.

Johns, A. 1999b. "The lexical semantics of affixal 'want' in Inuktitut". *International Journal of American Linguistics* 65(2): 176–200.

Johns, A. 1999c. "The lexical basis of noun incorporation in Inuktitut. Paper presented at the Workshop on Structure and Constituency in the Languages of the Americas, University of British Columbia.

Johnson, M. R. 1980. *Ergativity in Inuktitut (Eskimo), in Montague Grammar and in Relational Grammar*. Bloomington: Indiana University Linguistics Club.

Kalmar, I. 1979a. *Case and Context in Inuktitut (Eskimo)*. National Museum of Man Mercury Series No. 49. [Ottawa: Canadian Museum of Civilization.]

Kalmar, I. 1979b. "The antipassive and grammatical relations in Eskimo". In *Ergativity: Towards a Theory of Grammatical Relations*, F. Plank (ed.), 117–143. London: Academic Press.

KI Magazine [kinatuinamut Ilingajuk]. Fall 1999. Nain: OKâlaKatiget Society.

Lightfoot, D. 1999. *The Development of Language: Acquisition, Change and Evolution*. Oxford: Blackwell Publishers.

Lowe, R. 1985. *Siglit Inuvialuit Uqausiita Ilisarviksait/Basic Siglit Inuvialuit Eskimo Grammar*. [Available from Association Inuksiutiit Katimajiit, Université Laval].

Manning, C. 1996. *Ergativity: Argument Structure and Grammatical Relations*. Stanford: CSLI Publications.

Rasmussen, K. 1930. *Iglulik and Caribou Eskimo Texts. Report of the 5th Thule Expedition 1921–1924*, Vol. 7:3. Copenhagen: Nordisk Forlag.

Seigle, L. 1998. "Argument Structure and Antipassivization in Inuit". *Papers from the UPenn/MIT Roundtable on Argument Structure and Aspect*. MIT/WPL 32, H. Harley (ed.), 159–174.

Smith, L. 1982."An analysis of affixal derivation and complementation in Labrador Inuttut." *Linguistic Analysis* 10(2): 161–189.

Woolford, E. 1997. "Four-way Case systems: Nominative, ergative, objective and accusative". *Natural Language and Linguistic Theory* 15:181–227.

Subject and object in Old English and Latin copular deontics*

D. Gary Miller
University of Florida

The history of deontic expressions in several languages reveals some naturalness in (a) constructions involving BE plus infinitive/gerundial, (b) thematic object initially surfacing in the NOM, (c) reanalysis via case accommodation in neuters to a structure in which the thematic object surfaces in the ACC, and (d) animates being first to adopt the change obligatorily. Neuters permitted two analyses of the theme argument: (i) NOM subject; (ii) ACC object. BE and non-neuters of most word-classes favor the NOM subject analysis. In Latin, impersonals in *-um* favored an object analysis. In Latin and OE the possibility of analyzing the agentive dative as a quirky subject in the (OE) type *us is to ponder the word/what is us to ponder* shifted the cues in favor of an analysis of the theme as structural object, whence overt ACC objects.

1. Introduction

The history of deontic expressions equivalent to the type *the water is to boil* is discussed in Latin and English. It is argued that in both languages, as predicted by the presence of the verb BE, the thematic object could initially be expected to surface in the nominative. The morphological identity of NOM and ACC in the neuters could **accommodate** either a subject or object analysis. That ambiguity was exploited in both languages to innovate a type *one is to boil the water*, in which the thematic object surfaces in the ACC. In Latin, this type remained rare until the post-Classical period.[1]

In English, the type with NP movement was replaced by the new passive infinitive (*the water is to be boiled*), optionally with neuters (*the water is to boil* remains possible), obligatorily with animates (*he is to be loved*; **he is to love* is no longer grammatical, except as an active with implied object). A North Russian parallel shows that it is not accidental that (a) the construction originated with the theme argument in the NOM, or (b) the animates were the first to change. English insisted that the thematic object was in fact the structural subject, as evidenced by its NOM case in the new unambiguous passive structure. By contrast, in North Russian, the NOM was (re)analyzed as a structural object, and the animates were the first to shift to ACC.

Through the case-ambiguity of the neuters, the English type *what is to do* was reanalyzed from NP movement [*what is* [t *to do* t]], in which *what* was NOM, to WH movement with PRO subject [*what is* [PRO *to do* t]], in which *what* is ACC. That allowed for lexical subjects as well, hence the MnE type *what is one to do.*

2. The deontic gerundial in Latin

A typical function of nonfinite structures is deontic modality (obligation, etc.),[2] as in the gerund(ive) of necessity (with or without BE) in (1).

(1) a. tamen . hoc | veniundum . est . tibi
yet this come.GER.SG.NEUT is you.DAT
'still, this is (the place) you must come to' (D 620.7–8; SALI 233n.54) [?c-1ᵉ] (epitaph M. Statius Chilo)
b. eeis . rem . caputālem . faciendam .
they.DAT thing.ACC.SG.FEM capital.ACC.SG.FEM do.GER.ACC.SG.FEM
cēnsuēre (D 262.25; AI 278ff, 289ff) [S.C. de Bacch.: −186]
decree.PF.3PL
'they decreed that a capital charge should
be made against them' (trans. Gordon 1983:85)
c. reprimendum ... putō esse volūmen
compress.GER.SG.NEUT think.1SG be.INF roll.SG.NEUT
'I think the roll must be compressed' (Varro, LL 7.109)

The dative of "agent" (*tibi* 'you') in (1a) is normal in this construction (cf. Roby 1896: lxxi–lxxiv; Bolkestein 1980: 135ff; Bauer 1996) and must be (construable as) human (Bolkestein 1980: 138ff). For discussion of this combined experiencer-agent role, see Melis (1998). Type (1b) is frequent in early poetry: Plautus 20+X, Terence 6X (Risch 1984: §119). Though disputed by Aalto (1949: 83–84), a form of the verb BE (here *esse* 'to be') is implicit because it can be inserted, as in (1c) (see Draeger 1878: 820; Pariente 1981: 279; Risch 1984 §47; Vester 1991: 298).

As an extension of the impersonal type (1a), a neuter impersonal gerund plus ACC object alternates with the gerundive of necessity in some authors, especially Varro, as in (2a), from *de Re Rustica* ('On Agriculture'); contrast (2b), from *de Lingua Latina* ('On the Latin Language').

(2) Gerundive and Impersonal Gerund of Necessity (Varro)
    a. hōs veterānōs ex   campestribus locīs nōn emendum...
        these old.ACC.PL from plain   areas not buy.GER.SG.NEUT
        '(oxen) mature from the plain one should not buy (for badlands)'
        (RR 1.20.2)
    b. neque Ennius   cōnsuētūdinem   illam
        and.not E.NOM.SG.MASC practice.ACC.SG.FEM that.ACC.SG.FEM
        sequēns   reprehendendus
        follow.PRES.NOM.SG.MASC fault.GER.NOM.SG.MASC
        'nor should Ennius be faulted for following that practice' (LL 7.32)
    c. illud est potius advertendum
        'that is rather to be noticed' (LL 10.6)

The impersonal/nominative gerund occurs with object and without BE in (2a); (2c) is ambiguous because of the neuter: 'that is to notice' (*illud* 'that' is NOM subject or object)[3] or 'one should notice that' (*illud* is ACC object). The unequivocal gerundive (without BE) occurs in agreement with *Ennius* (NOM.SG.MASC) in (2b), by far the most frequent type. Even in Varro, who notoriously alternates between type (2a) and (2b), (2a) is rare except where neuters are involved (2c). Of the 36 impersonals cited by Aalto (1949:95) from Varro's RR, 11 have neuter plural objects, and 8 have objects of mixed gender or number. Gustafsson (1904:94) cites for Plautus (Pl) and Terence (Ter) the following figures: (a) impersonal alone (types *eundum est* 'one must go', *agendum est* 'one must act') 49×Pl, 15×Ter; (b) impersonal with neuter singular (type *faciendum est hoc* (*opus*) 'this (work) must be done; one must do this work') 35×Pl, 10×Ter; (c) neuter plural with agreement (type *haec* (*opera*) *facienda sunt* 'these (deeds) must be done') 60×Pl, 49×Ter. While acknowledging that in Gustafsson's second type [my (2c)] the neuter word can be subject of gerundive or object of impersonal gerund, Aalto (1949:148) opts for the latter, as does Strunk (1962:454), who takes type (2c) as originally equivalent to (2a) and pivotal for the creation of the predicative gerundive out of the impersonal gerund.[4]

I suggest rather that neuters were the original domain of the impersonal gerund. Contrary to Blümel (1979:86), who sees type (2a) as the older situation and does not want to discuss type (2c), that is plausibly the source of the impersonal construction by case accommodation (see McCreight 1988; Bhatt 1997). This account is well-grounded theoretically. Because of the verb BE, one initially expects the thematic object to surface in the NOM rather than the ACC (Wurmbrand 1998:126f, 148ff). The surface ambiguity of (2c) permitted reanalysis from 'that is to (be) notice(d)' to 'one should notice that', whence occasional generalization to allow type (2a), which attained productivity only after the Classical period. The reanalysis was facilitated by the impersonals in -*um*, including the gerund of necessity with intransitive verbs, type (1a).

3. The Old English deontic infinitive/gerundial with BE

The most common function of the *to* infinitive/gerundial with BE, since OE, was to express passive futurity and/or necessity. Callaway (1913:98) reports finding some 894 examples of the inflected infinitive of necessity or obligation. This section briefly overviews the historical development of that construction.

3.1 The NP-movement type

There were two deontic infinitival structures in OE. One type was active, often involved WH movement, allowed dative subjects, direct objects, and was replaced by an active construction. The other, involving NP movement, had no dative subject or ACC object, and was replaced by the construction with passive infinitive.[5] The examples in (3) are typical of the type with NP movement. More examples in Visser (1964–73:1460ff).

   (3) Deontic *to* Infinitive With BE (OE)
      a. for ðēof hē bið tō prōfianne: oððe tō slēanne
         oððe tō álīesanne (IneLaw 98 §20)
         'as a thief he is to be tested (tried), either to be slain or to be released'
         [prō fūre probandus est: vel occīdendus vel etiam redimendus]
      b. sē is tō lufianne 7 tō weorðianne ofer ealle ōðre ðing (WH 10c 207/145f)
         'he is to be loved & honored over all other things'

The literal construction of (3b) is *he is to love*, which is matched by German *er ist zu lieben* (Klöpzig 1922:378). The gloss on (3b) shows that this type was obligatorily replaced with the passive infinitive, while the literal construction is retained but active in sense (Klöpzig compares Germ. *er soll lieben*). These changes must be motivated.

The construction in (3) is the only one of its kind in existence until ca.1300 when the type *it is to be done* with passive infinitive was innovated (van der Gaaf 1928b: 108). The older type did not simply vanish, of course. Mannyng, for instance, had access to both, as in (4).[6]

(4) Formally Passive and Non-Passive Deontic Infinitive (ME)
    a. Þe old man wyst nat what was to do (HS 8486)
       'the old man did not know what was to be done'
    b. Þey byþ to be blamyd eft þar fore (HS 1546)
       'they are to be blamed afterwards for that'

By the time of Shakespeare, as noted by Klöpzig (1922: 387f), the passive infinitive prevails when the subject is a person, as in (5a), but the older construction prevails when the subject is a thing (5b).

(5) BE + INF (Shakespeare)
    a. His daughter is to be brought by you (Tam.Shrew 4.4)
    b. And little is to do (Macbeth 5.7)

Recall that in North Russian dialects animates in this type of construction were the first to adopt ACC rather than NOM objects according to the animacy hierarchy (Timberlake 1974: 70ff). In English, animate nouns obligatorily acquired the new productive passive infinitive, which clearly distinguished themes (passive subjects) from actors (active subjects), as in *the king is to do it*, but neuters could retain the older structure because there was no actor/theme confusion (cf. Fischer 1991: 180), e.g., in (5b) *little* is not going to be "doing" anything. It is not accidental that *they are to love* (*someone*) is unambiguously active in MnE and the subject is animate, while neuters can still be cast in the older construction (*things that are to boil ~ be boiled*).

With intransitive verbs in an English-type language the construction could not be passive (cf. Klöpzig 1922: 379), hence the *that is to come* type. It is not until c14 when, with the prior existence of a passive infinitive (Miller 2000a: §8.30), the active type *what am I to do* became possible (van der Gaaf 1931: 180; cf. Fischer 1991: 148, 1996: 129). However, early predecessors are attested; cf. (6), from Callaway (1913: 105); cf. Visser (1963–73: 1453).

(6) Non-Passive INF With BE = Predestined Future (OE)
   a. þæt hī þonne wǣron fram him ēce mēde tō onfōnne
      that they then were from him eternal rewards to receive
      (Bede 3.22.172 Sch 292.2371ff MS O) (cf. M 224.26)
      'that they would receive from him eternal rewards'
      [aeterna ab illō praemia essent perceptūrī (C&M 282.10f)]
   b. swā ys mannes sunu ēac fram him tō þrōwigenne (Gosp Mt 17.12
      'so is the son of man (predestined) to suffer at their hands' WS1)

In (6b), the construction with *fram* is not the passive agent phrase, as shown by the context, translating a Latin future active construction: *passūrus est ab eīs* 'will suffer from them' (i.e., 'at their hands'). (6b) illustrates a type of purposive infinitive (bordering on deontic) in an active sense with an intransitive verb (cf. van der Gaaf 1931: 177). Fischer (1991: 149ff) cites an impersonal variant in Dutch and Old English with a range of meanings from possibility to likelihood to necessity. (6a) illustrates that the BE plus *to* INF was (i) not necessarily passive (see below) and (ii) not necessarily deontic. This allows for mutual semantic influence. Specifically, I submit, type (6b) became deontic and influenced type (6a), which came to productively express the active deontic function (*they are to love someone*) after creation of the passive infinitive (*they are to love* → *they are to be loved*).

3.2 The deontic infinitive with WH movement

The other structural type of deontic *to* infinitive involved WH movement. This is clear from the absence of P-stranding (which occurred only with null operators in OE), dative subject, and possibility of an accusative object. This type was replaced by an active structure with nominative subject.

When the infinitive in this construction has a subject, it is in the dative case, as shown in (7).[7] More examples in Visser (1963–73: 353–354).

(7) Deontic Infinitive With Dative Subject (OE+)
   a. hæfdon ... geþeahte, hwæt tō dōnne wǣre (Bede 3.29.196 M 248.5)
      'they had deliberation (as to) what was to be done'
      [habitō ... cōnsiliō quid ... esset agendum (C&M 318.3)]
   b. þe him gerǣdað ǣfre hwæt him | tō dōnne sȳ
      7 hwæt tō forlǣtenne (WH 9 186/36f)
      'that ever advises him what he is to do and what to ignore'
   c. hwet is ūs tō dōnne (LHom 9.91/12)
      [*lit.* what is for us to do?] 'what must we do?'

(7a) is ambiguous as to NP movement (*what was* [t *to do* t]) or WH movement (*what was* [PRO *to do* t]). In (7b/c), on the other hand, the likelihood is that WH movement is involved, especially if the dative pronoun is a subject. If that is true, then the WH word is unequivocally an object. The assumption of WH movement is supported by the fact that this type never attests P-stranding. In reality, since 'what' is neuter, its case is impossible to determine. (7a) is the most ambiguous because there is no potential actor. In general, neuters have this ambiguity. Consider the examples in (8), cited by van der Gaaf (1931: 180), where WH movement is not at issue.

(8) Deontic INF With Case-Ambiguous Theme (OE)
  a. ūs is tō smēagenne ðæt word (ÆCHom 1.18 254/3)
     'we must ponder the word'
  b. ðæt mē sȳ   ān ðæra spella tō forlætanne
     that I.DAT be.SUBJ one of.the words to omit
     'that I am to omit one of those words' (GD 23.18f)

As in the Latin gerundive above, neuters are an important bridge between the active and passive structures because they can accommodate either subject (NOM) or object (ACC) case. The frequent type (7a) is the perfect bridge because it is unclear whether NP or WH movement is at issue. Ultimately, of course, *hwæt* must end up in a WH position, but in MnE *what was to be done, what* is also the structural subject of the passive verb. It is the surface ambiguity as to whether (7a) is active or passive that allowed for ACC objects, as in (9), cited by Callaway (1913: 102, 104).

(9) Deontic INF With DAT Subject and ACC Object (OE)
  a. ūs is tō biddenne drihtnes mildheortnysse (ÆCHom 2.33 286/231)
     'we must ask the lord's mercy'
  b. him is tō warnianne ðone rihtan dōm ðām ðe... (GD 340.29)
     'he is to warn (of) the proper judgment those that...'

With ACC objects there can be no question that the structure is active and the subject quirky. In light of the demonstration by Benveniste (1960) and others (see Kayne 1993; Harley 1995: 106–133, 194ff; Bauer 1996; Bhatt 1998; den Dikken 1998) that BE + DAT = HAVE in many ancient IE (and other) languages, including OE, it is not surprising that the usual ME successor to type (9) involved the verb *have*, as shown by van der Gaaf (1931: 183ff); cf. (10).

(10) Deontic HAVE + INF (ME)
   a. wat betere þen ich hwet ha haueð to donne (AW 13b.1 T31)
      'knows better than I what he has to do'
   b. (Ysaac) Thoght on thing he had to done (CM 3352)
      '(Isaac) thought on things he had to do'

The split between active and passive infinitive with BE (Miller 2000a §12.4) also provided a ME successor to (9) with non-quirky subject, as in (11), cited by Visser (1963–73:354), the only type used by Shakespeare (van der Gaaf 1931:185).

(11) Deontic BE + INF With NOM Subject (ME)
   a. We ... giu forbede ... þat gie ... I Be noȝte to preche (CM 19,329ff
      'we forbid you, that you are not to preach' Phys-E)
   b. he wist what he was to do (Wyclif, Sel. Wks. 1.120)
      'he knew what he was to do'

Since both types (10) and (11) survive intact into Modern English, no further discussion is necessary.

4. Historical overview of the English deontic infinitive

The deontic infinitive was an OE development from the purposive. Callaway (1913:200ff) argues that it was suggested by Latin because of its prominence in the translation tradition. In Early West Saxon, for instance, out of about 552 examples in Alfred and Wærferth, 478 correspond to the Latin periphrastic gerundial. Moreover, the construction does not exist in Gothic or Old Saxon (*ibid.* 239f). Where it occurs in Old High German, it generally corresponds to a Latin periphrastic gerundial (*ibid.* 240). Crucially, however, the construction was frequent in Old Icelandic as well as OE.

One must not confuse with structural borrowing the possibility that the construction was suggested by the translation tradition. The Latin construction was in fact quite different from that in OE and OI. Specifically, Latin did not use BE plus the infinitive, which is a very common construction in most of the older and many modern IE languages, including Romance (see Gippert 1978:90–100). I conclude that the construction was native (part of the grammatical competence of a speaker of OE) even if it was of limited practical use apart from the translation tradition (cf. Visser 1963–73:351, 1459). Los (1999:46) notes that the construction is frequently used by the translator of Bede's *Historia Ecclesiastica* independently of the source text.

The change from purposive to (passive) deontic in a copula clause is no major leap. In general, as noted by Lyons (1977:824), "there is an intrinsic connexion between deontic modality and futurity". Bybee et al. (1994:182ff) report a number of languages that use BE (or equivalent) + nonfinite form to express obligation. See also their paths of development (*ibid.* 240) and discussion of obligation as a "common agent-oriented pathway to future" (p. 258).[8]

To summarize, OE had a construction with BE plus infinitive that began as a purposive, and was contextually reanalyzed as expressing necessity, whence its use in the translation tradition for expected ("predestined") futures and the more typical deontic functions. There were two structures, one with NP movement, predicting the absence of any other subject (*pace* Visser (1963–75:352), who does not distinguish NP from WH movement). With intransitive verbs, the structure was not passive. Following the creation of the passive *to* infinitive, there was a split. The transitive (passive) structure underwent formal renewal with the new passive infinitive, initially where animate subjects were involved. In contrast to the deontic infinitive in North Russian, there was in OE no motivation for a NOM object analysis. North Russian tended to replace NOM with ACC objects, especially when animate. In ME, the animates were also the first to change, but in such a way that the NOM structural subject (theme argument) of the passive remained unambiguously that by requiring the new passive infinitive.

NP movement was the only type at some stage of prehistoric OE. Because of the case-ambiguity of the neuters, and the availability of matrix datives to be reanalyzed as infinitival subjects, theme arguments could be reanalyzed as objects, probably first in WH movement, then generalized to neuters in general where WH movement was not at issue. Since neuters could be ACC as well as NOM case, there was no problem accommodating either analysis. With non-neuters, however, NP movement continued to prevail with animates (especially pronouns) where there was no dative subject. With dative subjects, however, the structure was reanalyzed as active, and the thematic object was assigned ACC case.

The development of an ACC object of deontic infinitives with BE thus involved the same reanalysis as in the history of the Latin gerund above. Neuters provided the perfect bridge because of the formal ambiguity as to subject (NOM) or object (ACC) case. In particular, *what*, in *what is to do*, coupled with the surface ambiguity of whether the subject was null or empty, allowed for reanalysis from the older NP movement type [*what is* [t *to do* t]] to WH movement with PRO subject [*what is* [PRO *to do* t]]. That allowed for lexical subjects as well, hence the old dative of reference was reanalyzed as a quirky-case lexical subject (Miller 2000a:§8.15).

In ME the WH-movement type with quirky dative subject got replaced by *have* with nominative subject plus infinitive, parallel to the general trend of replacing DAT BE NP by NOM HAVE NP (*to me is a toy* → *I have a toy*), or by the old active *be* plus infinitive structure generalized from intransitive to transitive verbs.

5. Conclusion

The history of deontic expressions in several languages reveals some naturalness in (a) constructions involving BE plus infinitive/gerundial, (b) thematic object initially surfacing in the NOM, (c) reanalysis via case accommodation in neuters to a structure in which the thematic object surfaces in the ACC, and (d) animates being first to adopt the change obligatorily. Language differences reflect the analysis of the NOM theme argument as subject or object.

According to Lightfoot (1999:225), explaining language change requires only "(a) an account of how trigger experiences have shifted and (b) a theory of language acquisition that matches PLD [primary linguistic data] with grammars in a deterministic way." For copular deontics, the PLD with neuters (a frequent type because of questions with *what*) permitted two analyses of the theme argument: (i) NOM subject; (ii) ACC object. BE and non-neuters of most word-classes favor the NOM subject analysis. In Latin, impersonals in *-um* counterbalance the PLD in favor of an object analysis. In Latin and OE the possibility of analyzing the agentive dative as a quirky subject in the (OE) types *us is to ponder the word/what is us to ponder* shifted the cues in favor of an analysis of the theme as structural object, whence overt ACC objects. We have not isolated *the* deterministic cue (Lightfoot 1998, 1999) for any of the changes discussed here, but the parallel developments in Latin, North Russian, and Old English suggest that the surface ambiguity alone may be a sufficient cue to motivate (but not force) a change.

Abbreviations

ABL	ablative		ed. Thorpe (1844)
ACC	accusative	ÆLS	Ælfric, Lives of Saints
ÆCHom	Ælfric, Catholic Homilies [989+]		[992–1002] ed. Skeat (1881–1900)

AI	Wachter (1987)	INF	infinitive
AW	Ancrene Wisse [?a1200] ed. Tolkien (1962)	Lat	Latin
		LHom	Lambeth Homilies [ca. 1175] ed. R. Morris (1868)
Bede	Bede [c9ᵉ] ed. Miller (1890–98) and Schipper (1899)		
		LL	de Lingua Latina (Varro)
BenR(P)	Rule of St. Bene(dic)t, Prose [?965–975] ed. Schröer (1885–88)	MASC	masculine (in glosses)
		M	T. Miller (1890–98)
		ME	Middle English
C&M	Colgrave & Mynors (1969)	NEUT	neuter
CL	Classical Latin	NOM	nominative
CM	Cursor Mundi [a1325] ed. R. Morris (1874–93)	NP	Noun Phrase
		NR	North Russian
CP	Cura Pastoralis [890–896] ed. Sweet (1871–72)	OBJ	object
		OE	Old English
D	Diehl (1964)	P	phrase (after N, V, etc.)
DAT	dative	PASS	passive
DP	determiner phrase	PERF	perfect (in glosses)
FEM	feminine (in glosses)	Pl	Plautus
FUT	future	PL	plural
GER	gerundial	PRES	present participle
GEN	genitive	RR	de Re Rustica (Varro)
Gk	Greek	SALI	Vine (1993)
GD	Gregory's Dialogues [ca. 880–893] ed. Hecht (1900–07)	Sch	Schipper (1899)
		SG	singular
		SUBJ	subject
Gosp	Gospels [various dates] ed. Skeat (1871–87)	Ter	Terence
		WH	rel./interrog. word; Ā-movement
HS	Handlyng Synne (R. Mannyng) [ca. 1303] ed. Sullens (1983)		
		WH	Wolfstan, Homilies [c10ᵉ–11¹] ed. Bethurum (1957)
IE	Indo-European		
IneLaw	Laws of Ine [688–695] ed. Liebermann (1903–16) 1.26–46	WS	West Saxon

Dating conventions

To avoid the problem of BC/AD vs. BCE/CE ("Common Era") and obviate lengthy references ("second half of the 1st century BC(E)"), the conventions of Miller (1994) are adopted. For convenient disambiguation, 750 BC/BCE will be written [−750], roughly equivalent to [mid c −8], more simply, [c −8^m]. Most dates are approximate, signalled by [ca.] (= *circa* 'about') or equivalent. Following are the dating conventions used in this work:

[c10]	tenth century
[c10+]	begins in c10 and continues
[c11^b]	beginning of the 11th century
[c12^e]	end of c12
[c13^m]	middle of c13
[240–110]	240 BC/BCE to 110 BC/BCE
[110–240]	110 CE to 240 CE
[−110–240 CE]	110 BC/BCE to 240 CE
[ca.1150]	around 1150 (corroborated by independent evidence)
[?ca.1150]	the approximate date is not independently verifiable
[a1150]	before 1150
[p1150]	after 1150

Notes

* I wish to thank Jan Terje Faarlund for inviting me to join the Amsterdam Workshop on Grammatical Relations, and all the members of the workshop for a most fruitful discussion. A version of this paper has also profited from comments by Cynthia Allen, Phil Baldi, Olga Fischer, Brian Joseph, and many others.

1. *Gerundial* is used here as a generic term for *gerund* and *gerundive* when the distinction is not important. Latin texts are cited from standard Oxford editions unless otherwise indicated. A more complete discussion of Latin gerundials can be found in Miller (2000b).

2. Bhatt (1998) claims that modality is not inherent in the nonfinite structure or BE, but requires a covert modal. For Latin, the problem is that the variety of modal meanings of the gerundial overlaps with several modal verbs of different deontic nuance (see Bolkestein 1980: 137–149). The change from purposive to (passive) deontic in a copula clause is common (cf. Bybee et al. 1994: 182ff).

3. Nominative objects of "independent" infinitivals are not unusual, as shown by Timberlake (1974) and Babby (1991). From North Russian (NR) dialects at or above the 60th parallel, Timberlake (1974: 1, 13) cites (i-a), the archaicity of which is guaranteed by (i-b) from an Old North Russian text dated 1591.

(i) a. zemlja   paxat'
        land.NOM [is] plow.INF
        'it is necessary to plow the land'

b. emu   zemlja   paχatъ
    he.DAT land.NOM plow.INF
    'it is necessary for him to plow the land'

Timberlake (1974:226) gives a case-markedness account, arguing that NOM objects are permitted because the object requires less syntactic specification in the environment of a non-NOM subject. Pronouns, which are highest in animacy, were the first to require ACC objects, as in (ii-a), from Timberlake (1974:59, 71–72). Similarly, (masculine) animate nouns took (GEN-)ACC objects, as in (ii-b) (*ibid.* 64–65, 67–68).

(ii) a. ti   mja   ubiti
         you.DAT me.ACC kill.INF
         'you must kill me'
     b. a   poslati   sudiju   [1550]
         but send.INF judge.ACC
         'but it is necessary to send a judge'

According to Timberlake (1974:70ff), animates were the first to adopt ACC instead of NOM objects, and there are NR dialects to this day that have not generalized ACC to plural objects of independent infinitives. The reason is apparently that "animate objects typically must be more explicitly specified than inanimate objects" (*ibid.* 100), since animates prototypically function as agents and inanimates as patients, whence the animacy hierarchy (for recent discussion, see Comrie 1989:Ch.9). Only the feminine *a*-stems had a different form for NOM and ACC, so only they could be interpreted as substituting NOM for ACC, whence generalization of NOM objects to some other contexts in NR (Timberlake 1974:115ff). The same properties and constraints are found in Lithuanian, Latvian, and West Finnic (*ibid.* 182ff).

4. Aalto (1949:148–149) supports his case with the Greek *-téos* formation. He argues that *-téos* is not a real adjective because it takes no comparison, builds no derivatives, is predicative only, and only the neuter plural can be substantivized (cf. Lat. *vīsenda* 'sights' etc.). As in the Latin formation, the agent adjunct is assigned dative case. It can also be used impersonally with direct object, e.g., οὐδὲ λειπτέον τὴν τάξιν *oudè leiptéon tḕn táxin* (Plato, *Crito* 51b) '(you) must not leave the (your) post'. Since that is the preferred use (some 900 examples from (post-)Homer to Aristotle vs. only ca. 90 cases of a form of *-téos* agreeing with the subject), Aalto concludes that the impersonal was original and the agreeing form analogical to other verbal adjectives and participles. This, of course, has no necessary bearing on the development of the Latin gerundials, and Risch (1984:187–188) attributes the rarity of the impersonal construction in Latin, where it was "favored" only by Lucretius and Varro, to influence of the *-téos* constructions in Greek. Drexler (1962:438) makes the astute point that the construction corresponds to Gk. *-téos* but is not a syntactic Grecism, but comparable to the Latin undeclined infinitive in *-tūrum*, e.g., Plautus, *Truculentus* 400: *bona sua mē(d)* [FEM] *habitūrum omnia* 'I (FEM) was to have all his goods (everything he owns)', on which type see Blümel (1979). One can take this point further. Given (i) the strong influence of Greek constructions on Latin writers, and (ii) the preference for using *-téos* in the impersonal, it is reasonable to conclude that the reason the impersonal gerund + ACC object is so rare (except in the poet Lucretius and the linguist Varro) is that it was in fact marginal in Latin except with neuters which could be interpreted either way by accommodation. For all we know, it may have been more proper to southern Latin dialects with heavy Greek influence.

5. P-stranding in this construction seems to be non-existent, as expected with NP movement in OE (Miller 2000a §§8.21, 8.26). The one example I have come across, in (i), cited by van der Gaaf (1928b: 107), probably does not belong here.

(i) nis nān ōþer god ón tō gelȳfenne
'there is no other god to believe in'
(ÆLS 1.22.478/93)

While van der Gaaf includes (i) in a section which suggests the meaning should be 'no other god is to be believed in', the structure, with P-stranding, suggests rather that null operator movement is involved; cf. Skeat's translation 'there is no other God in whom to believe'.

6. In the interest of space, I ignore the lengthy interval between Wulfstan and Mannyng. Examples of the older construction as well as the one innovated ca.1300 are copiously documented in Klöpzig (1922), van der Gaaf (1928b, 1931), and Visser (1963–73).

7. It is impossible to prove that what is at issue here is a dative (quirky) subject. While it is true that quirky subjects are rare, they are less rare with infinitives. Specifically, numerous languages have infinitival subjects in the dative (Miller 2000a); cf. the English type *for us to go would be dangerous*. Moreover, the dative is replaced in the construction under consideration by a nominative subject in Middle English. It is also easier to motivate a direct object in the accusative if the matrix dative is reanalyzed as a subject.

8. Fischer (1991: 155f, 1996: 130f) claims that the deontic type *that question is to understand* arose from the "tough" type *that question is easy to understand*. The Latin -*nd*- formation shows that this is not a necessary assumption but, more to the point, there is no internal evidence for it. Moreover, crosslinguistically, both structures are extremely frequent but formal similarities between them are far from necessary (Latin and Greek being cases in point). Where they occur, the similarity can be attributed in part to pathways of development from a purposive and in part to the fact that both involve the verb BE. The lack of any direct connection between the two is further signalled by (i) the split in English between *that girl is pretty to look at* and **that girl is to look at*, which did not take place in Dutch (Hoekstra & Moortgat 1979: 152), and (ii) the fact that P-stranding in OE occurred only with infinitival complements of Group I (*pretty*) adjectives (Miller 2000a: §8.20), and not with Group II (*easy*) adjectives (*ibid.* §8.21f) or either type of deontic infinitive (*ibid.* §12.4f). Fischer (1991: 156) acknowledges that the deontic type "can only have developed from the 'easy'-construction." Finally, an account based on independent development of both from a purposive is well documented. This is supported by a number of *to* -*ing* purposives with deontic value; consider (i).

(i) a. hū fela sealma on nihtlīcum tīdum tō sinȝenȝe synt
'how many psalms at nightly times are for singing (= to be sung)'
(BenR(P) 9 [ch. heading].33.5f)
b. For here I telle what laborinthus is to menynge
'now here I tell what labyrinth is to mean' [Trevisa, Higden 1.311]

It is not accidental that in Modern English, *how many psalms are for singing*, despite being normally blocked by *are to be sung* and modal verb constructions, is readily interpretable either as a purposive or as a deontic.

References

Primary sources

Bethurum, D. (ed.) 1957. *The Homilies of Wulfstan.* Edition, introduction, and notes. Oxford: Clarendon.

Colgrave, B. and Mynors, R. A. B. 1969. *Bede's Ecclesiastical History of the English People.* Edition and translation. Oxford: Clarendon.

Diehl, E. (ed.). 1964. *Altlateinische Inschriften.* 5th ed. Berlin: de Gruyter.

Hecht, H. (ed.). 1900–07. *Bischof Wærferths von Worcester Übersetzung der Dialoge Gregors des Grossen über das Leben und die Wundertaten italienischer Väter und über die Unsterblichkeit der Seelen.* 2 vols. (BASPr. 5). Leipzig: Wigand. (Repr., Darmstadt: Wissenschaftliche Buchgesellschaft, 1965).

Liebermann, F. (ed.) 1903–16. *Die Gesetze der Angelsachsen.* 3 vols. Halle. Repr., Aalen: Scientia (1960).

Miller, T. (ed.) 1890–98. *The Old English Version of Bede's Ecclesiastical History of the English People.* Edited with a translation and introduction. (EETS 95–96, 110–111). London: Trübner. (Repr., 1959–63.)

Morris, R. (ed.). 1868. *Old English Homilies and Homiletic Treatises (Sawles Warde, and ߤe Wohunge of Ure Lauerd: Ureisuns of Ure Louerd and of Ure Lefdi, &c.) of the Twelfth and Thirteenth Centuries.* Series 1 (EETS 29, 34). London: N. Trübner.

Morris, R. (ed.). (ed.). 1874–93. *Cursor Mundi (The Cursur of the World): A Northumbrian poem of the XIVth century in four versions.* (EETS 57 [1874], 59 [1875], 62 [1876], 66 [1877], 68 [1878], 99 [1892], 101 [1893]). London: Kegan Paul, Trench, Trübner & Co.

Schipper, J. (ed.). 1899. *König Alfreds Übersetzung von Bedas Kirchengeschichte.* Leipzig: Georg H. Wigand.

Schröer, A. (ed.). 1885–88. *Die Angelsächsischen Prosabearbeitungen der Benediktinerregel.* (BASPr. 2). Kassel. (Repr., with appendix by Helmut Gneuss. Darmstadt: Wissenschaftliche Buchgesellschaft, 1964).

Skeat, W. W. (ed.). 1871–87. *The Holy Gospels: In Anglo-Saxon, Northumbrian, and Old Mercian versions, synoptically arranged, with collations exhibiting all the readings of all the MSS.; Together with the early Latin version as contained in the Lindisfarne MS., collated with the Latin version in the Rushworth MS.* Cambridge: CUP.

Skeat, W. W. (ed.). ed. 1881–1900. *Ælfric's Lives of Saints, Being a set of sermons on Saints' days formerly observed by the English Church.* (EETS 76, 82, 94, 114). London: Kegan Paul, Trench, Trübner. (Repr. in 2 vols.: Oxford: OUP, 1966).

Sullens, I. (ed.) 1983. *Robert Mannyng of Brunne, Handlyng Synne.* Binghamton, NY: Medieval & Renaissance Texts & Studies.

Sweet, H. (ed. and trans.). 1871. *King Alfred's West-Saxon Version of Gregory's Pastoral Care.* With an English translation, the Latin text, notes, and an introduction. (EETS 45, 50). London: Trübner. (Repr. 1958).

Thorpe, B. (ed.) 1844–46. *The Sermones Catholici or Homilies of Ælfric.* 2 vols. London: Ælfric Society. (Repr. 1971).

Tolkien, J. R. R. (ed.) 1962. *The English Text of the Ancrene Riwle, Ancrene Wisse: Edited from MS. Corpus Christi College Cambridge 402.* (EETS 249). Oxford: OUP.

Varro, M. T. [116–27]. ca. — 43. *De Lingua Latina* [On the Latin Language] ed. & trans. by R. G. Kent, Loeb Classical Library. Cambridge, MA: Harvard Univ. Press (1938, 1977, etc.).

Secondary sources

Aalto, P. 1949. *Untersuchungen über das lateinische Gerundium und Gerundivum*. Helsinki: Suomalaisen Tiedeakatemia [*Annales Academiae Scientarum Fennicae*, B 62:3.].

Alexiadou, A. and Wilder, C. (eds). 1998. *Possessors, Predicates and Movement in the Determiner Phrase*. Amsterdam: John Benjamins.

Babby, L. H. 1991. "Noncanonical configurational case assignment strategies". *Cornell Working Papers in Linguistics* 9: 1–55.

Bauer, B. L. M. 1996. "Residues of non-nominative syntax in latin: The *mihi est* construction". *Historische Sprachforschung* 109: 241–256.

Benveniste, É. 1960. "'être' et 'avoir' dans leurs fonctions linguistiques". *BSL* 55. (Repr. in Benveniste 1966: 187207.)

Benveniste, É. 1966. *Problèmes de linguistique générale*. Paris: Gallimard.

Bhatt, R. 1997. "Matching effects and the syntax-morphology interface: Evidence from Hindi correlatives".

Bhatt, R. 1998. "Obligation and Possession". In Harley 1998: 21–40.

Blümel, Wolfgang. 1979. "Zur historischen Morphosyntax der Verbalabstrakta im Lateinischen". *Glotta* 57: 77–125.

Bolkestein, A. M. 1980. *Problems in the Description of Modal Verbs: An investigation of Latin*. Assen: Van Gorcum.

Bruening, B. (ed.) 1997. *Proceedings of the Eighth Student Conference in Linguistics*. Cambridge, MA: Dept. of Linguistics, MIT [*MIT Working Papers in Linguistics* (MITWPL) 31].

Bybee, J. L., Perkins, R. and Pagliuca, W. 1994. *The Evolution of Grammar: Tense, aspect, and modality in the languages of the world*. Chicago:: Univ. of Chicago Press.

Callaway, M. Jr. 1913. *The Infinitive in Anglo-Saxon*. Washington, D. C.: Carnegie Institution.

Coleman, R. (ed.). 1991. *New Studies in Latin Linguistics*. Amsterdam: John Benjamins.

Comrie, B. 1989. *Language Universals and Linguistic Typology*, 2nd ed. Chicago: Univ. of Chicago Press.

Dikken, M. den. 1998. "Predicate inversion in DP". Alexiadou and Wilder 1998: 177–214.

Draeger, A. 1878. *Historische Syntax der Lateinischen Sprache*, Vol.1. 2nd ed. Leipzig: Teubner.

Drexler, H. 1962. "Über Gerundium und Gerundivum". *Gymnasium* 69: 429–445.

Fischer, O. 1991. "The rise of the passive infinitive in English". Kastovsky 1991: 141–188.

Fischer, O. 1996. "The status of *To* in Old English *To*-infinitives: A reply to Kageyama". *Lingua* 99: 107–133.

Gaaf, W. van der. 1928a. "The gerund preceded by the common case: A study in historical syntax". *English Studies* 10: 33–41, 65–72.

Gaaf, W. van der. 1928b. "The predicative passive infinitive". *English Studies* 10: 107–114.

Gaaf, W. van der. 1931. "*Beon* and *Habban* connected with an inflected infinitive". *English Studies* 1: 176–188.

Gippert, J. 1978. *Zur Syntax der infinitivischen Bildungen in den indogermanischen Sprachen*. Frankfurt am Main: Peter Lang.

Gordon, A. E. 1983. *Illustrated Introduction to Latin Epigraphy.* Berkeley:: Univ. of California Press.
Gustafsson, F. 1904. "De gerundiis et gerundivis latinis". *Eranos* 6: 81–97.
Gustafsson, F. 1906. "De gerundio iterum". *Eranos* 6: 6: 132–135.
Harley, H. B. 1995. Subjects, Events and Licensing. Ph.D. dissertation, MIT, Cambridge, MA.
Harley, H. B., (ed.). 1998. *Papers from the UPenn/MIT Roundtable on Argument Structure and Aspect.* Cambridge, MA: Department of Linguistics, MIT [MITWPL 32].
Hoekstra, T. and Moortgat, M.. 1979. "Passief en het lexicon". *Forum der Letteren* 20: 137–161.
Kastovsky, D. (ed.) 1991. *Historical English Syntax.* Berlin: Mouton de Gruyter.
Kayne, R. S. 1993. "Toward a modular theory of auxiliary selection". *Studia Linguistica* 47: 3–31.
Klöpzig, W. 1922. "Der Ursprung der *To Be To*-Konstruktion". *Englische Studien* 56: 378–389.
Langendonck, W. van and Belle, W. van (eds). 1998. *The Dative.* Volume 2: *Theoretical and contrastive studies.* Amsterdam : John Benjamins.
Lightfoot, D. W. 1998. "The development of grammars". *Glot International* 3: 3–8.
Lightfoot, D. W. 1999. *The Development of Language: Acquisition, change, and evolution.* Oxford: Blackwell.
Los, B. 1999. *Infinitival Complementation in Old and Middle English.* The Hague: Holland Institute of Generative Linguistics.
Lyons, J. 1977. *Semantics I and II.* Cambridge: CUP.
McCreight, K. L. 1988. Multiple Case Assignments. Ph.D. dissertation, MIT, Cambridge, MA.
Melis, L. 1998. "From form to interpretation: Building up the 'dative'-roles". In van Langendonck and van Belle 1998: 261–291.
Miller, D. G. 1994. *Ancient Scripts and Phonological Knowledge.* Amsterdam: John Benjamins.
Miller, D. G. 2000a. *Nonfinite Structures in Theory and Change.* Oxford: OUP.
Miller, D. G. 2000b. "Gerund and Gerundive in Latin". *Diachronica.* 17(2): 293–399.
Pariente, Á. 1981. "Las formas de gerundio y gerundivo". *Emerita* 49: 273–305.
Risch, E. 1984. *Gerundivum und Gerundium: Gebrauch im klassischen und älteren Latein: Entstehung und Vorgeschichte.* Berlin: Walter de Gruyter.
Roby, H. J. 1896. *A Grammar of the Latin Language from Plautus to Suetonius.* Part II, Book IV: *Syntax.* New York: Macmillan.
Strunk, K. 1962. "Über Gerundium und Gerundivum". *Gymnasium* 69: 445–460.
Timberlake, A. 1974. *The Nominative Object in Slavic, Baltic, and West Finnic.* Munich: Otto Sagner [Slavistische Beiträge 82].
Vester, E. 1991. "Reflections on the Gerund and Gerundive". Coleman 1991: 295–309.
Vine, B. 1993. *Studies in Archaic Latin Inscriptions.* Innsbruck: Institut für Sprachwissenschaft der Universität Innsbruck. [Innsbrucker Beiträge zur Sprachwissenschaft].
Visser, F. T. 1963–1973. *An Historical Syntax of the English Language.* Leiden: Brill.
Wachter, R. 1987. *Altlateinische Inschriften: Sprachliche und epigraphische Untersuchungen zu den Dokumenten bis etwa 150 v. Chr.* Bern: Peter Lang.
Wurmbrand, S. 1998. Infinitives. Ph.D. dissertation, MIT, Cambridge, MA.

The loss of lexical case in Swedish

Muriel Norde
University of Amsterdam

One of the most fundamental changes in the history of the Germanic languages was the loss of inflectional case marking. This paper will discuss the mechanisms involved in the decline of inflectional case systems with special reference to the loss of lexical case in Swedish. It will be seen that the decline of lexical case was by no means a straightforward affair. The tendency towards loss was powerfully counteracted by tendencies of maintenance, which managed to slow down the eventual collapse of the case system. Ultimately, these opposed tendencies can be identified as the conflicting interests of the speaker and the hearer, or ease of production vs. ease of perception. This will be illustrated by a case study in changes in prepositional case assignment.

1. Deflexion

1.1 Introduction[1]

Deflexion is one of the principal characteristics of the histories of the Germanic languages. With the exception of the peripheral languages (Icelandic and Faroese in the far North-West and High German in the South) and dialects spoken in remote areas, all Germanic languages underwent vast inflectional simplification, though to varying degrees. In (standard) Swedish, both verbal and nominal morphology were affected. Number and person marking on the verb, as well as the subjunctive, have been eliminated altogether. Nouns and adjectives are no longer inflected for case, and masculine and feminine gender merged into a common gender.[2] Nevertheless, (nominal) deflexion in Swedish was less profound than, say, deflexion in English. The categories of gender[3] and number have been preserved, and so have case marking on the pronoun (if in residual form) and the opposition between strong and weak inflection of the adjective (see Table 1).

Table 1. Nominal inflection in Old and Modern Swedish

	Old Swedish	Modern Swedish
nouns	3 genders 2 numbers 4 cases	2 genders 2 numbers 0 cases
adjectives	3 genders 2 numbers 4 cases "strong" vs. "weak" inflection	2 genders 2 numbers 0 cases "strong" vs. "weak" inflection
pronouns	3 genders 2 numbers 4 cases	2/3 genders 2 numbers 2 cases

Swedish is thus eminently suited for a study of the history of inflections, since it has developed from a relatively heavily inflected language — its inflectional morphology was very similar to that of Old Norse–to a language with very little inflection. What is more, the history of Swedish (Scandinavian)[4] is comparatively well recorded in a number of sources, both runic and written. The entire process of deflexion covered several centuries: it may have started as early as the Runic Swedish period, and was not yet completed by the beginning of the Early Modern Swedish period.[5]

1.2 The definition of deflexion

The term "deflexion" is potentially misleading: it suggests the mere loss of inflectional material, but what it really entails is the disappearance of grammatical categories. In the present context, deflexion thus refers to the loss of case as an inflectional category. This may be illustrated by the fate of the ending -*ar*, which was a PL.NOM[6] marker in some masculine and feminine declensions, a SG.GEN marker in some feminine declensions etc. Now, -*ar* has been lost as a FEM.SG.GEN ending, but it is still in use as a plural marker. We may thus say that one system of inflections merely gave way to another one (see further Norde 2000a).

On the other hand, the loss of a given category, say dative, does not necessarily imply that all endings expressing the dative disappeared simultaneously. MASC/NEUT.SG.DAT -*i* may be dropped in the earliest texts already, as in (1a) (though dative forms as in (1b) are more common). PL.DAT -*um*, on the other hand, is still attested in Early Modern Swedish, as in (1c) (see further Norde 1999b: 29ff.).

(1) a. *Huggar maþær hand af man* [...]
   chop-3SG man-MASC.SG.NOM hand-FEM.SG.ACC of man-Ø
   'If a man chops off another man's hand [...]' VgL: Sm4⁷
   b. *Hugger næsær af. manni.* [...]
   chop-3SG nostril-FEM.PL.ACC of man-MASC.SG.DAT
   'If [a man] chops off another man's nose [...]' VgL: Sm4
   c. *een quinna som* [...] *hadhe mykit lidhit aff mongom*
   a woman who had much suffered from many-PL.DAT
   läkiarom
   doctors-PL.DAT
   'a woman who had suffered much under a number of doctors'
   GVB 119–120

But the stage at which one ending is lost and another maintained appears to be (in the history of Swedish at least) a transitional one — eventually, all case distinctions in noun and adjective paradigms would disappear.

1.3 Internal and external factors

A number of language-internal factors that may have triggered deflexion in Continental Scandinavian (or Germanic in general) have been suggested. It will be obvious that internal factors alone are not a sufficient explanation for the disappearance of inflectional case, since they apply to *all* Scandinavian languages, Insular as well as Continental. It will be obvious, then, that extralinguistic factors will have to be taken into account as well. Considering the geographical position of the Insular Scandinavian languages, it seems natural to assume that the conservatism of Icelandic and Faroese is due to their peripheral location. Many authors (e.g. Torp 1982, Sandøy 1994, Braunmüller 1995) have observed that languages spoken in isolated, tightly-knit communities tend to allow more morphological irregularity than do languages spoken in large, open communities. In the case of Scandinavian, it may be relevant that the Continental languages were profoundly influenced by Middle Low German in the days of the Hanseatic League. It thus seems likely that processes of linguistic simplification, such as deflexion, are reinforced (if not prompted) by language contact (or possibly dialect contact, see Norde 1997b). In the following sections, I will confine myself to internal factors (see Norde 1997a: 27ff. and Norde 1997b for discussion of both internal and external factors).

1.3.1 *Phonological changes*

In his standard work on Germanic, Meillet (1922) asserts that deflexion is rooted in the Proto-Germanic accent-shift from a pitch accent to one of intensity on the first syllable of the word, a shift which Meillet (1922:71) characterizes as "un changement décisif". This fixed accent resulted in the gradual weakening of final syllables (among them inflectional endings) which inevitably led to deflexion: "C'est la ruine phonétique qui a précipité la simplification de la flexion" (p. 113).

This view is disputed by Liberman (1982: 249), who believes that deflexion is primarily a morphological matter, not a phonological one:[8]

> We do not know the ultimate causes of apocope, but it is a recurrent process in the history of the Germanic languages. Each time it must have been evoked by a force more powerful than the structural upheavals within the system of phonemes or prosodemes. It appears that the force in question smites not final syllables as such but the inflection, or, to put it differently, its quarry is not a phonetic but a grammatical entity.

A similar controversy is found in two papers on deflexion in the Continental Scandinavian languages. According to the first (Hansen 1956), the phonetic weakening of inflectional endings was merely a symptom of the loss of genitive and dative complements with verbs and prepositions. In reply to Hansen, Beito (1957) points out that in dialects in which some prepositions still govern the dative productively, only those dative forms that were most prone to reduction, i.e. the indefinite forms (e.g. (Old Norse) MASC.SG.DAT.INDEF. *-i*) had disappeared. The definite forms (e.g. (Old Norse) MASC.SG.DAT.DEF *-inum*) have been retained. Beito therefore concludes that the loss of the dative with prepositions was phonologically motivated.

To sum up, the view that the Germanic stress shift and subsequent reduction of final syllables is primarily responsible for the loss of inflections is not generally accepted. The most likely scenario is that phonological and morphological (morphosyntactic) changes intensified one another. As we have seen in Section 1.2, one and the same ending (*-ar*), was lost in one function (FEM.SG.GEN) but preserved in another (e.g. OSw MASC.PL.NOM; MoSw COMM.PL). Reduction of *a* and loss of *r* were certainly involved, as they affected both genitive and plural endings (see Norde 1997a: 100ff.), but the plural forms were "restored" (for details see Kock 1921: 210f.), possibly in part because the category of number has been retained.

1.3.2 *Morphological changes*
A second factor which dates back to Proto-Germanic is the emergence of independent (uninflected) roots (see e.g. Meillet 1922: 118f. and Werner 1984: 193ff.). In Proto-Indo-European, a noun was always a grammatical form, an inseparable unit consisting of a root, a stem suffix and a (cumulative) inflectional ending, as in MASC.SG.ACC *$dhogh^w$-o-m*. In the corresponding Gothic and Old Norse forms (both *dag* 'day') however, both the stem suffix and the inflectional ending have disappeared. After the emergence of such independent roots inflectional endings became, as Meillet (1922: 119) put it, "un accessoire", the significance of which gradually diminished. Furthermore, since inflections no longer form an inseparable unit with the stem to which they are suffixed, they may now detach themselves from their stems (Knudsen 1967: 11), as in s-genitive constructions (see 1.3.5).

Another morphological factor is mentioned by Wessén (1968: 147), who suggests that the internal inconsistency of the case system invited the levelling of case distinctions. A case form could be expressed by several endings and, conversely, a given ending could denote several forms. In other words, there was almost never a one-to-one relationship between form and function. The only case that was uniquely marked was the dative plural (*-um* in all genders of both nouns and adjectives) and the only non-homonymous case ending was SG.GEN *-s* of (some) masculine and neuter nouns. This factor cannot have been of decisive importance however, for the same was true for Old Norse, yet the four-case system has been retained until the present day in Modern Icelandic.

1.3.3 *Syntactic changes*
Other factors that may have been involved are of a syntactic nature. As we have seen in 1.3.1, Hansen (1956) believed that the loss of lexical case assignment was essentially a syntactic change, not one prompted by reductive phonological changes. In other works, deflexion is connected to changes in other parts of the grammar. Marold (1984: 319ff.), for instance, suggests that MASC.SG.NOM was lost in Continental Scandinavian because a fixed position for the subject had been established, as a result of which nominative marking was no longer required. Furthermore, there might be a relation between the decline of case

marking and the rise of definiteness marking (see Anward & Swedenmark 1997). These suggestions raise the obvious chicken-or-egg-question, and once more it becomes evident that it is impossible to single out one factor, be it a phonological, a morphological or a syntactic one.

1.3.4 *The rise of competing periphrastic constructions*

In the Old and Middle Swedish periods, the use of (primary and secondary)[9] adpositional constructions increased considerably, arguably to compensate for the loss of case as an inflectional category. This issue has been the subject of much debate in diachronic Germanic linguistics. Within grammaticalization studies, it is frequently observed that there exists a relation between nominal deflexion and the rise of periphrastic adpositional constructions: "[...] the decline of case inflections correlates with the introduction of spatial expressions for case marking — with the effect that locative adpositions [...] have assumed the function of the declining case inflections" (Heine, Claudi & Hünnemeyer 1991:121). At this point it is not clear however whether the relation between the loss of (structural) case and the rise of prepositional constructions should be conceived of as a *push chain*, i.e. that case became redundant when semantic relations formally expressed by inflections could be denoted with the help of adpositions alone; or a *drag chain*, i.e. that the increase in adpositional constructions was triggered by the loss of case. In other words, whether the increase in adpositional constructions preceded or followed the collapse of the case system, is as yet unclear.

Hjelmslev (1935:77), for example, suggests that new constructions *must* be developed before inflectional cases are lost. Skautrup (1944:275), on the other hand, observes for the history of Danish that case constructions had not yet been fully replaced by PP's when case inflections had worn away, but he does not provide us with any data. It is also conceivable that both changes simply occurred simultaneously and reinforced one another, as suggested by Lehmann (1985:312 and 1991:501):

> [...] it is futile to ask whether the grammaticalized prepositions oust the other case suffixes or whether, instead, the attrition of case inflection attracts the prepositions to fill the gap. It seems more appropriate to view adpositions and case affixes as being two stages of the same scale and both being grammaticalized simultaneously and in parallel (Lehmann 1991:501).

Furthermore, it should be borne in mind that the expansion of adpositional constructions at the expense of oblique case constructions was not as straightforward as it might appear. First of all, cases and adpositions had coexisted for a considerable period before the erosion of case endings set in; also in many other more or less highly inflected languages such as Latin, Russian or Icelandic both inflections and periphrastic adpositional constructions are found.

In this respect it is also important to note that the use of an adposition does not necessarily imply the loss of case, as the Old Swedish adpositions required themselves an oblique form of the noun. In other words, it is incorrect to regard the shift from case to adposition as a shift from synthetic to analytic structures. For instance, in (2b) and (2c) prepositional constructions are used instead of the dative in (2a), but the preposition *til* in (2b) takes the genitive case and the preposition *at* in (2c) takes the dative. Uninflected complements as in (2d) are very rare in Old Swedish. (Examples (2a–c) are from Schwarz 1878: 91–92).

(2) a. *Takær man annærs þræl lani* […]
 takes man other-GEN slave-ACC loan-DAT
 'If a man borrows another man's slave […]'
 b. […] *hæsten til laans taker*
 horse-the to loan-GEN takes
 '(he) borrows the horse'
 c. *Nu takær man pæninga at lane af andrum* […]
 now takes man money at loan-DAT from other-DAT
 'Now a man borrows money from another man'
 d. […] *som han fik honom til laan* […]
 which he gave him to loan-Ø
 'which he lent him' Mose 358

At this point it should be noted that an important question in a comparative study of two competing constructions is whether they can be said to express the same semantic relation. Jakobson (1971:28f.), for example, argues that case inflections and periphrastic constructions cannot be bracketed together:

> Auch das System der präpositionalen Fügungen ist nicht mit der flektierenden Deklination zu verwechseln, da die Sprachen, die beide erwähnten Kategorien besitzen, erstens die syntaktischen Verwendungen eines Kasus mit Präposition und ohne solche (mittelbare — unmittelbare Verbindung) einander entgegensetzen, und zweitens die Bedeutung der Kasus und der Präpositionen als zwei besondere Bedeutungsgattungen deutlich voneinander unterscheiden […] (cf. also Perridon 1993, Lehmann 1995:22 and Van Loon 1996:202).

Indeed there are often some subtle differences between the two types of constructions. For example, in the contrastive pair of examples in (3), the dative in (3a) denotes the recipient, whereas the PP in (3b) denotes destination (Schwarz 1878:70):

(3) a. *kastadhe* [...] *hanom äpplit*
     threw   him   apple-the
     '(he) threw the apple to him'
  b. *kasta til min thz äpplit*
     throw to I-GEN that apple-the
     'throw that apple to(wards) me'

Other differences can be found as well. The NP in the genitive case, for example, functions as a determiner (when it precedes the head noun)[10] but adpositional phrases do not. Thus, in the OSw genitive construction *konungxsins win* (king-GEN-the-GEN friend) 'the king's friend', the head noun is inherently definite and hence lacks the suffix of definiteness, but in adpositional constructions with *till* 'to' it is not (cf. Modern Swedish *vännen till kungen* (friend-the to king-the) 'the friend of the king').

1.3.5 *Deflexion and grammaticalization*

Deflexion involves a series of grammaticalization patterns: within grammaticalization studies, loss of inflections is regarded as the ultimate stage of grammaticalization (Lehmann 1995:171). This is predicted by the so-called unidirectionality hypothesis which forms the cornerstone of grammaticalization theory. This hypothesis may be illustrated by Hopper & Traugott's (1993:7) "cline of grammaticality":[11]

content item > grammatical word > clitic > inflectional affix (> Ø)

Inflectional affixes are located at the very end of this cline of grammaticality, which suggests that the only remaining change for them would seem to be loss. By and large, this is true — complex inflectional systems tend to erode and eventually disappear, as has happened in many Indo-European languages. It should be noted however that these changes need not occur. Morphological case is still going strong in languages such as Russian and Icelandic, and it is impossible to predict when these languages will lose their case systems, if at all. Furthermore, individual case suffixes may violate the unidirectionality hypothesis and become derivational suffixes or clitics. The best known example is the s-genitive in

English, Danish and Norwegian, which developed from a MASC/NEUT.SG.GEN ending to a phrase-final clitic (see further Norde 1997a and 2000a).[12]

Furthermore, fusional languages do not merely lose inflectional material — new inflections may arise as well. In late Middle Swedish, for example, a new plural marker was developed. Neuter nouns ending in a vowel, which formerly lacked a distinct ending in the nominative/accusative plural got a plural ending -*n* as a result of rebracketing of the definite form: *äpple-na* (apples-DEF) 'the apples' became *äpplen-a* (see Wessén 1968:200 and Norde 2000a for details).

2. The loss of lexical case

2.1 The Old Swedish case system

Like its close relative Old Norse, Old Swedish possessed four cases: nominative, genitive, dative and accusative. But the OSw case system has been simplified considerably when compared to reconstructed Proto-Germanic or Proto-Scandinavian (or even Old Norse) inflections. Old Swedish also differs from Runic Swedish, the language of the runic inscriptions.[13]

Table 2. Some Old Swedish nominal paradigms

	masculine a-stems	masculine u-stems	feminine ō-stems	neuter a-stems	masculine an-stems	feminine ōn-stems
NOM	fisker	sun	siang	skip	biti	vika
GEN	fisks	sunar	siangar	skips	bita	viku
DAT	fiski	syni	siangu	skipi	bita	viku
ACC	fisk	sun	siang	skip	bita	viku
NOM	fiskar	synir	siangar	skip	bitar	vikur
GEN	fiska	suna	sianga	skipa	bita	vikna
DAT	fiskum	sunum	siangum	skipum	bitum	vikum
ACC	fiska	syni	siangar	skip	bita	vikur

fisker 'fish'; *sun* 'son'; *siang* 'bed'; *skip* 'ship'; *biti* 'bit'; *vika* 'week'

OSw nominal paradigms were by no means maximally differentiated — singular dative and accusative forms, for example, had been levelled to a considerable extent. Roughly speaking, strong masculine and neuter nouns generally distinguish between dative and accusative in the singular (except when they end in a vowel) whereas strong feminine nouns and all weak nouns do not. Strong feminine nouns lack a distinct ending in both SG.DAT (only in the earliest texts a distinct form is attested in a limited number of nouns, e.g. *siang* 'bed' in Table 2) and SG.ACC. In the weak declensions (n-declensions), SG.GEN, SG.DAT and SG.ACC are identical, and this form is generally labelled OBLIQUE. The dative plural on the other hand, which is invariably -*um*, is always distinct from the various PL.ACC endings. Some paradigms are given in Table 2 (see further Noreen 1904:280ff. or Wessén 1968:94ff.).

2.2 Methodological problems

2.2.1 *Identifying changes in lexical case assignment*

In the course of the Old and Middle Swedish periods, lexical case assignment gradually disappeared. This is most evident with prepositions that governed the genitive or the dative, since these cases (particularly the genitive) were usually distinctly marked. Compare the contrasting pairs in (4) and (5):

(4) a. *han skal. gangæ til roms*
   he shall go to Rome-GEN
   'he shall go to Rome' VgL: ÆB12
 b. *Hon kom mz sinom døtrum til rom*
   she came with her-PL.DAT daughters-PL.DAT to Rome-?
   'she came to Rome with her daughters' ST 15
 c. *Hon kom till Rom*
   she came to Rome
   MoSw

(5) a. *Far mapær af landi* [...]
   goes man-MASC.SG.NOM from country-NEUT.SG.DAT
   'If a man leaves the country [...]' VgL: ÆB12
 b. *Han gig aff land*
   he went from country-?
   'He left the country' ST 205

Changes in prepositional constructions in which the prepositional complement was accusative are less easy to identify, since this case was only marked in the MASC.SG.ACC of adjectives, some definite forms[14] and some plural forms (cf. Table 4 and Table 6).

During the transitional stage at which the decline of lexical case had set in, the methodological problem of how to interpret suffixless forms presents itself. When a prepositional complement that was formerly marked for genitive or dative is uninflected, as in (4b) and (5b), there are in principle two possible analyses. According to the traditional scenario (e.g. Wessén 1965: 87), prepositions that used to govern the genitive or dative switched to the (mostly unmarked) accusative. In that case, *rom* in (4b) and *land* in (5b) would be labelled ACC.

Alternatively, the uninflected forms can be interpreted as zero.[15] In other words, the former analysis implies that lexical case is still productive whereas the latter implies that it has disappeared.

Thirdly, the unmarked forms could be analysed as "new" genitive or dative forms. In that case, the change from *roms* to *rom* would be purely morphological, not syntactic. That is, *rom* would still be glossed as GEN and there are no changes in case assignment — *til* continues to govern the genitive. This possibility will be further discussed in the next section.

These three claims are obviously mutually exclusive, so one has to state explicitly how changes in lexical case assignment are to be understood. To my mind, the first alternative is acceptable only when this is evidenced by unambiguous accusative forms whenever these are available. In Old and Middle Swedish this was not the case however. As we will see in Section 4 for example, the preposition *til* 'to' that used to governed the genitive does not generally switch to accusative, but only with a restricted number of noun phrases in an apparently opportunistic fashion. Thus, when there is no complete change to accusative with *all* forms, I see little reason to analyse *rom* in (4b) as accusative, for in that case, one would have to postulate two separate stages: one at which *rom* is inflected for accusative (i.e. when *til* shifts from genitive to accusative marking) and one at which *rom* is an uninflected base form (i.e. when lexical case is no longer productive). Needless to say, it will be impossible to establish when the former stage ends and the latter stage begins.

A similar problem arises with the third scenario. Evidently, lexical case is no longer productive in Modern Swedish–it would make no sense to analyse *Rom* in the MoSw equivalent in (4c) as a genitive form governed by *till*. Thus, at one point in the history of Swedish the genitive assigned by prepostions must have disappeared. If however suffixless forms are regarded as the mere result of morphological (or morphophonological) change and *rom* and *land* are interpreted as forms that are still marked for case, the loss of lexical case as a syntactic change is ignored.

2.2.2 *The interpretation of forms*

In addition, one needs to formulate strict criteria according to which prepositional complements are formally analysed. Inflectional paradigms presented in OSw reference grammars (e.g. Noreen 1904, Wessén 1968) are invariably idealized renderings of the rich variety of forms actually attested. This variety was mainly due to phonological changes that affected unstressed vowels and deletion of final *r*, which formed part of quite a number of OSw suffixes. Hence, one might also construct a more "pessimistic" OSw inflectional morphology, since reduced or even suffix-less forms may occur just as frequently as the full forms. When these two extremes are contrasted, as in Table 6 (p. 263), it becomes evident that the analysis of individual forms may become quite complicated.

In diachronic morphology, a fixed point of reference is indispensable however. In the discussion of changes in lexical case assignment, unequivocal criteria for distinguishing between genitive or dative and accusative or zero forms are required. For this purpose I will use the "idealized" paradigms that are given in Noreen's (1904) grammar of Old Swedish as a starting point, including the reduced variants of the suffixes. For example, -*ar* will serve as the point of reference for FEM.SG.GEN, including forms in which the vowel of this suffix is reduced and/or final *r* is dropped. Similarly, for MASC.SG.DAT I will use -*i*, even though this ending is increasingly omitted in the OSw period (see 1.2). It should be noted that the idealized forms are not reconstructed forms, or transferred from Old Norse. Even the bold forms in Table 6 are all actually attested and for this reason they form a valid starting point. Thus, both *sialar*, *sialær*, *siala* and *sialæ* 'soul' will be analysed as FEM.SG.GEN, but *sial* will not; *manni*, *manne* 'man' will be analysed as MASC.SG.DAT but *man* will not, even though this form is frequently attested in dative position (cf. example (1a) above). If this strict criterion were not applied, it would be impossible to reconstruct morphosyntactic changes such as the loss of lexical case assignment. All endings were eventually lost, and to my mind it makes little sense to posit an intermediary stage in which such forms as *sial* and *man* are considered as "new" genitive or dative "inflections". In addition, unless there is evidence of accusative complements after a given preposition, *sial* and *man* will not be regarded as accusative forms either (cf. the preceding section).

One potential disadvantage of this procedure however, is that suffixless forms were already quite common in "idealized" Old Swedish. Strong feminine nouns had already lost the distinction between SG.DAT and SG.ACC, and these forms will be classified as DAT/ACC.[16] One might object that the analysis of *sial* as FEM.SG.ACC or -ø in genitive position, but as FEM.SG.DAT/ACC in dative position is inconsistent, but this solution is to be preferred to one in which both are analysed as -ø or one in which *sial* is analysed as FEM.SG.GEN in genitive position.[17] In the former case, it would be impossible to know whether a given case with a given noun or declension could still be formally marked in Classical Old Swedish on which the ideal paradigms are based. In the latter case, it will be impossible to distinguish between inflected and suffixless forms and it might seem as if no change had occurred at all. One additional advantage of the proposed approach is that the data presented in tables and examples are unambiguous: even if the reader would disagree with the present formal analysis it will be clear how they are constructed with respect to the "ideal" OSw paradigms, and the reader will subsequently be able to interpret them his/her own way.[18]

2.2.3 Excursus: prepositions of rest and motion

In one notable group of constructions, the problems discussed in the preceding sections become particularly evident. These are prepositional constructions of rest and motion, in which a combination of the preposition and the case suffix serves to encode the grammatical relation. Such prepositions are commonly found in Indo-European languages — in Latin for instance, the preposition *in* takes the ablative to signify rest, as in (6a), whereas the accusative signifies motion, as in (6b). Similarly, Old Swedish uses both the dative and the accusative with the preposition *i* 'in', as in (7a–b).

(6) a. *in insula   vivere*
       in island-FEM.SG.ABL live
       'to live on an island'
    b. *in aquam   cadere*
       in water-FEM.SG.ACC fall
       'to fall into the water'

(7) a. *Dör han i   klostre.*
       dies he in monastery-NEUT.SG.DAT
       'if he dies in the monastery' VgL: ÆB9
    b. *Giuær maþær sik   i   klostær.*
       gives man   himself in monastery-NEUT.SG.ACC
       'if a man joins a monastic order' VgL: ÆB9

As a result of deflexion, such distinctions are no longer possible in Modern Swedish, which has to use adverbial *in* 'in' + prepositional *i* to signify motion, as in (8b), although in some cases single *i* can still be used, as in (8c).

(8) a. *hon sitter i   vardagsrummet*
       she sits   in living-room-the
       'she is sitting in the living-room'
    b. *hon gick in i vardagsrummet*
       she went in in living-room-the
       'she went into the living-room'
    c. *hon hoppade i sjön*
       she jumped in lake-the
       'she jumped into the lake'

In Old Swedish, the distinction between rest and motion does not consistently determine the choice between dative and accusative complements. Already in the earliest text, *Äldre Västgötalagen* (see Table 3), the preposition *i* 'in' may have an accusative complement in constructions denoting rest as in (9a), or a dative complement in constructions denoting motion as in (9b). The latter case is admittedly rare however (I found only one example), and as the accusative is correctly used in similar examples (even within one and the same sentence, as in (9c)), this might be a writing error.

(9) a. *Dræpær maþær   man   i*
       kills   man-MASC.SG.NOM man-MASC.SG.ACC in
       ölbenk   mæþ knivi.
       ale-bench-MASC.SG.ACC with knife-MASC.SG.DAT
       'if a man kills somebody on a drinking-bench with a knife' VgL: ÖM
    b. *Faldær. fæ   .i. mans   handæværki.*   [...]
       falls   cattle in man-MASC.SG.GEN handiwork-MASC.SG.DAT
       'if cattle falls into a man-made piece of work [...]' VgL: RB9
    c. [*Faldær. fæ .i. ...*] *ællær. annur þylik værk*
                              or   another such work-MASC.SG.ACC
       '[...] or into another such piece of work' VgL: RB9

Thus, *i* can take both dative and accusative complements and the choice between these two is not entirely determined by the motion-rest opposition. For this reason, it is impossible to assess whether an uninflected form is accusative or zero. It will be obvious, then, that prepositions such as *i* will have to be treated separately and with caution. As long as dative and (inflectionally marked) accusative forms are still attested (as is clearly the case in VgL), no form will be analysed as zero.

Table 3. Motion and rest with *i* in VgL (n = 64)[19]

	motion	rest
n	30	34
DAT	1	25
ACC	29	9

3. Least-effort strategies as principles of grammatical change

3.1 The speaker vs. the hearer

Deflexion in Swedish was a slow and complex process. As we have seen in Section 1.2, it did not merely entail the loss of inflectional material, as a result of reductive phonological processes or other changes discussed in 1.3. The question we have to deal with, therefore, is why a given morpheme disappeared in some syntactic environments but not in others, and why some suffixes were still used for a considerable period of time after the first signs of deflexion had become apparent. It will be seen that, apart from mere loss, a number of other tendencies can be observed as well. If the decline of lexical case is examined more closely, it will be seen that the tendency towards loss was counteracted by tendencies of maintenance. In other words, even though lexical case was to disappear eventually, it was temporarily slowed down by other developments which resulted in a stronger position of lexical case. In these sections, I will argue that these opposite tendencies can all be identified as least-effort strategies.

From a functional perspective, language change may be characterized as the interplay between two conflicting motivations: ease of production and ease of perception. Von der Gabelentz (1901:256) already observed that the relation between deflexion and alternative means of expressing case relations is rooted in the opposition between the inclination towards indolence (*Bequemlichkeitstrieb*) and the desire for clarity (*Deutlichkeitstrieb*). To put it differently, language change results from subtle shifts in the delicate balance between the speaker's and the hearer's least-effort strategies.

But as Hopper & Traugott (1993:64) rightly point out, economy of effort is a difficult concept. Little is known about what requires more or less effort on behalf of the speaker or hearer. Nevertheless, even with that reservation in mind, it is possible to formulate a rough but workable opposition between the speaker's and the hearer's interests. As far as the speaker's position is concerned, it is generally assumed that reducing the speech signal implies less effort whereas the hearer requires clear and preferably unambiguous input in order to perceive and process an utterance. When applied to inflectional case, these conflicting interests imply that a speaker might tend to reduce the inflectional ballast whereas the hearer needs as much grammatical information as possible in order to be able to parse the utterance correctly.

Not surprisingly, then, two of the principles discussed below are diametrically opposed to one another. One principle however, the principle of single encoding (see 3.4), appears to meet both the speaker's and the hearer's demands, and for this reason it may have been relevant for a relatively long period of time.

One might object that the least-effort principles are empirical generalizations rather than causative factors. Lass (1980), for instance, is particularly critical of such notions as "functional load" or "markedness". According to him, they have no predictive value or explanatory relevance, since they are based on a "simple and rather sloppy metaphor, with no empirical support that I know of" (Lass 1980: 93). I agree with Lass that the economy principle (see 3.2) should be conceived of as a metaphor which is unsuitable for predictions about the course or direction of language change. For if this principle were so omnipotent, one wonders why inflectional case was not lost in all Indo-European languages. The main reason for this appears to be that it is not the only principle at work, but counteracted by other principles, and it is probably impossible to predict which of the competing principles will turn out to be the most powerful one in a given situation. It will be understood, then, that the principles are used descriptively rather than predictively. Nevertheless, it will be seen that, as metaphors, they apply remarkably well to the changes discussed in Section 4. A meticulous empirical investigation may reveal how these tendencies gradually gain or lose importance in the course of deflexion.

3.2 The economy principle

The least-effort strategy on behalf of the speaker is frequently termed the economy principle. This principle is most often applied to phonological changes. According to Martinet (1955: 95), for example, the speaker fights a continuous battle against the inertia of the speech organs. In 19th century linguistics, the prevalent view was that the main motivation of the speaker is "to make things easy on our organs of speech, to economize time and effort in the work of expression" (Whitney 1868: 28, quoted from Jespersen 1922: 261). This view has met with considerable criticism (the critics Jespersen quotes dismiss it as "empty talk" and "worthless subterfuges now rejected by our science"), but

Jespersen himself does not reject the principle, even though there are many examples in which it is violated and it may not always be easy to establish which sound or combination of sounds is the easier one, "the instinctive feeling of all linguists is still in favour of the view that a movement towards the easier sound is the rule, and not the exception" (Jespersen 1922: 263).

As far as lexical case is concerned, the speaker might be tempted to omit the inflectional suffix on prepositional complements, since the preposition alone will suffice to express the grammatical relation. Surely more effort is required to pronounce *fra lawarþi sinum* (from lord-MASC.SG.DAT his-MASC.SG.DAT; VgL: RB11) than it would be to pronounce *fra lawarþ sin 'from his lord'. It should be noted however that deflexion does not exclusively result in shorter forms — it would be bizarre to claim, for instance, that MoSw *lagar* 'laws' is "more economical" than OSw PL.DAT *lagum*. As can be inferred from Table 2, the economy principle would only apply to the singular forms of strong declensions (and the plural forms of neuter nouns).

3.3 The principle of formally marked grammatical relations

It might seem that when the meaning of the utterance or the grammatical function of a given constituent can be derived from other grammatical means, such as fixed word order or periphrastic constructions (e.g. adpositional phrases), inflectional expression is no longer indispensable. Nevertheless, case marking of prepositional complements is remarkably persistent in all inflecting Indo-European languages. Even if part of the case system is lost, the prepositional complement may come to be marked for a different case. For example, in Swedish dialects which lost the genitive but retained the dative, the dative is used after the preposition *till* 'to(wards)', which used to govern the genitive (Reinhammar 1993).

In other words, there is a very strong tendency to maintain lexical case, even though it does not add anything to the meaning of the prepositional construction (except in the case of motion-rest prepositions discussed in 2.2.3). This tendency I will call the principle of formally marked grammatical relations.

The principle of formally marked grammatical relations may also be held responsible for the apparently arbitrary use of inflected forms after prepositions. As OSw inflectional contrasts wore away, it was not always possible to mark a given noun for the required case. Quite surprisingly however, this did not invariably lead to the immediate loss of lexical case assignment. As we will see in Section 4, a preposition could sometimes take complements of whatever case that still happened to be marked inflectionally, e.g. genitive with single MASC.SG. INDEF nouns, but accusative in MASC.SG noun phrases containing an adjective.

Similarly, the more distinctly marked definite forms of the noun may have been preferred to indefinite forms with nouns that had few case distinctions, such as n-stems (which in the singular only distinguished between nominative and oblique). In his interesting monograph on the suffix of definiteness in Old Swedish, Larm (1933) has shown that this suffix was not evenly distributed among the various nominal declensions in the OSw laws. A considerable part (in VgL even 50%) of the definite noun forms consists of nouns belonging to weak declensions. Furthermore, Larm observes that the MASC.SG.GEN.DEF form *bondæns* of the noun *bonde* 'yeoman' is found over twice as many times as the indefinite form *bondæ* in *Upplandslagen* (the law of Uppland).[20] According to Larm, this higher frequency is due to the "stronger pithiness" of the definite form. In my opinion, this stronger pithiness is also responsible for the relatively large share of definite forms of weak nouns, since these are unambiguously marked.

3.4 The principle of single encoding

The principle of single encoding may be defined as a subtype of the economy principle. It is interesting to note however that, unlike the economy principle, the principle of single encoding is not only advantageous to the speaker. As Newmeyer (1998: 136) points out, it is also more efficient for the hearer to parse grammatical information only once. In the present context, it means that it is more efficient (for the speaker and hearer alike) to mark case on only one single element in the noun phrase, instead of adding an inflectional suffix to all elements (concordial case).

Jespersen (1922: 348ff.) regarded the disappearance of concordial case — "the clumsy repetitions under the name of concord" — as a token of progress. For instance, Jespersen argues, the absence of concord between a noun and its dependent, gives English an advantage over French, for in English one can say *my wife and children* whereas in French the possessive pronoun has to be repeated in order to meet gender and number concord requirements: *ma femme et mes enfants*. Another example used by Jespersen is given below:

(10) a. opera virorum omnium bonorum veterum [Latin]
 b. ealra godra ealdra manna weorc [Old English]
 c. alle gode gamle mænds værker [Danish]
 d. all good old men's work [Modern English]

In Latin *virorum omnium bonorum veterum*, number (plural) and case (genitive) have been marked four times, gender twice; in Old English, case and number are expressed four times, whereas gender is not; in Danish, only plural is marked four times and case only once; and in English, finally, both case and number are denoted only once. In Jespersen's view, English thus represents the highest stage in a progressive linguistic evolution: "[...] as nothing is lost in clearness, this method as being the easiest and shortest, must be considered the best" (Jespersen 1922: 351).

The principle of single encoding may be illustrated by the loss of concordial case in Swedish. Old Swedish was originally a word-marking language, that is, all elements in the noun phrase had to be inflected for case, as is illustrated in examples (11a–d).

(11) a. *mykilhughæþær   maðþær   oc*
       proud-MASC.SG.NOM man-MASC.SG.NOM and
       girughær
       avaricious-MASC.SG.NOM
       'a proud and avaricious man' Vidh 14

  b. *innan enom   gardhe*
      in   one-MASC.SG.DAT yard-MASC.SG.DAT
      'in one yard' Mose 27

  c. *mz   allom   sinom   sonum*
      with all-PL.DAT his-PL.DAT son-PL.DAT
      'with all his sons' Mose 196

  d. *v   ens   salogs   manz*
      from a-MASC.SG.GEN blessed-MASC.SG.GEN man-MASC.SG.GEN
      munne
      mouth-MASC.SG.DAT
      'from a blessed man's mouth' Bur 205

This type of case marking disappears during the Old and Middle Swedish periods — in an increasing number of constructions, case is marked on one element in the NP only, as in (12a–c) (see further Norde 1997a: 128ff.).

(12) a. *een vnger   konung*
       a   young-MASC.SG.NOM king-Ø
       'a young king' ST 377

  b. *j synom   gardh*
      in his-MASC.SG.DAT yard-Ø
      'in his yard' ST 10

c. vtan   min   fadhers   wiliu
   without my-Ø father-MASC.SG.GEN consent-FEM.SG.OBL
   'without my father's consent' Did 2

The general tendency thus appears to be that only those elements are inflected that form part of maximally differentiated paradigms — usually strong adjectives and/or pronouns. In general, inflectional contrasts were better preserved with adjectives than with nouns, primarily because in Proto-Germanic some pronominal endings had been transferred to adjectives, probably under the influence of pronominal adjectives such as *all* and *other* (Werner 1984:204). This resulted in far more case distinctions in adjective than in noun declensions (except for the usual homomorphy of nominative and accusative with neuter nouns). In Table 4, these pronominal forms are printed in bold. In addition, suffixless forms are rare in strong adjective declensions (with the exception of FEM.SG.NOM and NEUT.PL.NOM/ACC). In this respect, strong adjectives differ significantly from nouns, where suffixless forms were far more common (even more so at the end of the OSw period), as a result of which noun inflections increasingly took on the character of Meillets accessories (cf. 1.3.2). For this reason, if the principle of single encoding is applied, it is usually the adjective which is inflected in adjective-noun NP's.

Table 4. Strong adjective inflection in Old Swedish

	masculine	feminine	neuter
NOM	langer	lang	**langt**
GEN	**langs**	**langrar**	**langs**
DAT	**langum**	**langri**	langu
ACC	**langan**	langa	**langt**
NOM	**langir**	langar	lang
GEN	**langra**	**langra**	**langra**
DAT	langum	langum	langrum
ACC	langa	langar	lang

lang- 'long' ("idealized" forms only)

Hence, in (12a) we find *een vnger konung*, not *een vng konunger; in (12b) we find *j synom gardh*, not *i syn gardhe.[21] The only exception to this pattern is MASC/NEUT.SG.GEN *-s*, which turned into a phrase marker, as in (12c) (see further Norde 1997a and Norde to appear1).[22]

It is also important to note that I have thus far only found examples of single case marking in singular noun phrases. It is tempting to assume that this is due to the lack of suffixless forms in plural paradigms (with the exception of neuter nouns) with both nouns and strong adjectives. In other words, neither with nouns nor with strong adjectives a suffixless form was available and hence the principle of single encoding could not be applied.

4. Case study: case assignment of the preposition *til*

In this final section, I will examine the loss of the lexical genitive which is governed by the preposition *til* 'to(wards)' (see Norde 1997a: 147ff. for details).

Til is a grammaticalized noun, derived from Proto-Germanic **tila-* 'goal' (cf German *Ziel*). In Proto-Scandinavian, it replaced the Proto-Germanic preposition *tō* (English *to*, German *zu*). Probably because of its nominal origin (as the head noun in genitive constructions), *til* originally governed the genitive:

(13) a. *Dauid kom rættelika til rikis*
 David came lawfully to power-NEUT.SG.GEN
 'David came lawfully into power' Mose 5
 b. *þær skulu all til toptær*
 they shall all to homestead-FEM.SG.GEN
 'they all belong to the homestead' VgL: IB7

But in the course of the Old Swedish period the use of the genitive after *til* rapidly decreases; in religious prose (Bur, Mose) suffixless forms even outnumber inflected forms when the prepositional complement is a bare noun. Feminine nouns, in particular, are mostly not inflected for genitive after *til*, as in *til sokn* (UL: KiB4) 'to (the) parish'; *tel trøst* (Bur 135) 'to solace'; *til hiælp* (Mose 13) 'to aid'. According to Nordling (1924: 396) more than two thirds of feminine nouns lack a genitive suffix in manuscripts until 1350. To a large extent, the lack of FEM.SG.GEN -*ar* was due to phonological change (cf. 1.3.1) — -*ar* was affected by both vowel reduction and r-deletion as a result of which probably only a mere schwa remained, which was easily dropped. However, this change is also in part syntactic, since MASC/NEUT.SG.GEN -*s*, which was not reduced at all, is also increasingly omitted (see below).

However, when *til* governs not a bare noun but a feminine definite noun or a feminine full noun phrase, genitive complements are still extremely common:

(14) a. *klandar han tompt   ok   alt þæt*
        claims he   homestead and all that
        til tomptinna   liggær
        to homestead-Ø-the-FEM.SG.GEN lies
        'if he claims the homestead and all that belongs to it' ÖgL: ES15

   b. [*þa   a*] *han eig vitu   num   til ennær   skipt.*
        then has he   not right except to one-FEM.SG.GEN piece.of.land-Ø
        'then he is not entitled to more than one piece of land' VgL: IB7

As far as full noun phrases are concerned, Nordling (1924: 390) suggests that the absence of genitive inflection with strong feminine nouns resulted in an increase in the use of the more distinctly marked adjectives, in order to denote the genitive case of the prepositional complement. Unfortunately, Nordling does not provide empirical support for his hypothesis, yet it does hold a certain appeal. It may also account for the relatively large share of definite genitive forms of strong feminine nouns which are, like the adjective forms, unambiguously genitive (see Table 5). The examples in (14) thus meet two principles simultaneously: the principle of single encoding and the principle of formally marked grammatical relations.

Table 5.   FEM.SG inflection in Old Swedish

	bare nouns	definite nouns	strong adjectives
NOM	færþ	færþ-in	lang
GEN	færþ-a(r), -æ(r)	færþ-inna(r), -innæ(r)	lang-(r)a(r), -(r)æ(r)
DAT	færþ	færþ-inni, -inne	lang-(r)i, -(r)e
ACC	færþ	færþ-ina, -inæ	lang-a, -æ

færþ 'journey'

With masculine full noun phrases, a different picture emerges — MASC.SG.GEN was *-s* for both nouns (in most declensions, see Table 6) and strong adjectives (see Table 4). Especially in (late) OSw religious prose, uninflected complements are more common than inflected ones, as in (15a), although it should be noted that quite a number of complements in *-s* have been preserved in fixed expressions.[23] However, in noun phrases containing one or several adjectives, these adjectives are frequently inflected for accusative, as in (15b).

Table 6. Noun inflections in some Old Swedish declensions

	(j/i)a-stems			(j/i)ō-stems		i-stems			u-stems[b]		consonant stems			r-stems
	MASC	NEUT		FEM		MASC	FEM		MASC	NEUT	MASC	FEM		MASC/FEM
SG.NOM	-er	–		–		-er	–		-er****, -er	–	-er	–	–	-ir, -er
GEN	-s	-s		-ar		-ar, -s	-æ, -s	-ar	-ar**, -æ, -s -s	-æ	-s	-ar	-s	-ur(s), -or(s)
DAT	-i	-i		[-u]ᵃ	–	-i	–	[-u]ᵃ	-i*	–	-i	–	–	-ur, -or, -r*
ACC	–	–		–		–	–		-****	–	–	–	–	-ur, -or
PL.NOM	-ar	–		-ar	-æ	-ir	-ir	-e	-ir*	-e	-er*	-er*	-e	-er*
GEN	-a	-a		-a	-æ	-a	-a	-æ	-a**	-æ	-a	-a	-æ	-ra*, -ræ*
DAT	-um	-um		-um	-om	-um	-um	-om	-um***-om	-om	-um	-om	-om	-rum*, -rom*
ACC	-a	–		-a	-æ	-i	-ir	-e	-i*	-e	-er	-er	-e	-er*

ᵃ This ending is so rare that it is excluded from Norén's tables, it is only mentioned as a characteristic of a handful of nouns (Norén 1904:301; 307).
ᵇ U-stems are very rare in OSW. Most masculine u-stems had already switched to a-stem inflection (Wessén 1968:9 and there is probably only one neuter u-stem: *fæ* 'property, cattle', which is a singulare tantum (Norde 1997a:97).
* with i-umlaut of the stem vowel
** with a-breaking of the stem vowel
*** with u-breaking of the stem vowel
**** with u-umlaut or u-breaking of the stem vowel
(For a brief survey of umlaut (vowel mutation) and breaking (diphthongization) in the OSc languages see Haugen (1976:152–153).

(15) a. *oc waldo   en ærlikan hærra til konungh*
         and elected-3PL an honest man to king-Ø
         'and they elected an honest man to be their king' Mose 19
    b. *tel en   mæstan   ok*
         to a-MASC.SG.NOM/ACC most.eminent-MASC.SG.ACC and
         mærastan.   [...] rican
         most.distinguished-MASC.SG.ACC   rich-MASC.SG.ACC
         kunugh.
         king-MASC.SG.ACC
         'to a most eminent and most distinguished rich king' Bur 497

Now, there are two potential reasons why accusative *-an* is used to mark the prepositional complement instead of genitive *-s* (following the principle of formally marked grammatical relations). First, when concordial case was lost, MASC/NEUT.SG.GEN *-s* developed into a phrase marker (cf. example (12c) and note 22). Consequently, since adjectives are overwhelmingly prepositive in Old Swedish, phrase-final *-s* is usually attached to the noun — examples such as (16a) are virtually absent.[24] For the same reason, such constructions as (16b) are not attested either. It thus seems that *-s* could no longer function as an "ordinary" inflection once it had been reanalysed as a phrase-marker. However, such phrase-marking constructions are only attested in adnominal position, not in prepositional complements (see Norde 1997a: 223ff. for theoretical discussion). Hence, a construction such as (16c) was not a possible alternative for a construction such as (15b) either. For this reason, MASC.SG.ACC *-an* was used in order to meet the principle of formally marked grammatical relations and the principle of single encoding.

(16) a. ?**vtan   mins   fadher   wiliu*
        without my-MASC.SG.GEN father-Ø consent
        'without my father's consent'
    b. **til mins   fadher*
        to my-MASC.SG.GEN father-Ø
        'to my father'
    c. **til min   fadhers*
        to my-Ø father-MASC.SG.GEN
        'to my father'

Secondly, adjectival MASC.SG.ACC may indicate a general shift from genitive to accusative with *til*. Further evidence of such a transition is provided by Latin accusative forms of foreign personal names and place names:[25]

(17) a. *En vngar cristen   suen talaþe tel andream*
       a young Christian lad spoke to Andreas-ACC
       'a young Christian spoke to Andreas' Bur 136
    b. *han war en aff them som kommo   til babylonem*
       he was one of those who came-3PL to Babylon-ACC
       'he was one of those who had come to Babylon' Mose 10

If however the general tendency was one from genitive to accusative marking, one could ask why definite feminine nouns and feminine full noun phrases (cf. examples (14a–b)) did not take part in this development, even though FEM.SG.ACC was distinctly marked in both the definite article and the strong adjective. The tentative answer to this question would be that with these noun phrases no such shift was necessary, since the unambiguous FEM.SG.GEN forms already met the principle of formally marked grammatical relations.

5. Conclusions

From the case study presented in the previous section it becomes evident that both the general tendency towards loss and the apparently enigmatic exceptions are ultimately determined by least-effort strategies. The economy principle, which eventually led to the loss of lexical case, was obviously the most powerful one. The genitive with *til* was fully productive at the beginning of the Old Swedish period, but in late OSw religious prose the share of genitival complements with *til* amounts to less than one third. The economy principle was however obstructed by the principle of formally marked grammatical relations. Unambiguous forms, when available, appear to have been preferred to mark lexical case relations, which may account for the inconsistencies in case marking after *til*. These conflicting tendencies may be characterized as the principal least-effort strategies on behalf of the speaker and the hearer respectively.

But these two principles do not suffice to describe the loss of lexical case in Swedish, since they do not cover the attested intermediary stage of single encoding, which can be characterized as a least-effort strategy that is beneficial to speaker and hearer alike. The principle of single encoding led to a relatively stable new type of case system—one in which only one element in the noun phrase was distinctly marked. For this reason, lexical case managed to maintain itself for a relatively long period of time after its decline had set in. Feminine noun phrases opted for genitive forms of definite nouns or adjectives, which were still formally marked. And if Nordling is right, full noun phrases (i.e. noun phrases containing a distinctly marked adjective) were increasingly preferred to uninflected bare feminine nouns. Masculine noun phrases, on the other hand, show a different pattern. Bare nouns are inflected for genitive (though an increasing number of these constructions are to be analysed as fixed expressions, cf. note 23), but full noun phrases for accusative. I have argued that the reason why MASC/NEUT.SG.GEN -s was not used as a single case marker was that it was probably no longer available as an inflectional suffix after it had turned into a phrase marker. Adjectival MASC.SG.ACC -*an*, on the other hand, was still inflectional and an unambiguous case marker.

It remains to be investigated what (internal and external) factors determine the strength of these principles in different languages at different points in time. It also goes without saying that more empirical research into prepositional case assignment is required, both to deal with the methodological problems discussed in 2.2 and to establish the relative significance of the various least-effort strategies involved. For this purpose, a scrupulous collection and analysis of available data is crucial. If only the initial situation (productive lexical case) and final result (no lexical case) were to be examined, it would seem that the loss of lexical case was an uninterrupted process and that the only relevant least-effort strategy was the economy principle. I will therefore conclude this paper with the following quote from Lass (1997:288), which eloquently illustrates the indispensability of a detailed account of intermediate stages in historical linguistics:

> If I drive from Edinburgh to London, make some stops for petrol, and take a brief trip east on the way to visit a friend in Cambridge, I can still be said (from the point of view of 'the accomplishment', or juxtaposition of initial and final states) to 'have driven from Edinburgh to London'. How I got there is another (kind of) story. [...] We seem usually to be thinking of macro-stories when we talk about 'change'; but the micro-stories are of enormous theoretical importance as well.

Notes

1. This paper forms part of my research project *Grammaticalization in its final stages: deflexion and related changes in Continental Scandinavian*, which is financed by the Netherlands Organization for Scientific Research (NWO). In the linguistic examples, the following abbreviations will be used: MASC: masculine; FEM: feminine; NEUT: neuter; COMM: common;

SG: singular; PL: plural; NOM: nominative; GEN: genitive; DAT: dative; ACC: accusative; OBL: oblique; INDEF: indefinite; DEF: definite; S: s-genitive.

2. It seems likely that the merger of masculine and feminine gender is related to deflexion, since the endings that distinguished masculine from feminine inflection were largely lost (Davidsson 1990:148).

3. In Modern Swedish, gender is not only marked on articles, pronouns and adjectives but also on nouns, that is, all plural endings are largely or even entirely confined to either common or neuter nouns. In this respect, Swedish is more conservative than Danish, where all productive endings are found with both common and neuter nouns, e.g. (COMMON) *stol/stole* 'chair(s) — (NEUT) *bord/borde* 'table(s)' (Swedish *stol/stolar* – *bord/bord*). We may thus say that the Danish case system was substituted by a number system (Hansen 1956:186). On gender in Swedish see also Norde (to appear) and Norde 2000a and references there.

4. A good introduction to the breakup of Proto-Scandinavian and the histories of the individual Scandinavian languages is Haugen 1976.

5. The main periods of the Swedish language are: *Runic Swedish* (RSw): 800–1225; *Old Swedish* (OSw): 1225–1375; *Middle Swedish* (MiSw): 1375–1526; *Early Modern Swedish* (EMoSw): 1526–1732; *Modern Swedish* (MoSw): 1732–

6. Old Swedish nominal inflections were typically cumulative, i.e. simultaneous realizations of gender, case and number.

7. For the abbreviations in references to law texts the reader is referred to the editions of these texts.

8. Another objection that is sometimes raised where phonological factors are concerned is that word-initial stress did not result in reduction or apocope in other languages, such as Finnish (Haugen 1976:285). In order to account for the difference between e.g. Germanic and Finnish, Van Coetsem, Hendricks & McCormick (1981:298) distinguish between two types of stress ("prominence" in their terminology): dominating (D) and non-dominating (ND) which they define as follows: "In a language with D type prominence (D type language), prominent syllables are perceived as more salient *at the expense* of the nonprominent syllables, regardless of the physical correlates. On the other hand, in a language with ND type prominence (ND type language), the perceived salience of prominent as against nonprominent syllables is less pronounced." Following this distinction, stress in the Germanic languages would be of the dominant type, whereas stress in Finnish would be of the non-dominant type. For criticism of the potential circularity of Van Coetsem's theory see however Riad 1998.

9. On secondary adpositions see Norde 1999 and 2000b. These are adpositions that were developed during a relatively late period, that is, they have no Proto-Indo-European origin. They are derived from lexical items — the noun *bland* 'blend', for example, grammaticalized into a preposition meaning 'among'.

10. In Old Swedish, the attributive genitive could both precede and follow the head noun; when it is postpositive, it does not function as a determiner (Norde 1997a:189ff. and 216ff.). In some MoSw constructions, the genitive functions as a modifier, which is formally expressed by the strong (indefinite) form of the adjective: *efter tre dagars intensivt arbete* (after [three day]s hard work) 'after three days of hard work' (Norde 1997a:74ff.).

11. It should be noted that quite a substantial number of counterexamples to the unidirectionality hypothesis have been cited. Janda 2000 notes that counterexamples to unidirectionality are mentioned in at least 29 works from before 1990 (i.e. before the discussion on unidirectionality became an issue). In addition, Janda mentions 30 works from the 1990s in which the unidirectionality of grammatical change is explicitly challenged. Also in one of the grammaticalization textbooks it is acknowledged that: "Extensive though the evidence of unidirectionality is, it cannot be regarded as an absolute principle. Some counterexamples do exist. Their existence, and their relative infrequency, in fact help define our notion of what prototypical grammaticalization is" (Hopper & Traugott 1993: 126).

12. More examples of Old Swedish inflectional suffixes becoming "less grammatical" are discussed in Norde (to appear) and 2000a.

13. There are some 3000 runic inscriptions in Sweden (Düwel 1983: 64), most of which date from ca. 950–ca. 1100. Unfortunately, there is a yawning gap between this Golden Age of runic inscriptions and the earliest OSw text, *Äldre Västgötalagen* (the older West Gautish law). This text was first written down around ca. 1225, but the oldest complete manuscript dates from the 1280s. From the 12th century there is no linguistic evidence, neither runic inscriptions nor manuscripts. The Runic Swedish period will not be considered in this paper.

14. Both OSw and MoSw possess a suffix of definiteness. In OSw, both the noun and the suffixed article were inflected (the so-called 'internal inflection'; see Norde 1997a: 105ff), as in *fisk-s-in-s* (fish-MASC.SG.GEN-the-MASC.SG.GEN) 'the fish'.

15. I will use the term "zero" (glossed Ø) to refer to forms that are no longer marked for case. Suffixless forms that already formed part of the ideal Classical Old Swedish paradigms will not be labelled Ø, but, for instance, MASC.SG.ACC (cf. Section 2.2.2 and note 17).

16. Only those feminine nouns that are still distinctly marked in SG.DAT (see Table 6) will be analysed as dative or accusative.

17. Another possibility would be to analyse *all* suffixless forms as -ø, as all nouns were once inflected for case (going back to Proto-Scandinavian, Germanic or even Indo-European). Since this paper deals primarily with the change from Old to Modern Swedish however, I have chosen to take Classical Old Swedish (which can still be said to possess a productive four-case system) as the point of reference.

18. Another obvious problem is dialectal variation — Old Swedish was not a standardized language, and in some varieties more forms that form part of the idealized OSw paradigms may have been suffixless from the earliest records onwards. I will let this problem rest for now.

19. *I* occurs 212 times in VgL (its spelling variant *j* included). These are not all prepositions — *i* may also be a verbal particle. For practical reasons, I only analysed the first 100 constructions in which *i* appears as a preposition. 64 of these constructions contained unambiguously marked complements (the others were DAT/ACC or OBL).

20. This law was enacted in 1296, the principal manuscript dates from the middle of the 14th century.

21. Note that it makes no difference whether or not noun and adjective inflection differ. In MASC.SG.NOM, the suffix is -*er* for both nouns and adjectives; in MASC.SG.DAT the suffix is -*i* for nouns and -*um* for adjectives.

22. The tendency towards phrase-marking, which is the essential first step in the development of the s-genitive, dates back to the OSw period. Examples from this period are admittedly rare, but in MiSw phrase-marking becomes increasingly common. It is thus interesting to note that this shift from concordial case to phrase-marking does not follow deflexion but occurs simultaneously.

23. Some examples from MoSw are *till sjöss* 'at sea' and *till skogs* 'to the forest'. This has been a productive pattern, since it is also used with nouns that are originally feminine (with a SG.GEN in *-ar*), e.g. *till sängs* 'to bed' (see further Norde 1997a:54f.).

24. In all the MiSw texts I examined, I found only one example in which *-s* is attached to the adjective only (see Norde 1997a:138n.).

25. It seems unlikely that these Latin accusatives are due to the fact that the corresponding Latin prepositions (in most cases *ad*) take the accusative in Latin, because *til* and *ad* are not cognate and Bur and Mose are no direct translations from Latin texts.

Sources

Old Swedish
Bur: *Codex Bureanus*. In: *Ett forn-svenskt legendarium* ed. by G. Stephens. (= *Skrifter utgivna av Svenska Fornskriftsällskapets samlingar* 8, 9, 12, 17, 18, 28) 1847–1858.
Mose: *Fem moseböcker på fornsvenska enligt Cod. Holm. A1* ed. by O. Thorell. (= *Skrifter utgivna av Svenska Fornskriftsällskapets samlingar* 212, 218, 223) 1959.
UL: *Upplandslagen enligt Cod. Holm. B199* ed. by S. Henning. (= *Skrifter utgivna av Svenska Fornskriftsällskapets samlingar* 240, 242) 1967–1969.
VgL: *Äldre Västgötalagen* ed. by E. Wessén. Stockholm: Norstedts. 1965. Previous edition in: *Corpus iuris Sueo-Gotorum antiqui I* ed. by H.S. Collin & C.J. Schlyter. Stockholm: Z. Hæggström. 1827.
Vidh: *Vidhemsprästens anteckningar*. In: *Corpus iuris Sueo-Gotorum antiqui I* ed. by H.S. Collin and C.J. Schlyter. 1827.
ÖgL: *Östgötalagen*. In : *Corpus Iuris Sueo-Gotorum Antiqui II* ed. by H.S. Collin och C.J. Schlyter. Stockholm: Z. Hæggström. 1830.

Middle Swedish
Did: *Didrikssagan* ed. by G.O. Hyltén-Cavallius. Stockholm: P.A. Norstedt & Söner. 1850–1854.
ST: *Siælinna thrøst I* ed. by S. Henning. (= *Skrifter utgivna av Svenska Fornskriftsällskapets samlingar* 209) 1954.

Early Modern Swedish
GVB: *Gustav Vasas Bibel*. In: *Nya Testamentet i Gustav Vasas Bibel under jämförelse med texten av år 1526* ed. by N. Lindqvist. Stockholm: Svenska Kyrkans Diakonistyrelsens Bokförlag. 1941.

References

Anward, J. and Swedenmark, J. 1997. "¡Kasus nej, bestämdhet ja! Om möjliga modeller av nominalböjningens utveckling i svenskan". In *Studier i svensk språkhistoria 4*, Patrik Åström (ed.), 21–34. Stockholm: Institutionen för nordiska språk.

Beito, O. T. 1957. "Har alle endringar i eit morfologisk system opphav i innhaldsplanet?". *Arkiv för nordisk filologi* 72:71–77.

Braunmüller, K. 1995. "Morphologische Undurchsichtigkeit — ein Charakteristikum kleiner Sprachen". In *Beiträge zur skandinavischen Linguistik*, K. Braunmüller, 53–80. Oslo: Novus Forlag.

Coetsem, F. van, Hendricks, R., and McCormick, S. 1981. "Accent typology and sound change". *Lingua* 53:295–315.

Davidsson, H. 1990. *Han hon den. Genusutvecklingen i svenskan under nysvensk tid.* Lund: Lund University Press.

Düwel, K. 1983. *Runenkunde*, (Zweite Auflage). Stuttgart: Verlag J. B. Metzler.

Gabelentz, G. von der. 1901. *Die Sprachwissenschaft, ihre Aufgaben, Methoden und bisherigen Ergebnisse*. (Reprinted. Tübingen: Tübinger Beiträge zur Linguistik 1969).

Hansen, A. 1956. "Kasusudvikling i dansk". In *Festskrift til Peter Skautrup*, 183–194. Aarhus: Universitetsforlaget.

Haugen, E. 1976. *The Scandinavian Languages*. London: Faber and Faber.

Heine, B., Claudi, U., and Hünnemeyer, F. 1991. *Grammaticalization. A conceptual framework*. Chicago: The University of Chicago Press.

Hjelmslev, L. 1935. *La catégorie des cas. Étude de grammaire générale*. Aarhus: Universitetsforlaget.

Hopper, P. J. and Traugott, E. C. 1993. *Grammaticalization*. Cambridge: CUP.

Jakobson, R. 1971 [1931]. "Beitrag zur allgemeinen Kasuslehre: Gesamtbedeutungen der russischen Kasus". In *Selected writings II*, R. Jakobson, 23–72. Den Haag: Mouton.

Janda, R. D. 2000. "Beyond "pathways" and "unidirectionality": On the discontinuity of language transmission and the reversability of grammaticalization". *Language Sciences*. 23(2–3):265–340.

Jespersen, O. 1922. *Language. Its nature, development and origin*. London: George Allen & Unwin Ltd.

Knudsen, T. 1967. *Kasuslære I: Inledning, nominativ, akkusativ*. Oslo: Universitetsforlaget.

Kock, A. 1921. *Svensk ljudhistoria 4*. Lund: C. W. K. Gleerup.

Larm, K. 1933. "Morfologiska faktorers inverkan på utbredningen av suffigerad artikel i lagsvenskan". *Arkiv för nordisk filologi* 49:374–385.

Lass, R.. 1980. *On explaining language change*. Cambridge: CUP.

Lass, R. 1997. *Historical Linguistics and Language Change*. Cambridge: CUP.

Lehmann, C. 1985. "Grammaticalization: Synchronic variation and diachronic change". *Lingua e stile* 20 (3):303–318.

Lehmann, C. 1991. "Grammaticalization and related changes in German". In *Approaches to grammaticalization II*, E. C. Traugott and B. Heine (eds), 493–535. Amsterdam: John Benjamins.

Lehmann, C. 1995 [1982]. *Thoughts on Grammaticalization*. München: Lincom Europa.

Liberman, A. 1982. *Germanic Accentology I: The Scandinavian languages*. Minneapolis: University of Minnesota Press.

Loon, J. van. 1996. *Endogene Factoren in de Diachrone Morfologie van de Germaanse talen*. Tongeren: Drukkerij George Michiels N. V.

Marold, E.. 1984. "Überlegungen zur Entwicklung der Substantiv-flexion in den skandinavischen Sprachen". In *Linguistica et philologica. Gedenkschrift für Björn Collinder*, O. Gschwantler et al. (eds), 307–330. Wien: Wilhelm Braumüller Universitäts-Verlagsbuchhandlung.

Martinet, A. 1955. *Économie des changements phonétiques. Traité de phonologie diachronique*. Berne: Éditions A. Francke.

Meillet, A. 1922 [1917]. *Caractères généraux des langues germaniques*. Deuxième édition. Paris: Librairie Hachette et Cie.

Newmeyer, F. J. 1998. *Language Form and Language Function*. Cambridge MA: MIT Press.

Norde, M. 1997a. *The History of the Genitive in Swedish. A case study in degrammaticalization*. PhD dissertation, University of Amsterdam..

Norde, M. 1997b. "Middle Low German-Middle Scandinavian language contact and morphological simplification". *Multilingua* 16 (4): 389–409.

Norde, M. 1999. "Förlust av kasus och sekundära adpositioner i fornsvenskan". *Tijdschrift voor Skandinavistiek* 20 (2): 25–64.

Norde, M. 2000a. "Deflexion as a counterdirectional factor in grammatical change". In *Language Sciences*. 23(2–3): 231–264.

Norde, M. 2000b. "The grammaticalization of adpositions in the history of Swedish". In *Proceedings of the Xth conference of Nordic and general linguistics*, Guðrun Þórhallsdóttir (ed.), 177–187. Reykjavík: Institute of Linguistics.

Norde, M. to appear. "The final stages of grammaticalization: affixhood and beyond". In *New reflections on grammaticalization*, I. Wischer and G. Diewald (eds). Potsdam.

Nordling, A. 1924. "Ur genitivens historia". In *Festskrift tillägnad Hugo Pipping*, 395–405. Helsingfors.

Noreen, A. 1904. *Altschwedische Grammatik*. Halle: M. Niemeyer Verlag.

Perridon, H. 1993. "On the relation between case and preposition". In *Sprache — Kommunikation, Informatik. Akten des 26. Linguistischen Kolloquiums, Poznán 1991*, J. Darski and Z. Vetulani, 359–365. Tübingen: M. Niemeyer Verlag.

Reinhammar, M. 1993. "Levande språkhistoria". In *Studier i svensk språkhistoria 3*, L. Wollin (ed.), 183–191. Uppsala: Institutionen för Nordiska Språk..

Riad, T. 1998. Review of F. van Coetsem *Towards a typology of lexical accent: "Stress accent" and "pitch accent" in a renewed perspective. American journal of Germanic linguistics and literatures* 10 (2): 307–312.

Sandøy, H. 1994. "Uten kontakt og endring?" In *Språkkontakt, dialektkontakt och språkförändring i Norden*, U.-B. Kotsinas and J. Helgander (eds), 38–51. Stockholm: Institutionen för Nordiska Språk..

Schwartz, E. 1878. "Om oblika kasus och prepositioner i fornsvenskan från tiden före år 1400". *Uppsala universitets årsskrift 1878*.

Skautrup, P. 1944. *Det danske sprogs historie I: Fra guldhornene til Jyske lov*. København: Gyldendal.

Torp, A. 1982. *Norsk og nordisk før og nå*. Oslo: Universitetsforlaget.

Werner, O. 1984. "Morphologische Entwicklungen in den germanischen Sprachen". In *Das Germanische und die Rekonstruktion der indogermanischen Grundsprache*, J. Untermann and B. Brogyanyi (eds), 181–226. Amsterdam: John Benjamins.

Wessén, E. 1965. *Svensk språkhistoria III: Grundlinjer till en historisk syntax.* (Reprinted. Edsbruk: Akademitryck 1992).

Wessén, E. 1968. *Svensk språkhistoria I: Ljudlära och ordböjningslära.* (Reprinted. Edsbruk: Akademitryck 1992).

Whitney, W. D. 1868. *Language and the Study of Language.* London.

The coding of the subject–object distinction from Latin to Modern French*

Lene Schøsler
University of Copenhagen

In order to understand and decode the message of a sentence, it is necessary to understand its basic argument structure. This implies e.g. that one must be able to identify the subject and distinguish this from the other elements of the sentence, in particular from the direct object. As linguistic patterns provide the speakers or writers with different types of construction with more or less transparency, it should be possible to identify the linguistic clues ensuring communication; e.g. the clues helping to distinguish the subject and the object. This distinction is in fact one of the crucial distinctions in syntax, and I will focus only on that distinction. I want to consider the following three factors, belonging to different grammatical levels, which may help to identify the elements of the sentence: the organising power of verbal valency: the nominal and verbal inflection and the word order. It will be shown that these factors cooperate in order to facilitate the identification of the subject and the direct object.

1. Introduction

This paper discusses the coding of certain grammatical relations from Latin to Modern French. The relations considered concern the subject, the verb and the object. The paper is based on the assumption that in order to understand and decode the message of a sentence, it is necessary to understand its basic argument structure. This implies e.g. that one must be able to identify the subject and distinguish this from the other elements of the sentence, in particular from the direct object. Put differently, in a communication perspective: the one who speaks or writes will normally organise his or her words in a way that make them understandable for the listener or the reader. It has been rightly argued that verbal communication is not just organised in order to be as transparent as possible. Still, it seems reasonable to me — and here I am following Smith (1995) — to consider that linguistic patterns provide the speakers or writers with different types of construction with more or less transparency. Consequently, it should be possible to identify the linguistic clues ensuring communication; e.g. the clues helping to distinguish the subject and the object. I find this distinction one of the crucial distinctions in syntax, and I intend to focus only on that distinction. For reasons that will be discussed in Section 4.1.1., the distinction between human subjects and human objects is important and that subtopic will be considered with special interest. In particular, I want to discuss the following three factors, belonging to different grammatical levels, which may help to identify the elements of the sentence:

- on the lexical level: the organising power of verbal valency,
- on the morphological level: the nominal and verbal inflection,
- on the linear level of the sentence: the word order.[1]

It is my intention to show that these factors cooperate in order to facilitate the identification of the subject and the direct object. By the term "identification" I mean the determination of which of several possible candidates in fact fulfil these functions. In the case of non expressed subjects or objects, the problem concerns the determination of the possible referents. Some grammatical categories of Classical Latin have disappeared, others have been maintained, but marked in different ways. I will draw the attention to the fact that the distinction between the subject and the direct object is one of the distinctions that have been maintained in spite of the loss of nominal declension, and that the distinction has even been reinforced in certain contexts in all Romance languages.

I will consider the development of French in a framework that can be summarised in the following way: Latin has a paradigmatic organisation of phrases, whereas Modern French has a linear organisation of phrases. The shift from one type of organisation to the other takes place before or during the early Middle Ages and is clearly linked to other different, well known morphological simplifications — see e.g. Bauer (1987). This change can be considered as an indication of the creation of noun phrases and verb phrases, which did not exist in Latin in the way these terms are normally used. The organisation of the noun phrase offers us a good illustration of these changes: in Latin, morphological agreement marks what belongs to a noun phrase and the linear ordering depends on pragmatic or stylistic considerations.[2] By the time of the first French texts, this has changed: the noun phrase is primarily marked via its linear ordering, and only secondarily by means of morphological agreement.

During the development of French, agreement tends to be reduced, and it is virtually absent from pronunciation in Modern French. The following two passages, from Cicero's *De Inventione*, in Latin and in Modern French, provide an illustration of the two ways of organising phrases.

> Quid nunc uobis faciendum est, *studiis militaribus* apud iuuentutem *obsoletis, fortissimis* autem *hominibus ac summis ducibus* partim aetate, partim ciuitatis discordiis ac rei publicae calamitate *consumptis* .... (Pro M. Fonteio, vol. vii, ed. Budé, p. 50).
>
> Que devez-vous donc faire aujourd'hui que *le goût des choses militaires s'est perdu* chez nos jeunes gens, que *les hommes valeureux et les chefs de guerre éminents* nous *ont été enlevés* tant par l'âge que par les discordes civiles et les malheurs qu'a subis la république; (p. 49).

In the Latin original we find two ablative absolutes, both discontinuous structures, which are translated into French finite and linear structures. The first ablative absolute, *studiis militaribus ... obsoletis*, is translated as a whole sentence *le goût des choses militaires s'est perdu*. The second, even more "scattered" than the first, *fortissimis ... hominibus ac summis ducibus ... consumptis* is also translated as a sentence *les hommes valeureux et les chefs de guerre éminents nous ont été enlevés*.

It is my claim that similar changes of organisation are found at the level of the verb phrase. These changes are less well studied than the changes in the noun phrase; I think, however, that they result in important reorganisations at the sentence level that took place during the period of Old and Middle French. The changes of the verb phrase to be considered in the following concern word order, prepositional marking of objects and the status of the direct object, overt or not. I will consider this latter point with special interest (Section 4.3.). In the following section, I shall first summarise traditional views of the relevant changes concerning verbal valency, declension, inflection and word order, occurring during the period under investigation.

We expect a *Latin* sentence to have been decoded by means of its inflection, without reference to word order. Apart from the contributions of Harm Pinkster (1991a,b, 1993) and Maria Selig (1991), there hardly exists any work on the importance of verbal valency for the comprehension of the Latin sentence.

Old French has been considered to be the first period of transition, during which the two-case declension, the only vestige of the Latin morphology, ensured the identification of the valency-bound elements, i.e. the subject, object, etc., until this function was taken over by word order. The exact moment when the morphology was substituted by the grammaticalisation of word order has been much discussed, but it is often conveniently placed at about 1300 (an intermediate period par excellence). Apart from my own contributions (see e.g. Schøsler 1984, 1991), the importance of verbal valency in decoding the sentence and in the identification of its valency-bound elements has not been much studied.

Traditionally, *Middle French* has a transitional position between Old French and Modern French. There exists little research into the point that interests us here. The two-case declension has vanished by this period, so one would expect that the fixation of word order has taken over as the means of identifying the valency-bound elements. However, the freedom of word order in Middle French, echoing the Latin order, is often stressed in studies on Middle French. There is no mention of verbal valency. In the absence of formal features distinguishing valency bound elements, one is tempted to conclude that oral or written communication was hardly possible in Middle French.

In *Modern French*, where only the personal and relative pronouns still preserve a declension, most scholars agree that we are seeing the end of a grammaticalisation process, leading from free to fixed word order, replacing the function of the Latin declension system.

In the following sections, it is my intention to show that the traditional views which I have just summarised are not sufficient. Firstly, the traditional direct causal relation between the abandoning of the declension system and the fixation of the word order does not survive a closer inspection of the facts (Section 2). Secondly, the importance of verb typology and of verbal valency has not been acknowledged (Section 3). And thirdly, additional features ensuring the formal distinction between the subject and the object function have not been taken into account (Section 4). My intention is to show how different factors, from the different grammatical levels, interact in order to ensure the transparency of grammatical relations and in particular to assure the distinction between the subject and the direct object. The increasing importance of these factors are the result of the reorganisation at the level of the verb phrase mentioned above. Section 5 contains my conclusion.

My investigation is based on a parallel examination of texts dating from the four separate periods. As many linguistic features, e.g. word order, depend among other things on the pragmatic and stylistic function of the text, it is most important to compare texts which are similar in these respects, that is, texts belonging to the same textual register. I have done my best to compare only similar texts. Cicero's *De Inventione* and *Rhetorica ad Herennium* in their Latin (abbreviation: INVI) and French versions constitute a specially suitable field of investigation, as the French versions are faithful translations: into Old French (abbreviation: JdA) by Jean d'Antioche (1282), and into Modern French (abbreviation (BOR) by Bornecque (1932). For further information on these versions, see the thesis of Michèle Goyens (1994). The Latin text and its translations have been placed at my disposal by Willy van Hoecke and his research group at the Catholic University of Leuven. Unfortunately there is no Middle French version of this text, so I have chosen the following Middle French texts for the comparison: *Les Chroniques de Froissart*, *Les Mémoires de Commynes*, *Les Quinze Joies du Mariage*, and *Cleriadus*. These Middle French texts have been placed at my disposal by Monique Lemieux and Fernande Dupuis, from l'Université du Québec à Montréal. All the texts are available in electronic form. I have included in my study the oldest French texts: *Les Serments de Strasbourg* (842), *La Prose de Sainte Eulalie* (IXth century), *La Vie de Saint Léger* (Xth century) and *La Vie de Saint Alexis* (XIth century).

2. Abandoning of the declension system ⇒ fixation of word order?

It is a well known fact that Latin had a rich nominal morphology: five declensions with six cases in two numbers. No Romance language has continued this system. Most of the Romance languages abandoned the nominal declension before the first vernacular texts (Italian, Catalan, Spanish and Portuguese), some first reduced it to a two-case system, separating a subject form from a non-subject form, and only later abandoned it completely (French and Occitan, Swiss Romance dialects). Roumanian is the only Romance language to have a surviving nominal declension, yet of a different kind (a nominative-accusative case opposed to a common genitive-dative case).

One of the traditionally very popular causes put forward to explain the disappearance of nominal declension in French is the fixation of the word order. It has been amply proven by statistical investigations of Old and Middle French texts, however, that word order remained rather free long after the abandoning of the nominal declension system — see Schøsler (1984), Chapters 5 and 6 with references and Vance (1997) containing statistics and ample discussion — and refutation — of the traditional view. Moreover, rules governing word order for feminine, i.e. essentially caseless, nouns and for masculine, i.e. declined, nouns have never differed, in spite of the difference in declension possibilities. Obviously, there is no direct causal relationship between the two linguistic changes, the abandoning of the declension system and the fixation[3] of the word order. This is also true for other Modern Romance languages; like French, Italian, Spanish and Portuguese have no declension, and yet, unlike French, they do not have a fixed word order in the sense given in note 3. On the other hand, the fixation of word order in French clearly marks the subject and the object of a sentence, so word order certainly did take over the original function of the declension system. Then, how was the subject/object distinction marked during the periods of instable case declension and free word order? And why was fixed word order introduced in French, unlike the other Romance languages? Let us consider the first question first and come back to the second question in the conclusion. The following section will illustrate the importance of the construction of verbs for the identification of the subject and the object.

3. The importance of verb typology and of verbal valency for the subject/object distinction

In terms of unambiguous subject/object distinction both verb typology and verbal valency, i.e. the syntactic structures and the semantic selectional restrictions on the valency bound elements, are of importance.[4]

I distinguish non-full verbs from full verbs. Non-full verbs are auxiliary verbs, copula verbs, support verbs[5] and modal or causal auxiliaries. Non-full verbs are characterised by the fact that they combine with an element which sometimes resembles a complement, a direct or a prepositional object, but for which there are particular selectional restrictions; this excludes the free substitution of this element by some other element. The particular restrictions concerning the element in question clearly mark this element as non-subject and thus facilitate the identification of an overt element having the grammatical function subject. The examples listed below illustrate the different types:

3.1 Non-full verbs

Copula and auxiliary verbs:

(1) a. *partes eius sunt duae* ... (INVI031–1)
 'there are two parts of it ...'
 b. ...*ont été plus avantageuses ou plus nuisibles* ... (BOR 1)
 '...have been more advantageous or more damaging ...'

Support verbs:

> c. ... *ait* plus *fait* de mal ou de bien (JdA II, 7–9)
>   '... has done more harm than good ...'
> d. ... *ce m'est avis* ... (JdA II, 30–32)
>   '...it seems to me that ...'
> e. ...*je me rends compte que* ... (BOR 1)
>   '... I realise that ...'

Modal auxiliaries:

> f. ... *propugnare possit* ... (INVI S, 8–10)
>   '...can defend ...'
> g. ... *peut profiter* ... *peut nuire*... (JdA II, 21–24)
>   '...can profit ...can damage...'
>   Causal Auxiliaries:
> h. *la sagesse me fait pencher* ... (BOR 1)
>   'wisdom makes me lean towards ...'

3.2 Full verbs

Full verbs can be divided into two classes: those that by definition are unambiguous with respect to the identification of valency bound elements, and those that create potentially ambiguous contexts. Let us consider these classes.

3.2.1 *"Unambiguous" full verbs*

If the verb is impersonal, the identification of the subject — which, in spite of the examples quoted below- is rarely expressed before the period of Classical French (before ca. 1600) — is unambiguous, as the referent is impersonal and as in French only impersonal pronouns can function as overt subjects. Examples:

> (2) a. *in omni dictione meminisse oportebit* ... (INVI033–1)
>   '...in any discourse it will be important to remember ...'
>   b. *En celui tens y avoit il un noble paintour* ... (XXXVIII I002–1 JdA)
>   'At that time there was a noble painter ...'
>   c. *nos vodrions qu'il semblast que* ... (XXXVIII 010–1 JdA)
>   'we would like that it to appear that ...'

If the verb is monovalent, there is no ambiguity in the identification of the subject, not even in Old French texts with their disintegrated declension system: a non-prepositional noun phrase or nominative pronoun is automatically identified as the overt subject, and the selectional restrictions of the verb helps identifying the referent of a non-expressed subject. Examples:

> d. *id quod per raro potest **accidere**...* (INVI033–1)
> 'which could very rarely happen ...'
> e. *... la greignor partie des dopmages **est avenue** ...* (JdA II, 12–13)
> '...the largest part of the damage has happened ...'
> f. *...il ...soit avis que nostre araisonement **voise** plus loinz...* (XXXVIII 010–1 JdA)
> '...it should appear that our reasoning should go further ...'

If the verb is a polyvalent full verb, and if the second valency-bound element is not a direct object, a preposition introduces the object and marks it unambiguously as non-subject. This is particularly frequent in the French periods and infrequent in Latin. I will come back to this point in Section 4.2. Examples:

> (3) a. *partes eius sunt duae, quarum utraque magno opere **ad** aperiendam causam et constituendam **pertinet** controversiam.* (INVI031–1)
> 'there are two parts of it, each of which is very important for the explanation of the cause ...'
> b. ***De** la confirmacion et **de** la reprehencion **deysmes** nos amplement et plus espanduement.* (XXXIX JdA I011–1)
> 'We will talk in a more ample and detailed way about the confirmation'
> c. *J'ai souvent et longuement **réfléchi à** la question ...* (BOR 1)
> 'I have often and for some time been thinking about...'
> d. *de l'arrogance **naît** la haine, de l'orgueil l'arrogance.*
> BOR XXVIII 042–1)
> 'Arrogance gives birth to hate, and pride to arrogance.'

3.2.2 *"Ambiguous" full verbs*

If the full verb is polyvalent, with a direct object, there is in principle a risk of ambiguity. The following is an example of an ambiguous construction:

> (4) *Adonques les Crotoniciens, par comun conseil, **amenerent** ensemble toutes les beles virgenes en un leu ...* (XXXVIII JdA I003–1)
> 'Then the C., by common decision, brought all the pretty young virgins to a place ...'

In (4) this grammatical ambiguity — concerning who are bringing whom to a certain place — is eliminated only because of our knowledge of the world, and in particular our intuition concerning the respective power of the virgins and the Crotonician men. In other cases, grammatical ambiguities like the one in (4) are eliminated by different grammatical factors. It is possible to distinguish at least four cases of grammatical elimination of ambiguity: semantic restrictions (5a–b), declension (6), difference in number or person (5a, 7) and word order (8b, 5a). When there are different valency-bound restrictions for the subject and the object, where the subject has the feature +human, and the object the features ±human, ±concrete, ±abstract, the identification of the elements of the sentence will present no difficulty, as in the following example:

(5) a. *Cele meisme raison* **regardames** *nos* ... (XXXVIII JdA I004–1)
'We considered this same reason...'

Ambiguity arises when the subject and another element of the sentence have the same valency-bound restrictions, as in the following example:

b. ... *vero ita sese* **armat** *eloquentia*, ... (INVI001–11, S 2, 8–10)
'...[who], however, thus arms himself with eloquence...'

Armat has the following restrictions for the subject: ±human, ±concrete, ±abstract; so *eloquentia* can be either the subject or in the instrumental case, an ambiguity which is not eliminated by its written morphological form.

Ambiguity is eliminated when the subject and/or the object are clearly marked with respect to case. This is illustrated in Modern French in the following translation of (5b), where the subject has an unambiguous nominative form (*qui*):

(6) ... *mais celui qui s'arme de l'éloquence* ... (BOR 1–3)

On the other hand, example (4) illustrates the ambiguity caused by the absence of case marking.

Ambiguity is eliminated when there is a difference in number and/or person between the subject and the object, as in example (5a) above, and example (7) below. The following example illustrates the importance of differences in number and person:

(7) *Nam cum et nostrae rei publicae detrimenta* **considero**
(INVI001–2, S 1, 3–4)
'Because, when I consider the disasters of our republic ...'

Whereas identity of number and person causes ambiguity, see again example (4).

If the subject is in the first or second person singular or plural, if it is neutral, or if the verb is in the imperative, the identification of the subject is unambiguous; see example (5a). Ambiguity arises if both the subject and the object are in the third person singular or plural; see example (4).

The grammaticalisation of word order makes a Modern French sentence unambiguous, as in the following example:

(8) a. *l'argumentation* **semble** *bien un moyen imaginé pour ...*
(BOR XXIX 44.044–1)
'the argumentation seems to be a means ... to ...'

See, however, example (3d) for a case of inversion in Modern French which is possible because of the unambiguous verbal valency.

In certain cases restrictions concerning word order can also be of importance in Old and Middle French, as in example (8b); here the word order is SOV, and could hardly have been interpreted as a case of OSV, as this word order is very rare in Old French and mostly found in the case of a relative pronoun as object constituent.[6]

b. *Et en tel maniere longuement pensant, la vive raison me* **mena** *meismement a ceste sentence que* ... (JdA II, 19–21)
'And considering this thoroughly, reason brought me to the following judgment...'

On the other hand, an example like (5a) with the word order OVS, might just as well have been interpreted as an instance of SVO — if it were not for the unambiguous first plural form of the verb; in such cases, word order does not facilitate the identification of the elements of the sentence. Put differently: in Old and Middle French word order sometimes offers clues to the identification of valency-bound elements, see e.g. example (8b) — in other cases it does not. In such stages of language where the function of the elements is not generally expressed by means of the linear ordering, we have what I call "free word order" (cf. the definition in note 3).

More often than not, several factors collaborate in order to ensure correct identification of the subject; see e.g. (5a), (8b), etc.

3.3 Conclusion of Section 3

The preceding analyses have shown that verbal typology and verbal valency have played an important role for the identification of valency elements and, consequently, for the interpretation of a sentence. This role must have been equally important during all the periods of the language and is certainly important for the identification of valency elements of the other Romance languages as well. Let us now concentrate on which additional features are at work in the so called "ambiguous" cases: polyvalent full verbs combining subjects and objects with the same valency restrictions.

4. Additional features ensuring the formal distinction between the subject and the object function

I will consider the following features: nominal declension (Section 4.1), prepositional marking (Section 4.2), obligatoriness of the valency bound elements (Section 4.3).

The importance of the nominal declension system for the subject/object distinction varies according to its stability. In the dialects that have a solid declension system, e.g. in the Northern and Eastern French dialects of the 12th and 13th centuries, declension contributed to the formal distinction between the subject and the direct object. However, we should never overestimate its importance, and only in exceptional cases is it the *only* factor to identify the valency bound elements, see Schøsler (1984), Chapter 1. Pinkster (1993:247) has similar results for Latin (my translation): "... lexical meaning of the verbal and nominal forms as well as the connection between these are based on the coherence of the sentences. It is only in a very small number of cases (definitely not more than 5%) that you have to resort to suffixes in order to avoid ambiguity of the sentence ... The inflectional system is consequently, to a certain point, redundant, as far as it gives an additional guarantee of the right indication or interpretation to a sentence." But let us have a closer look at the disappearance of the nominal declension in French.

4.1 The disappearance of the nominal declension

The breakdown of the nominal declension system can be described according to three axes: type of word, dialect, and chronology, the last two being closely linked.

4.1.1 *Type of word*
The progressive disappearance of declension in Old French during the Middle Ages has been studied in a corpus of Old French of some 5 million words by Pieter van Reenen from the Free University of Amsterdam and myself. Concerning the type of word, we have been able to show, see Reenen & Schøsler

(1997), that loss of declension starts in proper nouns before it reaches common nouns. Among common nouns it reaches inanimate nouns before it reaches nouns indicating humans and animals, feminines before masculines, adjectives before nouns, nouns before articles, nouns and articles before pronouns. In fact, all modern Romance — and Germanic — languages still conserve case declension at least in most personal pronouns. Loss of declension is found earlier in the plural than in the singular. In short, we find a very clear hierarchy–with the exception of proper nouns, however — showing the classes of inanimate, feminine and plural nouns, without articles, as innovative, whereas animate, masculine, singular, determined nouns and pronouns are conservative with respect to declension preservation. Except for proper nouns of persons, this hierarchy is consistent with that proposed in Andersen (1990). See Figure 1:

Early loss of declension:	Late preservation of declension:
Proper nouns[7]	Common nouns
Inanimates	Humans, animates
Feminine	Masculine
Adjectives	Nouns
Nouns	Articles
Nouns, articles	Pronouns
Plurals	Singulars

Figure 1

The relative propensity for innovation or conservatism in nominal types is consistent with a development seen already in Late Latin. Here we find a progressive elimination of case marking, especially of the clearest marking of case, the imparisyllabic marking, in the inanimate, feminine and plural nouns, whereas a clear declension system is conserved in animate, masculine and especially singular nouns. See e.g. the imparisyllabic nominative feminine in Classical Latin: *mansio, carbo*, accusative: *mansionem, carbonem*, made less clearly marked as nominatives in the later analogical reconstructed, but not attested, forms *mansionis, carbonis*. This elimination did not happen in the case of animate, masculine, singular nouns that preserved their clear, often imparisyllabic, declension, e.g. nominative: Latin *imperator* > Old French *emperere*; Latin *homo* > Old French *on*; accusative: Latin *imperatorem* > Old French *empereor*; Latin *hominem* > Old French *homme*. See Reenen & Schøsler (1988).

The declension preserving status of animate, definite masculine nouns and pronouns in this hierarchy is important. I interpret this as as an indicator that language needs special marking of referents caracterised by these features. Put differently: as this type of referents are likely to assume the subject function, they need to have their grammatical function marked clearly, e.g. as subject or non-subject, in order to avoid confusion. Thus, this hierarchy is consistent with that of the prepositional marking of direct objects found in other Romance languages, see Section 4.2.

4.1.2 *Dialect and chronology*

The loss of nominal declension moves from West to East. There is extensive loss of declension in the very first western Old French texts (ca. 1050), but declension is still strong in the northern and eastern parts of Northern France generally in the thirteenth century. The declensional system is totally abandoned by the end of the fourteenth century. This dialectal and chronological movement is well documented and illustrated in the maps of the two Atlases published by Dees et al. (1980 and 1987); see e.g. Map 206, Dees et al. (1980), below.

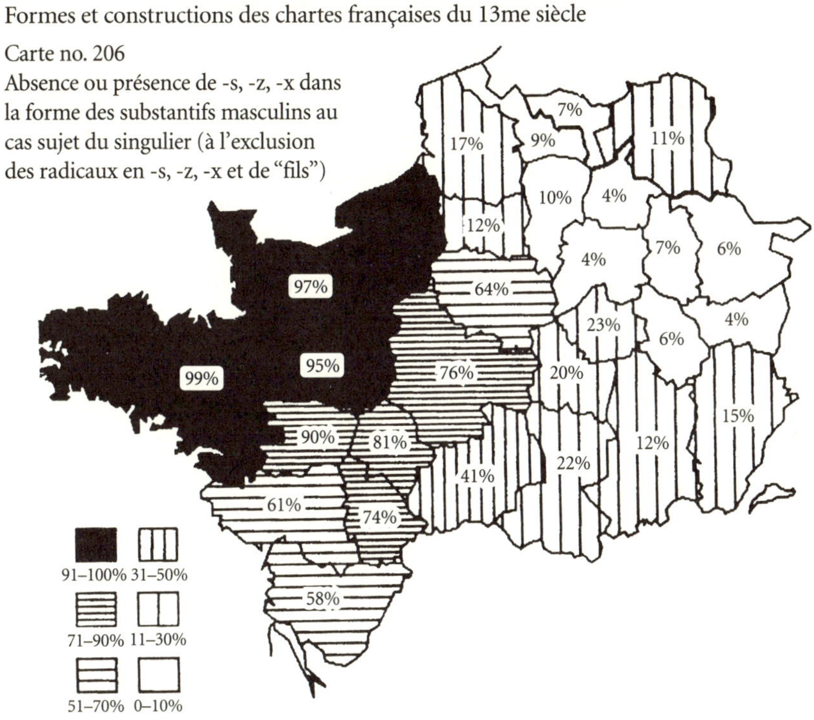
Formes et constructions des chartes françaises du 13me siècle
Carte no. 206
Absence ou présence de -s, -z, -x dans la forme des substantifs masculins au cas sujet du singulier (à l'exclusion des radicaux en -s, -z, -x et de "fils")
7%
17%
9%
11%
10%
4%
12%
7%
6%
4%
97%
64%
23%
4%
6%
99%
95%
76%
20%
15%
90%
81%
12%
41%
22%
61%
74%
58%
91–100%
31–50%
71–90%
11–30%
51–70%
0–10%

Map 206.

The dark areas are those with complete loss of declension (91–100% of absence of -s in singular, nominative, masculine nouns, i.e. "case errors"). White areas are declension preserving areas (0–10% of "case errors"). Intermediate areas have different shadings.

4.2 Prepositional marking

The case preservation type of word presented in Section 4.1.1 is — as mentioned above — consistent with the type of direct objects with prepositional marking found in different Romance languages — with the exception of human proper names, though. In fact, we find in Spanish,[8] Italian and Romansh dialects, and in Roumanian that a preposition, *a* (< Latin *ad*) or *pe* (from Latin *per*), marks the function of the direct object, but only if the direct object belongs to the type of animate, definite, individual nouns. See the following examples:

(9) Spanish:
   a. *no he visto a mi hermano; no le/lo he visto*
       'I have not seen my brother; I have not seen him'
   b. *quiero a Maria; la quiero*
       'I love Maria; I love her'
   Rumanian:
   c. *iubesc pe frate*
       'I love my brother' (Meyer-Lübke III: 374)
   Italian dialect of Sicily:
   d. *l'aviti visu a me frati?*
       'have you seen my brother' (Meyer-Lübke III:373)
   Romansh dialect (Vallader):
   e. *Nus vezzain ad Annina*
       'we see Annina' (Liver 1991: 86)

The introduction of a systematic prepositional marking of the direct (definite, individual, human) object is not relevant for French. However, in French, as in the other Romance languages, we generally find the introduction of prepositional phrases corresponding to Latin direct constructions of different cases. Example (9f), quoted from Tesnière (1976: 286) illustrates such a case. Moreover, it illustrates in French the creation of support verb constructions (see also examples (1c–e), which are per definition transparent (see Sections 3.0–3.1). As the number of prepositional phrases increase in French — and in the other Romance languages in comparision with Latin — non subject elements are increasingly marked by means of preposition. This facilitates the identification of the valency bound elements.

    f.   *tela milites deficiunt*
          les traits font défaut aux soldats
          'lit. arrows lack for the soldiers i.e. the soldiers are short of arrows'

4.3 Obligatoriness of the valency bound elements

I now come to the point concerning the difference between the periods under investigation that I want to discuss in details.

During my investigations of variation in valency patterns in the history of the French language, I have discovered important differences in the status of the valency bound elements. It is well known that the status of the subject has changed from optional in Latin, Old and Middle French to obligatory in Modern French, with respect to their overt presence in the sentence.[9] In traditional GB-terminology,[10] Latin, Old and Middle French have null subjects or subject pro-drop, whereas Modern French does not permit subject pro-drop. The status of the direct object, however, has never previously been examined in a diachronic perspective. In the following, I shall first shortly provide a typology of missing objects and of different conditions favoring or preventing ellipsis in general (4.3.1). Secondly, I shall provide the results for the diachronic study of ellipses (4.3.2).

4.3.1 Typology of missing objects and of conditions for ellipses

At least two types[11] of missing objects are normally distinguished: "generic ellipsis" and "anaphoric ellipsis".[12] In the first case there is no referent of the missing object in the linguistic or extra-linguistic context, in the second case such a referent exists. Let us consider some examples. In the sentence: *Pierre mange* (Peter is eating), the missing object is generic, meaning: Peter is eating [some unspecified kind of food]. Example (10a) is a generic example from spoken French quoted from Larjavaara (2000); in the translation, the missing generic object is indicated by means of #. Examples (10b–c) are generic examples from Latin (Cicero: *Trebatio* and Catullus), illustrating that non-anaphoric ellipsis permits to focus on the action of the verb.

    (10)   a.   'Il faut **éduquer, convaincre**, en aucun cas **contraindre**', nous dit le professeur Hirsch, tout en reconnaissant qu'il est plus difficile d'arrêter de fumer que de cesser de se droguer.
                  'One must educate #, convince #, in no case force # …'

b. *Quam sint morosi qui **amant***
'How they are wayward, those who love #.'
c. ***Odi** et **amo**. Quare id faciam, fortasse requiris. Nescio, sed fieri sentio et excrucior.*
'I hate # and I love #. You may ask me why it is so. I do not know, but I feel that it is happening and I suffer.'

In (10d), also quoted from Larjavaara (2000), the explicit object in the question *cette époque* (this epoch) is missing in the answer, but it is understood, in other words, it is a case of zero anaphora or "anaphoric ellipsis":

d. *Pourquoi avoir choisi cette époque? — Parce que j'**adore**.*
'Why have [you] chosen this epoch? — Because I love [this epoch]'

We have distinguished two main types of ellipses, let us now consider three factors conditioning the ellipses. First, there are thematic or pragmatic reasons not to express a valency bound element. Thus, old information is more easily omitted and still understood than new information. The ellipses of *cette époque* in (10d) illustrates this case. Secondly, there are syntactic conditions which favour ellipses — in Modern French, for instance a succession of questions and answers, infinitive constructions, and coordination favours ellipses. The ellipsis of *cette époque* in (10d) illustrates ellipses in a succession of questions and answers. Thirdly, text type or register is also relevant for the frequency of ellipses. Thus, we know that in French ellipses are more frequent in the spoken register than in the written, and more frequent in an informal register than in a formal register. Modern French legal texts, for example, have few ellipses if any. A fourth factor is related to the lexicon, i.e. we have verb specific ellipses.[13]

4.3.2 *Diachronic study of ellipses*

I have studied a series of transitive verbs (Schøsler 1999, 2000)[14] and have come to the following results for the three periods under investigation concerning the status of the direct object with respect to overt or covert realisation in sentences:

1. Latin
   - obligatoriness or optionality of direct objects are features of the individual verb — i.e. they are lexically determined;[15] this applies to "anaphoric ellipsis", as well as to "generic ellipsis";
   - there is no clear correlation between text type and optionality;
   - there is no clear correlation between chronology and optionality.

2. Old and Middle French
- obligatoriness or optionality are less evidently features of the individual verb, as all verbs tend to avoid non-expression of the direct object;
- provisional results suggest that especially objects with the feature +human tend to be obligatory;
- non-expression of other valency bound elements depend on the text type.

3. Modern French
- obligatoriness or optionality of direct objects are features of the individual verb — like in Latin;[16] this applies to "anaphoric ellipsis", as well as to "generic ellipsis";
- there is a clear correlation between text type and non-expression of valency bound elements (but no pro-drop of the subject): formal register avoids non-expression, informal register favours non-expression.

The results clearly point to Old and Middle French as a separate period, with special rules concerning obligatoriness of the direct object that differ from those of both the preceding and the following periods. Let us now look at some statistical evidence concerning the nominal objects of the early French period. It appears from Figure 2 that objects tend to be expressed, except in two typical cases: a personal pronoun preceding a dative, as in *Alexis* v. 283 (example 11a), and combined with the pro-verb *faire*, as in *Alexis* v. 415 (example 11b):

(11) a. *cil* [le] *li aportet* (v. 283)
 'he gives [it] to him'
 b. [*doüses/Le gunfanun l'emperedur porter*],
 Cum [le] *fist tis predre e li tons parentez* (v. 415)
 'as your father did and his entire family'

text	nominal direct objects	expressed nominal objects	non-expression of objects
Serments 1 & 2 842	7	7	0
Eulalie 882	14	14	0
Léger 950–1000	64	64	0
Alexis 1040	192	190	2 (11a, 11b)

Figure 2. Nominal direct object in the oldest French texts; tokens

Examples from the later periods of French show the same tendency as the early texts to avoid non-expression of the direct object. Let us have a closer look at some typical examples presented in (12). They show a stage of evolution with optional subjects and defective noun declension and relatively free word order. This means that isolated sentences containing transitive verbs may be ambiguous as to the identification of the valency bound elements. This is especially relevant for verbs which combine human subjects and human objects, as in the cases quoted in (12):

(12) a. *Cum veit le lit, esguarda* **la pulcela** (Eulalie v. 56)
'As saw {3.pers.SG} the bed, saw {3.pers.SG} the young girl'
b. [*Vait par les rues ...*/*Altra pur altre*], *mais* **sun pedre** *i ancuntret* (Alexis v. 213)
'... but met {3.pers.SG}his father there'
c. *ciel Laudebert fura buons om / et* **sanct Lethgier** *duis a son dom* (Léger v. 197–198)
'this L. was a good man/and Saint L. accompanied{3.pers.SG} to his home'
d. *Monseignor Gavain et son hoste / Ont a deus fenestres trové* (Perceval 8294–5)
'Sir G. and his host/found{3.pers.PL} at two windows'

These four examples are ambiguous without their context, as we have no semantical, no morphological and no word order features telling us whether the nouns quoted here, and marked in bold, function as subjects or as direct objects. However, my statistical evidence points to them as being direct objects, not subjects, as transitive verbs generally tend to avoid non-expression of the direct object, as we have already seen — but certainly not to avoid ellipses of the subject, which are indeed frequent. Closer inspection of the texts show that these nouns are in fact all direct objects. Consequently, I propose the following rule for the interpretation of sentences like these: whenever we have a transitive verb and a noun that is a potential candidate for either a subject or an object function, it is interpreted as an object. If this rule is correct, it explains how Old and Middle French handled this type of constructions, and may be why they were handled like this. In fact, the rule makes the potentially ambiguous sentences unambiguous. We do however find some pragmatically motivated cases of non-expression of direct objects, especially in particular contexts, e.g. direct discourse and coordinated sentences. But the overall picture is that objects, especially human objects, are most often explicitly mentioned, unlike many subjects. Put differently: in Latin and Modern French the expression or non-expression of the direct object is lexically determined (i.e. valency-bound). In Old and Middle French the expression of the object is not lexically determined, but seems to be grammatically required.

How can we explain the differences concerning the status of the object: optional or obligatory, as observed in the three periods? As suggested already, I think that the obligatory presence of objects in Old and Middle French is linked to the ambiguity of sentence analysis. This ambiguity is due to the following four factors: the absence of a transparent nominal declension, the progressive blurring of verbal morphology,[17] the absence of a fixed word order and the frequent pro-drop of subjects.

Generally speaking, the thematic structure of sentences plays an important part in the identification of valency bound elements in a sentence — but in Old French, the four factors just mentioned may create ambiguities, especially with the type of verbs studied so far. The obligatoriness of objects prevents this type of ambiguity. Thus, I suggest, the object has become obligatory in order to avoid grammatical ambiguity. Objects remained obligatory until another important change took place in Middle French, which was the increase in the number of sentences with overt subjects, especially pronominal subjects. The importance of the presence of the subject pronouns is twofold; it implies:

- an explicit indication of the subject, as the personal pronoun in the nominative has an unambiguous form in the singular and in the third person plural; and as the pronominal subject, which has become clitic, has a tendency to precede the finite verb (except in questions), it implies furthermore:
- a grammaticalised word order: subject–verb. This means that the progressive increase in the presence of subject pronouns prepares for the grammaticalisation of word order in Modern French (see e.g. Fleischman 1992). After the generalisation of the subject, the obligatory presence of the direct object was no longer necessary and its presence became optional.

This hypothesis has two advantages: (1) it fits the chronology of the change and (2) it proposes a specifically French explanation for changes that did not happen in other Romance languages.

5. Conclusion

In the introduction, I have introduced three factors that contribute to the identification of the subject and the direct object. My description of the relative importance of these factors from Latin to Modern French has shown that the role of nominal (but not pronominal) declension has diminished from Latin to Middle French and that the fixation of word order arrived later, so that the latter cannot have caused the former (Section 2). On the other hand, verbal valency has been important during all periods (Section 3). In some contexts, valency has even increased its importance. The obligatory presence of a direct object in Old and Middle French is a factor related to valency, for it functions as a means for the identification of valency bound elements. In other Romance languages the introduction of prepositional (animate) objects had a similar effect (Section 4). Thus, during the transition from Latin to Modern French we see not only the well known shift from a paradigmatic (or synthetic) organisation of phrases to a linear (or analytical) ordering of phrases, but also a less well known shift from less transparent towards more transparent, hence redundant, sentence structures.

Middle French is distinct from Old French as regards the two points mentioned above, concerning the consequences of the generalised use of subject pronouns in this period. This implies not only an increase in the importance of the pronominal morphology — and hence a compensation for the loss of declension of nouns and adjectives which took place at about the same time — but also an increase in the importance of word order, as pronominal subjects — that are mostly preposed — compensate for the progressive disappearance of the verbal endings. In describing the developments in this way, I by no means wish to imply a causal connection between, on the one hand, the loss of inflection and, on the other hand, the generalisation of the pronouns and the grammaticalisation of word order. The connection between these phenomena is much more complicated and has been subject to discussion in e.g. Schøsler (1984) and Vance (1997).

Finally, a few concluding words concerning grammatical categories. Several Classical Latin categories have been lost in the Romance languages, e.g. the morphological passive system, the declension system with its five types, three genders and six cases. Some of the functions of these morphological distinctions have been taken over by other, essentially analytical factors, others, e.g. the neuter, have simply been abandoned. In the case examined here, we have found a preservation of the grammatical distinction between subjects and objects. During the entire period, this distinction is marked by means of different, cooperating factors, thus assuring a redundant marking. Moreover, we find an introduction of the distinction between human and non-human as a basic linguistic category both in French and in the other Romance languages. This new distinction often cooperates with the subject/object distinction in potentially ambiguous sentence types, i.e. sentences which combine human subjects and human objects — and these are the types especially considered in this paper.

Appendix 1: Selection of verbs studied

In general, the verbs examined are chosen in order to present a possible combination of human subjects and human objects, which is a potential source of confusion. Table 3 contains Latin verbs, Table 4 Modern French verbs. See also Schøsler (1999).

Table 3. Examples of Latin Verbs examined

Verb	valency (Happ)	Happ76	(a) Plautus	(b) Cicero etc	(c) Corpus Iuris	(d) Vulgata	(e) Merovingian Latin
accipio	SO(PO)	oblig.O	oblig.O	oblig.O	oblig.O	oblig.O	oblig.O (1 opt/11)
accuso1 = function as accusator	S	*	*	opt.O	opt.O	*	no ex.
accuso2 = accuse	SO	*	oblig.O	SO	*	few ell.	no ex.
adiuvo	S(O)	opt.O	?	opt.O	no ex	opt. O (16 opt/56)	opt.O (3opt/3; pr.part.)
amo 1 (=to be in love)	S	no ex	opt.O	no ex.	no ex	no ex	no ex
amo 2	SO	no ex	SO	oblig. O	no ex	few ell. (3 opt/56)	oblig. O
appello	SOOP	oblig.O	no ex	oblig.O	opt.O	few ell.	no ex.
attingo	SO	oblig.O	opt.O	few ell.	oblig.O	no ex.	no ex.
audio	S(O)	opt.O	opt.O	opt.O	no ex.	opt.O 50%	opt. O 12opt/54
claudo	–	no	no ex	oblig.O	no ex.	oblig. O	O; 1 ex
cognosco	SOPO	oblig.O	oblig.O	few ell.	opt. O few O	opt. O	few ell. 3 opt/18
converto	–	no ex	no ex	oblig.O	no ex.	few ell.	oblig. O (5 ex.)
decipio	–	no ex	oblig.O	oblig.O	opt. O	opt. O 8 opt/50	O; 1 ex
dedignor	–	no ex	no ex	oblig.O	no ex.	no ex	no ex
defendo1 (=act as defensor)	S	S	S	S	S	no ex.	
defendo2	S(O)	opt.O	oblig.O	oblig.O	oblig.Ono ex oblig.O	no ex	
destruo	*	no ex	no ex	oblig.O	no ex	no ex	no ex
dono	SO (ABL)	oblig.O	oblig.O	oblig.O	opt.O	opt.O	oblig.O 3 ex.
dubito	S(O)	opt.O	oblig.O	oot.O	opt. O 25 opt/144	opt.O	fex ell. 2 opt/3
duco	SO(PO)	Oblig.O	few ell.	few ell.	few ell.	OBL.O	oblig.O 1 opt/9
excrucio	–	no ex	few ell.	oblig. O.	no ex	no ex	no ex

Verb	valency (Happ)	Happ76	(a) Plautus	(b) Cicero etc	(c) Corpus Iuris	(d) Vulgata	(e) Merovingian Latin
facio	SO	Oblig.O	few.ell.	oblig.O	opt.O 19 opt/100	opt.O 30 opt/200	opt.O 13 opt/77
fugio1 = flee	SO	Oblig.O	oblig.O	oblig.O	oblig.O	oblig.O	no ex.
fugio2 = run away	S	no O	no O	no O	no O	no O	no ex
judico1 (=act as a judge)	S	no O	no O	no O	no O	no O	no ex
judico2 (=evaluate)	SO	Oblig.O	opt.O	opt.O	opt.O	opt.O	oblig.O 4 ex
laedo	–	no ex	1 opt./7	opt.O	no ex	no ex	no ex
laudo	S(O)	opt.O	oblig.O	opt.O	oblig.O 2 ex.	opt.O	oblig. O 2 ex.
monstro	SO	Oblig.O	opt.O	oblig.O	oblig.O 2 ex.	oblig.O	no ex.
percipio	–	no ex	few ell.	oblig.O	no ex	no ex	no ex
perdo	SO	Oblig.O	oblig.O	oblig.O	oblig.O	oblig.O	oblig.O 4 ex.
ploro	–	no ex	opt.O 3 ex.	opt.O	*	opt.O 10 opt/46	no ex.
precor	SO	no ex	opt.O	oblig.O	no ex	oblig.O	oblig.O
punio	–	no ex	no ex	oblig.O?	no ex	no ex	no ex
sequor	SO	opt.O	opt.O	opt.O	opt.O	opt.O	oblig.O 1 ex.
teneo	–	no ex	opt.O	oblig.O	no ex	no ex	no ex
traho	–	no ex	oblig.O	oblig.O	no ex	no ex	no ex
vinco	–	no ex	opt.O	opt.O	no ex	no ex	no ex

Proportion of opt.O/oblig.O per column: 12/14; 12/21; 9/7; 11/9; 3/most ex.

The sources are: (a) Preclassical Latin of Plautus; (b) Classical Latin of Caesar, Cicero (all texts); later periods: Apuleius, Augustin, Boetius; (c) Digesta, Corpus Iuris; (d) Vulgata; (e) 200 pages of Merovingian Latin. Valency patterns. Proportions of obligatory ~ optional objects. S = subject, O = object, PO = prepositional object, OP = object predicate; in the first column brackets indicate optionality. The result of the investigation is that obligatoriness or optionality of direct objects are features of the individual verb.

Table 4. Examples of Modern French verbs examined

Verb	(a) Busse & Dubost	(b) GARS	(c) PROTON
accepter	S+hum oblig.O+/-hum	6 opt.O/41	opt.O-hum; oblig.O+hum
accuser1	S+hum oblig.O+hum (de quelque chose opt.)	3 opt.O/11	opt.O-hum; oblig.O+hum
accuser2	S+hum oblig.O-hum (de quelque chose oblig.)		
aider	S+hum opt.O+hum (à quelque chose opt.)	6 opt.O/79	oblig.O
aimer	S+hum opt.O+hum or oblig.O-hum (NB!)	32 opt.O/375 all O = -hum	opt.O-hum; oblig.O+hum (NB!)
appeler	S+/-hum oblig.O+hum (opt. Quelque part)	opt.O in the sense "phone"	= "call" oblig.O = "phone" opt.O
atteindre1	S+hum oblig.O+hum	oblig.O	oblig.O +/-hum
atteindre2	S-hum oblig.O-hum		
clore	S+/-hum oblig.O-hum	few ex.	
conduire1	S+hum oblig.O+hum (opt. Quelque part)	1 opt.O/14	oblig.O=+hum; trivalent
conduire2	S-hum opt.O+/-hum oblig. quelque part		opt.O=-hum; divalent
connaître	S+hum oblig.O+/-hum	40 opt.O/314 most 0 = -hum	opt.O-hum; oblig.O+hum
convertir	S+hum oblig.O +/-hum	no ex.	
décevoir	S+/-hum opt.O+/-hum	6 ex., obligatory O	oblig.O+hum
dédaigner	S+hum oblig.O+/-hum	no ex.	opt.O-hum; oblig.O+hum
défendre	S+hum oblig.O+/-hum (contre opt. +/-hum)	47 ex., all obligatory	oblig.O+/-hum
détruire	S+/-hum oblig.O+/-hum	9 ex., all obligatory	opt.O-hum; oblig.O+hum
donner	S+/-hum oblig.O+/-hum (à quelqu'un opt.)	421 ex, many senses main type: 18 opt.O	opt.O-hum
douter NB: PO	S+hum de quelque chose	2 opt.O/12	
écouter	S+hum opt.O+/-hum		opt.O-hum; oblig.O+hum
faire	S+hum oblig.O-hum	4228 ex.	oblig.O-hum
fuir	S+hum oblig.O+/-hum	no ex.	oblig.O+/-hum
jeter	S+hum oblig.O+hum quelque part opt.	1 opt.O/40	opt.O-hum
juger	S+hum oblig.O+/-hum	3 opt.O/14	opt.O-hum; oblig.O+hum
louer (praise)	S+hum oblig.O+/-hum (de/pour quelque chose opt.)	no ex.	
montrer	S+/-hum oblig.O+/-hum (à quelqu'un opt.)	6 opt.O/23	opt.O-hum; oblig.O+hum

Verb	(a) Busse & Dubost	(b) GARS	(c) PROTON
percevoir	S+hum oblig.O+/-hum	2 ex. all obligatory	
perdre	S+hum oblig.O-hum	19 ex. all obligatory	oblig.O+/-hum
pleurer	S+hum oblig.O+/-hum	no ex.	
prier	S+hum oblig.O+hum (evt. pour) oblig.subord. sentence	5 ex. all obligatory	oblig.O+hum
punir	S+/-hum oblig.O+/-hum (pour/de opt.)	5 ex. all obligatory	
suivre	S+/-hum oblig.O.+/-hum	23 opt.O/86	opt.O-hum; oblig.O+hum
tenir1	S+hum oblig.O+/-hum	2 opt.O/ca. 10	opt.O-hum; oblig.O+hum
tenir2	S-hum oblig.O-hum		
trahir1	S+hum oblig.O+/-hum	no ex.	
trahir2	S-hum obligO+/-hum	no ex.	opt.O-hum; oblig.O+hum
vaincre	S+hum oblig.O+/-hum	no ex.	oblig.O+hum

Proportion of opt. vs. obligatory O: 5 opt.O/32 oblig.O; ca. 13 opt.O/ca. 89 oblig.; ca. 15 opt.O/20 oblig.O

The sources are: (a) the Valency dictionary of Busse & Dubost; (b) study of the Spoken French corpus "GARS" 600.000 occ.; (c) the valency dictionary of PROTON. The result of the investigation is that obligatoriness or optionality of direct objects are features of the individual verb.

Appendix 2: Illustrations of three factors favouring or preventing ellipsis

As mentioned in Section 4.3.1., we find:
1. thematic or pragmatic reasons not to express a valency bound element — old information being more easily omitted than new information;
2. there are syntactic conditions which favour ellipses — in French e.g. a succession of questions and answers, infinitive constructions, and coordination favours ellipses
3. text type or register is also relevant for the frequency of ellipses e.g. informal register has more ellipses than formal, spoken register more than written.

The following two passages provide illustrations of these factors; (a) is an Old French text from the 12th century illustrating the numerous ellipses (marked by #) of (fictional) spoken, informal register with a succession of questions and answers; (b) is an Old French legal text of the 14th century illustrating the avoidance of ellipses in written, formal register essentially providing new information. The text has only one ellipsis: a missing object following an infinitiv, indicated by #. In Modern French we find the same differences, thus, a case similar to (a) is seen in example (10a) above.

(a) *– Dame, fet il, la force vient*
de mon cuer, qui a vos se tient;
an ce voloir m'a mes cuers mis.
– Et qui # le cuer, biax dolz amis?
– Dame mi oel #. — Et les ialz, qui #?
– La granz biautez que an vos vi #.
– Et la biautez qu'i a forfet?
– Dame, # tant que amer # me fet.
– Amer #? Et # cui? — # Vos, dame chiere.

Chrétien de Troyes *Yvain* v. 2017–2025

– My lady, he said, the power comes / from my heart, that loves you / my heart has put me into this disposition. / And what [# has put into this disposition] the heart, dear friend?/ My lady, my eyes [# have put my heart into this disposition]. — And the eyes, what [has put the eyes into this disposition?] / The great beauty that I saw in you [# has put the eyes into this disposition] / And what has my beauty caused? / My lady, [# your beauty has caused] so much that [it] has made me love [# someone]. / Love [# someone]? / And [# love] whom? — [# love] you, dear Lady.

(b)
Sacent tout chil ki cest escrit veront et oront, ke Dierins Makes a donnét a loial moituerie, dou jour de may ki vient prochainnement, pur IX. ans ki sont a venir nouuielement, l'un apries l'autre, a Jehan Kauee, toutes les tieres que li dis Dierins a a Baudegnies, a droite moitiet.

Et doit li dis Jehans entrer en le ditte moituerie au jour de may deuant dit, ki sera l'an mil ccc. et XIX.

Et doit chius Jehans Kauee, tout le cours des IX. ans, les tieres ahaner bien et loiaument, c'est a savoir, les ghieskieres en quarte roie et de saison, et semencier de boinne semence et loial, de tel semence ke as dittes tieres apiertenra, et les bles de mars ausi, tout ensi et en tel maniere c'on use ens ou liu, et semer bien et loiaument de tel semence c'as tieres apiertenra, ensi que deuant est dit.

Et doit li dis Jehans les tieres des bles et des mars ahaner, cescun an, sans deroyer ne refroissier #.

Et quant che venra a cescun aoust des IX. anees deseure dittes, li dessus dis Jehans Kauee doit markander, pour li et pour le dit Dierin, de missonner le bles et les mars a mies tout le muis et le plus lealment k'il pora, sans fraude et sans boisdie, et en tans c'on en doit markander.

Et quant li dis Jehans en ara markandét, il doit moustrer le markiet au dessus dit Dierin, u a sen remanant, se de lui defaloit; se il li plaist, tenir puet li dessus dis Dierins le markiet que chius Jehans ara fait ensi que deuant est dit. (Chartes tournaisiennes du XIVe siècle, V, 1318)

Let everybody who will see and hear this letter know that Dierens Makes has given in loyal bail, from the day of May next to come, for nine years to come, again, one year after the other, to Jehan Kauee, all the lands that the mentioned Dierins owns at Baudegnies, in two equal halves.

And the mentioned Jehan has to come to the mentioned bail, on the day of May mentioned before, which will be in the year one thousand three hundred and nineteen.

And this Jehan Kauee throughout the nine years, has to labour the fields, faithfully and loyally, that is to say, the fallow lands every fourth furrow and in time, to sow good seed, and loyal, with such seed as suits the mentioned fields, and the March wheat also, all the same and in such a way people usually do in this place, and to sow well and loyally with such seed as suits the fields, such as was said before.

And the mentioned Jehan has to cultivate the wheat and the March wheat fields every year, without interruption or change of crops.

And when it comes to each August of the nine years mentioned above, the previously mentioned Jehan Kauee has to arrange, for himself and for the mentioned Dierin, to harvest all the wheat and all the March wheat, as loyally as he can, without fraud and without deceit, and at the time that one should arrange this.

And when the aforementioned Jehan has arranged it, he has to show the arrangement to the above mentioned Dierin, or to his caretaker, if he is not there; if he wishes, the above mentioned Dierens can accept the arrangement that this Jehan has made, as was said before.

Notes

* I am indebted to Roger Wright for many helpful comments on the form and content of this paper. I thank J.C Smith and Nigel Vincent for interesting and useful discussions of previous versions of this paper.

1. In this study I do not consider the pragmatic structure, that is, the organisation of information — known or new — and its codification on the syntactic level, in the sense used by Givón (1984, 1991). For further information on the pragmatic level, see Reenen & Schøsler (forthcoming) and Nedergaard Thomsen (1996).

2. However, according to Charpin (1991), word order at least facilitates identification of the elements forming a complement, although not the syntactic function of the elements.

3. By the term "fixation of the word order" I here understand a rule governed linear ordering of the valency-bound elements **that indicates their respective syntactic functions**. By "free word order" I understand that the linear ordering of the valency-bound elements **does not indicate their respective syntactic functions**. More specifically, I do not imply by "free word order" the absence of rules governing the ordering of the elements of the sentence other than syntactic, e.g. pragmatic.

4. In this section I shall make use of the verbal typology elaborated and justified in Schøsler & Van Durme (1996).

5. Support verbs are verbs combined with nominal extensions.

6. See Marchello-Nizia (1995), the observations on which she bases the schemes 7: OnSnV (*un escuier li rois apele*) and 8: OnSpV (*un escuier il apele*) in **main clauses** (p. 52ff.). Additionnally, *me* is an unambiguous non-subject form.

7. Proper nouns of persons fossilise rapidly, and sometimes in the nominative form.

8. Meyer-Lübke also quotes an indefinite, rather strange example: *fueron a buscar a un médico* (they fetched a doctor, cf. Meyer-Lübke III: 372). According to Meyer-Lübke III: 373, Portuguese also have prepositional direct human object, as illustrated by the following example: *aquele a quem amo* (the one that I love). However, this does not seem to bee correct, the appropriate Portuguese way of saying "the one that I love" is without preposition: *aquele quem amo*.

9. In the following I shall use the term "obligatory", "obligatoriness" in the sense of "no pro-drop" and the terms "optional", "non-expression" or "optionality" in the sense of "null NP" or "pro-drop", see Ouhalla (1994: 275ff.).

10. See e.g. Rizzi (1986), Ouhalla (1994) and Vance (1997).

11. Following Fillmore (1986) and Fillmore & Kay (1993), Lambrecht & Lemoine distinguishes not two but three types of missing objects: (i) "la réalisation zéro infinie" or "generic ellipsis", (ii) "la réalisation zéro libre" and (iii) "la réalisation zéro définie"; however, (ii) and (iii) can be subsumed as "anaphoric ellipsis", as proposed in Larjavaara (2000: 101).

12. In a very interesting study, Sæbø (1996) follows Shopen in the distinction between indefinite (=generic) and definite (=anaphoric) ellipses. Sæbø proposes that a zero argument is anaphoric iff the predicate triggers a presupposition involving it (1996: 195). The article provide a clear analysis of the notions involved in the definition, e.g. presupposition in Discourse Representation Theory, anaphoric and non-anaphoric presupposition, zero anaphora, ellipsis, and examples concerning different predicates (lexically determined ellipses). I wish to thank John Ole Askedal for having drawn my attention on Sæbø's article.

13. These four factors are studied in details in Schøsler (1999 and 2000); see Appendix 1 for verb specific ellipses and Appendix 2 for illustrations of the first three factors.

14. See examples of examined verbs in Appendix 1.

15. Implicitely, this is also the analysis of Happ (1976).

16. This is also the analysis of Busse & Dubost (1977). Note however, that this way of putting it does certainly not imply that optionality is a feature of the same lexical verb, from Latin to Modern French.

17. Let us not forget that — in opposition to the other Romance languages–most verb forms are ambiguous with respect to person and number in French.

Sources

1.a Latin text:
De Inventione (Cicero); = INVI
Rhetorica ad Herennium
(Electronic version elaborated by W. van Hoecke, of the Catholic University of Leuven)
Other electronic corpora

1.b Old French texts:
Les Serments de Strasbourg,
La Prose de Sainte Eulalie,
La Vie de Saint Léger,
studied in: Koschwitz, E. (1964): *Les plus anciens monuments de la langue française.* II: Textes critiques et glossaire, 6ème édition, München, Max Hueber Verlag
La Vie de Saint Alexis,
studied in: Storey, Christopher (1934): *Saint Alexis. Etude de la langue du manuscrit de Hildesheim, suivie d'une édition critique du texte d'après le manuscrit L.* Paris, Droz
Translation of Cicero by Jean d'Antioche (1282) (Electronic version elaborated by W. van Hoecke, KUL, Leuven) = JdA.
Chrétien de Troyes: *Yvain*

1.c Middle French texts:
Les Chroniques de Froissart,
les Mémoires de Commynes,
Les Quinze Joies de Mariage,
Cleriadus,
(Electronic versions elaborated by M. Lemieux and F. Depuis, of the University of Quebec in Montreal)

1.d Modern French texts:
Translation of Cicero by Bornecque (1932),
(Electronic version elaborated by W. van Hoecke, KUL, Leuven) = BOR.
The electronic corpus of GARS, at Université de Provence; corcordances established by J.-P. Adam from the GARS group.
PROTON: Dictionnaire électronique des verbes du français, Université Catholique de Leuven.

References

Andersen, H. 1990. "The structure of drift". In *Historical Linguistics 1987. Papers from the 8th International Conference on Historical Linguistics*, H. Andersen and K. Koerner (eds), 1–20. Amsterdam: John Benjamins.

Bauer, B. 1987. "L'évolution des structures morphologiques et syntaxiques du latin au français". *Travaux de Linguistique 14/15*: 95–107.

Busse, W. and J.-P. Dubost. 1977. *Französische Verblexicon. Die Konstruktion der Verben im Französischen*. Stuttgart: Klett-Cotta.

Charpin, F. 1991. "Ordre des mots et identification de l'objet". *Stemma* 1: 25–34.

Dees, A. et al. 1980. *Atlas des formes et des constructions des chartes françaises du 13e siècle*. Tübingen: M. Niemeyer [Beihefte zur Zeitschrift für romanische Philologie Band 178].

Dees, A. et al. 1987. *Atlas des formes linguistiques des textes littéraires de l'ancien français*. Tübingen: M. Niemeyer Verlag [Beihefte zur Zeitschrift für romanische Philologie Band 212].

Fillmore, C. J. 1986. "Pragmatically controlled zero anaphora". In *Proceedings of the Twelfth Annual Meeting of the Berkeley Linguistics Society*, K. Nikiforidou et al. (eds). Berkeley: BLS Inc.

Fillmore, C. J. and Kay, P. 1993. Construction Grammar Coursebook. Ms. Berkely: UCB.

Fleischman, S. 1992. "Discourse and diachrony: The rise and fall of Old French SI". In *Internal and External Factors in Syntactic Change*, M. Gerritsen and D. Stein (eds), 433–473. Berlin: Mouton de Gruyter.

Givón, T. 1984, 1991. *Syntax. A Functional-Typological Introduction*, vol 1–2. Amsterdam: John Benjamins.

Goyens, M. 1994. *Emergence et évolution du syntagme nominal en français*, Berne: Peter Lang.

Happ, H. 1976. *Grundfragen einer Dependenzgrammatik des Lateinischen*, Göttingen: Vandenhoeck & Ruprecht.

Lambrecht, K. and Lemoine, K. 1996. "Vers une grammaire des compléments zéro en français parlé". *Travaux linguistique du Cerlico* 9: 279–310.

Larjavaara, M. 2000. *Présence ou absence de l'objet. Limites du possible en français contemporain*, PhD. dissertation, University of Helsinki.

Liver, R. 1991. *Manuel pratique de Romanche. Sursilvan — Vallader*, Romanica Rætica 4^2, Edizun Lia Rumantscha.

Marchello-Nizia, C. 1995. *L'Evolution du français. Ordre des mots, démonstratifs, accent tonique*. Paris: Armand Colin.

Meyer-Lübke, W. 1899, [1972]. *Grammatik der Romanischen Sprache III, Romanische Syntax*. Hildesheim.

Nedergaard T. O. 1996. "Pronouns, word order, and prosody". *Acta Linguistica* 23: 131–138.

Ouhalla, J. 1994. *Introducing Transformational Grammar. From rules to principles and parameters*, London: Arnold.

Pinkster, H. 1991a. *Latin Syntax and Semantics*. London: Routledge.

Pinkster, H. 1991b. "Evidence for SVO in Latin?". In *Latin and the Romance Languages in the Early Middle Ages*, R. Wright (ed.), 69–82.London: Routledge (paperback reprint, Penn State Press, 1996)'

Pinkster, H. 1993. "Chronologie et cohérence de quelques évolutions latines et romanes". In *Actes du XXe Congrès International de Linguistique et Philologie Romanes*, Tome III, 239–250. Tübingen: Francke Verlag.

Reenen, P.Th. van and Schøsler, L. 1988. "Formation and evolution of the feminine and masculine nominative singular nouns in Old French *li maison(s)* and *li charbons*". In *Historical Dialectology, Regional and Social*, J. Fisiak, (ed.), 505–545. Berlin: Mouton de Gruyter.

Reenen, P. Th.. van and Schøsler, L. 1997. "La déclinaison en ancien et en moyen français, deux tendances contraires". In *Le moyen français, Philologie et linguistique, Approches du texte et du discours* (Nancy, septembre 1994), 595–612. Paris: Didier.

Reenen, P.Th.van and Schøsler, L. Forthcoming. "Pragmatic parameters in Old French. topic continuity and topic change in the main clause in Old French. The pragmatic function of the particles *ainz, apres, donc, lors, or, puis, si*".

Rizzi, L. 1986 "Null Objects in Italian and the Theory of *pro*". *Linguistic Inquiry* 17: 501–58.

Schøsler, L. 1984. *La déclinaison bicasuelle de l'Ancien Français, son rôle dans la syntaxe de la phrase, les causes de sa disparition*. Odense [Etudes Romanes de l'Université d'Odense 19].

Schøsler, L. 1991. "Les causes externes et internes des changements morpho-syntaxiques". *Acta Linguistica Hafniensia* 23: 83–112.

Schøsler, L. 1999. "Réflexions sur l'optionnalité des compléments d'objet direct, en latin, en ancien français, en moyen français et en français moderne". *Etudes Romanes* 44: 9–28.

Schøsler, L. 2000. "Le statut de la forme zéro du complément direct en français moderne", *Etudes Romanes 47, Le françis parlé: corpus et résultats*, 105–129.

Schøsler, L, and Van Durme. K. 1996. *The Odense Valency Dictionary*. Université d'Odense [Odense Working Papers in Language and Communication 13].

Selig, M. 1991. "Inhaltskonturen des 'Dativs'. Zur Ablösung des lateinischen Dativs durch *ad* und zur differentiellen Objektmarkierung". In *Connexiones Romanicae. Dependenz und Valenz in romanischen Sprachen*, P. Koch, and Th. Krefeld (eds), 187–211. Tübingen: M. Niemeyer [Linguistische Arbeiten 268].

Smith, J.C. 1995. "Perceptual factors and the disappearance of agreement between past participle and direct object in Romance". In *Linguistic Theory and the Romance Languages*, Smith and Maiden (eds), 161–180. Amsterdam: John Benjamins.

Sæbø, K.J. 1996. "Anaphoric presuppositions and zero anaphora". *Linguistics and Philosophy* 19: 187–209.

Tesnière, L. 1976. *Eléments de Syntaxe Structurale^2*. Paris: Klincksieck.

Vance, B.S. 1997. *Syntactic Change in Medieval French. Verb-second and null subjects*. Dordrecht: Kluwer [Studies in Natural Languages and Linguistic Theory 41].

Changes in Popolocan word order and clause structure*

Annette Veerman-Leichsenring
University of Leiden

The Popolocan languages (Otomanguean, Mexico) have historically a VSO basic word order. The subject is encoded in the verb, in some verbs subject and human object. For pragmatic reasons a subject or object may be moved into the preverbal position. The preverbal argument, often marked by a focus marker, is repeated after the predicate by a nominal or pronominal form — one may say to restore the basic word order. The four Popolocan languages are affected by a change from a VSO into an SVO word order. However, each language shows a different stage of this development by using or omitting the coreferential terms and the focus marker.

Comparable observations are made with reference to the instrumental and comitative categories. The encoding in the verb of these arguments is gradually replaced by the use of prepositions, in some languages together with word order changes, each language showing a different degree of development.

As the vast majority of Popolocan speakers are bilingual, these developments are likely to be influenced by the Spanish SVO order.

1. Introduction

The increasing use of the Spanish language in Central America has resulted in a high degree of bilingualism in the majority of the Native American speech communities there. It is generally assumed that in such a situation, the influence from the dominating language occurs primarily in the vocabulary and that morphological and syntactic structures are affected in a later phase. Whereas the discreteness of its character makes it rather easy to detect lexical borrowing from Spanish, changes in the morphosyntactic and syntactic structure of a language take place more gradually and can less easily be ascribed to external factors.

In this article I will focus on certain changes in word order and clause structure. Section 2 sketches in short terms the actual situation of the Popolocan languages and their internal relationship. Some characteristics which are relevant for this article are mentioned in the third section. The fourth section is dedicated to word order changes in relation to the use of coreferential pronouns and the marking of preverbal arguments. Section 5 analyses developments in the instrumental and comitative categories in relation with word order and the introduction of Spanish prepositions. Conclusions are summarized in the last section.

Apart from the titles mentioned in the list of references, this study is based on field notes I made during several stays in Popoloc, Chocho and Ixcatec villages. Examples that do not explicitly indicate the source of reference, are drawn from these field notes.

Data from Metzontla Popoloc are prevailing since more syntactic and morphosyntactic details are available of that dialect.

2. Popolocan languages and their genetic relationship

The Popolocan language family consists of four languages: Mazatec, Ixcatec, Chocho and Popoloc. They are spoken in Mexico some 250 kilometres south of Mexico City in a more or less continous area in the States of Puebla, Oaxaca and Veracruz. Mazatec has the largest number of speakers (about 80,000) and is genetically and geographically the most distant member. Many studies have been dedicated to this language; however, the dialectal variety is considerable and the descriptive material is rather fragmentary for most of the dialects. Ixcatec, with no more than ten speakers left, occupies a somewhat ambiguous position by sharing a number of innovative developments with Chocho and Popoloc and others with Mazatec. The close genetic relationship between Popoloc (about 10,000 speakers) and Chocho (about 1,000 speakers)[1] can be established easily by comparison of vocabularies and morphological structures.[2]

3. Some characteristics of Popolocan

The four languages are tonal and highly fusional. A one-to-one relationship between form and meaning is frequently lacking and a sharp distinction between inflection and derivation is difficult to establish. A large number of the lexical roots function in various word classes where they are adjusted with distinct nominal or verbal affixes.

Nouns are not inflected for their grammatical function which is defined by word order and semantic features of the verb or the noun itself.

It is generally assumed that the Popolocan languages are historically VSO with the verb occupying the initial position of a neutral sentence. The verb is the center of gravity of the proposition encoding tense, aspect and/or mode, the person of the actor, or both persons of actor and recipient/beneficiary in one portmanteau morpheme. Ambiguities due to the presence of two third person actants are generally avoided by contextual information. A non human object is not encoded in the verb.

Although in varying degrees, coreferential pronouns are used in the four languages to repeat a preverbal subject or object argument after the verb. With the use of such a pronoun, the basic VSO word order is restored in a certain sense. A subject or object argument is fronted to the verb for the purpose of focalisation. In some languages, the preverbal argument is followed by a specific marker to mark it as focus.

Differences in the use of coreferential pronouns and, in a lesser degree, the marking of the preverbal argument, reveal different stages in a change towards an SVO order in the four Popolocan languages.

Causative, ingressive and passive verbs are derived by prefixation. Instrumental as well as comitative predications are formed by suffixation; in both cases the valency of the verb is extended by an extra argument which has mostly but not exclusively an instrumental or comitative meaning.

The class of prepositions includes a relatively high number of Spanish loans, which are mostly used redundantly with verbs already including a semantic feature of direction, place or source, as in 'go to', 'come from', 'arrive at', or verbs containing already an instrumental or comitative suffix.

4. Word order, coreference and marking of preverbal arguments

In Popoloc, the verb continues to precede subject and object arguments in a neutral, unmarked sentence. However, a subject or object argument is often moved into the preverbal position for pragmatic purposes. In these cases, the transposed argument is repeated after the predicate in a nominal or pronominal form. In the following examples, the preverbal argument is followed by the marker na^3, glossed M, to enhance the focus value of the preverbal argument.

(1) kã³ši¹ tu¹mʔe¹na¹ na³ ku¹še¹ndʔe¹ tu¹me¹ ³
    all   my.money M   spent   CO:money
    'It is all my money that is spent'.

(2) tu³tʔe¹na¹ na³ thu¹a¹ tu³tʔe²
    my.feet   M   clean   CO:foot
    'My feet, they are clean'.

The coreferential term follows the verb immediately. In the preceding examples, the coreferential term is a noun which repeats in an unaccented and uninflected form the noun of the antecedent. Only in Popoloc, coreference may be optionally expressed by a full noun. More often, coreference is obligatorily expressed by a pronoun which is morphologically related to the lexical classifier used in the antecedent, as in example (3). In either case, there is a clear semantic and formal relationship between the antecedent and the coreferential term.

(3) tī¹ ka³-nia³   na³ tʔa²khia² ka³
    the CL-strawmat M   I.sell   CO:leaf
    'It is the strawmat that I sell'.

A rather extensive set of lexical classifiers is used to indicate the semantic category to which the noun belongs, as the class of trees, flowers, animals etc., or the class of human beings, male or female, married or marriageable grown-ups, children, etc. As a morphologically related coreferential pronoun corresponds to each of these classifiers, the number of pronouns is equally extensive.

Actually, the coreferential term that follows the predicate has two functions: a grammatical one, to refer back to a preverbal subject or object argument, and a semantic one, to indicate the generic class to which the head noun of the preverbal argument belongs. In the Popoloc examples given above, the marker M is additionally used to focus the preverbal argument. However, the marker might have other functions in a sentence, such as to connect clauses, to introduce direct speech, or to mark the end of an adjectival phrase. Although its use is somewhat dependent on stylistic factors, the marker is rather consistently used after a preverbal subject or object argument in Popoloc.

Although subject arguments are often fronted to the verb in Chocho, coreference is only optionally applied in this language. Moreover, it is exclusively expressed by pronouns. Another important difference from Popoloc is that the noun of the antecedent may contain a classifier which is not morphologically related to the coreferential pronoun, or that a classifier is not used at all. So, different from Popoloc, a semantic and formal relationship between the antecedent and the coreferential pronoun is not always apparent, as in example (4):

(4) hngu¹ nya³ ka³   xu³na¹ be²-ci¹nga² ba²   nu³nde³
    one dog small never P-lies   CO:animal ground
    'A little dog, (that) never lied down on the ground'.
    (Angulo and Freeland 1935: 126; adapted transcription).

Such a formal disconnection between the classifier and the coreferential pronoun is also caused by dissimilar phonological developments, as in the next example, which shows that a high degree of rhotacism has affected the unaccented coreferential pronoun ru^3, but not the classifier.

(5) sa¹ tu³-ce³   še¹ma¹ ru³
    the CL-lemon dry   CO:fruit
    'The lemon is dry'.

Another example of disconnection between the antecedent and the anaphoric term, is provided by the pronoun ni^2, which is used to express respect in coreference with names which may contain one out of a variety of classifiers, such as ta^1- for male reverential names or na^1- for female reverential names. Although I could not trace any classifier synchronically related to the pronoun ni^2, cognate terms used as classifiers in the other languages, Popoloc ni^2, Ixcatec mi^2-, Proto-Mazatec *hmi^4- (Kirk 1966 set 138) and Proto-Popolocan *hmi (Gudschinsky 1959a set 198), makes it plausible that a classifier *ni^2- have been used in an earlier stage of Chocho too. So, in this case, the grammatical function of the coreferential pronoun, i.e. to refer back to a preverbal subject or object argument, is overruled by the semantic function, i.e. to indicate the honorific class to which the referent of the preverbal argument belongs. In this case, the coreferential pronoun developed an independent semantic value which allows its occurrence with any antecedent associated with the expression of respect.

Likewise, the familiar pronoun ri^3 corefers with nouns that refer to adult male persons, which may contain the classifier $řu^2$- or no classifier at all. The value of the pronoun ri^3 seems to be predominantly a semantic one, viz. to indicate a familiar relationship to the referent, and not so much a grammatical one, dictated by the rules of word order.

(6) su³a¹ řu²-gringo çō³   ri²
    this CL-gringo is.afraid CO:person
    'This American man is afraid'
    (Angulo and Freeland 1935: 125, 126; adapted transcription).

As the number of classifying prefixes is more limited in Chocho than in Popoloc, the number of coreferential pronouns is considerably smaller too and an appropriate coreferential pronoun is not always available. The fact that coreferential pronouns are often omitted in Chocho, suggests that a VSO order is no longer felt as the only and unconditional basic one in that language.

A sentence marker is used in Chocho too, and its functions coincide largely with those of the Popoloc marker. The main difference is that it is not used after a preverbal argument, at least, not in the Chocho data I collected in 1996/97. This supports my hypothesis that an argument in preverbal position is not necessarily the focus in Chocho.

The Ixcatec texts included in Fernández de Miranda's vocabulary (1961) show consistently that in this language, different from Chocho and Popoloc, a preverbal subject or object argument is generally not repeated after the verb by a noun or pronoun. Moreover, the use and number of coreferential pronouns in Ixcatec is even more limited than in Chocho. Only three pronouns with an obvious coreferential function could be attested in the available material, where only *ba* is used in a consistent manner in coreference with animal names containing the classifier $ʔu^2$-.[4]

(7) tu^{1}nda^{2}ʔa^2 ʔu^2-šyee^1 fi^{2}ka^{2}hu^2 ba^3 ka^{2}hndu^3
he.has   CL-his.ox   goes.with   CO:animal   mountain
'He who owns an ox, takes it to the mountain.'
(Fernández de Miranda 1961: 178).

The other two pronouns, *da* coreferring with male names and *kua* with female names, occur very sporadically. In the seven texts which Fernández de Miranda (1961) analyzed, the pronoun *da* occurs only once. Moreover, in this case the pronoun appears to refer back to a rather distant argument, which strongly suggests that the pronoun is not used for grammatical reasons but for pragmatic ones, namely to recall into the memory a syntagmatically distant actant or to avoid ambiguity between different third person actants. In the next example, the use of the pronoun *da* indicates that it was the soldiers who were hitting and that the guns were in the hands of the soldiers.

(8) di^2-soldadu... kwa^{1}řha^{2}ši^2 da^3 ya^{2}štu^{3}hwee^3 da^3
CL-soldier   hit.with   CO:man   his.gun   CO
'The soldiers (...) they hit with their guns.'
(Fernández de Miranda 1961: 188).

The coreferential pronouns figure in the same positions as the Chocho and Popoloc ones, i.e. directly after a verb or a noun inflected for third person. However, different from Chocho, they seem to be used exclusively when a corresponding generic noun or classifier is present in the preceding text. The coreferential pronoun *ba* is interesting from a historical point of view. It is related to the Ixcatec classifier of animal names $\mathit{?u}^2$- and a reflex of the proto form *ku^2a, which is composed of the root *ku^2 'animal' plus a deictic vowel *a. The Ixcatec pronoun *ba* is cognate with the coreferential pronouns for animals in Popoloc, ba^2, and Chocho, ba^3, which indicates that the pronoun was already used in the proto language underlying Ixcatec, Chocho and Popoloc.

My own field notes (see also Veerman-Leichsenring, in preparation) reveal that a preverbal argument is incidentally marked most probably for pragmatic reasons, to enhance its focus value, and not for syntactic necessity. I have the impression that in Ixcatec an SVO word order is becoming, or has become already, the neutral one and that coreference, with the exception of the animal pronoun, is mainly applied for pragmatic reasons.

Some texts are available in three Mazatec variants belonging to three distinct dialect clusters, viz. the Huautla dialect of the highland cluster, the Jalapa dialect of the valley cluster and the Chiquihuitlán dialect which is spoken in one isolated village only (see Gudschinsky 1958).

As coreference is obviously concomitant with the movement of argument phrases, I checked the available texts specifically for the presence of coreferential terms.

In the Chiquihuitlán texts (A.R. Jamieson 1977a,b; C. Jamieson, not dated), only two coreferential pronouns occur: *ča* for male names and related to the male classifier *ča-*, and *ču* for animals and related to the animal classifier *ču-*. The coreferential pronoun *ču* is also used when the animal name contains an unrelated classifier or no classifier at all. This causes a similar disconnection between the antecedent and the coreferential pronoun as we have observed for Chocho. So the morphological relationship between the noun and the coreferential pronoun may be lacking in this language too. The following examples illustrate the use of pronouns to refer back to an earlier mentioned argument in the Chiquihuitlán dialect. The coreferential pronoun in example (9) is morphologically related to the classifier *ča-*. In the other two examples, such a relationship is lacking.

(9) tinuʔū ča-ništi nuhu cuidadu ta
 tell CL-child you.REV attention because
 cakʔuīī kamaʔa ni ča
 no.fear very no CO:male
 'Tell your boys to be careful because they have no fear at all.'
 (C. Jamieson, not dated)

(10) sa³kuaʔ³⁴ hya³⁴ hā² nē²⁴ ši³ skuae⁴¹ ču¹⁴   la³nka¹⁴ ⁵
     as   eagle he M   that   will.see co:animal child
     'As the eagle will see the children (...)'
     (A.R. Jamieson 1977a: 175)

(11) kui⁴nči²rae²⁴   na⁴šī² ši³ kua⁴nih⁴¹   ču⁴
     he.will.look.for mule that will.transport co:animal
     'He will look for mules for the transport.'
     (A.R. Jamieson 1977b: 132)

Only a few examples containing morphologically related pairs of nouns and pronouns could be traced in the one available Jalapa de Díaz text (Schram and Schram 1979).

(12) nda³ šʔā³ ha²ā¹ ku²ma² ndyi³na¹šu¹ ndo³
     man poor then became rich   co:man
     'The man who was poor, became rich.'
     (Schram and Schram 1979: 21; adapted transcription)

(13) nghi²ko³šu¹ ho¹o³   ki³čo³
     took.up   co:people machete
     'They found the machete.'
     (Schram and Schram 1979: 87; adapted transcription)

In (12) the pronoun retained its supposed grammatical function, i.e. it corefers with a preverbal argument. In (13), however, it corefers with an argument that is not explicitly mentioned by a noun. As the semantic value of the attested pronouns is very broad, viz. 'man', 'animal', it seems plausible that the retention of these forms is due to their frequent usage.

The use of a very limited number of coreferential pronouns in the Chiquihuitlán and Jalapa dialects resembles the situation in Ixcatec. Although it is possible that more pronouns could be traced in a larger body of texts, it is unlikely that the total number is much larger.

As the use of a coreferential pronoun is not attested in the Huautla texts at my disposal (K. Pike 1948; E.V. Pike 1949; Gudschinsky 1959b; F.H. Cowan 1963; G.M. Cowan 1965), this dialect seems to be the most innovative variant with respect to word order. In fact, a verb medial word order seems to be the unmarked, neutral one in actual speech. Although markers as *xo¹* 'quoted' and *ʔni³* 'indeed', and possibly a low tone, are added to words or phrases for pragmatic reasons, no evidence is found for a specific focus value of the argument in preverbal position.

To summarize, Popoloc retained the Proto-Popolocan VSO word order as the basic one and applies coreferential terms, pronouns as well as nouns, when a subject or object is fronted to the preverbal position; the focus value of the preverbal argument is often enhanced by a sentence marker.

Ixcatec and Mazatec replaced the VSO order by an SVO one. The basic character of this order makes the use of a coreferential term after the verb superfluous. However, in both languages, some coreferential pronouns are present as the vestiges of an old system but which are mainly used for pragmatic reasons.

Chocho occupies the intermediate position. VSO still seems to be the basic order although SVO orders are not always marked obligatorily. The use of coreferential terms is limited and their grammatical value seems to be replaced by a semantic one.

5. Comitative and Instrumental categories, prepositional phrases and word order

In different Popolocan languages and dialects, the verb stem is followed by a suffix which expresses that the sentence contains an instrumental (INSTR) or comitative (COM) argument. The INSTR as well as the COM suffix is inflected for person. A COM suffix indicates that the subject/actor together with another person, the co-actor, are fulfilling the action referred to by the verb. The verb adds an INSTR suffix, when the sentence contains an argument which refers to the instrument with which the action is performed, or to the source, cause or purpose of the action. However, the precise grammatical value of the INSTR argument varies among and within languages. The COM as well as the INSTR suffix extends the valency of the verb. The INSTR argument generally precedes the predicate whereas the COM argument follows. This allows the reconstruction of a basic word order for sentences containing an INSTR and a COM argument as

$$*I^{instr}VS^{actor}C^{co\text{-}actor}O.$$

Specific phenomena related to a decreasing use of INSTR and COM suffixes, such as changes in word order and the use of prepositional phrases, are indicative of developments which are probably influenced by Spanish syntax.

The INSTR suffix is productively used in Popoloc verbs with a lexical meaning that admits an argument expressing an instrument, location or cause. These arguments are by nature non-human third person noun phrases. In the

Popoloc dialects of Metzontla, Tlacoyalco and Otlaltepec, the INSTR suffix is obligatorily encoded in the verb when the INSTR argument precedes the verb, as the following examples show.

(14) yo²o¹ letra mahina ci¹khi³ʔ-ší²ʔ   ka²yu¹u²vi¹ na¹nku² šū³ū²
     only letter machine is.written-INSTR both   side   paper
     'The paper is written on both sides with only machine letters.'
     (Williams & Longacre 1967: 170)

(15) para   que vittha   na tomi   rroganche-ší   na tattita
     in.order that he.came PL money   to.take.out-INSTR PL man
     'So they got enough money to take the man out (of the hospital).'
     (Machin 1977: 103)

(16) ka³ši¹ na³ molde tʔu¹na²-ši²
     all   M   mould is.made-INSTR
     'Everything is made with a mould.' (Veerman-Leichsenring 1991: 412)

The preverbal INSTR argument is not followed by a specific marker as is the case with preverbal S and O arguments. This indicates that the preverbal position of the INSTR argument is the unmarked, neutral one. The INSTR suffix is optionally applied when the corresponding argument follows the predicate. Sentence (17) shows the presence of the INSTR suffix and (18) its omission although in both cases the INSTR argument follows the verb.

(17) tʔa²nda²ku¹xu³ʔū²-ši²-na² tī¹ šaʔ
     become.old-INSTR-1   the work
     'I get old with the work.'
     (Veerman-Leichsenring 1991: 416)

(18) kā³i¹ tī¹ figura kue¹kʔu¹na² na³ puru molde
     all   this figure were.made   M   only mould
     'All these figures were made with a mould only.'
     (Veerman-Leichsenring 1991: 414)

In the Atzingo and Tlacoyalco dialects of Popoloc, the use of the INSTR suffix seems to be optional and not dependent on the position of the INSTR argument. However, in Tlacoyalco Popoloc a preposition is used when the INSTR suffix is not applied.

(19) xidaña   ntao koniší kochío
     he.chops meat with   knife
     'He chops meat with a knife.' (Machin 1980: 5)

A COM suffix is added to the Popoloc verb when the sentence contains an argument referring to an accompanying person:

(20) the³the³xu¹-kʔu³   sē¹ tī¹ tʔe¹   sē¹
 they.are.living-COM.3 REV the his.parent REV
 'they (rev.) are living with their parents.'
 (Veerman-Leichsenring 1991:430)

In most Popoloc dialects, the COM argument immediately follows the verb occupying the position which is normally occupied by the subject/actor. Usually it is the co-actor who is referred to by a noun whereas the person of the subject/actor is indicated by inflection of the COM suffix. If both arguments are nominal, one occupies the preverbal position where it is generally followed by a focus marker. Example (21) shows that the grammatical ambiguity of the two arguments is parallelled by an underdifferentiation of the semantic functions.

(21) tī¹ ndu³a³ na³ tʔi²-ku³   ši¹nʔa³
 the man   M   drinks-COM my.husband
 'The man drinks with my husband', or:
 'With the man drinks my husband.'
 (Veerman-Leichsenring 1991:302)

Some cases of the use and forms of the COM suffix could be attested in an 18th century Popoloc manuscript I discovered in the Latin American Library of Tulane University in 1991 (Ms. 1760; Veerman-Leichsenring 1995):

(22) cuechruya   quian ngo se chin
 committed.sin COM.1 one REV woman
 'I committed sin with a woman.' (Ms.1760:35)

(23) cuechruya   cuâ   cjaguà
 committed.sin COM.2 your.sister
 'You committed sin with your sister.' (Ms.1760:35)

As the COM elements in these examples do show inflection (in adapted transcription *kiá* for the first person and *kua* for the second), whereas the verb stem is unchanged, it may safely be assumed that the COM elements are suffixes.

Studies which deal with Popoloc dialects other than Metzontla, hardly mention the COM category, and the small quantity of data I could trace in the available texts is not sufficient to detect dialectal characteristics.

The INSTR and COM suffixes are mutually exclusive in Metzontla Popoloc. When the sentence contains an INSTR as well as a COM argument, only one of the arguments is encoded in the verb, though I could not discover any criteria according to which one argument is selected instead of the other.

In the Ocotlán dialect of Chocho, the COM as well as the INSTR argument follows the verb. However, instead of the encoding in the verb, a prepositional phrase is used. The following examples are taken from Veerman-Leichsenring 2000.

(24) bʔa¹rxa³ ri¹ ku³ ngu² nda³
hit   CO with a   stick
'He (the man) hit with a stick.'

(25) sua¹ ri¹ çua¹   ri¹ ku³ ma¹ ri¹
he   CO comes CO with me CO
'He (the man) comes with me.'

The preposition ku^3 that figures in these examples, can be conveniently translated by the Spanish preposition *con*. It seems plausible that formal and semantic similarities have favoured the use of the prepositional phrase instead of the COM suffix. Contrary to expectation, ku^3 is not followed by the independent first person pronoun $xā^1$ in example (25), but by the enclitic pronoun ma^1 and another copy of the referential marker. As it is only in the verb phrase that two enclitic pronouns can be used together, the preposition seems to have retained the characteristic of the comitative verb expressing the persons of the actor and the co-actor.

My hypothesis that the substitution of the COM suffix by a prepositional phrase is favoured by formal and semantic similarities between the COM suffix and the preposition, is supported by the fact that in the same dialect a particle $ṣe^3$ is added to the verb when the sentence contains an argument which refers to the source, destination or cause of an action as in examples (26) and (27), i.e. in those cases where the particle cannot be translated by the Spanish preposition *con*. Apparently, the particle $ṣe^3$, which is most probably cognate with the Popoloc INSTR suffix $-ši^2$, is not replaced by the Spanish preposition *con* because of the absence of formal and semantic similarities.

(26) sua¹ ya³ da³xī³   ṣe³ ya³ Nia¹ʔ
you REV come.down from CO hill
'You descend from the hill.'

(27) sa¹ u²nia³ bʔe¹ ṣe³ ba³ xi³nda³
the dog   died of CO hunger
'The dog died of hunger.'

The preposition *ndie*, the adapted form of the Spanish preposition *de*, is sometimes inserted when the argument refers to a source. This redundant use of two prepositions signals that the Chocho *se³* form is becoming a semantically empty form.

(28) u²sta² çua³ se³ ndie du³su³ʔ
already comes from from Tamazulapan
'He comes already from Tamazulapan.'

The INSTR suffix that Mock mentions in her study of 1977, shows a stronger similarity with the form and distribution of the Popoloc INSTR suffix than I could establish on the basis of my field notes. This is most probably due to developments which have taken place during the twenty years between her and my registrations. Mock mentions the use of an INSTR suffix *-ší²* when an INSTR argument precedes the verb which is in agreement with the usage in Popoloc.

(29) či²ʔ ndu¹ nče²ʔdu³ tu¹na²-ši²   či²ʔ
pot M   clay   is.made-INSTR CO
'The pot is made with clay.' (Mock 1977:141)

(30) ši¹-xōā¹ʔ ndu¹ čoa¹³-ši²   ri¹ ku²nča³
CL-Juan M   comes-INSTR CO Oaxaca
'John comes from Oaxaca.' (Mock 1977:143)

However, when the INSTR argument follows, the preposition *ku³* is used instead of the INSTR suffix:

(31) ta²ʔša² ku³ rxa¹³
smash with your.hand
'Smash it with your hands!' (Mock 1977:140)

Her examples suggest that in the language phase she registered, this happens only when the argument has an instrumental value, i.e. when replacement by the Spanish preposition *con* is possible.

In Ixcatec, INSTR and COM arguments are encoded in the verb by distinct suffixes. However, a strong regression in the use of both suffixes can be observed when we compare Fernández de Miranda's texts with my field notes. In her texts, a suffix *-ší²* or *-šī²* is used rather regularly to encode an INSTR argument. It is also used when the argument follows the verb, as in example (32).

(32) kwa¹řha²-ši² da³ ya²štu³hwee³ da³
 hit-INSTR CO his.gun CO
 'they (the soldiers) hit with their guns.'
 (Fernández de Miranda 1961: 188)

According to my own field notes, an INSTR suffix is only used with a causal or locative argument, as in (33) and (34), and the preposition ka^2hu^2 is used with an instrumental argument, as in (35) and (36).

(33) sa² u²-ni²ña³ ʔme²-ši² ba² hi²ndia²
 the CL-dog dies-INSTR CO hunger
 'The dog dies of hunger.'

(34) sa² la²ʔĩ¹ la³ ku¹xi²ʔe²-ši³ ngi²wa³
 the child M was.born-INSTR Coixtlahuaca
 'The child was born in Coixtlahuaca.'

(35) ba²ne² ka²hu² rxa²
 he.eats with his.hand
 'He eats with his hands.'

(36) ku¹ce²tʔua¹ na²ʔnde² ka²hu² i²nda³
 you.cleaned floor with water
 'You cleaned the floor with water.'

The Ixcatec COM suffix shows a comparable behaviour. Only a restricted number of verbs, such as 'to go with someone', 'to take', 'to come with someone', 'to bring', 'to eat, to drink or to play with someone', add an inflected COM suffix. The following examples are drawn from my field notes.

(37) sa¹ mi²čʔa² la² fi²-ka²hu² ngu² či²xi³
 the woman M go-COM.3 a jar
 'The woman carries a jar.'

(38) i¹la³ na² fi²-kua³ ngu² či²xi³
 you M go-COM.2 a jar
 'You carry a jar.'

(39) i²ni¹ u²šta¹ma¹-kui² sa² la²ʔĩ¹
 we play-COM.1PL the child
 'We play with the child.'

With other verbs, a preposition ku^2 or ka^2hu^2 marks the comitative argument.

(40)　su²a¹ kua¹mi¹ da¹ ku² i²na¹na³
　　　he　talked　co　with me
　　　'He talked with me.'

(41)　i²na¹na³ kua¹mi¹na² ku² i²la³
　　　I　　　talked　　　with you
　　　'I talked with you.'

Compared with the other Popolocan languages, the Mazatec texts show a rather different structure with regards to the marking of INSTR and COM arguments. This is undoubtedly related to the early separation of Mazatec from the Popolocan common language.

In the Jalapa dialect, the grammatical functions of INSTR and COM merged into one suffix. As in Metzontla Popoloc, the instrumental argument precedes the verb.

(42)　ku²ma² čū²　su²wa²šu¹u³ ni²　ši²　ki²cʔĩ¹-ko³
　　　became clean alone　　　　thing that he worked-INSTR
　　　'It became clean alone with the thing he worked with.'
　　　(Schram and Schram 1979:21)

In the Chiquihuitlán dialect, one preposition marks the COM as well as the INSTR argument:

(43)　hbae² koh³ šu⁴ta⁴ča²naʔ³⁴ nki³hña²
　　　I.go　with my.parent　　field
　　　'I go with my parent to the field.'
　　　(A.R. Jamieson 1977b:127)

(44)　ʔi³škā¹⁴ ši³　na⁴ši⁴ntya³⁴ ne⁴ koh³ le⁴ʔba¹⁴ ka³ba²khĩ²⁴
　　　where that boulder　M　with hoe　we.broke
　　　'Where there were boulders, we broke up (the ground) with a hoe'
　　　(A.R.Jamieson 1977b:128)

The Huautla dialect seems to distinguish the two categories. As Gudschinsky reports (1959b), in this dialect an instrumental enclitic ni^3 -which is obviously not cognate with the INSTR marker in the other Popolocan languages-, may be added to the verb when the sentence contains an instrumental argument. One of her examples is:

(45) ti³⁴   ti¹si¹ša¹   ni³   ki⁴ti⁴ma²³
the.boy is.working INSTR hoe
'The boy is working with a hoe.'
(Gudschinsky 1959b: 85).

A suffix or enclitic ni^3 appears rather frequently in the Huautla texts where its precise grammatical value is not clear in every instance. Quite often, it seems to emphasize the foregoing word and only in a few cases it is unambiguously connected with an instrumental or locative argument. In the Huautla texts analyzed by E.V. Pike (1949), a suffix -kao is added to the verb to encode the presence of a COM or an INSTR argument.

(46) ca²khẽ⁴-kao⁴-nia³ ka²nto⁴ša⁴ʔnta⁴
she.ate-COM.3-me chicken.soup
'She ate chicken soup with me.' (Pike 1949: 291)

(47) hnko³ sa¹³   la⁴   ki³sʔe³ nka³ kʔoa⁴sʔĩ² ki³ski³ʔnta¹-kao⁴
one   month perhaps became that like.that cried-INSTR.3
'It was probably a month that she cried with it like that.' (Pike 1949: 290)

The suffix -kao^4 is furthermore used in the Huatla dialect to derive comitative and causative verbs:

$vi^3šã^3$ 'to marry' — $vi^3šã^3$-kao^4 'to marry with someone'
(Pike and Gudschinsky 1957: 58).

To summarize, in Popoloc, distinct suffixes are added to the verb to encode the presence of a COM or INSTR argument. In a neutral word order the INSTR argument precedes the verb without additional marking; the COM argument follows the verb. In some Popoloc dialects (Atzingo and Tlacoyalco), the encoding in the verb is optional when the INSTR argument follows the verb. A preposition is used in the Tlacoyalco dialect when encoding fails.

In Chocho, a preposition ku^3 connects the verb with the INSTR as well as with the COM argument. However, when the argument refers to a location or a cause, a preposition se^3 is used, which is most probably cognate with the Popoloc INSTR suffix -ši.

Ixcatec agrees largely with Chocho. Both arguments, INSTR and COM, appear in the postverbal position and INSTR as well as COM arguments are expressed by a prepositional phrase. The suffix -$ši^2$ is nowadays only added to the verb when the clause includes an argument with a causal or locative meaning.

The few examples I found in Mazatec with regard to INSTR and COM categories, show different patterns. In the Jalapa dialect, COM and INSTR suffixes collapsed in one suffix and the INSTR argument precedes the verb. In Chiquihuitlán Mazatec, one preposition is used for both categories. Although a COM suffix seems to be generally used in Huautla Mazatec, it is not clear how the INSTR category is represented in that dialect.

6. Conclusions

The modern Popolocan languages have been undergoing syntactic changes which can be ascribed to an increasing influence of the Spanish language. Languages and dialects show different phases in the development of these changes.

The shift from a basic VSO order towards an SVO order is accompanied by a proportional loss of coreferential pronouns. With a strict VSO order and an abundant use of coreferential terms, Popoloc is the more conservative member of the Popolocan family. The adaptation to the Spanish word order seems to be fully reached in the Huautla dialect of Mazatec, where an SVO order is the unmarked, neutral one and coreference is not applied at all. In some languages (Ixcatec and the Mazatec dialects of Jalapa and Chiquihuitlán), a few coreferential pronouns are used in a very limited way. They are most probably the remnants of an older system. Chocho, where the VSO order is affected already and the number of coreferential pronouns is rather reduced as compared with Popoloc, seems to be in a transitional phase.

The observed differences in the use and number of coreferential pronouns show a relationship with the varying degrees in which lexical classifiers are used in the four languages. The morphosyntactic value of the generic classifiers seems to be vanishing in Mazatec, Ixcatec and Chocho. The decrease in the number of coreferential pronouns may have favoured this development.

Also the structure of the Spanish sentence expressing instrumental and comitative arguments by means of prepositional phrases, (*pega con un palo; me voy con mi padre*), has influenced the sentence structure of the modern Popolocan languages. The more conservative structure is again observed in Popoloc where the INSTR argument occupies the initial position in an unmarked sentence and where it is encoded in the verb by an INSTR suffix inflected for person. However, in some Popoloc dialects (Atzingo, Tlacoyalco), in Ixcatec and in Mazatec, the INSTR argument may follow the verb as in the Spanish sentence. In these cases, the INSTR suffix is often omitted as its presence is felt to be superfluous when the INSTR argument immediately follows. The use of a preposition instead, as happens in Chocho, Ixcatec and Tlacoyalco Popoloc, completes the adjustment to the Spanish structure. The development may be represented as

$\text{Instr Verb}^{\text{instr}} > \text{Verb}^{\text{instr}} \text{ Instr} > \text{Verb Prep Instr}.$

The COM suffix underwent a somewhat different change. The COM argument follows the verb in each language, where it occupies the position and fulfils a similar semantic role as the subject/actor. In fact, the person of the subject and the person of the comitative argument are co-actors. Popoloc and Huautla Mazatec retained the encoding of the COM argument in the verb. However, most probably influenced by the use of the prepositional phrase in Spanish, the COM suffix has been reanalysed as a preposition in Chocho, Ixcatec and the other Mazatec dialects here included. The fact that the form of the Spanish preposition *con* is rather similar to the form of the uninflected COM suffix *-ku* must have contributed to this reanalysis and to the contraction in one form of the INSTR and COM markers. This hypothesis is supported by the fact that a suffix which is cognate with the Popoloc INSTR suffix, is still applied in Ixcatec and Chocho when the argument refers to a cause or a location, i.e. in those cases where the meaning of the structure does not allow an interpretation with the Spanish preposition *con*. So it seems plausible that the form of the Spanish preposition together with the order Preposition + Noun, has motivated the use of the preposition *ku* followed by the comitative argument in several Popolocan languages and dialects.

Comparison of the Ixcatec and Chocho data mentioned in Fernández de Miranda 1961 and Mock 1977, with the data I registered in 1996/97, shows that fundamental changes have taken place in a relatively short period. Such a rate of structural changes can only be explained satisfactorily in relation to the strong increase in bilingualism during the last decennia of the past century.

Notes

* I acknowledge the Netherlands Organization for Scientific Research (NWO), the Research School of Asian, African and Amerindian Studies (CNWS) of Leiden University and the Institute for Anthropological Research of the Universidad Nacional Autónoma de México (UNAM) for providing the opportunity to do the research for this article.

1. The numbers of speakers here included are impressionistic, based on my own observations and of those of the authorities in situ.

2. According to lexicostatistical and glottochronological calculations (see Swadesh 1967 and Fernández de Miranda 1956), Mazatec was the first language to split off, about 25 minimal

centuries (m.c.) ago. Then followed Ixcatec about 13 m.c. ago, whereas Chocho and Popoloc started to separate from each other about 8 m.c. ago.

3. The phonemic symbols have much their traditional values. A raised number [1] indicates a high tone, [2] a mid tone, [3] a low tone, and [4] a lower than low tone; ʔ represents a glottal stop, ř a retroflexed trill, c̣ a retroflexed affricate, ṣ a retroflexed sibilant, and N a voiceless alveolar nasal. In some examples, the transcription is adapted to the one generally used in this article. The gloss CO means coreferential noun or pronoun, CL classifying prefix, M focus marker, REV reverential, INSTR instrumental, COM comitative, PREP preposition, PL plural and 1, 2, 3, first, second and third person respectively.

4. As the coreferential pronoun assimilates its tone to the last tone of the preceding word, tones are not marked in the Ixcatec citation forms.

5. The indication of two tones on morphemes in the Mazatec examples refers to tone clusters.

References

Angulo, J. de and Freeland, L. S. 1935. "The Zapotecan linguistic group: A comparative study of Chinanteco, Chocho, Mazateco, Cuicateco, Mixteco, Chatino, and specially Zapoteco proper and its dialects". *International Journal of American Linguistics* 8: 1–38; 111–130.

Cowan, F. H. 1963. "La mujer del agua arrastradora: un texto mazateco". *Tlalocan* IV(2): 144–146.

Cowan, G. M. 1965. *Some Aspects of the Lexical Structure of a Mazatec Historical Text*. Norman: Summer Institute of Linguistics and University of Oklahoma.

Fernández de Miranda, M. T. 1956. *Glotocronología de la familia popoloca*. Mexico: Instituto Nacional de Antropología e Historia [Museo Nacional de Antropología, Serie Científica 4].

Fernández de Miranda, M. T. 1961. *Diccionario ixcateco*. Mexico: Instituto Nacional de Antropología e Historia.

Gudschinsky, S. C. 1958. "Mazatec dialect history. A study in miniature". *Language* 34: 469–481.

Gudschinsky, S. C. 1959a. "Proto-Popotecan: A comparative study of Popolocan and Mixtecan". *International Journal of American Linguistics* 25(2) (Supplement) [Indiana University Publications in Anthropology and Linguistics, Memoir 15].

Gudschinsky, S. C. 1959b. "Mazatec kernel constructions and transformations". *International Journal of American Linguistics* 25: 81–89.

Jamieson, A. R. 1977a. "El origen del nombre del pueblo de Chiquihuitlán, Oaxaca". *Tlalocan* 7: 173–179.

Jamieson, A. R. 1977b. "Chiquihuitlán Mazatec tone". In *Studies in Otomanguean Phonology*, W. R. Merrifield (ed.), 107–136. Dallas: Summer Institute of Linguistics and University of Texas.

Jamieson, C. Not dated. His father's mules [a Chiquihuitlán text]. Not published.

Kirk, P. L. 1966. Proto-Mazatec phonology. Dissertation. University of Washington..

Machin, P. 1977. *Discourse Markers in Northern Popoloca*. Arlington: University of Texas.

Machin, P. 1980. "The clause of Northern Popoloca". *SIL- Mexico Workpapers* 3: 1–19.

Mock, C. 1977. *Chocho de Santa Catarina Ocotlán*. Mexico: El Colegio de México, Centro de Investigación para la Integración Social and Instituto Lingüístico de Verano [Archivo de lenguas indígenas de México 4].

Ms.1760: *Text in Popoloc of Tepexi de Rodriguez*. Latin American Library, Tulane University, New Orleans. PM 3641.T4 LAL Rare.

Pike, K. 1948. *Tone Languages: A technique for determining the number and type of pitch contrasts in a language, with studies in tonemic substitution and fusion*. Ann Arbor: University of Michigan Press.

Pike, E.V. 1949. "Texts on Mazatec food witchcraft". *El México Antiguo* VII: 287–294.

Pike, E.V. and Gudschinsky, S.C. 1957 (revised ed.). *Vocabulario Mazateco* (Huautla). Mexico: Instituto Lingüístico de Verano.

Schram, T.L. and Schram, J.L. 1979. "Mazatec of Jalapa de Díaz: About the thunderman". In *Discourse Studies in Meso-American languages*, L.K. Jones (ed.), 2: 15–27. Dallas: Summer Institute of Linguistics and University of Texas.

Swadesh, M. 1967. "Lexicostatistic classification". In *Handbook of Middle American Indians*, N.A. McQuown (ed.), V: 79–115. Austin: University of Texas.

Veerman-Leichsenring, A. 1991. *Gramática del popoloca de Metzontla*. Amsterdam and Atlanta: Rodopi.

Veerman-Leichsenring, A. 1995. "Un documento popoloca del siglo XVIII". *La "découverte" des langues et des écritures d'Amérique*. [Actes du colloque international, Paris, 7–11 septembre 1993, Amerindia 19/20]. Paris,A.E.A.

Veerman-Leichsenring, A. 2000. *Gramática del chocho de Santa Catarina Ocotlán*. Leiden: Research School of Asian, African and Amerindian Studies (CNWS) of the Universiteit Leiden, and Instituto de Investigaciones Antropológicas of the Universidad Nacional Autónoma de México (UNAM).

Veerman-Leichsenring, A. In preparation. Gramática del ixcateco.

Williams, A.F. and Longacre, R.E. 1967. "Popoloca clause types". *Acta Linguistica Hafniensia* X (2): 161–186.

Index

A

accusative 69, 123, 124, 133n, 249-254, 258, 260, 262, 264-266, 268n, 269n
adjective 284, 292
adposition 246-248, 257, 267n
Afrikaans 8, 131
agent 31, 137, 138
agreement 8, 167, 220n
ambiguity 291
animate 138, 284, 286
antifocus 179
argument structure 273
article 284
aspect 18, 20, 32, 59, 167, 305
Atzingo 312, 318, 319
auxiliaries 25, 31, 43, 51, 53, 56, 137, 146, 150, 278–279

B

background 187, 191, 193, 194, 200
Bagvalal 164, 168
bleaching 15–17, 58
Botlikh 164, 168

C

case 7, 65f, 100f, 205f, 241f
  case assignment 241, 245, 250-252, 257, 261, 266
  case system 214, 241, 245, 246, 248, 249, 257, 265, 267n, 268n, 277
Catalan 277
catatagm 177
categorical structure 173, 176, 178
Chechen 161, 162, 167, 168
Chiquihuitlán 309, 310, 317, 319
Chocho 304, 306-309, 311, 314, 315, 318–320, 321n

chronology 288
clitic 130
coding 273
comitative 311, 313-318, 320, 321n
common nouns 284
communication 273, 274, 276
concord 258, 259, 264, 269n
content syntax 173
Continental Scandinavian 243, 244, 246
copula verb 278
corpus 271, 283, 294, 300

D

Danish 12, 31, 66, 82, 171, 174–186, 189–201, 246, 249, 258, 259, 267n
Dargi 162-165, 167, 169
dative 65f, 100f, 211, 228, 243-245, 247-254, 257
declension 274–279, 281, 283–286, 291, 292
definite 284, 286
deflexion 241-244, 246, 248, 253, 255–257, 267n, 269n
deontic 223, 224, 226–232
dependency 176
determiner 108, 248
dialect contact 244
direct discourse 290
discontinuous structures 275
distributional test 176
drift 5
Dutch 6, 15, 34-37, 44-46, 53, 54, 56, 131, 228, 236n

E

economy principle 256-258, 265, 266
ellipsis 287–289
English 5-7, 9, 11, 17, 25, 27, 28, 30-36, 44-46, 52, 53, 59, 112, 131, 207, 215, 223, 224, 227, 230, 236n, 242, 249, 258, 259, 261
epistemic 27, 28, 58
ergativity 11, 68, 206, 209
experiencer 31
expression syntax 173

F

Faroese 7-9, 12, 65, 66, 68, 69, 89–92, 94n, 132, 241, 243
feminine 243, 249, 250, 252, 260-262, 265, 284
focus 158f, 179, 197, 200
formal register 288–289
French 7-10, 35, 54, 258, 273-280, 283, 284, 286-289, 291, 292, 296, 297, 300n
Frisian 34, 37, 56, 131
full verbs 278
fundament 179

G

gender 241, 242, 258, 259, 267
genitive 220, 244, 245, 247-252, 257-259, 261, 262, 264, 265, 267n, 269n
Georgian 19, 22, 23, 61
German 5-10, 15f, 65f, 102, 131, 226, 241
Germanic 241, 243-246, 249, 260, 261
gerund 224–226, 231
governance 176
grammatical categories 274, 292
grammatical distinction 292
grammatical levels 274
grammaticality cline 248
grammaticalization 15f, 173, 206, 246, 248, 276, 282, 291, 292

H

hierarchy 284
Huautla 309, 310, 317-320

human 69, 78, 284, 286, 289, 292
human objects 274, 290, 292, 293
human subjects 274, 290, 292, 293
hypotagm 177

I

Icelandic 3, 7-10, 12, 65f, 99f, 202n, 241, 243, 245, 247, 248
iconic 174, 186–191
inanimate nouns 284
incorporation 210, 211, 217, 219n
individual 209, 285, 286
Indo-European 7, 12, 21, 91, 102, 173, 174, 176, 204, 233, 245, 248, 253, 256, 257
infinitive 32, 50, 55–56, 123f, 226f
inflection 132, 172, 275, 292
inflectional case 241, 243, 256
informal 288–289
instrumental 304, 305, 311, 315–319
Insular Scandinavian 66, 91, 243
Inuit *see Inuktitut*
Inuktitut 5, 205f
Inuttut 209, 211-214, 216, 218
Italian 8, 277, 278, 286
Ixcatec 304, 307-311, 315, 316, 318-320

J

Jalapa 309, 310, 317-319

L

language contact 4, 244
Latin 3, 5-8, 10, 11, 22, 54, 67, 133n, 223-225, 228–232, 247, 253, 258, 259, 264, 269n, 273-277, 280, 283, 284, 286–294, 300n
least-effort 255, 256, 265, 266
less transparent 292
lexical case 93, 241f
lexical level 274
linear level 274
 ordering 282
 structures 275

M

masculine 266, 284
Mazatec 304, 307, 309, 311, 317–320
Metzontla 304, 312, 313, 317
Mexico 3, 5, 303, 304
Middle English 3, 150, 152, 233, 236n
Middle French 8, 275–277, 282, 287, 289-292
Middle Low German 244
minimalism 15, 56
modal auxiliaries 278
modal particle 41
modal verb 17
Modern French 273–277, 281, 282, 287-292
Modern Swedish 242, 243, 251, 253, 267
morphological level 274

N

names 209, 211
neuter 249
new information 288
nominal declension 274, 283
nominal morphology 277
nominative 68, 99f, 171f, 205–209, 214, 218, 223, 225, 228, 232, 234n, 246, 249, 258, 260
non-full verbs 278
North East Caucasian 3, 5, 159, 160, 168
North Russian 223, 227, 231-234
Norwegian 9, 11, 66, 76, 79, 80, 83, 84, 88, 94n, 96, 115, 132, 133, 171, 174-178, 186, 192, 193, 249
noun 216, 217, 241, 242, 263, 274–279, 284, 292, 305–311, 313
null subjects 287
number 241, 242, 245, 258, 259, 267n

O

Oaxaca 304
object 71, 74, 77, 97, 177, 207, 223f, 273f
obligatoriness 283, 287
oblique subjects 65f, 100f
Occitan 277

Old English 3, 6, 9, 28, 137, 140, 141, 144, 146–148, 206, 226, 228, 232, 233, 258, 259
Old French 275-277, 279, 282-284, 291, 292, 297, 300-302
Old German 27, 46, 230
Old Icelandic 65, 97, 99f, 175, 230
old information 288
Old Norse 7, 9, 10, 72–75, 77, 78, 81–90, 94n, 115, 133n, 176, 180, 202, 242, 244, 245, 249, 252
Old Swedish 103, 242f
Otomanguean 5, 303

P

paradigm 243, 249, 250, 252, 253, 260, 261
parameter 3, 7, 27, 66
passive 9–12, 20, 31, 46, 52, 67, 83, 88, 100, 102, 105, 119, 120, 138, 142, 143, 148, 149, 223f
periphrastic construction 246, 247, 257
personal pronoun 111, 291
phrase-marker 264, 266
plural 284
Portuguese 277, 278, 299n
pragmatic function 276
preposition 58, 80, 244, 246, 247, 250–254, 257, 261, 275, 280, 283, 286, 287, 303–305, 311, 312, 315–320
  prepositional objects 292
  prepositional complement 250-252, 257, 262, 264
pronominal subject 291
pronoun 229, 284, 285, 289, 291, 292
proper name 286
proper noun 284, 299n
Proto-Germanic 244, 245, 249, 260, 261
Proto-Indo-European 245
Proto-Scandinavian 249, 261, 267n, 268n
Puebla 304

Q

quantifier float 104, 115
quirky subject 83, 84, 223, 229, 232

R

raising 25, 32, 33, 52, 59, 60, 84, 88
reanalysis 43, 45–47, 55, 58, 59, 194, 197, 223, 226, 231
reduction 245, 261
referent 175, 279, 287
reflexive 128, 130
register 288
reinterpretation 174, 177, 190–193, 197–199
relative clause 178
rheme 179
Romance languages 6-8, 10, 11, 274, 277, 278, 283–286, 291, 292, 300
Roumanian 277, 286
Runic Swedish 242, 249, 267n, 268n
Russian 102, 161, 223–224, 227, 231–234, 247, 248

S

Scandinavian 6-9, 11, 12, 31, 65, 66, 75, 78, 84, 85, 87, 89-91, 93n, 104, 112, 131, 132, 171, 172, 174-176, 179-181, 187, 191, 193, 194, 198, 199, 202n, 242-244, 246, 266n, 267n
singular 284
Spanish 8, 9, 277, 278, 285, 286, 303-305, 311, 314, 315, 319, 320
stress shift 245
structural case 10
stylistic function 276
subject 65f, 100f, 171f, 178, 223f, 273f
subjectless sentence 8

support verb 278, 279, 286, 299n
Svan 19, 20, 23, 24
Swedish 5, 66, 125, 171, 174, 175, 178, 241-243, 251, 253, 255, 257-259, 265
Swiss Romance 277

T

text type 288, 289
textual register 276
theme 31, 179, 227, 229
thetic construction 177
topological field 37
topological frame 187
transparency 273, 274, 276

U

Udi 159, 160, 164-167, 169n
unidirectionality 248, 249, 268n

V

V2 24, 38, 40, 41, 174, 175, 182, 183, 185, 187, 193, 194, 197-201
valency 174, 177, 179, 190, 198, 273f
Veracruz 304
verb typology 278, 282

W

word order 173, 193, 204, 257, 273, 274, 275-278, 282, 290-292, 305
word-marking 259

Y

Yiddish 7-10, 37

Z

zero 251, 252, 254, 268n

In the STUDIES IN LANGUAGE COMPANION SERIES (SLCS) the following volumes have been published thus far or are scheduled for publication:

1. ABRAHAM, Werner (ed.): *Valence, Semantic Case, and Grammatical Relations. Workshop studies prepared for the 12th Conference of Linguistics, Vienna, August 29th to September 3rd, 1977.* Amsterdam, 1978.
2. ANWAR, Mohamed Sami: *BE and Equational Sentences in Egyptian Colloquial Arabic.* Amsterdam, 1979.
3. MALKIEL, Yakov: *From Particular to General Linguistics. Selected Essays 1965-1978. With an introd. by the author + indices.* Amsterdam, 1983.
4. LLOYD, Albert L.: *Anatomy of the Verb: The Gothic Verb as a Model for a Unified Theory of Aspect, Actional Types, and Verbal Velocity.* Amsterdam, 1979.
5. HAIMAN, John: *Hua: A Papuan Language of the Eastern Highlands of New Guinea.* Amsterdam, 1980.
6. VAGO, Robert (ed.): *Issues in Vowel Harmony. Proceedings of the CUNY Linguistics Conference on Vowel Harmony (May 14, 1977).* Amsterdam, 1980.
7. PARRET, H., J. VERSCHUEREN, M. SBISÀ (eds): *Possibilities and Limitations of Pragmatics. Proceedings of the Conference on Pragmatics, Urbino, July 8-14, 1979.* Amsterdam, 1981.
8. BARTH, E.M. & J.L. MARTENS (eds): *Argumentation: Approaches to Theory Formation. Containing the Contributions to the Groningen Conference on the Theory of Argumentation,* Groningen, October 1978. Amsterdam, 1982.
9. LANG, Ewald: *The Semantics of Coordination.* Amsterdam, 1984.(English transl. by John Pheby from the German orig. edition *"Semantik der koordinativen Verknüpfung"*, Berlin, 1977.)
10. DRESSLER, Wolfgang U., Willi MAYERTHALER, Oswald PANAGL & Wolfgang U. WURZEL: *Leitmotifs in Natural Morphology.* Amsterdam, 1987.
11. PANHUIS, Dirk G.J.: *The Communicative Perspective in the Sentence: A Study of Latin Word Order.* Amsterdam, 1982.
12. PINKSTER, Harm (ed.): *Latin Linguistics and Linguistic Theory. Proceedings of the 1st Intern. Coll. on Latin Linguistics, Amsterdam, April 1981.* Amsterdam, 1983.
13. REESINK, G.: *Structures and their Functions in Usan.* Amsterdam, 1987.
14. BENSON, Morton, Evelyn BENSON & Robert ILSON: *Lexicographic Description of English.* Amsterdam, 1986.
15. JUSTICE, David: *The Semantics of Form in Arabic, in the mirror of European languages.* Amsterdam, 1987.
16. CONTE, M.E., J.S. PETÖFI, and E. SÖZER (eds): *Text and Discourse Connectedness.* Amsterdam/Philadelphia, 1989.
17. CALBOLI, Gualtiero (ed.): *Subordination and other Topics in Latin. Proceedings of the Third Colloquium on Latin Linguistics, Bologna, 1-5 April 1985.* Amsterdam/Philadelphia, 1989.
18. WIERZBICKA, Anna: *The Semantics of Grammar.* Amsterdam/Philadelphia, 1988.
19. BLUST, Robert A.: *Austronesian Root Theory. An Essay on the Limits of Morphology.* Amsterdam/Philadelphia, 1988.
20. VERHAAR, John W.M. (ed.): *Melanesian Pidgin and Tok Pisin. Proceedings of the First International Conference on Pidgins and Creoles on Melanesia.* Amsterdam/Philadelphia, 1990.

21. COLEMAN, Robert (ed.): *New Studies in Latin Linguistics. Proceedings of the 4th International Colloquium on Latin Linguistics*, Cambridge, April 1987. Amsterdam/Philadelphia, 1991.
22. McGREGOR, William: *A Functional Grammar of Gooniyandi*. Amsterdam/Philadelphia, 1990.
23. COMRIE, Bernard and Maria POLINSKY (eds): *Causatives and Transitivity*. Amsterdam/Philadelphia, 1993.
24. BHAT, D.N.S. *The Adjectival Category. Criteria for differentiation and identification*. Amsterdam/Philadelphia, 1994.
25. GODDARD, Cliff and Anna WIERZBICKA (eds): *Semantics and Lexical Universals. Theory and empirical findings*. Amsterdam/Philadelphia, 1994.
26. LIMA, Susan D., Roberta L. CORRIGAN and Gregory K. IVERSON (eds): *The Reality of Linguistic Rules*. Amsterdam/Philadelphia, 1994.
27. ABRAHAM, Werner, T. GIVÓN and Sandra A. THOMPSON (eds): *Discourse Grammar and Typology*. Amsterdam/Philadelphia, 1995.
28. HERMAN, József: *Linguistic Studies on Latin: Selected papers from the 6th international colloquium on Latin linguistics, Budapest, 2-27 March, 1991*. Amsterdam/Philadelphia, 1994.
29. ENGBERG-PEDERSEN, Elisabeth et al. (eds): *Content, Expression and Structure. Studies in Danish functional grammar*. Amsterdam/Philadelphia, 1996.
30. HUFFMAN, Alan: *The Categories of Grammar. French lui and le*. Amsterdam/Philadelphia, 1997.
31. WANNER, Leo (ed.): *Lexical Functions in Lexicography and Natural Language Processing*. Amsterdam/Philadelphia, 1996.
32. FRAJZYNGIER, Zygmunt: *Grammaticalization of the Complex Sentence. A case study in Chadic*. Amsterdam/Philadelphia, 1996.
33. VELAZQUEZ-CASTILLO, Maura: *The Grammar of Possession. Inalienability, incorporation and possessor ascension in Guaraní*. Amsterdam/Philadelphia, 1996.
34. HATAV, Galia: *The Semantics of Aspect and Modality. Evidence from English and Biblical Hebrew*. Amsterdam/Philadelphia, 1997.
35. MATSUMOTO, Yoshiko: *Noun-Modifying Constructions in Japanese. A frame semantic approach*. Amsterdam/Philadelphia, 1997.
36. KAMIO, Akio (ed.): *Directions in Functional Linguistics*. Amsterdam/Philadelphia, 1997.
37. HARVEY, Mark and Nicholas REID (eds): *Nominal Classification in Aboriginal Australia*. Amsterdam/Philadelphia, 1997.
38. HACKING, Jane F.: *Coding the Hypothetical. A Comparative Typology of Conditionals in Russian and Macedonian*. Amsterdam/Philadelphia, 1998.
39. WANNER, Leo (ed.): *Recent Trends in Meaning-Text Theory*. Amsterdam/Philadelphia, 1997.
40. BIRNER, Betty and Gregory WARD: *Information Status and Noncanonical Word Order in English*. Amsterdam/Philadelphia, 1998.
41. DARNELL, Michael, Edith MORAVSCIK, Michael NOONAN, Frederick NEWMEYER and Kathleen WHEATLY (eds): *Functionalism and Formalism in Linguistics. Volume I: General papers*. Amsterdam/Philadelphia, 1999.

42. DARNELL, Michael, Edith MORAVSCIK, Michael NOONAN, Frederick NEWMEYER and Kathleen WHEATLY (eds): *Functionalism and Formalism in Linguistics. Volume II: Case studies.* Amsterdam/Philadelphia, 1999.
43. OLBERTZ, Hella, Kees HENGEVELD and Jesús Sánchez GARCÍA (eds): *The Structure of the Lexicon in Functional Grammar.* Amsterdam/Philadelphia, 1998.
44. HANNAY, Mike and A. Machtelt BOLKESTEIN (eds): *Functional Grammar and Verbal Interaction.* 1998.
45. COLLINS, Peter and David LEE (eds): *The Clause in English. In honour of Rodney Huddleston.* 1999.
46. YAMAMOTO, Mutsumi: *Animacy and Reference. A cognitive approach to corpus linguistics.* 1999.
47. BRINTON, Laurel J. and Minoji AKIMOTO (eds): *ollocational and Idiomatic Aspects of Composite Predicates in the History of English.* 1999.
48. MANNEY, Linda Joyce: *Middle Voice in Modern Greek. Meaning and function of an inflectional category.* 2000.
49. BHAT, D.N.S.: *The Prominence of Tense, Aspect and Mood.* 1999.
50. ABRAHAM, Werner and Leonid KULIKOV (eds): *Transitivity, Causativity, and TAM. In honour of Vladimir Nedjalkov.* 1999.
51. ZIEGELER, Debra: *Hypothetical Modality. Grammaticalisation in an L2 dialect.* 2000.
52. TORRES CACOULLOS, Rena: *Grammaticization, Synchronic Variation, and Language Contact. A study of Spanish progressive -ndo constructions.* 2000.
53. FISCHER, Olga, Anette ROSENBACH and Dieter STEIN (eds.): *Pathways of Change. Grammaticalization in English.* 2000.
54. DAHL, Östen and Maria KOPTJEVSKAJA TAMM (eds.): *Circum-Baltic Languages. Volume 1: Past and Present.* n.y.p.
55. DAHL, Östen and Maria KOPTJEVSKAJA TAMM (eds.): *Circum-Baltic Languages. Volume 2: Grammar and Typology.* n.y.p.
56. FAARLUND, Jan Terje (ed.): *Grammatical Relations in Change.* 2001.
57. MEL'ČUK, Igor: *Communicative Organization in Natural Language. The semantic-communicative structure of sentences.* n.y.p.